THE IDEA OF FREEDOM IN ASIA AND AFRICA

THE MAKING OF MODERN FREEDOM

General Editor: R. W. Davis

Center for the History of Freedom
Washington University in St. Louis

THE IDEA OF FREEDOM IN ASIA AND AFRICA

Edited by Robert H. Taylor

STANFORD UNIVERSITY PRESS
STANFORD, CALIFORNIA
2002

Stanford University Press
Stanford, California

Printed in the United States of America

Library of Congress Cataloging-in-Publication Data

The idea of freedom in Asia and Africa /edited by Robert H. Taylor.
p. cm. — (The making of modern freedom)
Includes bibliographical references and index.
ISBN 0-8047-4514-5 (acid-free paper)
1. Developing countries. 2. National liberation movements—Asia. 3. National liberation movements—Africa. 4. Nationalism—Asia—History—20th century. 5. Nationalism—Africa—History—20th century. 6. Imperialism. I. Taylor, Robert H.. II. Series.

D883.134 2002
323'.095—dc21 2002001138

This book is printed on acid-free, archival-quality paper.

Original printing 2002

Last figure below indicates year of this printing:
11 10 09 08 07 06 05 04 03 02

Typeset at Stanford University Press in 10/13 Trump Mediaeval

< >

Acknowledgments

This volume has been generously supported by a grant from the Lynde and Harry Bradley Foundation and a gift from Carolyn and Joseph Losos of St. Louis. As always, we are also grateful for the support of Washington University.

Series Foreword

THE STARTLING AND moving events that swept from China to Eastern Europe to Latin America and South Africa at the end of the 1980s, followed closely by similar events and the subsequent dissolution of what used to be the Soviet Union, formed one of those great historic occasions when calls for freedom, rights, and democracy echoed through political upheaval. A clear-eyed look at any of those conjunctions—in 1776 and 1789, in 1848 and 1918, as well as in 1989—reminds us that freedom, liberty, rights, and democracy are words into which many different and conflicting hopes have been read. The language of freedom—or liberty, which is interchangeable with freedom most of the time—is inherently difficult. It carried vastly different meanings in the classical world and in medieval Europe from those of modern understanding, though thinkers in later ages sometimes eagerly assimilated the older meanings to their own circumstances and purposes.

A new kind of freedom, which we have here called modern, gradually disentangles itself from old contexts in Europe, beginning first in England in the early seventeenth century and then, with many confusions, denials, reversals, and cross-purposes, elsewhere in Europe and the world. A large-scale history of this modern, conceptually distinct, idea of freedom is now beyond the ambition of any one scholar, however learned. This collaborative enterprise, tentative though it must be, is an effort to fill the gap.

We could not take into account all the varied meanings that freedom and liberty have carried in the modern world. We have, for example, ruled out extended attention to what some political philosophers have called "positive freedom," in the sense of self-realization of the individual; nor could we, even in a series as large as this, cope with the enormous implications of the four freedoms invoked by Franklin D. Roosevelt in 1941. Freedom of speech and freedom of the press will have their place in the narrative that follows, certainly, but not the boundless calls for freedom from want and freedom from fear.

We use freedom in the traditional and restricted sense of civil and political liberty—freedom of religion, freedom of speech and assembly, freedom of the individual from arbitrary and capricious authority over persons or property, freedom to produce and to exchange goods and services, and the freedom to take part in the political process that shapes people's destiny. In no major part of the world over the past few years have aspirations for those freedoms not been at least powerfully expressed; and in most places where they did not exist, strong measures have been taken—not always successfully—to attain them.

The history we trace was not a steady march toward the present or the fulfillment of some cosmic necessity. Modern freedom had its roots in specific circumstances in early modern Europe, despite the unpromising and even hostile characteristics of the larger society and culture. From these narrow and often selfishly motivated beginnings, modern freedom came to be realized in later times, constrained by old traditions and institutions hard to move, and driven by ambition as well as idealism: everywhere the growth of freedom has been *sui generis*. But to understand these unique developments fully, we must first try to see them against the making of modern freedom as a whole.

Historians continue to argue about whether freedom in Africa and Asia is essentially a gift from the West or mainly an indigenous growth. We contend that this is the wrong way to frame the question. To maintain, as we do, that modern freedom had its roots in early modern Europe is not to suggest that it subsequently grew there alone, in isolation, to be exported only in its fully perfected state at some later date. That was clearly not the case for two good reasons. The first is that by the time Europeans finally ceased to be present on the two continents mainly as traders on sufferance and began to establish themselves as territorial powers, which in both cases began in the second half of the eighteenth century, modern freedom as we have defined it was far from being fully developed. The second reason is that in the century and more that it took to fashion freedom into a recognizably modern form, Africans and

Asians were evidently part of the dialogue and process by which this was accomplished.

The Indian case will help to make these points clear. In 1759 Robert Clive and a largely Indian force beat the French and their Indian allies, and with the acquisition of Bengal made the British East India Company a territorial power in India. The British government did not take long to make itself a partner in the governing of the new territory. Though neither the company officials in London nor the British government wished it, the early years in India were a period of conquest, which speeded up markedly after 1800. Those who drove the conquest were men on the spot, ambitious governors general and military men; but the troops which accomplished it, albeit with British officers, were overwhelmingly Indian. Though more Europeans were added to the mix after the Mutiny in 1857, the rank and file remained heavily Indian right to the end of the empire.

The fact that imperial rule was established and sustained by Indian troops suggests the importance to the British of these Indian allies. And when in the 1830s British officials began to give serious thought to regularizing civil government in India, they again sought Indian allies. In the course of discussions about introducing government-sponsored English education in India in 1833, Thomas Babington Macaulay declared that whether or not it would ultimately bring Indians to demand British liberties, he did not know, but: "Whenever it comes, it will be the proudest day in English history." Macaulay was sure that it would not happen for a long time.[1]

But to look at the other side of the question, what liberties would Britain have been able to exemplify in 1833? When Macaulay spoke, colonial slavery had not yet been abolished, though a bill for that purpose would be carried in the same year. While Protestant and Roman Catholic minorities had been granted full citizenship a few years before, Jews would have to wait until 1858. Freedom of speech and assembly were regularly being suspended in Ireland. And as for political participation, while the first parliamentary reform act of 1832 had greatly reduced corruption and increased the size of the electorate, it had done so at the cost of considerably raising the property barriers to qualification for the vote. It would take two more re-

[1]Bernard Porter, *The Lion's Share: A Short History of British Imperialism, 1850–1983* (2d ed., London 1984), 20–21.

form acts and an act establishing equal electoral districts before Britain could call itself a democracy. This did not occur until 1885, the same year in which the Indian National Congress was formed. Even then about a quarter of adult men and all adult women were left unenfranchised, and would remain so until after World War I, by which time Indians had begun to press very insistently for self-government. In 1833 modern freedom in Britain was still very much a work in progress.

Macaulay is often remembered for his sweeping dismissal of the cultures of India and Arabia; but the educational reform he proposed and himself put in place in India in 1835 was not only warmly received but had actually been strongly lobbied for by many in the educated elite of India, mostly Brahmans, who though trained up in the traditional way were distressed that there was no longer much call for their learning. Macaulay's immediate objective appealed to them mightily. What Macaulay wanted, he said, was to produce a class educated in English ways "who may be interpreters between us and the millions whom we govern."[2] That is to say these English-educated Indians were to become the civil servants and professional men who would have the most to do with the mass of the people. This role the Brahman elite was delighted to assume.

British promises in 1833, however, were not matched by performance. On the renewal of the company's charter in 1833 it had been promised that there would be no discrimination against any candidate for official employment on account of race or creed. But in fact Indians did not rise much above the lower levels of administration. They were invaluable as village heads and local magistrates and in the various ranks of clerkdom, but experience proved that they could not aspire to the higher ranks of political administrators.

In 1858, after the Mutiny, when the British government assumed the direct rule of India from the company, the pledge of 1833 was renewed by royal proclamation. But, for all practical purposes, the pledge was no more honored than it had been earlier. In 1861 an act made Indians eligible for high court judgeships, but for many years thereafter only one was actually appointed. A few were nominated to legislative councils, where they were swamped by European colleagues. Yet from 1854 onward the situation was, or at any rate

[2]Ibid.

ought to have been, most embarrassing for the British government. In that year, several years before the end of company rule, competitive examinations were instituted for admission into the Indian civil service. The next year Parliament endorsed the same principle for the British civil service. Implementation did not go very far until 1870 when Gladstone's first government instituted measures which finally established the examination system for entry into all branches of the domestic civil service. This was one of a series of measures implementing the vaunted liberal principle of equality of opportunity, and the model was the Indian civil service. As far as Indians were concerned, however, there was a problem: until 1893 all examinations were held in London. Such blatant ruses made the British government an easy target for charges of hypocrisy.

These charges did not fail to come, crudely from the growing vernacular press and with a politeness so extreme as to suggest the strong possibility of sarcasm from the new Indian National Congress founded in 1885. The Congress pledged itself to urge by strictly constitutionalist means the establishment of responsible government in India; that is to say one in which the executive is responsible to an elected parliament. This form of goverment was first proposed by Lord Durham for Canada in 1839 (six years after Macaulay's 1833 speech). At the time Lord John Russell, the British colonial secretary, declared, perhaps somewhat disingenuously, that he did not understand what responsible government was. Since then, as well as in Canada it had been taken up in Australia, New Zealand, and South Africa. Now Indians were asking for the same.

Clearly those Indians were not following any narrowly British model, and certainly not one that the British government was pressing upon them. Rather they settled on a model that had been tried and proven sound by other countries in the empire. That is, they were following an imperial model, in an empire of which they were a part (as of course were the British of the metropole) and one which was developing a corporate life of its own.

From the beginning the Indians had taken a cool and practical view of British policies, very much aware of their own interests. They had watched the growth of British liberties and had kept abreast as well of developments in the wider empire. They were clearly drawn to what was happening in the self-governing colonies now transforming themselves into what would be called dominions and beginning to assume control of their own external as well as internal affairs. Canada, Australia, and New Zealand, at least, would ultimately press on further, to independence under liberal and democratic institutions. For a long time the Indians would have been pleased to follow the same route; and they finally did, though often obstructed by the British government and perhaps partly for that reason forced to see their independence born in blood in 1947. What should never have been in doubt, however, was the new republic's fierce attachment to liberal and democratic institutions, as Indira Gandhi found in 1975 when she tried to suspend them. The world's largest democracy has successfully weathered many trials since then. And India still remains attached to the Commonwealth, no longer merely British in fact or in name.

A series editor must be indulged in his duty to show how this volume follows from those that have gone before. Robert Taylor and his colleagues, all leading scholars in their own fields, will however demonstrate with infinitely greater learning, expertise, and sophistication the delicate, and not so delicate, interactions that have produced the idea of freedom in Asia and Africa.

The Making of Modern Freedom grows out of a continuing series of conferences held at the Center for the History of Freedom at Washington University in St. Louis. Professor J. H. Hexter was the founder and, for three years, the resident gadfly of the Center. His contribution is gratefully recalled by all his colleagues.

R.W.D.

<>

Contents

CONTRIBUTORS

William J. Foltz
Yale University

Sheldon Garon
Princeton University

James L. Gelvin
University of California, Los Angeles

Sudipta Kaviraj
School of Oriental and African Studies
University of London

Benedict J. Tria Kerkvliet
Australian National University

Andrew J. Nathan
Columbia University

Robert H. Taylor
University of Buckingham
(Emeritus)

Crawford Young
University of Wisconsin, Madison

THE IDEA OF FREEDOM IN ASIA AND AFRICA

Introduction

ROBERT H. TAYLOR

THERE ARE UNIVERSAL ideas of freedom to be found in the diverse intellectual and political traditions of the globe. The ways of conceptualizing and operationalizing the implications of ideas of freedom have been heavily influenced by the global trade in ideas which has grown exponentially during the past 200 years. In Africa and Asia, the conceptualization of freedom for individuals and societies has been heavily influenced by the translation of specific European or American ideas of freedom into new political and social contexts. In this volume we are attempting a preliminary assessment of some of the causes and consequences of this process. Africa and Asia too often have been portrayed in Western accounts as having no historical purchase on ideas of freedom; but as in any effort to appreciate the historical processes of change which created the modern world, their complex histories must be appreciated in their own right. As the chapters in this volume reveal, these societies have had their own ideas of the proper degree of autonomy by the individual relative to the authority that the state and other institutions can and should have over him or her.

The range of issues and topics which could be dealt with in a volume of this kind seems almost endless. We have attempted to concentrate on only those few which can assist in making some coherent comparative analysis of changing conceptualizations of freedom relative to the state and political authority and action. However, when these questions are examined with any kind of historical regard to the specificity of particular societies and their histories, it quickly becomes apparent that the discussion cannot be divorced from ideas of freedom in regard to other institutions, most particularly the economy and the family. The totality of life as perceived by individuals in their own specific historical context shapes both debate and action over the idea of freedom.

The creation of the modern bureaucratic republic as the near universal standard of what is today considered legitimate political authority is the result of political processes which have occurred since the American revolution and the nineteenth-century rise of European imperialism. Republicanism was a powerful expression of one idea of freedom and individual autonomy vis-à-vis established authority. Imperialism was another powerful expression not only of the great might of industrial society but also of the apparent invincibility of the ideas of social and political organization which underlay the economic and military power of European states. The ideas of the imperialists, however, were not imposed upon an African and Asian *tabula rasa*, but upon peoples and societies which were both appalled by, and attracted to, the strength and vigor of the societies which had the capacity to dominate and remake their institutions. But nineteenth-century imperialism carried within it the seeds of its own destruction by bringing with it a vocabulary of freedom which stimulated new ways of conceptualizing and acting upon existing concepts and opened up new debates about old ideas in the societies across Africa and Asia, as well as their new world diasporas.

Asian and African anti-colonialism and nationalism are frequently recognized as the primary political consequences of the imperialist epoch. The second half of the twentieth century is equally noted as the period in which ideas of freedom represented by the vocabulary of nationalism triumphed. And in global political terms, this is an obvious truism. But within African and Asian societies, debates about the specific local meanings of these ideas for a variety of human and social institutions have been equally, if not more, important. Nationalism justified democracy and republicanism. These encouraged broadened dialogues about freedom which American and European ideas encapsulated in the concept of "individual freedom" engendered in political and social thought in Africa and Asia, as elsewhere.

Modern world history looked at from the perspective of the authors of this volume is not the tale told to many of us in history classes half a century ago. This is not a book about the expansion of Europe and the bringing of freedom to peoples who had no conceptual references outside their own narrow existence. What is remarkable is the simultaneity of the spread of modern ideas of freedom throughout the globe. There were no followers and leaders, though the domination of the Western officials and scholars in describing this historical process has frequently obscured this elementary point. Freetown, the name taken by former slaves who settled in what is now Sierra Leone in 1788, was the product of the ferment of revolts for freedom by African slaves forced into the global diaspora which imperialism created. With the growth of a European presence in East Asia, intellectuals in the Confucian ruling groups in China, Japan, and Korea debated the implications for ordered society of the ideas about liberty of John Stuart Mill and other authors which the traders brought with them. The Indian civil service and the germs of mass political parties emerged on the Indian subcontinent at the same time as these institutions of the modern state began to appear in England. Africans and Asians, however, were not just reacting to the notions brought from the West. They were, in many cases, changing the meaning of imported ideas in order to make them appropriate for their own conditions. The success of those Asian and African monarchies which survived despite imperialism and the rise of the republic ideal—Japan, Siam, and Ethiopia being the most obvious—is a demonstration of the success of adaptation despite the overwhelming odds which ended in the political subjugation of most of Asia and Africa. Even for the colonialized, Western ideas could be attractive, or at least stimulating, and, most importantly, could be used to defeat the West. But the domestic consequences have led to unforeseen outcomes.

We have had to ignore many issues in this volume which, were we to do complete justice to our topics, would require more elaborate and thorough analyses. In part this is a consequence of who we are. It is perhaps presumptuous of a small group of North American academics and one Indian residing in London to attempt to describe the biography of ideas of freedom in Africa and Asia. But there are limits to time and limits to budgets which make that necessary. Also, perhaps there is an advantage in the sense that we are attempting to interpret an historical process to readers who are largely unfamiliar with the stories we are retelling. Those who live in Africa and Asia know what we are attempting to delineate without the need for a book like this.

Aware of our intellectual limitations, none of us has attempted to examine any of the classical texts and traditions of African and Asian societies in order to delineate the intellectual roots of many of the ideas we are assessing. We are taking these as givens without subjecting them to the intellectual subtlety which they deserve. This book is not a history of ideas but more an analysis of how ideas have shaped history. Other scholars, more deeply steeped in the literature and traditions of Asia and Africa, must pursue those topics.

This is, in a sense, a book about translation. And translation became a motif which ran through our discussions in preparing the volume. Words for freedom, or what some would see in modern discourse as unfreedom, could be found in every language and culture. People knew what was not freedom because most African and Asian societies, like most early modern European societies, had ideas of social status and hierarchy which defined for individuals the limits of their freedom. People were designated as free or slave, as free or bondsman, as belonging to a particular caste or a class, in an elaborate hierarchy of social and political relationships. Wherever one was in these complex social structures, now often disparaged as "traditional" or "feudal," there was a vocabulary which made clear what one could and could not legitimately undertake. The moral order of the society provided a legitimizing rationale for these limitations.

In such societies, the language of freedom was often expressed in a language of implied obligation and assumed self-restraint. Translating Western ideas of positive freedom into cultures which had such traditions led to some curious and misleading linguistic confusions. Unintended nuances became attached to words, turning an idea which had a positive connotation in one culture into a negative concept in another. For example, *ziyou* in Chinese was translated as freedom or liberty but in fact stems from a word which literally means "from oneself," which has a selfish connotation. The original meaning was negative, doing things as one wishes, without regard to the social constraints which should be observed by any civilized person. In many of the languages of the societies examined in this volume, values such as freedom which are posited as a positive in English and American political discourse in translation have less positive, and sometimes negative, nuances. But what is true of ideas of freedom is also true of other concepts in political thought and practice.

In Burmese, for example, the introduction of the concept of the individual having a public role in political life, through the introduction of elections in a polity which until the 1880s had known only monarchical forms of authority, required political thinkers to innovate in order to encapsulate a new political practice. Rather than just transliterating the English word into Burmese, as was sometimes done, a neologism, *naingngandaw,* was coined for the English word "politics." Literally translated, *naingngandaw* contains implications about politics which are not found in the English concept of politics for it means "the conquered area's affairs" or perhaps "the kingdom's affairs." Young Burmese writers, such as Aung San, searching for a classical Burmese concept which more completely conveyed the idea of popular sovereignty and public choice in politics, could only find a lengthy poetical expression which would clearly not do in political debate: "internal affairs; the ruler's affairs are as broad as a cumulus cloud—the colour of a chicken egg, the *pauk* tree with a parakeet."

Sudipta Kaviraj, in discussion with his fellow authors, drew our attention to one element in our analysis which is perhaps a feature of difference between the Western intellectual traditions and those of the societies of Asia and Africa. He contended that in India, and perhaps by implication elsewhere in Asia and Africa, there was no self-conscious tradition of social theorizing in the Western sense until very late in the historical process. But the absence of self-conscious theories of freedom does not mean that when Western ideas entered into Indian, initially Bengali, intellectual and practical life, they replaced or supplanted existing ideas. There were no enormous shifts in social mentalities on the question of freedom. Rather there was a forced reflection on the meaning of the foreign concept as measured against indigenous ideas and practices. As Sudipta Kaviraj argued, the transformation of concepts was internal to traditional intellectual constructs and not some new superstructure which subjugated and replaced ideas.

A volume of this kind which consciously attempts to discuss the intellectual and political experiences of whole continents over a 200-year period faces even further problems in ensuring that its purpose is understood. Asia and Africa are no more single entities than is the West. We write of the "West" aware of the fact that during the entire period of concern there were in parts of Europe very different ideas of freedom from the Anglo-American traditions we are normally reflecting upon. But just as Portuguese, Spanish, and French ideas often came into colonial political discourses before English and American ones did, so too German ideas had a significant impact in parts of Africa as well as in the Middle East, Japan, and China. There was no one single or homogenous set of ideas to be translated, but a plethora from which to pick and choose. Similarly, legal traditions and ideas of justice and the meaning of the market varied in European traditions then as they do today.

Moreover, just as the entities which we now conceive as making up the political map of the West did not exist two centuries ago in the forms they do today, neither did the juridical entities of Africa and Asia. We are in most cases not writing about a single social and political entity over a 200-year period. Rather, we are using the current political constructions of these continents to help explain what were necessarily more complex historical processes of state formation which involved indigenous ideas and practices confronting external forces with their own intellectual logics and power. In no case was there a simple one-on-one relationship, but rather a manifold of complex and changing pressures and resistances. What people read competing Western ideas of freedom as meaning for themselves depended upon where they were and what they wanted or needed to take from what was on offer.

A lesson often overlooked in discussions of freedom in the West, but which comes through clearly in the chapters in this volume, is the Janus-faced nature of the concept. The gaining of a new freedom may result in the loss or diminution of another right or freedom. Historically derived structures in a society may deny freedom but provide protection to the individual or the group. The expansion of individual autonomy often gives rise to the creation of rules and laws which only the sometimes oppressive rule of law and lawyers seems capable of maintaining in highly structured, law-bound societies. The interaction of these conceptualizations of freedom provides grist for the mill of many historical and still continuing local debates about the nature of freedom in a particular context. Yet freedom has meaning only in a particular context, and the achievement of freedom for the individual as an individual may, for example, result in the loss of freedom for the same individual in the context of his or her family or social associations.

The Janus-like character of freedom was revealed in the saga of anti-colonialism during the past century. The successful end of colonial rule in Asia and Africa during the past 60 years led to the emergence of a number of regimes whose elites, while espousing the language of liberty and individual freedom to attack colonial rulers and their legacies, often created institutions and structures which limited political choice and liberty in the name of economic and social justice. The ambitions of postcolonial governments to create prosperity through economic and social planning, sometimes on huge scales, often resulted in the creation of elaborate security states frequently as oppressive as the colonial regime they replaced. Often ending in outright military government and financial bankruptcy, many of these regimes have fallen in recent years to the same arguments for freedom which their founders invoked a generation earlier.

What tentative conclusions can one draw from these preliminary analyses of the ideas of freedom in Africa and Asia as they have evolved in thought and practice during the past 200 years? Two impressions which initially appear to be contradictory emerge. First, that there has been a dramatic penetration of the European discourse on freedom into these societies, one which has changed their histories. Second, that every society contains its own internal strengths, which allow it to address issues of freedom from the vantage point of its own cultural preconceptions and preoccupations.

Whether cultures are merging as a result first of imperialism, then anti-imperialism, and now globalization can be read either way from these conclusions. What is clear is that people think about freedom and its realization. This speaks for the universality of freedom that underlines the diversity of historical ways of thinking about it. Freedom is an idea which was not merely discovered once and then spread round the world like a new commodity. Rather, freedom and its institutions emerge and reemerge out of the concrete circumstances of individuals' lives in history. The story of freedom knows no cultural barriers and continues to unfold in unexpected ways.

Itineraries of Ideas of Freedom in Africa: Precolonial to Postcolonial

CRAWFORD YOUNG

Narratives of the idea of freedom in the Western context tend to privilege seminal writings in the history of political philosophy or liminal moments in the evolution of a liberal democratic constitutional state. But the definition of freedom largely developed through political conflict in a multitude of sites, with an overarching struggle between centralizing states and societal forces. Other volumes in this series trace in detail this elaboration of the idea of freedom in the early modern Western state.[1] This long process involved the transformation of medieval notions of particularized liberties and franchises belonging to free subjects or corporations into a universalized concept of basic freedoms as the common property of human beings. Intense civil strife over religion eventually led to toleration of dissent, an ethos which spilled from the sacred to the secular domain. Centuries of struggle between sovereigns and society over the ultimate locus of legitimate authority produced representative government and constitutional democracy; the subject, in the process, became citizen. The revenue imperative of the state, frequently driven by recurrent wars, compelled rulers to bargain acknowledgment of parliamentary rights for fiscal concessions. Entrenchment of property rights became not only the cornerstone of economic freedom, but also the guarantee of individual autonomy.

The itineraries of the idea of freedom in Africa contrast sharply with those of Western states in a number of ways. If freedom requires its negative other of unfreedom to become an object of conscious reflection, then one must seek it in more sites than in the high politics of states. In the African context, interrogations concerning freedom and varying degrees of its absence are encountered in such spheres as personal status, gender, identity group, and religious membership, as well as unfolding state-society relationships. The ultimate sources of unfreedom, in much of the reflection upon it, are external to Africa: the Atlantic slave trade, colonial subjugation, great-power imperial pretensions, globalizing capitalism. Not all these aspects can receive adequate treatment within the confines of a single chapter; the focus here is the political realm. But other dimensions require acknowledgment.

The chapters in this volume devoted to Asia deal with one or two countries only, while the pair examining Africa purport to cover much or all of the continent. This apparent anomaly reflects common practice in comparative historical and political studies. There are a large number of sovereign entities in contemporary Africa (53), and in precolonial times an uncounted multitude existed; but there are many overarching commonalities, particularly in the nature of Africa's relationships with the external world from the fifteenth century onward. Large similarities in the nature and imprint of the African colonial state left a broadly comparable legacy across the continent. The contemporary African political universe is unusually inter-communicating in its intellectual currents and state politics, a fact symbolized through repeated rhetorical claims of a vocation of unity and their organizational embodiment in the Organization of African Unity (OAU) and the 2001 launching of the African Union. Left undefined in much of the discourse is whether Africa is a political and geographic concept, or a racialized one limited to the sub-Saharan regions. I prefer the continental version, though many writers set aside the Arab tier of states to the north. Whatever the limits to extending the lens this broadly, paradoxically one may argue that a more accurate overall portrait emerges through a continental perspective than through projection upon the continent of more specific analysis drawn from a small number of states.

The structure of this chapter is shaped by the crucial premise that the idea of freedom takes form as the antithesis to unfreedom. Unfreedom defines three major historical moments, which I examine in turn. Each of these constituted a field of metaconflict over the idea of freedom. The first moment was the Atlantic slave trade and its much smaller Arab-led counterpart, the impact of which in Africa became massive from the seventeenth to the nineteenth centuries. Freedom, as a powerful and eventually triumphant idea, meant the abolition of unfreedom, or chattel slavery. In a second historical moment, from the last quarter of the nineteenth century until the 1950s and 1960s, unfreedom in Africa had as primary referent colonial subjugation and oppression. The idea of freedom found embodiment in the movement for anti-colonial liberation and national independence. Unfreedom was defined once again in the 1960s and 1970s, as the newly independent states mostly became predatory authoritarian regimes. The idea of freedom now spread into multiple sites: democratization, economic liberalization, human rights, gender equality. In examining these three historical moments, I will also illuminate the particularity of the African itinerary of the idea of freedom through occasional comparison with historical paths of ideas of freedom in the Western world, which were the focus of earlier volumes in this series.

This chapter therefore explores African ideas of freedom beginning with the slave trade era in the two centuries before the sudden and dramatic subjugation of virtually all of the continent in the last quarter of the nineteenth century. There follows an examination of colonial subordination and reactions to it, which culminated in the rise of anti-colonial nationalism after World War II, and of the particular meanings to the swelling demand for freedom. In the immediate postcolonial moment, across the continent the dominant political form was a patrimonial autocracy, under single party or military auspices or both. Freedom as discourse and practice was regarded as an eventual by-product of the rapid development an empowered and expanded state would accomplish, with or without the benefit of formalized socialist doctrine. The disappointment of these hopes and the widespread conviction of state failure, by the 1980s, brought issues of freedom back into sharp focus in both old and new ways: democratization, economic liberalization, gender relations, human rights. Although the most recent period is primarily covered in chapter 2, I will conclude by examining the proliferating fields of freedom in the present.

An important part of the corpus of ideas regarding freedom in contemporary Africa, whether the issue is the rule-of-law state or gender equities, is of external derivation, a product of the intensive impact of colonial occupation, Western education, and Christian missions upon the African intellectual universe. In the world at large, an idea of freedom became ascendant during the twentieth century, codified in such seminal documents as the 1948 United Nations Universal Declaration of Human Rights and a ramifying array of declaratory documents since then. Yet indigenous itineraries are also important. Ideas, even if external in origin, achieve their motivating force when internalized, reformulated in terms of the contextual specificities, and syncretized with an indigenous heritage.

≺ I ≻

Slavery as the Negation of Freedom

In much of Africa historically, clear distinctions existed between free and unfree status. Upon this difference was erected the Atlantic slave trade, which in the western parts of the continent commercialized, politicized, and enlarged the realm of slavery, as well as ultimately generating the processes leading to its abolition. The marketing of African slaves in the Americas began in the sixteenth century, but assumed massive proportions only at the end of the seventeenth century.[2] Gaining momentum in the nineteenth century was a secondary slave raiding and trading zone, whose mercantile centers were Khartoum and Zanzibar, and whose primary agents had Arab antecedents. A far older slaving network had been central to earlier trans-Saharan commerce, depositing a significant number of sub-Saharan African captives in northern Africa and smaller numbers in the Iberian peninsula during the Middle Ages. By the seventeenth century, the magnitude of the trade set in motion a far-reaching political reconfiguration within Africa; new or expanding states became specialized in slave supply, while others emerged for defensive purposes.

Within Africa, the persons of unfree status were not viewed as simple chattel property, but rather as subordinated persons attached to the community.[3] Dependent status often originated in capture and raiding, but also in pawning or voluntary exchange of subordination for protection by small groups unable to survive on their own. Slave status involved a range of disabilities, related to role in community affairs, marriage, kinship, labor service obligations, access to land, and perhaps above all status respect. Slave labor in a number of instances was indispensable to the political economy and was used on a large scale (for example, East African coastal regions under Zanzibari rule, the Sokoto caliphate in northern Nigeria, the Abomey kingdom in Benin). The numbers involved could be substantial, a third or more of the population in some parts of West Africa.[4] However, slaves over time could be incorporated into the kinship structure of the society and over generations could erase their subjugated status, though memories of slave ancestry might linger.

Nonetheless, deeply embedded in the practice of slavery, even for those who avoided the horrors of the Middle Passage on slave ships to the Americas, was unfreedom. The stigma and disabilities attached to the status made its undesirability evident, without benefit of enlightenment doctrines of human equality. The widespread phenomenon of slave flight, when colonial occupation appeared to offer alternatives, makes clear that freedom as antithesis to slave status was part of the social consciousness. Many African communities share with the Sereer villages in Senegal an origin myth rooted in flight from and hatred of slavery, and refuge in inaccessible forests.[5]

The lexical representations of unfreedom in sundry African languages reflect the nature of the free/unfree binary in indigenous terms. The Swahili term for slaves, *watuma,* literally means someone sent to perform duties. It was often linked to a companion term, *wasenji,* or savages of a lesser form of humanity. Zambian scholar Chisanga Siame, in an intriguing analysis of concepts of freedom, suggests that in Bemba and other Zambian languages, "freedom" appears almost exclusively as the antithesis of "slavery."[6]

Slavery was a singularly comprehensive form of unfreedom: social death, in the eloquent exegesis of Orlando Patterson.[7] The abolition movement in Europe and North America, whose first success was the prohibition of slavery in Britain in 1772, formulated an initial doctrine of African freedom and foreshadowed early notions of African liberation among an emergent diaspora intelligentsia in the West Indies and North America. African unfreedom was exported to the Americas through the Atlantic slave trade, creating a nexus whose communication nodes were passageways for political ideas. Freed slaves from Nova Scotia and Britain settled in what is now Sierra Leone beginning in 1788; the name they gave their settlement, Freetown, amply measures the resonance of the idea. So does the national slogan adopted by the neighboring freed slave settlement in Liberia, first established in 1822, upon Liberian independence in 1847: "the love of liberty brought us here." At the same time, subliminal limits of this early concept of freedom are clearly expressed; the "love of liberty" was a special possession of the freed slave settlers and did not extend to the indigenous populations over whom they held exclusive sway for the first century of Liberian independence.

The struggle against slavery was appropriated by the expanding colonial powers themselves at the height of the African partition; in 1889–90, European diplomats assembled at Brussels for an antislavery conference, whose conclusions were then invoked as a pretext for further conquest. Freedom in personal status could be enforced, ran the argument, by subordinating the populace to alien rule. The contradiction between this commitment and the practical requirements of the institutionalization of hegemony created multiple dilemmas for the early colonial state. In places such as northern Nigeria, coastal East Africa, and portions of West Africa under French rule, the local economy and thus the fiscal basis of the colonial state depended upon slave agricultural production. A 1901 Colonial Office dispatch regarding northern Nigeria captured the dilemma: "The institution of domestic slavery, so far as its practices are not repugnant to civilisation, must be maintained in some form and under some name until another system of labour supply can be substituted for it."[8] Indeed, it was not fully abolished until 1936. Slatin Pasha, an Austrian renegade in the service of the early British administration in Sudan, warned his subordinates at the same time that "if in an official document I find again that he calls Sudanese servants 'slaves' - a finger from his right hand will be cut off."[9]

The idea of freedom can also be seen as a performance, enacted at the outset of the colonial period by widespread desertion and flight by slaves in Africa, as well as by African slaves in the Western hemisphere, dating from the sixteenth century. In colonial Africa, other avenues of escape included enlistment in the colonial armies, which in their first days were often largely composed of ex-slaves, especially the African contingents of the French army (*Tirailleurs Sénégalais*) and the British West African Frontier Force. Early Christian missions offered refuge and free status, and at times purchased captives to create embryonic Christian communities.

Slavery as a site of unfreedom and fount of ideas of liberation faded by the 1920s. Although it subsisted in submerged social practices here and there, and remained engraved in status memories, it ceased to serve as catalyst for notions of freedom, supplanted by the larger issue of colonial occupation itself. The issue has not wholly evaporated, however, remaining alive in Mauritania, where contentious debates persist around the status of the Harratin, former black slaves of the dominant Moor component of the population. Although the French colonial state officially abolished slavery, a further decree terminating slave status was promulgated as recently as 1980, and some challenge official explanations that Harratin who remain dependent clients of Moor families do so by choice.[10]

In some parts of West Africa, a different form of status, distinguishable from free or noble categories by its stigma-bearing functions, was found in "casted" groups. Included among them were blacksmiths, leather-workers, praise-singers, and some others. These generally endogamous groups shared with slaves a status carrying diverse exclusions.[11] The caste system lacks the comprehensive ritualization and ideological formulation of its South Asian counterpart, and it is thus less far-reaching in its social consequences and in its discursive impacts on concepts of freedom. Although it has persisted in popular consciousness and social relationships into the postcolonial period, its relative importance fades in the urban environment. Casted groups clearly ranked above slaves, excepting slaves who served as soldiers for the military aristocracies. Their degree of unfreedom, entirely internal to the societies concerned, did not connect to the larger discourses surrounding slavery and its abolition, or subsequently liberation from colonial rule; this perhaps explains why, although the status difference and its disabilities were central to social relationships, the caste system never became salient in larger political debate about freedom.

≺ II ≻

Precolonial Precursors of Freedom

Apart from such categories of marginalization, in many parts of Africa contemporary ideas of freedom find precolonial precursors in practices and rituals of consent in the exercise of rule. Such a linkage plays an important part in currents of African political thought which insist on indigenous lineages of liberty and democracy. Although a form of precolonial democracy was far less prevalent than some have claimed,[12] rulers in many areas operated within a framework of customary restraint which imposed important limits on capricious exercise of authority. Rulers might be subject to "destooling," or removal by the community for major transgressions. They were often expected to consult with variously constituted leaders, elders, lineage heads, or others acknowledged as speaking for elements of the community. In their jural role, they were expected to draw upon an established set of customary understandings in mediating, adjudicating, and punishing. The idiom of consent in governance above all conferred a sharing of responsibility for rule among leading elements in society and constraints upon arbitrary use of power, without being framed explicitly in the vocabulary of freedom. It was no less real in bequeathing an ethos which could potentially graft onto concepts of democracy, and in providing a reservoir of ideas, perhaps drawing upon an idealized reconstruction of the past, which can serve contemporary purposes.

Beyond the ritualization of consent, unarticulated notions of freedom were implicit in the highly decentralized nature of political structures in large parts of the continent.[13] A wide range of freedom for those unencumbered by servile status in these regions, although not a reflected doctrine, was embedded in everyday practice. The relative absence of historicized concepts of freedom noted in the chapters on China and Japan is explained by the long-standing existence of elaborated state institutions capable of disciplining the subject, and attendant state ideologies supplying a narrative of legitimation to such hegemony. In settings where centralized statecraft was largely absent, the subsistence-oriented kin and village-based units experienced little constraint in daily social choices. Perhaps the relative absence of restraint imposed by higher authorities was only a banal form of freedom. Nonetheless, naturalized in the normative codes of decentralized political societies, expectations of minimal restraints meant that colonial subjugation was experienced not simply as alien rule, and the imposition of vexatious fiscal and labor requirements, but as a loss of freedom in the modalities of everyday livelihood.

Precolonial Africa had its share of military conquest states, slave-raiding polities, or theocratic sultanates issuing from Islamic revolutions, as well as a millenial tradition of centralized state institutions in the Nile valley and Morocco; but in many areas political power was highly dispersed. A number of factors inhibited the creation of centralized power capable of enforcing unfreedom. Resources to support institutionalized state structures were often meager, and the limited tribute in kind which might be extracted could not support an elaborate superstructure of power, nor extensive modalities of rule. The low population densities of most of Africa until recent decades had important consequences for the possibilities of centralized rule. In many regions, sparse settlement opened the exit option for disaffected groups. If an ambitious ruler sought to enforce new constraints upon subjects, freedom could be regained by migration beyond the reach of the would-be state. Rulers without subjects faced ruin; the threat of withdrawal was a potent constraint.

Another customary practice of everyday freedom was found among pastoral populations. In the extensive low rainfall areas of the continent, partially or wholly pastoral modes of livelihood were indispensable. Although pastoralists are sometimes state-creators (the Fulani in West Africa from Mauritania to Cameroon), they are resistant to control by settled populations.[14]

States that did have centralized power often had a degree of effective authority only in their core area. Beyond lay a zone of fluctuating influence where rule was limited to sporadic exaction of tribute. The paradigm of such a state was the Moroccan kingdom, with its well recognized zone of settled government (*makhzan*) and land of dissidence (*siba*) which bore some resemblance to the southeast Asian "galactic state" examined in chapter 5.

Thus, in seeking antecedents to an idea of freedom in Africa, we find some elements in the nature of the varieties of precolonial encounter with would-be state-builders. In much of rural Africa there was no authority able to control production, extract resources, and regulate social practices.[15] By default, freedom—understood as the absence of restraint from above—was an everyday experience and an unarticulated norm.

Precolonial socioeconomic practice offers important insights into the particular contours of African notions of freedom in another sense. In striking contrast to the Western pathway to expanding freedom, in Africa notions of property rights of the individual played little role. One finds nothing resembling the Lockean joining of property to life and liberty as constitutive elements in personal freedom. In Europe, the sanctity of property was a critical bulwark against the expanding claims of the early modern absolute state. Real property, at the time, was the ultimate source of economic value and the final bastion of individual autonomy. But in Africa possession of land could have no comparable role.[16]

Limited population meant that the scarce factor of production was labor, not land. Control over the productive energies of persons, whether by kinship and family structure, local community customary practice, subordinated status, or some degree of centralized political authority, was key; land was abundant. In much of Africa, land was a communal good, with impermanent use rights ceded by a community leader to a household unit. Members of the community readily obtained such use rights; what was abundant could not be denied. Thus issues of private land ownership, and property rights as the cornerstone of freedom, played no historic part as forerunners of notions of personal liberty.

The idea of implicit right in such land tenure regimes, as well as in the restrictions upon the concentration of authority intrinsic to the environment, suggests another important dimension of embryonic notions of freedom: their rooting primarily in kin group or local community, and not the individual per se. Land was vested in the community, and not by custom alienable to the individual as a permanent asset. Dethroning a ruler or flight beyond reach is normally a response of the community, not an assertion of individual right. The individual could draw upon no normative justification in customary value systems for solitary resistance; the individual fugitive could survive only by attaching himself as a subordinated dependent to another community. Around such an observation emerged in postcolonial politics a major justification for socialist orientation and communal or collective agricultural policy ethos, most systematically argued by former Tanzanian president Julius Nyerere.[17] African societies were essentially communal, ran the argument. The incipient idea of freedom was expressed in the cooperative endeavor of the local community; the most basic resource of a rural society, land, belonged to the community, and production systems were embedded in an array of reciprocities which assured the basic security of all. The "possessive individualism" of capitalism and rooting of individual rights in property were thus seen as alien to the African heritage.

This reading of the heritage carried wide authority in the early years of independence; more recently, it has fallen on hard times.[18] The household unit was the normal base entity in everyday production. The product of the land accrued to the family, not to the community as a whole. In pastoral areas, animals had kin group owners as well. Thus the moral economy of an overwhelmingly rural society included household grounding of production and consumption, although suffused with a communal dimension by the dense linkages of reciprocal obligation which bound together the village, lineage, and migratory groups. Efforts to erect postcolonial collective agricultural policies upon the communitarian thesis invariably failed, rejected by local communities as a denial of household freedom.

The spread of universal religions contained yet another notion of freedom. Both Christianity and Islam have African roots extending back to the first millenium of the present era. In the century immediately preceding the colonial partition, both were expanding into new areas. Embedded in both theologies is the concept of a community of believers, ultimately equal in their submission to or faith in God, as *umma* or *res christiana*. Unfree status was reserved to the unbeliever.

Conversion, for many, was thus a personal act of liberation. It was also frequently an act of community, as entire local units followed their leaders into the new faith. Entry into the new religious community incorporated the converts into a new and cosmopolitan intellectual universe, with their centuries of theological debate around the consequences, rewards, and obligations of faith. The scriptural sources became a privileged library for political language of protest, and subsequently liberation. At the same time, religious membership brought subordination to its prescriptions and its authorities, not all of which advanced the idea of freedom. Much less an avenue to a highly personal and individual salvation, the Christian mission station and congregation and the Islamic mosque community provided a new framework for enactment of communal attachments. In the Islamic case, religious practice was frequently mediated through Sufi brotherhoods, with extensive collective obligations implicit in disciplehood.

Conversion, still very limited south of the Sahara in 1800, accelerated in the nineteenth century, and became massive in the twentieth. Christianity and Islam were not for the most part directly competitive in their recruitment of new believers, in good measure because colonial states, while generally favoring Christian missions, precluded on security grounds evangelization in zones where Islam was already established. There was competition, sometimes heated, between Protestant and Catholic missions. Within each of these religious traditions, there was a negotiated allocation of territories to particular mission orders or denominations. The politics of conversion, in short, did not give rise to anything remotely resembling the religious wars in Europe in the early modern era, nor to the consequent doctrines of freedom and toleration as necessary for religious peace.

≺ III ≻

The Colonial State and the African Subject: Unfreedom Redefined

Germs of an idea of freedom can be discerned in the early reactions to the ramifying European encroachment leading to the colonial partition. The deepening threat of alien rule was most dramatically experienced where it was accompanied by large-scale spoliation of lands, as in Algeria or southern Africa, or particularly rapacious and brutal collection of tribute and taxes, as in the two Congos. The earliest statements of what became African nationalism, in the middle of the nineteenth century, by Alexander Crummell, Edward Blyden (Liberians of African-American and West Indian origins respectively), and others, link to assertions of racial dignity a discourse of African rights. In their first formulation, these are joined to a message of Christian redemption and acquisition of "civilization" as an obligatory passageway to liberation; in Crummell's words, "Africa is the victim of her heterogeneous idolatries."[19]

These, of course, were not the only voices of protest of colonial conquest. However, in their message of resistance, the epic leaders of African combat against imperial occupation—Samory Toure in Guinea, Lat Dior in Senegal, Kabarega in Uganda, Abd-el-Kader in Algeria, and many others—lacked access to the Western realm of the written word, unlike Crummell and Blyden. The justifications of their struggles, which mobilized large followings, thus were erased from the written record; their thought became reduced to the single dimension of symbols of resistance.

The rapid imposition of colonial rule virtually everywhere in Africa in the final quarter of the nineteenth century entirely reconfigured the context within which questions of freedom arose. The African became the mere subject of the sovereign will of an alien ruler. The imperatives of colonial occupation required the rapid construction of comprehensive structures of domination.[20] The intensely competitive nature of the colonial partition drove the metropolitan powers to revive the doctrine of "effective occupation" at the 1884–85 Berlin Conference. Proprietary title was secure only if a basic superstructure of hegemony was demonstrably in place. At the same time, metropolitan treasuries and parliaments required that colonial occupation be self-financing. In most of Africa, no significant revenue flow existed; survival of the newly established colonial state depended upon appropriating subjects' labor.

The most important colonial occupants, Britain, France, and Belgium, were well established constitutional states by the time of their African expansion. Of the key colonial powers, only Portugal, for most of the colonial period, was an autocratic state at home (as were also minor or short-lived colonizers such as Italy, Germany, and Spain). For all colonial occupants, a sharp distinction was drawn between the African subject and the metropolitan citizen, justifying the denial of the rights of the latter to the former. The African was a mere "native," unprepared and unfit for the exercise of freedom. Even in the French case, where a patina of assimilationist ideology born of the French Revolution periodically entered state discourse, the legal distinction between metropolitan citizen and colonial subject was sharply defined.[21] A robust arsenal of arbitrary legislation emerged everywhere, empowering the administrative armature of the colonial state to arbitrarily punish the subject; paradigmatic in this respect was the French *indigénat* code, which offered a menu of dozens of elastic offenses (such as disrespect to a colonial officer or rumor-mongering) permitting summary punishment.

The actual colonial establishments were quite small; in proportional terms, the number of British administrators in Nigeria, relative to population, was far less than in India. Until World War II, the very circumscribed fiscal resources of the colonial territories permitted no more. Thus the consolidation of alien authority required an intermediary layer of African auxiliaries. The costly application of brute force could be economized if the intermediaries enjoyed a modicum of customary legitimacy. Accordingly, incumbent rulers or favorably disposed members of chiefly lineages were preferred choices to provide the local interface of state and subject, a preference given doctrinal content by the Lugardian ideology of "indirect rule," most systematically employed by Britain and Belgium.[22] In the absence of suitable candidates with customary claim to chiefly office, Africans connected to the state apparatus, preferably conversant with the language of the colonizer, might be invested. The element of consent and implicit social contract in a number of indigenous polities gave way to a unilateral chiefly accountability to the colonial superstructure: thus what Mahmood Mamdani, in a well-turned phrase, terms "decentralized despotism" as the inner essence of the colonial state.[23]

The capacious sweep of state authority embedded in the doctrine of sovereignty, unconstrained by effective constitutional restraints on state-subject relations or the emergence of a self-conscious "civil society" laying claim to being ultimate repository of sovereignty, conferred upon the colonial state a scope of authority limited only by its practical capacities. Emblematic was the proclamation, by King Leopold II of Belgium, as the second article of the decree announcing his sovereign proprietorship of the "Congo Free State" (subsequently Belgian Congo), that all "vacant land" was state domain. Because the only land deemed occupied was that under immediate cultivation, well over 95 percent of the surface was covered by regalian prescription. The scope of sovereignty claimed essentially unlimited labor service from the subject, as well as in most areas a substantial fraction of the cash proceeds of his labor through the capitation taxes.[24]

Despite its circumscribed resources, the colonial state from 1900 to 1945 was able to achieve its most central aims, in part because these were limited. Social action was small, and education was mostly delegated, before World War II, to Christian missions. The state was able to squeeze enough from its African subjects to maintain basic order and security (little threatened in the interwar years), to construct a basic network of roads (in major part through conscripted labor), to enforce a basic tax payment, to assure a labor supply to those opening mines or plantations, and to induce or impose the cultivation of cash export crops productive of customs revenue. In the context of the times, these were no small accomplishments.

In emergencies, such as the two world wars, the colonial state, with depleted European personnel, proved able to mobilize remarkable numbers of African troops and to sustain a war economy. By way of example, French survival in World War I owed much to its manpower reserves in Africa; mobilized for the trenches were 177,000 Algerians, 54,000 Tunisians, 37,000 Moroccans, and over 190,000 recruited in the sub-Saharan territories; of these, nearly 25,000 perished.[25]

The contradictions between the constitutional rights of the citizen, well developed in the metropolitan order of most colonial states, and command relationships with the African subject were sustained by the juridical wall of separation between colonial territories and the home domain. Metropolitan law, even in an imperial order such as the French which had sporadic recourse to a discourse of assimilation, did not apply to the African colonies unless specifically extended. In addition, the subject for the most part was subordinated to separated indigenous legal systems, applied through the intermediary customary institutions, partially codified and monitored by the colonial authority.

Thus, the realm of legal process, a critical terrain for the evolution of ideas of freedom in the West, was much less propitious for the African subject during high colonialism. In colonial public law, one can identify three distinct legal spheres. Relations among Europeans, and between Europeans and Africans, were governed largely by criminal and civil codes drawn from the metropole. This part of the legal order guaranteed the physical security of the Europeans clustered around the institutions of colonial hegemony and underwrote the sanctity of property and contract required for their economic activity.

A second sphere, exclusively African, was that of customary law. Conflicts which involved only African subjects, especially if unrelated to overall colonial security, were relegated to these tribunals, to be resolved according to customary norms, provided these were not "repugnant to civilized standards." Under the tutelage of the colonial state, customary law became over time subtly transformed. In the words of one influential study, colonial state monitoring of customary law "changed the nature and use of custom. It could no longer be primarily a political resource in a continued re-negotiation of status and access to resources. Custom became a resource of the instruments of government, rather than a resource of the people."[26] Further, customary law (except for *shari'a* in Islamic zones) had an encapsulating impact, being particular to a given ethnic community as presumed bearer of custom. Thus, argues Mamdani, "Encased in custom, frozen into so many tribes, each under the fist of its own Native Authorities, the subject population is, as it were, containerized."[27]

A third sphere, between these two, lay in the broadly defined arbitrary authority of the local European officer, who for most of the colonial period also presided over a local court. There was ample legislative authority in all colonial systems arming the territorial agents with sanctions for the recalcitrant or insubordinate. A modicum of discretion was needed in the exercise of command authority, to avoid provoking disorder. But the skilled practitioner had wide latitude.

In spite of the authoritarian essence of the colonial state, some interstices of freedom existed, which grew over time. The legal system did offer some such openings. In some areas, particularly coastal West African towns and South Africa, African barristers or legally knowledgeable persons were able to gain access to courts to challenge administrative actions concerning African status or land issues by the early years of the twentieth century. By the 1930s, the gradual crystallization of an African legal profession in British and French-ruled Africa had begun to create a cadre skilled in the litigation of rights which often had a subtext of freedom.

Settlers and immigrants constituted another breach in the wall of colonial sovereignty. For settlers from the metropolitan community, their status as citizens traveled in their luggage. Immigrants from southern Europe or the Levant might be relegated to alien status, but could not be subject to indigenous authorities. Indians in eastern and southern Africa enjoyed some sponsorship of their legal standing from the Raj, and claimed a distinct status as citizen-subjects of the Empire. Settlers in particular demanded a representative voice, and in areas where they were numerous leveraged their citizen standing into precocious control of the colonial state itself (Algeria, Southern Rhodesia, South Africa). A handful of enclaves of African voice subsisted, if only by accident (the four old communes of Senegal, the Creole community in Freetown).[28] In the French and Portuguese cases, the discourse of assimilation created a narrow passageway through which, prior to World War II, a small number of Africans could formally be acknowledged as citizens by internalizing metropolitan cultural norms and identification.

One of the legitimating concepts justifying colonial occupation was the notion of "civilization," a property intrinsic to Europe but absent in the wild domains subdued by imperial conquest. The zone of civilization was a land where freedom reigned; thus the acquisition of its cultural traits implied an escape from autocracy. Initially the concept of "civilization" carried heavy racial overtones; the elaboration of colonial rule in Africa coincided with the most virulent moment in the sad history of racism. The African subject, as a "native" of racial stock whose inferiority was assumed, lacked in European eyes the attributes of "civilization" necessary to enjoy civil liberties. The empirical measures became closely associated with the cultural practices of the respective colonizers: thorough mastery of the colonial language, conversion to Christianity (though for the French and British Islam would also do), Western education, adoption of the everyday cultural norms of the metropole. By the interwar period growing numbers of Africans met these standards and could invoke the lapidary Cecil Rhodes dictum: "equal rights for all civilized men."

In turn, until World War II, the educated African was a reformer rather than a rejecter of the colonial state. The grievances expressed and freedoms sought pivoted about the recognition of educated Africans as partners in colonial state management, as entitled voices in the organs of representation, as legitimate entrants into the respectable professions on the basis of their credentials and qualifications, and as persons whose mastery of the norms of European cultural practices merited ending the indignities of racial discrimination. Although these claims found only partial satisfaction, by the interwar period the educated African was increasingly exempt from the vexations applicable in the countryside (*indigénat* code, compulsory labor service, customary court jurisdiction). In return, many of the clerks, messengers, teachers, and interpreters gave loyal service to the state. So also did many of the chiefs, many of whom now had some education.

For the rural African, not yet attuned to discourses of freedom formulated in abstract forms, the terms of engagement with the colonial state revolved around issues of security and livelihood. As chapter 5 argues, order and security may have a high priority when memories of violence and unrest are relatively fresh. The nineteenth century, in much of Africa, was a time of widespread dislocation and insecurity: the predatory state-building of slave merchants such as Rabah and Msiri in central Africa, the aggressive expansion of the Zulu military state and the eddies of warfare it unleashed in southern Africa, the last round of Fulani *jihads* in West Africa, the Yoruba civil wars in Nigeria, in addition to the wars of colonial conquest. After the harsh years of its initial imposition, colonial occupation brought a relative degree of security of household and livelihood. This may help explain the infrequency of rural challenge during high colonialism, and the settled belief before World War II that, except for north Africa, the colonial system was secure for the foreseeable future.

Religious community was another site of legitimacy for the colonial order until its final years. For the Christian missions, the colonial state guaranteed security and freedom of operation for the evangelical endeavor. In return, the missionaries and the growing indigenous cohort of pastors, priests, and catechists found the blanket of colonial security assured the most important freedom of all: of worship and evangelization. Islam, although initially regarded as a singularly dangerous adversary for its capacity for organizing resistance on a scale transcending ethnos and polity, came to be viewed as a potential partner if managed with care. The epic sagas of the Qadiriyya warrior Abd-el-Kader in Algeria, the Sudanese Mahdi (god-guided one) Muhammed Ahmed, or the Somali "Mad Mullah" Muhammad 'Abdille Hassan, were well known to colonial state builders. The exemplary lessons they provided were well learned; the successors of the Mahdi in Sudan became honored figures in the colonial pantheon, and the British in 1914 successfully represented themselves to Sudanese subjects as defenders of the faith against the perfidious Turks. Similar cultivation won for the French the willing collaboration of the leaders of the Mouride and Tijaniyya orders.[29] The tone is conveyed by the celebrated letter to all Tijanis by Al Hadj Malick Sy on September 8, 1908:

> Adhere fully to the French government. God—may He be blessed and exalted!—has granted victory, grace and favor particularly to the French. He has chosen them to protect our persons and our goods. That is why we

> must live in perfect harmony with them. Let them hear nothing concerning us which would not have them rejoice.
>
> Before their arrival here, in effect, we lived on a footing of captivity, of murders and of pillages. Had they not come we would still be in such a condition. Do not consider yourselves unfortunate in fulfilling the obligations they have established. For on sound reflection, in fact, it is clear that this is a contribution which they ask of you, and not a burden they impose upon you.[30]

An assurance of freedom is key: the liberty for Islam to expand and prosper, without fear of colonial power being utilized to impose Christian missions.

From the early stages, colonial state behavior was subject to exposure and criticism by liberal and left voices in the metropole. The grotesque abuses of the Congo Free State under King Leopold were subjected to a storm of criticism in the first decade of the twentieth century, playing a part in forcing Belgium to assume full responsibility for the colony.[31] The vast land spoliations in southern Africa, Kenya, and Algeria triggered ineffectual but not insignificant protest from groups such as the London Aboriginal Rights Association. In 1931, the International Labour Organisation organized a major conference on allegations of forced labor in Africa; the French and the Belgians in particular (as well as independent Liberia) were subject to embarrassing revelations.

A muted but prescient voice of the African diaspora began to be heard in the series of Pan-African conferences initiated in 1900; although in the early years most participants were West Indians or African-Americans, the conferences did introduce themes of African rights and freedom, though not before 1945 liquidation of the colonial system. In the late nineteeth century, such liminal forerunners of subsequent African nationalism as J. B. Africanus Horton of Sierra Leone and Edward Blyden of Liberia had spoken of eventual African self-rule.

≺ IV ≻

African Freedom as Political Independence

The expansion and direct expression of an idea of freedom on a major scale was to await the post-World War II era. In 1945, the last and most important of the Pan-African conferences took place. It was mainly African in participation and animated by future heads of state Kwame Nkrumah of Ghana and Jomo Kenyatta of Kenya. The demand for full African liberation was strident and explicit. The international normative order was now transformed, and a right of self-government was inscribed in the 1945 United Nations Charter. Whereas the core players in the international system prior to the war were the major colonial powers themselves, after 1945 the world order was structured by the global rivalry between the United States and the Soviet Union, both of which by different logics favored the dissolution of the colonial order. Britain had committed itself to eventual self-rule for the African colonies in 1938, although the time frame was still in centuries. The postwar French constitution extended citizenship to the colonial subjects, and the *indigénat* was abolished in 1946; although self-government was ruled out by the 1945 Brazzaville conference defining postwar French colonial policy, the African colonies were to enjoy a democratic destiny in a loosely defined greater France. Vague thoughts of an eventual Eurafrican polity in Belgian Africa, confederated with Belgium, began to germinate.

African political discourse, however, altered the terms of the debate. The transcendent negation of freedom, the very definition of unfreedom, was colonial rule, or in the case of South Africa apartheid and white minority government. The achievement of freedom was the liquidation of the colonial system throughout Africa. "When I talk of freedom and independence for Africa," wrote Nkrumah, "I mean that the vast African majority should be accepted as forming the basis of government in Africa."[32] In different tonalities, the writings of such influential figures as the West Indians Frantz Fanon and Aime Cesaire; African nationalist figures such as Leopold Senghor, Kwame Nkrumah, Amilcar Cabral, or Julius Nyerere; widely read journals such as *Présence Africaine* in Paris; and seminal documents such as the 1956 African National Congress Freedom Charter in South Africa created a manifesto of freedom around the overarching theme of destroying colonialism and apartheid.

Political space was opened to rapidly burgeoning African nationalist movements, as representative institutions with African participation took form. Once the inevitability of eventual transition was accepted, the colonial state experienced a fundamental metamorphosis. One by one the innumerable barriers to the enjoyment of citizen rights mirroring those in the metropole began to fall. Respectable decolonization could occur only through the establishment of political institutions replicating the constitutional model of the colonizing power. The freedom conferred by grant of independence was embodied in the institutional forms which reflected the particular contours of the struggle to displace the early modern absolutist states with representative democracies. To the extent that colonial state managers retained a tutelary role during the transition, they could only operate from the sole blueprint for free government which they knew: that of the home country. African nationalists, at the time, sought no other formula; even as they fought colonial power, their own education and socialization had schooled them to hold the institutions of the imperial occupant in high regard as exemplary models of freedom.

One important issue in defining a path to postcolonial freedom was identifying who was to be its bearer. In Algeria, the French in their costly struggle to preserve Algeria as an integral part of the Republic through the 1950s argued that the object of freedom was the individual Algerian; there was no organic Algerian human collectivity which could make legitimate claim to liberation.

The goal of France, through the complete integration offered in the 1958 Constitution, was freedom for all individual Algerians within the Republic by their reclassification as citizens unencumbered by a higher intermediate identity as Muslims and Algerians. In the 1930s, such a formula might have had at least temporary success; Ferhat Abbas, subsequently for a time leader of the Algerian Provisional government in exile during the independence war (1954–62), famously wrote in the late 1930s:

> If I had encountered the Algerian nation, I would be a nationalist. Men who have died for a patriotic ideal are honored and respected every day. My life is worth no more than theirs. And yet I will not die for the Algerian fatherland, for this fatherland does not exist. I have not encountered it. I have questioned history. I have questioned the living and the dead. I have visited the cemeteries. No one has spoken to me of such a thing. You cannot build upon the wind. We . . . link our future once and for all to that of French endeavor in this country.[33]

But as the forces of African liberation gathered speed such sentiments became archaic expressions.

Another colonial formula for identifying the bearers of freedom was to vest the entitlement in racial communities, each of which could be viewed as an equal partner. This line of reasoning shaped successive franchise arrangements in the terminal colonial period. The French employed until 1956 a dual electoral college in sub-Saharan Africa, with one roll for French residents and officially assimilated Africans, and a second, vastly more numerous one for the rest of the African population; the two colleges received equal representation. Belgium employed a similar formula of gerrymandered urban districts designed to produce some kind of racial parity in the first elected municipal councils in 1958. Britain deployed the notion of racial partnership in east and central Africa through the 1950s. The last white regime in apartheid South Africa, in its final desperate effort to preserve remnants of white hegemony, tried to bargain for a modified version of such racial group rights. African nationalist leaders, supported by a global consensus that freedom of participation and representation must weight all individual human beings equally, could never accept a derogation from international norms such as racial group rights, which would annul their own birthright as a majority population.

A somewhat different variant of this issue arose in the decolonization dialogue in Nigeria. Here the issue was whether the instrumentality for achievement of freedom was at the national or regional level. The fateful choice was driven as much by Nigerian political dynamics as colonial preferences. The Northern Region, obsessed by its relative backwardness in cadres carrying the credentials for senior administrative appointment and fearful of southern domination, insisted with the backing of British tutors on regional self-government first, with a Nigerianized federal government to come later. Regional administrations were in the hands of political formations dominated by the three large ethnoregional blocs, Yoruba, Igbo, and Hausa-Fulani, and constituted Nigerian initial postcolonial politics as an unstable three-player ethnic game, with the nearly 40 percent of the population who belonged to other, smaller groups cast as permanent minorities. Political freedom, at the moment of Nigerian independence, essentially translated into the regional hegemony of the three large ethnic groupings.

A comparable dialectic occurred with respect to the colonial administrative federations of Afrique Occidentale Française and Afrique Equatoriale Française, with the important differences that the territorial subdivisions were not ethnic in character, and that the consequence of locating self-governing political structures at the territorial level in 1956 was the dismantling of the larger units. Political freedom was thus attained by a dozen territorial units rather than two. The territories that perceived themselves as prospective financial providers for the poorer territories, such as Ivory Coast, Benin (then Dahomey), and Gabon, insisted on the breakup.

The colonizers played for time but were confronted with an ever-foreshortening horizon of transition. Colonial forms of rule, through the 1950s, became prescriptively illegitimate through the emergence of a Third World voice in the international arena. The futility of military repression and its enormous costs became evident in the Dutch failure to reestablish postwar authority in Indonesia and the French disaster in Indochina; these instances eclipsed the British ability to crush Mau Mau in Kenya 1952–56 and the Communist insurgency in Malaya. In Africa, the failure of the French military deployment of 500,000 to crush the Algerian liberation movement, and a comparable failed Portuguese effort in its African territories, clearly established the inevitability of African independence.

"Freedom" as transcendent political goal, with the rise of anti-colonial nationalism, thus had as primary referent alien rule. Colonial subjects, in this doctrine of protest, achieve standing and rights only collectively as members of a community defined by the territorial geopolitics of the colonial partition. The cultural complexity of the states to emerge from the colonial order and the uncertain affective bonds of their prospective citizenries necessarily brought an awareness of their potential fragility. The compelling need both for solidarity in anti-colonial challenge and for consolidating the unity of the new state gave a collective cast to the idea of freedom. *Uhuru* (freedom), in the 1950s slogans, was joined to *umoja* (oneness).

A curious dialectic emerged, little noted at the time, between the norms of state institutions erected under the tutelage of the withdrawing colonial rulers and the discourses of anti-colonial liberation. The former privileged the ideas of individual right embedded in the liberal constitutional state, while the latter stressed the collective right of the new nation presumed under construction. "Democracy" was thus a newly discovered but foundational value for respectable withdrawal for the colonizer, but instrumental norm for the anti-colonial movement, a means to the transcendent end of immediate independence. The basic freedom to organize, to hold political meetings, to launch newspapers, to travel through the territory without restriction, was of immense benefit. So too were the frequent elections in the 1950s, which provided a focal point for nationalist mobilization. But the essential value of these freedoms was their utility in the combat against colonial rule, rather than their intrinsic worth.

≺ V ≻

Vanishing Freedom: The Illusion of the Integral State

The contradiction between the prevailing visions became apparent after independence. For the successor nationalist elite, the core imperatives were accelerated development and consolidation of the potentially fragile postcolonial state through "nation-building." "Freedom and development," declared Tanzania President Julius Nyerere in a 1968 speech, "are as closely linked together as are chicken and eggs! Without chickens, you have no eggs; and without eggs you soon have no chickens. Similarly, without freedom you get no development, and without development you very soon lose your freedom."[34] The very essence of freedom was overcoming poverty, ignorance, and disease. The imperative of national unity was the obverse of the same coin. "At the present stage of Ghana's economic development the whole community must act in the national interest," wrote Kwame Nkrumah. "In fact most of our development so far has had to be carried out by the Government itself. There is no other way out."[35] The pursuit of true freedom thus required unified, disciplined collective action carried out through the state. For secure existence and international respectability, states required nationhood, and thus "nation-building" by an energetic ruling group.

Based upon these premises, the idea of "democracy" as a liberal polity, placing supreme value on individual right and competitive multi-party electoral politics, gave way to a more jacobin notion of a unified popular will, represented by the dominant nationalist party, bearer of an historic mission of creating a single national identity and rapid development. The instrument for this intoxicating goal was the single party, marshaling all national energies in pursuit of a relentless struggle against underdevelopment. Although the single party formula long ago lost credibility, at the moment of African independence respected academic voices as well as the most prestigious leaders of the independence generation argued its validity as an instrument of democracy as well as development. The most elegant formulation is found in the 1965 Tanzania Presidential Commission on the Establishment of a Democratic One Party State. This document fully endorses a wide array of basic freedoms, although it rejects the notion of reducing them to a bill of rights. Its authors develop a well-argued brief for the processes of candidate selection and internal party procedures which intend to foster full discussion and free debate. The Commission rejects the notion that party membership should be limited to an ideological elect; such a view is "at variance with democratic principles and, in particular, with the principle of democracy as understood in traditional African society." The party is a mass organization "through which any citizen of goodwill can participate in the process of Government."[36] At a philosophical level, running through the document is a painstaking effort to reconcile the values of freedom and democracy with the axiomatic necessity of a single party structure.

The initially persuasive force of such arguments to many notwithstanding, in practice single parties soon fused with the state apparatus to form exclusionary political monopolies. The imperatives of preserving power and reproducing incumbent rule inevitably trumped the values of liberating mass participation and political rights of the individual citizen. Electoral process became a plebiscitary ritual. As well, over time the exercise of rule required a pattern of rewards to locally influential persons, as the initial legitimacy of leadership in the struggle for political independence faded. Initially on a small scale, diversion of public resources into patronage distribution by the 1970s became a major drain. By the middle 1960s, the loss of political momentum was evident, made visible by a dramatic wave of military coups (Algeria, Nigeria, Ghana, Congo-Kinshasa, Benin, and Central African Republic within a few months). The military in turn usually reconstituted their own single party systems, unable to justify prolonged army rule on the basis of the unique qualification of the military to govern.

The civil liberties extended belatedly by terminal colonial regimes were soon rolled back. Arbitrary statutes, often surviving from colonial times, were dusted off and enforced: preventative detention laws, requirements for permits for meetings, master and servant ordinances. All media were the monopoly of the party-state. Organizations were forced to become mere party appendages. State security agencies established networks of informers, and a climate of fear and suspicion took form among the public. Although the intensity of the repressive atmosphere varied—relatively mild in a Senegal or a Tanzania, much harsher in the Guinea of Sekou Toure—the pattern was general.

Beyond the monopolization of political power, another crucial trend was the rapid expansion of the government apparatus, driven by a vision that the state was the necessary theologian, architect, manager, and proprietor of development. This collectivizing demiurge drew sustenance from some other premises of modern statecraft which enjoyed commanding authority at the moment of African independence. It also built upon trends well in progress. From the 1920s, developmentalism was an important theme in the colonial discourse of legitimation, although its accomplishments were modest until World War II. But during the final colonial decade, as colonial power in retreat struggled to control and extend the timetable of transition, there was an extraordinary development of social infrastructure. Swelling colonial revenues fueled by the commodity boom for African exports and the first substantial metropolitan public capital investment in the African colonies brought a unique moment of a "life more abundant" for most strata of the African population. The rapidly growing ranks of young Africans armed by education with new aspirations for mobility and uplift expanded the audience for nationalist parties and injected into the language of liberation a commitment to a redoubled pace of progress which would attend independence. The terminal colonial state itself took partial ownership of the developmental process, creating agricultural marketing monopolies, planning offices, and state development banks.

"Developmentalism" in its 1960 version demanded a strong, centralized state capable of a planned and directive role, able to override recalcitrant social forces and assume control over colonial capital. To secure these ends, across the continent rulers married the autocratic heritage of the colonial state with the instruments of political monopoly forged in anti-colonial struggle, or created in its wake. Freedom in its essence was a collective good, to be realized in the developmental nation-state. The seeming possibility of such visions was enhanced by expanding state revenue, substantial aid from the former colonial power, and new access to international assistance.

These views on the centrality of state-led development were held not only by African leaders, but by mainstream development economists of the day, of diverse persuasions; "the congruence of Marxian and non-Marxian economic thought on the development issue," writes Killick, "was a rather remarkable and mutually reinforcing one."[37] This consensus, in Africa, intersected an additional potent factor shaping development thought in 1960: the belief that another core site of unfreedom was capitalism itself, as experienced in colonial Africa. In its visible manifestations, it was as alien as the colonial state itself. This view was intrinsic to socialist doctrine, widely espoused by the younger generation of intellectuals, but by no means limited to them. The economy was overwhelmingly in the control of the colonial corporations, with the secondary niches in wholesale commerce and retail trade often occupied by pariah entrepreneurs from South Asia, the Levant, or the Mediterranean. African participation in colonial capitalism was blocked by diverse restrictions, beginning with the reluctance of European banks to lend to Africans. One may recall that in the itinerary of ideas about freedom in Europe one important site of struggle between rulers and the propertied classes involved property rights and fiscal policies; in this battleground important individual rights and liberties were won. But in newly independent Africa nothing comparable could occur. Private property and attendant rights were overwhelmingly an issue which concerned only Europeans and immigrants from outside Africa. Relatively few Africans at the moment of independence had any stake in a liberal market economy.

Thus, whether or not regimes adopted some form of socialist ideology, the trend toward parastatalization of the economy was general. Colonial capital was a particular target, subject to diverse nationalization or indigenization measures. Even in a state such as Ivory Coast, one of the few overtly to proclaim its commitment to a capitalist strategy of development, the state, ran the argument, necessarily had to act as surrogate capitalist, given the absence of indigenous entrepreneurs with the means and the vocation to create new industries. Thus Ivory Coast, like most other African states in the 1980s, found itself with many dozens of state enterprises, most of dubious or negative profitability. In officially socialist Tanzania, former economic advisor to the Tanzanian government Reginald Green noted with satisfaction that by the mid-1970s, 80 percent of the medium and large-scale economic activity lay in the public sector, a figure higher than those for Soviet bloc states a comparable time after the imposition of Stalinist socialism.[38]

The product of the political monopoly and economic command state was a would-be integral polity, which dreamed of realizing a comprehensive design of perfected hegemony. Although not universally held, this vision influenced state-building projects from the late 1960s well into the 1970s. The state through its single party sought unrestricted dominance over civil society, whose participation was channeled, limited, and disciplined through the party's ancillary organizations in charge of organizing particular sectors (labor, youth, students, women, traders). Thus unfettered, the state is free to pursue a rational design for the future and amply to reward the ruling class for its governance services. In such a vision, the idea of freedom could have meaning and value only in its collective form.

≺ VI ≻

State Crisis and Multiple Sites of Freedom

The African project of the command state resembled in some respects the absolutism of the early modern European state, but it collided with a very different normative environment.[39] Ideas of freedom, codified in the 1789 French Declaration of Rights, had become not only universalized as concepts, but also globalized. Democracy and attendant civil rights, by the 1990s, was an obligatory model for full international respectability. The singular form of autocratic state which had become general in the 1960s in Africa, initially relatively impervious to internal or external critique of its human rights deficit, progressively weakened in the 1980s under the weight of its multiple policy failings. Civil society, which initially responded to state predation by disengagement and exit, by the late 1980s, sustained by a globalized discourse of freedom, challenged authoritarian modes of rule.[40] A once quiescent international human rights community now spoke with loud voices, providing copious documentation of state abuses.

The vision of the integral state was negated in the 1980s crippling indebtedness, stifling over-expansion of the state apparatus, and disastrous economic performance, which paved the way for the democratic opening of the 1990s and the rebirth of a differently conceived idea of freedom. Notions of liberty germinated in civil societies alienated by states which in the popular imagination were little more than predators, pirates, or even vampires. Such dystopic visions of the state drew upon what Celestin Monga, in a piquant formulation, terms the "anthropology of anger." For several decades, he suggests, "the rules of the political game and the social game (concerning power, status, wealth, and domination) were unilaterally determined by Africa's authoritarian states, and people feigned to accept these rules when in fact they constantly adjusted their behavior to escape domination and to circumvent the most coercive structures."[41] Civil society, a term which, significantly, came into common use in Africa only in the 1980s,[42] found or forced open new space for the open expression of ideas and opinions, and for formation of organizations outside the tutelage and control of the state. This rapidly expanding nongovernmental sector built upon the ramifying international discourse of rights and enjoyed powerful sustenance from major international forces, persuaded of the "failure" of patrimonial autocracy as a modality of rule in Africa. The stage was set for the contradictory and turbulent era of the 1990s, with the idea of freedom playing a far more comprehensive role than in the past, but competing with the legacy of state decay, far-reaching economic crisis, warlords and rogue militias, and other forces of disintegration.

The democratic era of the 1990s, in spite of its disappointments and limitations, situated ideas of freedom in a multiplicity of sites, opened many new debates, and revived older ones on making freedom authentic by rooting it in an indigenous heritage. Particularly noteworthy among the array of associations were human rights groups, created in most countries by dedicated and often courageous activists. The global library of freedom doctrines provided critical resources to such groups. So also did strategic alliances with the international human rights community, particularly such organizations as Human Rights Watch and Amnesty International which could bring pressure to bear upon the donor community. To some extent, the donor community incorporated requirements to respect human rights into their package of conditions for access to aid, which most African states desperately needed. Through the human rights campaigns, the languages of freedom percolated into the political realm in significant ways.

The incapacity of the economic command state had produced a burgeoning informal economy, in which individuals sought the elemental freedom to survive through eluding state regulation.[43] The inability of states to sustain their proprietary and controlling role, by the 1990s, opened opportunities for free endeavor in the public economic realm as well. Although the "structural adjustment programs" imposed by the international financial institutions and donor community fell far short of creating full market economies, a degree of liberalization did occur. The protocols of freedom in their economic dimension were in a process of redefinition, as the earlier animus toward capitalism as the alien handmaiden of colonialism and avatar of unfreedom slowly dissolved.

African women, liberated from the stifling single party control of their voice, opened new discursive space around ideas of freedom by insisting on its gender applications.[44] Drawing upon universal discourses, and energized by their involvement in the 1985 Nairobi and 1995 Beijing United Nations conferences on women's rights, a growing number of women's organizations Africanized gender discourses, to repel the charge of some male adversaries that such values were alien impositions of "Western feminists."[45] Forceful and frequently effective claims were made to enlarge the freedom of women in such issue areas as land rights, inheritance, succession, marriage, and access to education.

Group consciousness acquired a degree of legitimacy as a locus of freedom. Ethnicity in 1960 was widely perceived as backwardness, as mere "tribalism." Yet it became one more refuge from the command state, and emerged in the liberalized environment of the 1990s as a more publicly accepted social phenomenon, though many countries continue to proscribe political parties organized on the basis of ethnicity or religion. In the influential words of the late Nigerian intellectual Claude Ake, an authentic African democracy "will have to recognize nationalities, subnationalities, ethnic groups, and communities as social formations that express freedom and self-realization and will have to grant them rights to cultural expression and political and economic participation."[46]

In the context of virtual bankruptcy of many states and their incapacity to fund social services, religious congregations had often filled the void and thus served as another site of freedom. Church-related organizations have been particularly numerous in the proliferating non-governmental organization sector since the 1980s. They have supplied the basic organizational infrastructure for diverse humanitarian relief operations by the international community. Here and there, Islam provides a channel for charitable and social service endeavors, outside the state framework. In Algeria, for example, the enrooting of an important Islamist current in Algerian society during the 1980s is in part explicable by the role of the mosque in ministering to basic needs of urban popular sectors which felt abandoned by the state. The enhanced importance of religious community as social refuge as well as place of worship increased its role in the enunciation of societal values and the translation of constitutive elements of an African lexicon of freedom into localized idioms.

The forces of recovery and rejuvenation in Africa draw upon multiple sites of expression of ideas of freedom. Pressures of decay and disintegration have been produced by large zones of interpenetrated civil strife, the marginalization of Africa in the global economy, and the incapacity of the international financial institutions and Western donor community to find effective means and doctrines of assistance. The outcome of the interplay of these and of the huge challenge of a transition from the would-be integral state, with its autocratic colonial heritage, to an economically and politically liberalized polity, is far from clear. Unfreedom now has new sources, both internal—violence and disorder, with marauding and plundering militias—and external—the relentless imposition of "structural adjustment" programs perceived as impoverishing the populace. The historic vitality of ideas of freedom, as they are naturalized in Africa, is certain. But equally clear is the challenge they face to overcome forces of disorder and decline.

2

African States and the Search for Freedom

WILLIAM J. FOLTZ

> Our mistake was not in our demand for freedom; it was in the assumption that freedom—real freedom—would necessarily and with little trouble follow liberation from alien rule.
>
> Julius Nyerere, 1976[1]

FREEDOM, in the specific form of the elimination of formal colonial rule, came to sub-Saharan Africa as part of the worldwide "winds of change," which after World War II swept aside the presumption that large parts of the tropical and nonindustrial world would—and should—be ruled by Europeans and those of European descent. This presumption was replaced by the expectation that, for better or worse, the regions that had come under imperial rule now would be governed as independent and sovereign states, with boundaries essentially the same as those of the former colonies.

Since their independence, the 48 states in sub-Saharan Africa have moved through a series of complex relations with the many forms of freedom. Often, these relations have pitted freedom—or freedom of maneuver—for the political elite against the freedom and human rights of ordinary citizens. The end of colonization and the formal transfer of power to African nationalist politicians produced a juridical form of freedom, freedom *of* the African state, admitting it to membership in the international society of sovereign states. Poor, weak, and dependent on outsiders, the African states sought—with some skill—to use that sovereignty to increase their margin of maneuver in the international arena, an arena at the same time a source of danger and a source of political support and of material gain. That search sought *freedom for the African state.* The rewards of such maneuver, if rewards there were, accrued always to the state's central leadership and its select clients, but rarely to ordinary Africans. For many of them the state, whether under military or civilian control, was a source of repression and deprivation, to which they responded in age-old African fashion either by migrating beyond the reach of state agents or by dropping out in place and weaving a set of social and economic relationships independent of the state. This constituted a search for *freedom from the African state.*

The end of the Cold War, coinciding with the end of the economically disastrous decade of the 1980s, weakened the hold on power of some of Africa's most authoritarian regimes and emboldened some individuals and civil organizations to seek to bring about a more democratic order: a search for *freedom within the African state.* The same world events made possible a change in the norms of how Africa's states related to one another. The absolute defense of sovereignty yielded ground to a recognition that one state's repressive behavior could perhaps legitimately be a concern to neighboring states—and indeed African states as a whole—and that intervention to preserve a freely chosen government could be not only legitimate, but perhaps even imperative. This I term a hope that it would be possible to defend and even extend freedom *through the African state system.*

≺ I ≻

Freedom For the African State

The African states, the first wave of which became independent in the decade from 1957 (Ghana) to 1966 (Botswana), were born poor and weak. Their structures of state authority inherited from the colonial regime were poorly articulated, shallow in depth, and limited in substantive and geographic scope. These structures had for the most part sufficed to maintain the colonial regime in power at tolerable cost to its masters, with local instruments of power backed up by an imperial reserve of military force and economic plums that could be shifted throughout the empire at the metropole's direction to quell individual perturbations of colonial order. Imperial authority was exercised most effectively in the area around the capital and around any concentrated mineral resources, attenuating with distance into the countryside where it was often exercised through local chiefs and religious authorities enjoying varying degrees of legitimacy.[2]

The new African leaders had proved their skill in the hothouse environment of post-World War II decolonization politics: mobilizing popular grievances to embarrass the colonial administration without, however, breaking off dialogue; organizing enough of a political movement or coalition to win the elections held just before independence was granted. These were men of political talent, sometimes considerable political talent; but they knew little about running the economy and had only limited administrative experience. Gaining greater control over the political hinterland and finding ways for the state to penetrate society and extract tax revenue and other resources needed for the state apparatus to function were imperative and challenging tasks. These tasks were essential if the state was to survive long and strong enough to build a nation out of the congeries of peoples included within the country's inherited and internationally-recognized borders.

From the point of view of state leaders, the political freedom that was put in their hands at independence, or seized shortly after by coup d'état, was threatened by actions and actors in the economic realm over which the state had little control. As Tanzania's Julius Nyerere put it,

> [A] government immediately discovers that it inherited the power to make laws, to direct the civil service, to treat with foreign governments, and so on, but that it did not inherit effective power over economic developments in its own country. Indeed, it often discovers that there is no such thing as a national economy at all![3]

The most modern and profitable parts of the economy were controlled by Europeans, often through transnational mining and trading companies. Within Africa many of the intermediate administrative and entrepreneurial roles were taken by other outsiders—Lebanese in west and central Africa, South Asians in east and southern Africa. This uncontrolled economic realm, poorly understood by the new leaders, seemed to pose a political threat, all the more dangerous in that its operations were veiled from public eye and extended beyond state borders. It raised the specter of replacing colonialism with an even more insidious "neo-colonialism" labeled by Ghana's Kwame Nkrumah (with a bow to Lenin) "the last stage of imperialism."[4] Nor were such fears entirely fanciful. The attempt of

Moïse Tshombe to split off the mineral-rich Katanga province from the rest of Congo in the mid 1960s was bankrolled by major Belgian, British, and French financial concerns.[5]

The seemingly logical response to the neocolonial threat to the new-found freedom was to bring as much of the economy as possible under the control of the political elite by nationalizing existing firms, setting up state corporations, and strictly controlling exports and imports—all in the name of "African Socialism." With minor variations in ideological gloss, African Socialism was installed as economic doctrine across the continent from Senegal to Tanzania. Those countries, like the Cote d'Ivoire and Kenya, that eschewed the African Socialist label nonetheless built heavy and inefficient state sectors. Whatever the label under which they operated, and whatever the mix of self-serving and disinterested motivations, politicians sought to tame the political risk posed by the market economy by subordinating it to their own control.

The consequences were severe. Asians and Lebanese in particular were victimized; administrators were denied employment; entrepreneurs had their shops expropriated or were forced to buy protection by taking on politically safe African partners. In the most extreme case, Uganda's Idi Amin simply forced the entire Asian population out of the country, whether or not they were Ugandan citizens—with predictably devastating consequences for his country's economy. In theory a bold exercise of sovereign power in the name of the people, such "socialist" actions marked the weakness of the new political elites and the tenuous nature of their relationship to the larger society. In retrospect, such widely adopted policies may be seen to have had a disastrous effect on the economic life of most African countries:

> Africa's growth (measured as annual average change in GDP) averaged just 0.8% per year over the 25-year period 1965 to 1990. By contrast, growth in the seven fastest-growing developing countries outside Africa averaged 5.8% and growth in the rest of the developing world averaged 1.8%.[6]

The political impact of such anti-market measures was equally deleterious, providing easy opportunities for the creation of a neopatrimonial political order, one in which the state apparatus was bent to serve a clientele of cronies at the service of the state's master. Such an order was financed by rakeoffs from state-sector enterprises and other corrupt rent-seeking practices.[7] These policies might have effectively defended the political elite's freedom of maneuver, but they sapped the strength of the state and cost the African population dearly.

Weak at home, the new African states were objectively weaker abroad. Unable to project power effectively within their own boundaries, they had even less ability to project power or influence beyond them. In that sense all African states really were born equal: whatever the differences in size or natural endowments, during the first years of independence none of them had the ability to coerce another. The new African states did have one trump card they could play in the international arena, however; that was the juridical sovereignty that came with officially recognized membership in the international community of sovereign states. (In recognition thereof, the day of admission to the United Nations was likely to be celebrated with almost as much official pomp as independence day itself.) The African states exercised sovereign rights because the international community decreed that they were sovereign states (that is, they were "constitutionally independent" entities claiming both territory and population), whether or not they had conquered or effectively held their national territory or whether or not they dispensed with neocolonial economic and political ties with powerful outsiders. African leaders sought first to protect and actualize that sovereignty, then to use it as a tool for extending control at home and for increasing their margin of maneuver internationally. In a Cold War setting, they could use sovereignty to extract resources from abroad by trading symbolic goods, such as votes in the United Nations or public expression of ideological fealty, to one or another Cold War patron in exchange for tangible benefits.[8]

The Organization of African Unity (OAU), created in 1963, became the vessel and symbol of African states' sovereignty. The OAU has often been seen—erroneously—as a failed attempt at continent-wide, pan-African political unification.[9] Rather, it was a knowingly-crafted instrument to protect state sovereignty and the pre-eminent role of chief of state. Five out of the seven OAU charter's founding "principles" defend either state sovereignty or presidential pre-eminence. Nothing in that charter is designed to weaken any leader's freedom of action in his domestic realm. At its first anniversary meeting, on the initiative of Tanzania's Julius Nyerere, the OAU appended to the charter the provision that the existing colonial boundaries must remain unalterable, except through peaceful neighborly agreement. This provision defined and circumscribed the field of action in which a political leader could operate freely. As one founding leader, Mali's Modibo Keita, set forth the paradox, "African unity demands of each one of us complete respect for the maintenance of the present boundaries of our respective states."[10]

The OAU has served to amplify the voice of independent African states on those issues on which their leaders are agreed. These have included notably the liberation of southern Africa from white and colonial rule, a matter of direct and vital concern for neighboring states. These independent states on the southern African front line became, willy-nilly, hosts to armed liberation movements. This exposed them to retaliation, initially from the Portuguese. Then, after Angola and Mozambique became independent, they were savagely punished by Rhodesia and South Africa. When Rhodesia became independent in 1980 under the name Zimbabwe, it became a major target of South Africa's destabilization efforts.[11] Zambia, too, paid a price for Kenneth Kaunda's harboring headquarters for South African, Rhodesian, and Namibian liberation movements; the "high price of principles" one sympathetic scholar called it.[12]

The southern African freedom struggle was also of political and normative concern to states further away. African elites did feel their own freedom diminished by what they saw as the continued enslavement of other Africans. As Nyerere put it, "No African state is secure in its independence, and no African can rest secure in his own status as a free citizen of the world while any Africans are held in colonial subjugation."[13] Some states that neglected their OAU membership dues still contributed to the OAU's semi-autonomous African Liberation Committee, which provided the liberation movements with money and military equipment. Perhaps the major contribution the African states made to southern African liberation was keeping alive the issue of freedom from colonial rule and racial discrimination by insisting that they be heard at international gatherings and then throwing the norm of freedom in the face of the international community, which most of the time would happily have forgotten about issues of freedom in southern Africa.

While African states varied in the intensity of their commitments to southern African causes (French-speaking African leaders were in general less involved than their Anglophone and Lusophone colleagues), public appearance of commitment and unity of effort were strictly enforced.[14] In international forums, the OAU succeeded in imposing the norm that African states would control the agenda for discussion of issues involving any part of Africa. It also worked effectively in such forums to increase Africa's share of benefits, from UN Security Council seats, to multilateral aid, to secretarial jobs. On such matters the OAU secretariat leads the caucus to produce a solid bloc of African votes. On other sorts of issues, African states are free to vote according to their, or their leader's, interests, including encouraging one or another outside power's beneficence by lining up and voting "right" on matters of that power's concern.

The superpower rivalry of the Cold War produced an ideal atmosphere for African states to maneuver freely in their own interests and to extract resources as clients of the super-patrons. This was minor stuff for the superpowers; it was a matter of central importance to the African states. As Christopher Clapham puts it, "The relative insignificance of Africa to the superpowers meant that their activities on the continent were in practice fuelled by the agendas of African actors every bit as much as by their own."[15] Total aid flows extracted from the superpowers made clear that political and strategic concerns rather than economic criteria dominated decisions about where aid should go. The top six sub-Saharan African recipients of U.S. aid, economic and military combined, during the Cold War were Ethiopia, Kenya, Liberia, Somalia, Sudan, and Zaire.[16] Soviet aid was massively concentrated in just two states, Angola and Ethiopia. With the possible exception of Kenya, it would be hard to come up with a list of countries with systematically worse records of economic development.

The Arab-Israeli dispute provided another opportunity for African states to use their juridical sovereignty to manipulate more powerful international actors. Following the 1973 Yom Kippur war and the sudden rise in Arab oil revenues, all black African states broke diplomatic relations with Israel. The Arab states returned the favor by creating the Arab Bank for African Economic Development (BADEA), which funneled resources to African states, Muslim and non-Muslim alike.[17] The African diplomatic boycott of Israel remained intact until broken by Zaire's Mobutu in 1982 in exchange for substantial military and economic assistance plus a "promise to help polish the tarnished image of Zaire and its president in Washington's corridors of power."[18] As was the case with superpower assistance, the bulk of aid went into state security—rather, security for those who led the regime—and into the pockets of members of the ruling group.

≺ II ≻

Freedom From the African State

Resources that accrued to the African state from its creative use of juridical sovereignty or from windfall profits derived from the export of highly valued national resources, like petroleum, bauxite, or diamonds, could in theory have been used to cement a mutually supportive bond between state and citizen.[19] More often than not, however, they allowed a hypertrophied state to survive as, in Thomas Callaghy's felicitous phrase, a "lame leviathan."[20] This misshapen monster did little, or little positive, for ordinary Africans, particularly those who lived far away from the capital and did not share ethnic or regional affinity with those who controlled the state.

Rather, the state preyed upon the people. Part of this predation might be centrally controlled and co-ordinated, with profits collected by the state apparatus on behalf of the ruler and his immediate political family. Some of it was decentralized and poorly-ordered freebooting, as state agents were given license to supplement (or replace) their salaries by squeezing the local citizenry. As the Camerounian phrase has it, "The goats graze wherever they are tethered."[21] Paradoxically, rents from export of highly-valued natural resources often worsened rather than improved the lot of the ordinary citizen. Most immediately, it was often the case that inhabitants of producing areas suffered environmental damage. This was the plight of Nigeria's Ogoni people; their fishing resources and farmland were polluted by international oil companies, but virtually none of the royalty payments to the government ever returned to ameliorate the Ogoni's lot.[22] More generally in Africa the export of highly valued resources, petroleum in particular, appears to have a *depressing* effect on economic growth, probably by increasing governmental corruption.[23] As a result, frustrated, ordinary citizens have sought freedom *from* the African state.

Some of this frustration produced aggression directly in the form of rebellion against the state. The goal of such rebellion was occasionally the most radical form of political freedom, secession from the state and recognition of the seceding entity as a new sovereign state. The principal examples are Biafra's ultimately unsuccessful attempt to secede from Nigeria, Eritrea's successful secession from Ethiopia after 30 years of war, and the ongoing struggles in Senegal's Casamance and in southern Sudan. Given the fragility and the ethnic complexity of virtually all African states, it is remarkable that the number of serious secession movements has been so small, and their success so limited.

Secession, of course, ran strictly against the African state system's norm of preserving territorial integrity and the inherited colonial boundaries. The only clearly successful and internationally recognized secessionist movement so far, that of Eritrea, came about finally by peaceful agreement with a new set of Ethiopian rulers, with whom they had coordinated their struggle against Ethopia's egregious Marxist dictatorship. Eritrea's secession also constituted support for the OAU's boundary norm: Eritrea had been an Italian colony prior to World War II, shortly after which it was annexed by Haile Selassie's Ethiopia.[24] The same would be true if Somaliland (once a British colony) sustained its secession from Somalia (once an Italian colony) or if Western Sahara (once a Spanish colony) reversed Morocco's de facto military annexation.

More common than secession has been rebellion to seize the state itself, or at least its capital, and thereby the sovereign recognition that goes with it. The first and most persistent of such rebellions broke out in Chad in 1965. Initially a rural jacquerie protesting arbitrary and extortionate behavior by state agents, it turned into widespread factional warfare, which over the next fifteen years virtually destroyed the state structure before, in 1982, one faction leader established control at the center and began rebuilding a formal state apparatus.[25] The civil wars in Uganda (1981–86), Ethiopia (1974–91), Rwanda (1990–94), Liberia (1990–97), and by some accounts Mozambique (1980–93) all took the form of oppressed or excluded groups fighting their way from the periphery into power at the center to free themselves from oppressive rule by those who had been controlling the center.

These were cases of extreme action, however. More commonly,

disaffected groups sought simply as much as possible to avoid contacts with a state whose agents were always ready with exactions, but seldom able or willing to deliver services. Picking up and voting with one's feet has long been a traditional means by which African communities have reacted to harsh or feckless rulers.[26] In more recent times, a considerably greater population density and a diminution of free arable land have constrained that option. Though most African states continue to be hospitable to refugees, they are increasingly lodged in formal camps at international expense. It is not just war and civil strife that have made the African continent the greatest producer of and home to refugees and the internally displaced, some 5.3 million or 28 percent of the world's total at the end of 1998 by the calculations of the United Nations High Comissioner for refugees.[27] For these, the search for freedom leads to exile and life under conditions approaching incarceration under international humanitarian auspices.

Less dramatically and less visibly, Africans have sought freedom from state exactions by dropping out in place. This has been particularly true in the economic realm. States complain that peasant production has dropped, though farmers appear to be as busy as ever and climatic conditions remain constant. Goran Hyden has interpreted this evasive behavior as an atavistic reaction of an "uncaptured peasantry" to return to an ancestral "economy of affection."[28] More convincing research shows that economic activity is as lively as ever, but it quite rationally avoids government-controlled marketing boards and official purchasing agents and customs officers in favor of more remunerative private circuits.[29]

Some of these black or gray market operations are highly sophisticated and remunerative—enough so that government agents can be bribed into looking the other way.[30] Such a system can survive as a self-reinforcing tacit bargain and has a number of characteristics: the state leaders and immediate entourage derive income directly or indirectly from the international sector (royalties, foreign aid, profits from sales of state assets); the state provides only minimal services to the citizenry at large, thus putting few demands on state income, most of which accrues to the leaders; local state agents, minimally remunerated by the state, are paid off by the local community and encouraged to go into business for themselves; and finally, the local community for the most part is left alone in exchange for leaving government and its treasury to the leader and making no demands for services from the state. This system can be contrasted with the bargain struck in the "development states" of the Middle East analyzed in chapter 3, in which the citizen yields his political rights to an authoritarian state and receives in return a reasonable level of economic benefit. The African bargain is closer to the old Soviet bargain between workers who pretended to work for state enterprises, which pretended to pay them. In the African version, the peasant pretends to be governed, so long as the state only pretends to govern.

Such arrangements can remain reasonably stable for long periods of time. Mobutu Sese Seko, perhaps the most egregious case, stayed in power in Zaire for 30 years, during which he presided over the steady impoverishment of state and society. This impoverishment has been most evident in the deliquescence of physical infrastructure, the transport and power-generating networks in particular. Their collapse, of course, made it all the more likely that large parts of the population would free themselves from any involvement with the state.[31]

Such a regime could retain its simulacrum of national sovereignty only so long as neighboring states and rebel movements were too weak, too preoccupied, or too inhibited to topple the stumbling state, or so long as outside powers would provide military support, including armed intervention, to defend the state *in extremis*. At various times the United States, France, Belgium, Israel, and Morocco did intervene militarily to save Mobutu's rule in Zaire. The end of the Cold War removed a prime incentive for such protective intervention, and in 1996 a loose coalition of neighboring states and a small number of Zairois rebels toppled the Mobutu regime with surprising ease.

≺ III ≻

Freedom Within the African State

The Cold War's end provided an external shock that changed the internal dynamics of politics and set loose forces seeking to end ruling groups' grip on an authoritarian state. Signs of change appeared with remarkable speed. By 1991 "the great majority of regimes had declared their commitment to the principle of multi-party democracy."[32] Between 1990 and 1994, 16 states made a transition to some form of multi-party democracy.[33] The annual Freedom House reports give a general idea of the magnitude of the shift. Freedom House characterizes states as "free," "partly free," and "not free." In 1987, only 2 sub-Saharan African countries were judged "free" (Botswana and Mauritius); 15 were judged "partly free," and 30 "not free." A dozen years later, the judgments were 8 "free," 24 "partly free," and 16 "not free." (The sums differ, as Eritrea was not rated as a state in 1987.) Freedom House also rates countries on two dimensions of freedom, "political rights" and "civil liberties," ranging from 1 (the most free) to 7 (the least free). In 1987 the average figures for freedom of political rights was 5.8 and for civil liberties it was 5.7. In 1999, the figures had improved to 4.5 and 4.4.[34] For the first time a significant number of Africans could envisage a search for freedom *within* the African state.

These political initiatives took place against a painfully supportive economic background. The 1980s had been sub-Saharan Africa's worst economic decade, with regional per capita GDP declining by 1.2 percent per annum. This disastrous economic performance eventually had political consequences. It certainly made it much harder to convince ordinary Africans that authoritarian government might be a necessary condition for economic growth. If there were to be any truth in Kwame Nkrumah's famous injunction "Seek ye first the political kingdom and all else shall be added unto ye," a new type of politics was to be required. The message was amplified by events in eastern Europe: as the Berlin Wall came down, the incapacity of the Marxist command economy and of the state apparatus that ruled it were revealed for all to see. As one disabused African Marxist reflected:

> The radical one-party regimes, which have been justifying their rule on socialist principles of "democratic centralism" and emulating the Soviet bloc practice of governing, found themselves without any theoretical justification, and they soon resorted to the old argument that, because of "tribalism," Africa was not yet ready for a pluralist democracy . . . The leaders who resorted to such an argument were seen to be ready to denigrate the dignity of the African simply in order to continue to remain in power.[35]

Following the December 1988 southern African peace settlement, which led to the withdrawal of Cuban and South African troops from Angola and the independence of Namibia, the Soviet

Union drastically cut its remaining support to African client regimes, even trying with little success to collect payment for past delivery of military hardware. It would be too much to claim that the Western countries all promptly cut support for their authoritarian clients; France in particular continued to look out for the interest of select Francophone leaders. Particularly favored were Rwanda's Habyarimana and Zaire's Mobutu. Formerly under Belgian rule, Rwanda and Zaire were both Francophone, but had never been part of the French colonial sphere. Not only did France see these countries as new recruits for the Francophone *chasse gardée* in Africa, it saw them and their leaders as standing in the way of expanding Anglo-Saxon (and Tutsi) influence in Africa.[36]

A succession of American ambassadors might lecture Kenyan president Moi about human rights, but not to the point that the ambassadorial words might jeopardize the U.S. Navy's access to Mombasa's port facilities. Yet the straws were in the wind. In 1991 the United States refused to intervene in Liberia to save the erratic President Doe. In 1993 it effectively terminated aid to Mobutu's regime and three years later worked actively to facilitate his removal from power. "Democratization assistance," ranging from training of electoral officials to financial support for human rights organizations, became a significant proportion of USAID's African programs.[37]

In 1990, French President Francois Mitterrand shocked the Franco-African Summit at the seaside resort of La Baule when he said that henceforth France's economic and military assistance would be conditioned on a state's progress toward democracy, and that those regimes refusing to make such progress could not count on French intervention to save them from popular protests.[38] Although other motives were also involved, French policy gave point to Mitterrand's pronouncement when a few months later, despite having a significant military force in the area, the French army did nothing to prevent the violent overthrow of Chad's Hissein Habre, the African chief of state most publicly critical of the La Baule speech.

The decade that opened with France's refusal to intervene in Chad closed with its refusal to reverse a coup d'état toppling the president of the Côte d'Ivoire, once the proud center of French influence in Africa. The principle that France will not intervene militarily to save autocratic African leaders from the consequences of their misrule seems to have become well established. Active pressure for democratization has come more slowly. Both Mitterrand and his successor, Jacques Chirac, have fallen back on words to the effect that democratization will come at the pace set by "an African rhythm."[39] The rhythm, one may guess, is not expected to be that of a quick-step.

The international financial institutions (IFIs), notably the World Bank and the International Monetary Fund, but also the African Development Bank, edged away from their long-standing policy of abstaining from comment on their African clients' internal affairs. While words like "political freedom" and "democracy" remained too blunt for most international bankers to use in public, "good governance," defined in the World Bank's words as "the practice by political leadership of accountability, transparency, openness, predictability, and the rule of law,"[40] became an official goal. An African state's rate of progress toward this goal might help determine an IFI's largesse.

South Africa's dramatically successful transition to a freely elected government in 1994 presided over by the international superstar, Nelson Mandela, set an example of democracy in action that few on the continent could ignore or dismiss.

Taken together, these external factors, interacting with domestic pressures, opened a political space in which Africans seeking political freedoms could maneuver. Where not savagely repressed, myriad organizations belonging to the broad category of "civil society" stepped to the fore, much as civil organizations ranging from syncretist churches to trade unions to ethnic-based "friendly associations" had helped provide the social infrastructure for nationalist independence movements some 40 years earlier.[41] Some of these were mere fronts for autocratic rulers, rural bigmen, or unsuccessful politicians left over from another era. Others demonstrated unexpected vitality and organizational capacity and called forth financial support (and some political protection) from Western non-governmental organizations (NGOs) and aid agencies. It has been estimated that in 1996 $5.5 billion were dispersed in sub-Saharan Africa by NGOs, either from their own money or as operators for government and international organization agencies.[42]

Both the vitality and the political limitations of civil society were demonstrated in eleven countries by national conferences, which brought together a wide spectrum of civil society organizations to challenge the prevailing political order.[43] In some cases, for example Congo-Brazzaville, these declared themselves sovereign and ushered in a new, if ultimately unstable, political order. In others, autocratic rulers, for example Togo's Eyadema, successfully outmaneuvered and bought off the claimant forces. Even then, political space was widened.

Press freedom expanded at a startling rate throughout the 1990s, admittedly from a very low level. Today it is a rare African capital that does not have an opposition newspaper, if not a good dozen of them, alongside the government's official mouthpiece. Radio is still the most effective mass medium in Africa, and local and locally-controlled radio stations broadcasting in local languages have blossomed.[44] Even a poor country like Mali counted over 20 stations by 1995 and 80 by the end of the century.[45] Ghana's 40 private stations are reported to have played a major role in preventing government thugs from stealing the 2001 presidential election, won by the opposition.[46] The usual caveats must apply. Government self-glorification focused on the leader still dominates most official broadcast and press output. Outspoken or merely curious journalists too often face harassment, or worse, and the opposition press rarely reaches high levels of responsibility and accuracy. Still the contrast with the stifling media world of the 1980s is remarkable.

While attention predictably has focused on elections and the democratic replacement of old autocrats, freedom has advanced along less obvious paths. Decentralization of decision making and administration, a World Bank priority, has reduced the monopoly of power in national capitals, a monopoly notoriously to the disadvantage of the more remote rural populations. The democratically elected Konare government in Mali is perhaps in the lead in decentralization; but Museveni's Uganda, whose National Resistance Movement brooks no challenge to its political dominance at the national level, nonetheless has decentralized much decisional power to regional and local Development Councils. A careful World Bank study concludes that decentralization "facilitates increase in voting, lobbying, contacting and so on," but warns "If the evidence tells us anything, it is that the higher-ups are not going to allow decentralization bodies to dominate the development agenda."[47]

Decentralization in Africa is likely to come about more through weakness at the center than through the government's careful planning. Freedom from control from the center in many African countries has given new vitality to long-suppressed traditional village practices in place of the homogenized version of "national folklore" put forth in the name of national unity. Villagers may turn to NGOs or charismatic religious movements for communication with the outside world. This social and cultural liberation may go hand in hand with liberation of "a rich and complex political life, more or less autonomous in relation to the national-level political sphere."[48] However desirable such decentralization of powers may be, it carries its own hazards, in Africa as elsewhere. Local bigmen, whose interests may be sharply at variance with those of much of the population, may monopolize control of newly decentralized agencies.[49] As the experience of Western countries like France and the United States has shown, local politics offers its own opportunities for corruption and abuse of power. Africans are not likely to remain unaware of such opportunity.

All the new politically competitive regimes are obliged to function without a society-wide institutional base fully supportive of a free political order. Political leadership too often lacks connection with a popular base. A common feature is the reemergence of old-line politicians left over from the independence struggle, whose appeal is based on little more than name recognition and promises of patronage. In other cases, leaders command the support only of ethnic fragments. Benin, population five million, registered 63 political parties for the 1998 election with few ideological or programmatic distinctions in evidence. Building a more adequate institutional base for a democratic order will take time, during which may develop a tradition of democratic practice and of tolerance toward political opponents. These are not easily taught or quickly learned; rather tradition must be established and reinforced over time, and tolerance must be learned through experiment and experience.

Meanwhile, one must be aware that Africa's increase in political freedom is not irreversible. Six of the fifteen countries Freedom House judged "partly free" in 1987 had slipped back into the "not free" category in 1999. Only two of Africa's smallest countries, Benin and Mauritius, meet Samuel Huntington's "two turnovers" test for consolidated democracy: there must be two elections in which the party in power is defeated and peacefully turns over the reins of government to the opposing party.[50] Similarly, one must be aware that African ideas of freedom are unlikely to lead to the same democratic expectations and practices as are current in the West, just as one should not expect the myriad peoples of sub-Saharan Africa's 48 states to share identical understandings of basic political terms like democracy and freedom.

An ingenious study by Frederick Schaffer probed a cross section of Senegalese Wolof-speakers to ascertain the political connotations of the Wolof word *demokaraasie*, and how that term differs from the French *démocratie* and the Anglo-American understanding of *democracy*. Central to *demokaraasie*, a highly valued ideal, are norms of mutuality, such as group consensus, reciprocity, and evenhanded distribution of benefits. Competitive elections are a key part of *demokaraasie*, but the relationship between voter and candidate is mediated by communal concerns. Voters in the same social networks (village, family, religious community) seek to reach agreement on a common electoral choice to which individual members bind themselves. Reciprocity includes the obligation on elected officials to provide material rewards to those who have supported them. Finally, those who have acceded to positions of power should exercise that reciprocity in an evenhanded manner, sharing fairly and equally with those who have supported them. Lack of evenhandedness would break the implicit contract between citizen and ruler and threaten the integrity of the social community. Consensus seems to be the key: if electoral passions fracture consensus, they work against *demokaraasie*, and if command is required to achieve consensus, so be it. As one member of a Muslim religious community explained, "Our *demokaraasie* is to do what the marabout orders."[51]

A similar study by Mikael Karlstrom among rural Baganda in East Africa's Uganda explored the political connotations of *eddembe ery'obuntu*, the usual translation of "democracy."[52] Rather than emphasizing the fair distribution of electoral spoils, *eddembe ery'obuntu* refers above all to the freedom for a community and its individual members to be treated in a humane and civil manner. This would include freedom from severe political or social disorder, freedom of ordinary individuals to have their complaints and opinions heard by those in power, and fair and equal treatment by authorities. Equality of treatment is paradoxically based on a premise of inequality. At any level of social organization, from the family to the state, one person must represent the "pinnacle" of power and authority before which all others are equally subject. Without such a focus of authority, it is thought, disorder will reign and freedom will founder. Political parties are viewed with some suspicion as cause for freedom-threatening disorder and division.

In Zambia, speakers of ChiBemba contribute yet another set of nuances. *Ubutingwa*, which is etymologically related to *eddembe ery'obuntu* through the root *ubuntu*, the quality of being fully human, is the common word for freedom. It is opposed to *ubusha*, slavery, a term used by extension to refer to the way Africans were treated under colonial rule and which evokes still powerful communal memories of Arab slave-raiding. "In ChiBemba and other Zambian languages, when one refers to national independence, one is simultaneously referring to the freedom of the citizens. There is no way to describe a country's independence apart from the people."[53] Referring to both personal and national freedom, *Twalipoka ubuntungwa* would be translated "we have attained the status of a free people." That sense of positive freedom persists, even though government may act in a high-handed manner and political party toughs may force ordinary Zambians to avoid public criticism of those who control the state.[54]

The differences among the three understandings of political freedom would seem to reflect the different political experiences of the Senegalese Wolof, the Ugandan Baganda, and the Zambian Bemba. The Wolof have had a long tradition of political clientelism and mostly peaceful electoral participation since well before independence. They expect concrete rewards for their political participation and freely concert their votes to increase their chances of big rewards. The Baganda have experienced long periods of bitter civil war and savagely capricious authoritarian rule. They see order and hierarchy as requisites for social and political freedom. Under colonial rule the Bemba were incorporated into the southern African racial order, which routinely added personal indignity to political subordination. Membership in a community freed from foreign rule constitutes a highly valued positive freedom. One must expect equivalent differences in the ways other African peoples understand and practice democracy, freedom, and legitimate authority.

For all the fragility of Africa's democratic transitions, by the mid-1990s it became possible to think seriously of finding some forms of political freedom within some African states.

≺ IV ≻

Freedom Through the African State System

As changes in the larger external environment facilitated the growth of freedom within African states, so the spread of national democracies affected, at least on the surface, the norms and expectations governing relations among African states. Key to this movement are two normative shifts. First is reduced tolerance for those chiefs of state who seize power through coups or other violent means. Second is the questioning of the non-interference in internal affairs norm and, to a lesser extent, the territorial integrity norm. Tolerance for those seizing power through violent means was attacked by several chiefs of state at the July 1999 OAU summit meeting. As the OAU Secretary-General, Salim Ahmed Salim, put it: "The makers of coups d'état no longer have a place with us . . . They may no longer expect to be invited to OAU meetings and to the next summits."[55] The OAU's threat had little apparent deterrent effect: in the months following Salim's announcement military coups overthrew the governments of Côte d'Ivoire and Comores. Still, the OAU stuck to its new principle. The two leaders of the coups stayed away from the next summit. Thus was the strict sovereignty norm breached in the service of a higher political good. The limits of that breach were equally in evidence. The July 2000 annual summit was held in Lomé, Togo, and according to OAU tradition, the host chief of state was installed as OAU chairman for the coming year. The Togolese president, Gnassingbe Eyadema, was still in power 37 years after assassinating his predecessor in independent Africa's first coup d'état. The new strictures were clearly not to be retroactive.

In opposing future coups d'état the OAU acted in a manner that would respect the political liberties of ordinary citizens, but would do so by privileging and protecting the continued tenure of incumbent leaders. It would seem that regimes that come to power through violence are no less opposed to future coups d'état than are those that come to power through democratic elections.

The non-interference and territorial integrity norms had been conceived primarily as part of the independence-era sovereignty bulwark against neocolonialism and less subtle interference with African states' freedom by non-African forces. As such, they were complemented by the normative injunction "African solutions to African problems," an injunction for outsiders to stay clear while the African states, in effect, washed their dirty linen at home. Once it became clear that a problem was not caused by extra-continental interferences, but rather took the form of conflict between neighboring states or even an intra-state communal conflict that spilled across borders, "African solutions" might require jettisoning "non-interference" in the name of a higher and more pressing good.

In 1979, when in response to repeated provocation Tanzania's troops marched into Uganda and overthrew the tyrannical and murderous rule of Idi Amin Dada, most of the continent's leaders breathed a private sigh of relief, while publicly deploring this violation of Uganda's sovereignty. Nigeria, then under civilian government, led the complaints. Hardly a voice was raised in Tanzania's support, and no state came to Tanzania's aid. Twenty years later, norms had changed: Nigeria's military government, with the formal blessing of its Economic Community of West African States (ECOWAS) partners, had proudly supervised elections in Liberia while its soldiers led the assault on Sierra Leone's capital city to throw out a military junta and restore a freely elected president to office. The OAU itself had created a "Mechanism for Conflict Prevention, Management and Resolution" whose mandate included dealing with intra-state disruptions that threatened regional order. As a preparatory document made clear, the Mechanism should operate according to a norm that approved "intervention" of those "outside forces" that would "facilitate prevention and/or resolution, particularly on humanitarian grounds . . . given that every African is his brother's keeper."[56] In his last appearance before the OAU as South Africa's president, Nelson Mandela told the assembled OAU chiefs of state "we must all accept that we cannot abuse the concept of national sovereignty to deny the rest of the continent the right and duty to intervene when behind those sovereign borders, people are being slaughtered to protect tyranny."[57] Two months later South African and Botswanan troops went into Lesotho to put down a mutiny, at considerable cost to lives and property, and to restore the elected civilian government.

At issue is the balance between freedom of sovereign state action from outside interference on the one hand, and protection of the citizenry on the other from the breakdown of civil order and the egregious violation of human rights by the state. The tension over this balance displayed itself on the world stage at the 1999 opening of the United Nations General Assembly. The UN Secretary General, Ghana's Kofi Annan, spoke forcefully in support of "this developing international norm in favor of intervention to protect civilians from wholesale slaughter." Annan was directly challenged by Algeria's Abdelaziz Bouteflika. Speaking as the then chairman of the OAU, Bouteflika proclaimed that "interference can only occur with the consent of the state concerned . . . We remain extremely sensitive to the undermining of our sovereignty . . . because sovereignty is our last defense against the rules of an unequal world."[58]

A recent project to supersede the OAU with an African Union illustrates the tension perfectly. Article 4(h) of the draft constitution allows interventions by the African Union "as a whole" in serious circumstances such as genocide and crimes against humanity. This is balanced by Article 3(b) which sets the AU's objective to include "to defend the sovereignty, territorial integrity and independence of its member states."[59]

No simple rule will suffice to strike the balance; African states, like others, will come down for or against a particular humanitarian intervention depending on their immediate interests. A balance that would be consonant with previous African practice would maintain strong non-interference norms insofar as the issue involves interference from non-African powers, while allowing greater tolerance for intervention by Africans—particularly multilateral intervention under African international auspices.

It will take more than a shift in norms, however, to confront the prime challenge for the new millenium, freeing large parts of the continent from armed violence perpetrated against Africans by Africans. These conflicts are fueled by the dispersion, throughout the continent, of small arms that are a residue of Cold War deliveries and post-Cold War sales of surplus equipment. They are paid for by the export of readily exploitable natural resources. Three categories of armed violence challenge the African state system to produce a systemic response. These are internal violence, often ethnic or regional, that spills across the border to affect neighboring countries (Sudan, Rwanda, Burundi); warlord conflict in the absence of effective state structures (Somalia, Liberia, Sierra Leone); and most serious, regional war caused by the collapse of a major state (Democratic Republic of Congo, bringing in Angola, Namibia, Zimbabwe, Uganda, Rwanda, Burundi, and others). These are truly "African problems," and having declared that Africans should solve them, the continent's leaders find that they lack the economic and military means, and often the political will, to do so. As a sympathetic appraisal concluded, "The OAU mechanism has so far been largely ineffective in managing Africa's conflicts."[60]

The outside world shows little enthusiasm for direct military intervention in these complex conflicts, which lend themselves poorly to classic peacekeeping doctrine. The United States, leery of anything that might resemble its fiasco in Somalia, and France, cautious after its controversial role in Rwanda, have sought a more indirect involvement. Both countries have undertaken to train selected African military units in skills needed for peacekeeping and peace enforcement and to provide standardized equipment, particularly communications equipment, so that an international but wholly African force can function effectively in the field. Britain has mounted a robust training force to support the military efforts of the Sierra Leone government and the substantial force mandated by the United Nations Security Council. The Scandinavian countries have made their own expert contributions to training African troops, notably by supporting the peacekeeping training institution in Zimbabwe.[61]

Arms, training, and money can come from outsiders, but the political will must come from Africans themselves. That may well involve a willingness to intervene in the role of one's African brother's keeper, but it must involve a political will, backed by organizational capacity, to resolve problems at the level of the state without exporting them to the neighboring countries or the continent as a whole. Without effective states, no larger state system, or intervention by outsiders, will be able to nourish or protect the freedoms to which, increasingly, Africans aspire.

Developmentalism, Revolution, and Freedom in the Arab East: the Cases of Egypt, Syria, and Iraq

JAMES L. GELVIN

To many observers in Europe and North America, the dramatic events of recent years, from the confrontation at Tiananmen Square to the collapse of the Soviet Empire, demonstrated that a new global democratic dispensation was about to emerge. Conversely, many also assumed, in the words of Lisa Anderson, that a "country's failure to embrace [democracy] is evidence of political perversity or moral obtuseness on the part of its citizenry."[1] If the same observers were to undertake a search for that "perversity" or "obtuseness," it seemed they could do no better than to look in the Arab East (Egypt and the Asiatic Arab world) where it appeared to be concentrated and where few if any social scientists placed much stock in the likelihood of democratization. Most surveys charting current prospects for liberalization and democratization either ignore the region completely or rate the potential for the development of democratic institutions and respect for individual freedoms there as "low."[2] While evidence to contradict such an assessment is certainly meager, a comparable deficiency has not prevented specialists from providing more optimistic assessments about other regions.[3] However valid the pessimism may prove to be, the vehemence with which the case against the possibility of liberalization and democratization in the Arab East is presented demonstrates that the roots of such pessimism must be located elsewhere.

As Edward Said and others have argued for more than two decades, the current popularity of smug, neo-Weberian analyses of "Islamic civilization" with its "bloody borders" and "history gone wrong" represents just a suggestive tip of an Orientalist iceberg which has until recently colored academic scholarship not only about the Arab East, but about the Middle East as a whole.[4] For centuries the Middle East has played the essential role of counterpoise to Enlightenment and post-Enlightenment discourses of freedom and state: the Middle East, as constructed by Montesquieu, J. S. Mill, Marx, Weber, and Wittfogel, was fabricated to serve as the essential "other" against which the notion of a dynamic, progressive, and civilized "West" might be honed. In its role as foil, the region has enriched the social science lexicon by providing examples of "oriental despotism," "sultanism," the "Asiatic mode of production," and "hydraulic civilization."

Orientalist scholarship has commonly attributed the so-called backwardness and despotic nature of the Middle East to a number of factors. Some Orientalists have pointed to factors intrinsic to the region: Islam, the integration of religion and politics, the continuous domination of society by a warrior caste, state ownership of land, the legacy of centralization left by empires whose viability depended upon large-scale investment in irrigation works, heterogeneous ("mosaic") societies impossible to unify except through coercion, and patriarchy. Others have looked to any one of a number of "absences" to explain the region's stagnation and propensity for authoritarianism, thus placing responsibility for the deficiencies of the Arab East on the lack of rational legal and bureaucratic institutions, civil society, a middle class, corporate structures, private ownership of land, and even an intrusive but "reformative" European colonialism. As has been well established elsewhere, none of these prohibiting factors stands up to close scrutiny.[5] Not only is the empirical foundation upon which they rest weak with respect to the Middle East, but they present a mythologized and ideologized narrative of the rise of capitalism and freedom in Europe as well.

Take, for example, the question of Islam and freedom. By presenting Islam as timeless, undifferentiated, self-enclosed, and entirely operative, Orientalist scholarship disregards the complex interplay among religious belief, cultural norms, and social, political, and economic structures—an interplay that enables Islam simultaneously to affect and be affected by social processes. Political and religious elites have, of course, found in Islam justifications for despotism. But Islam has been used for opposite ends as well. Beginning in the nineteenth century, Islamic modernists, living in cultural centers exposed to the ideas and institutions associated with an expanding world economy and the colonial encounter, sought to demonstrate the compatibility of Islamic tenets with Enlightenment ideals and Western political philosophy. From the Young Ottomans (whose writings and activities in the 1860s influenced the Ottoman constitutionalist movement of 1876) through Muhammad ᶜAbduh and the more contemporary Muhammad ᶜImara, ᶜAbbas Mahmud al-ᶜAqqad, and Khalid Muhammad Khalid, Islamic modernists have sought to reconcile Qurʾanic allusion and religious tradition with contemporaneous political ideals imported from the West. In their hands *shura* (consultation in which Muhammad and the first caliphs engaged with community leaders) became parliamentarianism, *bayᶜa* (the pledges exchanged between the caliphs and their followers) became constitutionalism, and *ijtihad* (the procedure, rooted in Islamic legal practice, of using reason to accommodate Islam to changing circumstances) became the principle that justified adapting Islam to Auguste Comte's "spirit of the age."[6]

Because intellectuals and belletrists in the region have, over the course of the past two centuries, championed myriad political philosophies, from liberal democratic to despotic, the search for some ideal-typical "concept of freedom" associated with the Arab East (or, as we are reminded in chapter 6 below, any other region) is a fool's errand. Rather than looking to Islam or some other unique, transcendent source for the current spate of authoritarian regimes in the Arab East, then—or, conversely, engaging in apologetics which invoke the inherently democratic and egalitarian nature of Arab/Islamic society and the purely contingent or exogenous roots of contemporary authoritarianism—it is necessary to locate the bases of that authoritarianism historically. Fundamentally, the question to be addressed when investigating the course of freedom in the region is not a conceptual but a practical one: why is it that certain concepts of freedom have been empowered and not others?

The primary locus of political power in the modern world is, of course, the state. Two interrelated phenomena have enabled the states of the Arab East to consolidate and consistently reinforce their capabilities. First, starting at least as far back as the mid-nineteenth century, both political elites and, increasingly over time, non-elites began to frame their political aspirations in terms of a developmentalist ethic. Developmentalism emerged as a contingent ideological response to the integration of the region into the world economy.

The doctrine garnered support as a result of the structural changes induced by integration—changes that created and inspired new classes of ideological producers and consumers and lent credence to their beliefs. In those areas of the Arab East in which structural change was most profound, developmentalism has been an essential prerequisite for political legitimation—and in numerous cases has provided the principal criterion for that legitimation.

In its simplest form, developmentalism called for the adoption of institutional forms and technological tools necessary to achieve autonomous economic growth and bring the nation to the stage of "modernity." In its nationalist manifestation, developmentalism was inextricably connected to the quest for national independence: full economic growth, it was believed, could be accomplished only through a complete political separation from colonial domination. In its populist manifestation (which was frequently, but not necessarily, associated with nationalism), economic growth was a *sine qua non* for realizing social justice and uniting political leaders with the masses they claimed to represent in a singular national project. As the state became the primary site of political contestation during the late nineteenth and early twentieth centuries, and particularly as the mobilized segments of the population increasingly came to distrust the capacity of even the nationalist bourgeoisie to respond effectively to social inequality and structurally-induced underdevelopment, developmentalism became identified with state-guided economic development (etatism).

The second phenomenon that has enabled states in the Arab East to consolidate and reinforce their capabilities has been their access to externally-generated sources of revenue. This revenue, which economists categorize as "rent" (income accrued by states from sources other than taxation), has consistently provided essential economic support for many states in the region; indeed, in several cases (Jordan, Saudi Arabia) dependence on rents from foreign assistance coincided with the formation of the state itself. In no other area of the world have states been so reliant on income derived from rent, whether in the form of direct petroleum revenues, remittances sent home by workers abroad to make up for domestic economic deficiencies, or foreign assistance (from the West, the Soviet Union, and petroleum exporters to their less fortunate neighbors). Overall, rent collection has enabled states in the region to maintain themselves as the central locus of economic power. Revenues thus accumulated have endowed those states not only with coercive power, but with capacities for social engineering and ideological production necessary for the manufacture of consent as well.

While conventional accounts frequently divide the states of the region into discrete "developmentalist" and "rentier" categories, such a division must be made circumspectly. In virtually every state in the Arab East, developmentalist strategies and rent collection have acted serially or in conjunction to strengthen state power. In the wake of the Suez War, for example, when Gamal Abdul Nasser's anti-imperialist stance and propaganda campaigns popularized the Egyptian model throughout the region, the developmentalist/etatist policies adopted by the Egyptian government became the legitimizing norm throughout the Arab East, even in places such as Saudi Arabia and Lebanon that lacked Egypt's revolutionary experience and tradition of state centralization.[7] This, in turn, compelled political elites in those states to reassess their government's role in fostering economic development and/or social welfare. In the 1960s, for example, Saudi Arabia experimented with many of the administrative practices usually ascribed to the revolutionary republics of the region, particularly in the realm of revenue extraction, centralized economic planning, and corporatist forms of interest representation (see below).[8] During the presidency of Fuʾad Shihab, which followed the political crisis of 1958, the Lebanese government adopted similar policies to rein in the "rabid competition of Lebanese capitalism"[9] and bridge the gap between rich and poor.

On the other hand, the revolutionary republics of the Arab East (Egypt, Syria, Iraq) have never successfully weaned themselves from their dependence on rents derived from foreign assistance, remittances, and, particularly in the case of Iraq, oil. Before the disastrous war with Iran, oil income accounted for more than half the Iraqi GDP, while at the beginning of the 1990s non-tax revenue accounted for one-third and one-quarter of government revenues in Egypt and Syria—fractions that solidified the dominant role of the state in the national economy at a time when it appeared that weak economic performance would force a decisive retrenchment.[10]

The attempt to divide the states of the Arab East into distinct rentier and developmentalist categories may thus be infeasible. Indeed, as a result of the aforementioned factors, a cross section of states in the region hold significant political attributes in common. As will be seen below, many of the peculiarities social scientists have ascribed to "rentier states"—the linkage between political loyalty and economic reward, the degeneration of politics into disputes over resource allocation, the fragmentation of society (frequently along newly solidified kinship, ethnic, and religious lines) into competitive units as a result of those disputes—currently hold for "developmentalist states" as well.[11] The fact that these attributes have come to define political life throughout the Arab East makes it impossible to counterpose "rentier states" against "developmentalist states" when assessing the prospects for liberalization and democratization in the region.

Developmentalism and rentierism have not, however, affected all states of the region equally, particularly during the formative stages of institutional development. Some states (Jordan, the Gulf States) were constructed by or at the sufferance of European imperial powers in frontier areas or on the outer fringes of the Ottoman Empire. Isolated from the strictures of the Ottoman imperial center and governing territories relatively insulated from the disruptive effects of the world economy, these states have successfully employed policies of selective rent allocation to maintain the dominance of a fairly compact group of political elites centered around a royal court. Other states (Egypt, Syria, Iraq) share a different set of defining characteristics. Unlike the previous group of states, the combination of the incorporation of their territories into the world economy during the nineteenth century and their subjection to foreign control established the parameters that delimited their post-independence economic and social systems. Furthermore, all three were dominated at the time of independence by political elites who had been steeped in ideological currents that had incubated in the late Ottoman Empire, the West, or both. Finally, in the period stretching from the late 1940s through the 1960s, all three experienced abrupt political upheaval that empowered regimes that both embodied and drew their legitimacy from the developmentalist aspirations of their populations. The evolution of these states, and the impact of that evolution on the structures of governance and the disposition of freedom, is the subject of the remainder of this chapter.

≺ I ≻

The Historical Roots of the Developmentalist Ethic and Its Ramifications

The Ottoman Empire held dominion over most of the Arab East from the beginning of the sixteenth century through World War I. While at its inception the empire provided a formidable challenge to its adversaries, beginning in the seventeenth century the fulcrum of international power began to shift decisively to an economically and militarily expansive West. Toward the end of the eighteenth century, Ottoman elites attempted to arrest the decline in relative Ottoman power by undertaking a program of military reorganization and administrative centralization. While individual initiatives launched during the first half of the nineteenth century did register success, foreign interference, domestic resistance, and the almost overwhelming complexity involved in reforming an administrative system that integrated informal as well as formal controls doomed the global aims of defensive modernizers to failure.

Further hampering these early efforts to revitalize the Ottoman Empire was the difficulty of undertaking measures designed to strengthen the administrative capabilities of the imperial center at a time when the strongest international power and the empire's main foreign ally, Great Britain, was also the most forceful champion of Liberal economic and political dogmas. The British imposed free trade policies on the Ottoman Empire, most pointedly through the 1838 Treaty of Balta Liman which substantially lowered Ottoman import and export duties and outlawed government monopolies. To garner British military and political support during the so-called Muhammad ᶜAli crisis (when the governor of Egypt challenged Ottoman authority in the Asiatic provinces of the Ottoman Empire) and the Crimean War, the Ottomans promulgated two imperial decrees, the terms of which were inspired by doctrines of political Liberalism. The *Hatt-i Sharif* of Gulhane (1839) and the *Islahat Fermani* (1856) (the latter purportedly dictated to the imperial chancellory by the British ambassador to the Ottoman court) promised "perfect security for life, honor, and property" for all Ottoman subjects and religious liberty and equality for the non-Muslim inhabitants of the empire.[12] The thin stratum of Westernizers who aspired to infuse the empire with internationally recognized standards of civilization naturally supported the adoption of Liberalism as official doctrine; few others were convinced. Among the latter category were political elites who accepted the same modernist assumptions that had spawned Liberalism but who, like many state-builders in non-core European states, found the specific precepts of Liberalism to be distasteful and/or an insufficient basis for imperial revival.

Beginning in the middle of the nineteenth century, and accelerating during the reign of Abdul Hamid II (1876–1909) and the subsequent period of Young Turk rule, the approach taken by Ottoman political elites to strengthen state power changed substantially. Impressed by the examples of German and Italian unification, Ottoman authorities abandoned piecemeal approaches toward "modernization" for a more comprehensive state-building strategy that had increasingly gained currency through the works of such litterateurs as the Young Ottoman Namik Kemal. In the words of Turkish historian Selim Deringil,

> The Ottoman sultan, the Meiji emperor, the Russian tsar, the Habsburg emperor were all drawn towards the twentieth century at different tempos, but down broadly similar paths. All invested in a recharged state mythology, which they sought to inculcate through mass education. All invested to varying degrees in the inevitable technical trappings of modernity: railways, the telegraph, factories, censuses, passports, steamships, world fairs, clock towers, and art-deco palaces. All looked to each other to see how their peers were playing the role of "civilized monarchy." This process of emulation among the crowned heads of the world had a definite competitive bent, but the model was inevitably the concept of modernity as seen in the core cultures of Western Europe, perhaps even more specifically, the France of the Second Empire.[13]

Essentially, by the last quarter of the nineteenth century rulers of imperia throughout the world embarked on ambitious programs designed to restructure fundamentally their empires, using as their model the more successful nation-state. Accordingly, the Ottoman state promulgated official ideologies, which it attempted to disseminate through an expanded, state-directed educational system and through state-controlled media outlets. It attempted (at various times and with varying degrees of success) to establish uniformity in legal, Islamic, and linguistic practice. After the Young Turk revolution, it encouraged the transformation of Ottoman subjects into Ottoman citizens through the opening up of the political process and the promotion (within controlled conditions) of mass participation in politics.[14] The state also assumed direct responsibility for economic development, backing away from the free trade policies that had solidified its integration into the world economy. As will be seen below, the economic policies adopted by the Ottoman state during the period spanning the second half of the nineteenth and the early twentieth centuries had an effect on ideological production that equalled that of the dissemination of official ideologies or state-directed attempts to standardize cultural norms.

Ottoman etatism took a variety of forms. Although attempts to establish state-run factories failed—most of the factories established during the 1840–60 period closed their doors in the face of Western competition and shortages of skilled workers and available investment capital—the state soon embarked on an ambitious project to foster private industrial production by reorganizing guilds, sponsoring industrial exhibitions, assembling cooperative associations for industrial production, offering tax breaks to entrepreneurs, founding a school of industry, setting production standards, and raising customs duties. The Ottoman state attempted to attract foreign investment capital by offering concessions for building telegraph lines, railroads, and tramways and for expanding port facilities in Istanbul and Beirut. In 1867 the state established the Industrial Reform Commission to encourage a variety of industrial enterprises in Istanbul, ranging from silk weaving to iron working. The Ottoman state's attempt to address the agricultural crisis of the third quarter of the nineteenth century—an attempt marked by the establishment of agricultural schools and an Agricultural Bank to issue credits to impoverished farmers (thereby undermining the power of rapacious private lenders), by the distribution of seed, and by the assembly of teams of agronomists that roamed the countryside offering advice to peasants—was so intrusive that, in the words of one historian, "during the nineteenth century, the state began to encroach upon life in the countryside in a manner hardly seen, if ever, during the long centuries of the Ottoman imperium."[15] In all, by the beginning of the twentieth century more than half a million Ottoman civil servants managed a host of activities commonly associated with modern nation-states, from the administration of hospitals to the construction and maintenance of essential infrastructure.[16]

While the Ottoman effort to foster industrial and agricultural development yielded mixed results in the economic realm, it had a marked effect on the public's attitude toward government and economic doctrine. For example, the outlines of an economic consensus uniting the politically-active inhabitants in the territory that later became Syria began to emerge at least as far back as the beginning of the twentieth century. According to Yahya Sadowski, from the late Ottoman period to the present day a dominant strain in Syrian political discourse has consistently affirmed a belief in a strong state that not only would act to ensure economic development and the well-being of the population, but would limit excessive exploitation and foster equity by intervening, if necessary, to ensure social justice.[17] Similar support for economic development and a strong, interventionist government was expressed by the ex-Ottoman officers, trained under the Young Turks, who formed the inner circle of the monarchy established (under British tutelage) in Iraq after World War I.[18] During the Iraqi monarchic period, which lasted until 1958, these doctrines were disseminated to a wider audience by extra-parliamentary political groups, which linked them to issues of social justice and national independence.[19]

The spread of developmentalism was, if anything, even more pronounced in Egypt during the latter half of the nineteenth century. While Egypt had been a juridical part of the Ottoman Empire since 1517, its history differed from other provinces of the empire for three reasons. First, beginning in the early nineteenth century, Egypt was governed by a dynasty founded by Muhammad ᶜAli, who had seized control of the province in the wake of the Napoleonic invasion of 1798. To ensure Ottoman acquiescence to his dynastic ambitions, Muhammad ᶜAli initiated a far-reaching program of state centralization and forced economic development which both expanded and enhanced state capabilities. Second, Egyptian reliance on monoculture (the cultivation of cotton, which with cotton seed made up 86 percent of Egyptian exports by 1913[20]) resulted in both colonial-style development and Egypt's integration into the periphery of the world economy. Finally, the British occupation of Egypt, which lasted in one form or another from 1882 to 1956, not only ensured continued colonial-style development and economic integration, but provoked a reaction in the form of the first nationalist movement in the Arab East. Egyptian nationalism, like other nationalisms engendered under similar circumstances, both espoused an aspiration to participate in universal progress and condemned the colonizing power for blocking that participation.[21]

While the specific factors that affected Egyptian political and economic development in the nineteenth century differed from those at work in the rest of the Ottoman Empire, the ideological ramifications of that development were much the same. Thus, when the first British high commissioner, the Earl of Cromer, attempted to impose free trade policies on Egypt, he met with widespread resistance and was forced to back down. By the outbreak of World War I, political and economic elites in Egypt were in "near universal agreement"[22] that Egypt had to abandon monoculture and orient toward industrial development, not only to escape the vagaries of the international market but to ensure the welfare of increasing numbers of unemployed peasants migrating to urban centers from the countryside.[23] The example of British economic mobilization during World War I, along with resentments generated by British monopoly and marketing practices and the explosion of nationalist sentiment in the immediate aftermath of the war, served to reinforce the overlapping developmentalist and etatist impulses that had begun to emerge a century earlier.

The victorious entente powers dismantled the Ottoman Empire in the aftermath of World War I. They remanded the Arab Asiatic provinces of the empire to mandatory control by Britain (which received mandates for Iraq, Palestine, and [Trans-]Jordan) and by France (Lebanon and Syria). With the exception of Iraq, which achieved independence in 1932, the former Ottoman territories remained as mandates through World War II. Egyptian political history followed a different course during this period: in December 1914 the British made Egypt a protectorate, severing the ties connecting it with the Ottoman Empire; and in the wake of a nationalist revolt in 1919, Britain unilaterally declared Egypt conditionally independent. Renegotiating the terms of "conditional independence" would remain a pivotal issue in Egyptian politics until 1954.

Although the mandates had been imposed on subject populations as a "sacred trust of civilization" to prepare them for the "strenuous conditions of the modern world,"[24] and although Egypt had achieved conditional independence early on during the interwar period, the so-called "liberal experiment" or "liberal age"[25] in the

Arab East appears as such only if one considers the formal trappings of democratic life. True, parliaments were convened, political parties formed, constitutions promulgated, secular rights institutionalized, and newspapers published. But in all three countries the franchise was limited, parliaments were unrepresentative, associational life was restricted and often curtailed, and political parties and newspapers were subject to dissolution and censorship. Governments in Egypt, Syria, and Iraq were weak and unstable and governed at the sufferance of the imperialist powers that maintained a presence throughout the region. In Egypt, the British, the palace, and their political allies actively conspired against unfettered parliamentary rule; in Syria, it was the French; in Iraq, the British and the Iraqi military.

In the first decades following World War I, nationalist parties in the Arab East concentrated on the goal of gaining or confirming national independence; economic and social concerns played only a subsidiary role in their programs. In part, this was a natural outgrowth of the distribution of political and economic power in newly or soon to be independent states, which circumscribed the capacity of nationalist parties to effect social change. Additionally, the social composition of the dominant nationalist parties curtailed their enthusiasm for such change. In Syria and Iraq, the agrarian policies of the mandatory powers accelerated the consolidation of large freehold estates; the preoccupations of nationalist parties and parliamentary politics reflected the political power of the landed nobility. A similar phenomenon occurred in Egypt, where large landowners increasingly took on leadership roles in the most popular nationalist party, the Wafd,[26] and where, as a result of the king's power to dissolve parliament and appoint governments, the Wafd had little opportunity to govern anyway. In all three countries, agrarian interests could and did find common ground with advocates of industrialization on a variety of relatively painless social and economic initiatives, including the expansion of educational opportunity, infrastructural development, centralized planning, state-supported incentives for private enterprise, and even moderate attempts to overcome inequities in the agrarian sector through the sale of state lands and the organization of agricultural cooperatives. But once rudimentary and politically uncontestable programs had run their course, developmentalist coalitions dissolved.[27]

In spite of the relatively short shrift initially given to economic policy by independence-minded nationalist movements and the instability of developmentalist coalitions, however, during the period that began with the armistice and culminated with the establishment of military regimes support for developmentalism and etatism not only continued but broadened. This occurred for three reasons: the activities of the first Arab bourgeoisie, the enlargement of the politically mobilized population, and institutional development promoted by foreign powers.

Although denigrated by the self-justificatory propaganda of revolutionary regimes (and by historians who have all too frequently approached their pronouncements uncritically), the prerevolutionary accomplishments of the Arab bourgeoisie were far from negligible.[28] Beginning in the 1920s in Egypt (and somewhat later in Syria and Iraq) the bourgeoisie came into its own, propelled by the "basic" investments cited above, the end of colonialist monopoly policies, favorable circumstances for industrial investment spawned by the Great Depression (cheap labor, a dwindling of imports, tariff wars, and, with declining profitability in the agrarian sector, an increase in capital available for industrial investment), and the activities of the Middle East Supply Center (see below). Its members diversified their holdings, participated in government planning commissions (such as the Development Board of Iraq, founded in 1950), experimented with new strategies for capital accumulation (business groups, non-family based joint stock companies), and engaged in joint ventures with foreign capital. Most significantly, groups of industrialists and their allies (the Bank Misr group in Egypt, the *iqtisadiyyun* in Syria) began to espouse the doctrine of economic nationalism—developmentalism within the framework of an independent nation-state. Whether compelled by true belief or (more cynically) by the opportunity to gain partisan advantage over foreign-national and/or so-called "comprador" capitalists whose interests were aligned with those of the imperial powers, economic nationalists achieved "a remarkable ideological hegemony"[29] for their ideas among the politically-active middle classes. All told, as a result of the efforts of the Arab bourgeoisie, after the 1930s the dominant nationalist discourses in Egypt, Syria, and Iraq included a conspicuous economic as well as political component.

But it was not just the activities of the Arab bourgeoisie and their sometime supporters among the dominant nationalist parties that made economic nationalism an integral part of the nationalist program. During the 1930s, the organizational and ideological character of political activity began to undergo a radical transformation in the region. Structural changes in land ownership, Depression-era poverty, and the lure of expanded employment and educational opportunities in the cities precipitated an unprecedented migration from the countryside to urban areas in Egypt, Syria, and Iraq. As urban populations increased, so did the constituency available for political mobilization. The political parties and associations that emerged, splintered, and reformed during this period (from assorted communist parties and Muslim brotherhoods to the Syrian Social Nationalist Party, the League of National Action [Syria], the National Democratic Party [Iraq], the Wafdist Vanguard and Young Egypt) differed from the nationalist parties that had previously dominated the political field not only because they were tightly structured and possessed a middle-class leadership and middle-class and lower middle-class constituency, but because the doctrines they championed went beyond mere calls for political independence. Forming at a time when the battle for political independence had been all but won and the consensus on developmentalist strategies had splintered, these political groupings articulated programs that addressed the social and economic concerns of ever-widening layers of the population.

Further strengthening the hand of indigenous forces committed to economic nationalism were the obtrusive activities of the Great Powers, which facilitated the realization, however limited, of developmentalist and etatist programs during the period that stretched from the 1930s through the 1950s. As a result of colonial/mandatory presence and/or the exigencies of war, Britain, France, and the United States introduced into the region new administrative structures, many of which had only recently been instituted in the West in response to the Depression or World War II. These structures augmented the capabilities of governments, habituated populations to closer governmental supervision of economic affairs, raised popular expectations, and opened up fresh possibilities for developmentalist currents. For example, during the Depression French mandatory authorities in Syria introduced measures to stabilize the economy and maintain order similar to the welfare-state policies introduced by the Popular Front government in France. But once price supports, wage guidelines, labor codes, poor relief, subsidization of consumer goods, and the like were enacted, urban Syrians increasingly viewed them as an obligation of, not a benefaction from, government, making their revocation well-nigh impossible.[30]

The activities of the Middle East Supply Center (MESC) reinforced etatist sentiments even further. Initially designed by the Allies to collect data on consumer needs in the region so that cargo space on freighters might be allocated more efficiently, the MESC over the course of World War II took on the tasks of regulating imports, guiding and supporting industrial investment, distributing essential commodities, and supervising production. Abetted by war-induced shortages and military consumption, manufacturing output in Egypt thus increased by 40 percent and investment in Syrian industry quadrupled during the war years.[31] Postwar governments in Syria, Egypt, and Iraq maintained the planning and regulatory agencies established by the MESC. Overall, then, the activities of the MESC not only set a standard for state-led economic development but provided the developmental blueprint for postwar governments to follow.[32]

The agitation of indigenous capitalists, the new political formations, and the intrusive activities of foreign powers redefined the criteria for political legitimation for ever-expanding segments of the population and forced a response from the "old guard" politicians who dominated parliamentary politics. From 1942 through 1950, for example, Egyptian governments enacted (although rarely enforced) bills that guaranteed free primary and secondary education, workman's compensation, and social security. Egyptian governments decreed the establishment of a central bank and passed other measures regulating industrial contracts, working conditions, joint stock companies, and foreign investment.[33] Upon taking power in 1950, the Wafd leadership proclaimed that, after securing the evacuation of British forces from the Suez Canal zone and the unity of the Nile Valley, fostering economic development and realizing social justice would be the two primary goals of the new government. The Wafdist interior minister, Fu'ad Sirag al-Din, went so far as to proclaim the Wafdist parliamentary deputies to be "socialists" (although he later assured the U.S. ambassador, "I own eight thousand feddans [roughly 8,320 acres]. Do you think I want Egypt to go communist?").[34]

The Syrian Constitution of 1950 presents an even clearer view of the penetration of official political discourse by developmentalist ideals during this period. Although the constitution retained the basic political framework that had been established under French mandatory rule, legislators appended to the document a 28-article "Bill of Rights"—the first of its kind in the Arab East. While not ignoring political rights entirely, the Syrian Bill of Rights dealt almost exclusively with economic and social issues—from articles guaranteeing the right of citizens to free public education and employment to an article requiring the Syrian assembly to ensure that private property "performs its social function." Most tellingly, although the constitution and Bill of Rights were promulgated after the first postwar military coup d'état in the region, the parliament that passed them was controlled by the business-dominated People's Party whose concern for economic and social justice had been goaded not only by popular sentiment, but by the desire to expand the internal Syrian market.[35]

≺ II ≻

Military Rulers in Pursuit of a Policy

Beginning in 1949 and continuing for the next two decades, cliques of military officers launched coups d'état against civilian politicians in Egypt, Syria, and Iraq and then against already empowered military regimes in Syria and Iraq. By the time of the initial coups cells of Free Officers had gestated for three years in the Egyptian army and for six in the Iraqi. Although they had formed in opposition to the imperialist presence and civilian mismanagement of military affairs, they, like their military counterparts in Syria, seized power when they did for opportunistic reasons: to avert arrest (Egypt), to deter budgetary cutbacks (Syria), to take advantage of advantageous military deployment (Iraq). Under such precipitous conditions, there was little time for programmatic deliberation, a factor compounded among the Free Officers of Egypt and Iraq by the conscious decision, taken early on, to avoid potentially divisive ideological debates within the ranks. Rather than proffering a grand ideological vision, the officers claimed to be acting as the guardians of constitutional or democratic life whose actions would end the abuses, ineptitude, and treason of the old regimes.[36] In the Egyptian case, which provided the model for subsequent military takeovers, the Free Officers referred to themselves and their action merely as a "movement"; only later did they retrospectively overstate their purposefulness by replacing the word "movement" with "revolution."[37]

This is not to say, however, that the military conspirators who seized power between 1949 and 1958 were ideologically barren. As urban dwellers, graduates of military academies, and the products of lower middle- or middle-class upbringing at a time when those strata formed the epicenter of new political currents, military officers were steeped not only in the political controversies of the day, but also in a milieu which provided them with a set of unarticulated assumptions about modernity and progress. Once in power, even such a relatively unimaginative officer as Husni al-Zaᶜim of Syria or ᶜAbd al-Karim Qasim of Iraq was instinctively drawn to the sorts of developmentalist policies that came to be associated with all military-led revolts in the region. Colonel al-Zaᶜim, who ruled for only three months, reportedly proclaimed "Give me five years and I will make Syria as prosperous and enlightened as Switzerland" shortly before he was deposed; and in spite of General Qasim's notoriously mercurial personality, the land reform, labor, housing, health care, and educational initiatives that he promoted made him a hero to thousands of Baghdadis who volunteered to defend his regime on the eve of its overthrow.[38]

Similar tacit assumptions permeate both the seemingly banal six-point program of the Free Officers of Egypt presented in January 1953 and Nasser's *Philosophy of the Revolution*. In the historical section of the latter document, the anti-imperialist Nasser even argued that the project of modernization launched by the Free Officers was the continuation of a process begun by Napoleon's invasion of Egypt in 1798:

> [With Napoleon] our modern awakening began . . . While new thoughts and opinions washed over us, we had not reached a stage of development that would have enabled us to make proper use of them. Our minds were still in the thirteenth century, although we possessed a few of the attributes of the nineteenth and twentieth centuries. We tried to catch up to the caravan of human progress, but we were five or more centuries behind. The pace has been frightening and the journey has been draining.[39]

Thus, the military officers who took power in the late 1940s and 1950s neither represented a radical break from the past nor did they present themselves as such. Indeed, their initial programs were decidedly mainstream, indistinguishable not only from the programs that had circulated among the politically-mobilized middle and lower middle classes from whom they sprang and to whom they looked for support, but from those formulated by Anglo-American modernization theorists as well.

Like the modernization theorists, the officers believed in the nation-state as the fundamental unit of development and in "modernity" as the goal of national policy. They claimed for themselves, as the vanguard of the "new middle class," an historic role in guiding their nations to modernity: because the "new middle class" was the only stratum of society created by and ideologically committed to modernity, it was the only stratum that could destroy traditional social and economic relations that had obstructed modernization.[40] As presented in the discourse of the military conspirators during this period, the military assumed power to end "corruption" (private profit-seeking by economic elites which impeded directed development), "feudalism" (agrarian accumulation which, they believed, diminished the availability of development capital, inflated the political power of agrarian magnates, and promoted "corruption"), and "imperialism" (not only foreign presence but the monopolistic trade practices imposed by colonial governments and the relations of dependence which sustained underdevelopment). The defeat suffered by Arab armies in the First Palestine War (1948) played a central symbolic role in the discourse of the military conspirators in part because it incorporated images of "corruption," "feudalism," and "imperialism" within a single signifier: the defeat served as a reminder of the inherent inability of existing parliamentary governments to further the national interest by fostering "modernity" and thereby to resolve the problem of imperialism once and for all.

Both modernization theorists and the military officers who took power shared another attribute as well: their equivocal attitude toward political democracy. In contrast to those development experts who, in the wake of the Iranian Revolution, have equated "modernization" with political disruption, both groups believed that planned economic development would eradicate destabilizing social inequities and engender the political stability that was the *sine qua non* for democracy. Hence, the six-point program of the Free Officers of Egypt and the four-point program of the Free Officers of Iraq juxtaposed reaffirmations of the transitional nature of military rule and the goal of democratic restoration with promises of land reform: in addition to the economic and political benefits that would accrue from providing the peasantry with greater buying power and from enervating agrarian magnates by expropriating their assets, modernization theorists and military officers alike viewed land reform as a means of preventing the spread of unrest among land-hungry peasants and their unemployed counterparts who had migrated to the cities. Sayyid Marᶜi, who administered the first land reform legislation enacted by the Free Officers and who obviously sought to gain from his comments at least grudging acquiescence from landowners by appealing to their socially conservative instincts, explained it as follows:

> We all remember the days preceding the revolution of July 1952; we remember how the Egyptian village became restless as a result of dangerous agitation; we remember the events which led to bloodshed and destruction of property—for the first time in the history of the Egyptian village. Would the large landowners have preferred to be left exposed to the wind blowing through this unrest, exploiting want and poverty, until it became a tempest uprooting everything . . . and endangering, perhaps, the peace of our entire fatherland? Do they not fare better under stable conditions, the income from the land being given to its tillers and its price to its former owners to be invested by them in the development of Egyptian industry and commerce?[41]

But planned economic development not only fostered political stability, it required political stability as well. Thus, like modernization theorists, the military officers who took power couched their developmentalist impulses within a discourse of order that belied their otherwise populist orientation and their stated commitment to the rapid restoration of democracy. Immediately after the Free Officers took power in Egypt, for example, regime spokesman Rashed el-Barawy warned the West,

> Western powers have always criticised the anarchy of representative life and lack of stability in certain regions. The Army's movement declared, in its statements, that its object was to establish the desired stability which is essential for the economic and social progress and the maintenance of security in the Middle East. Any interference on the part of [foreign] Powers

would have been considered as a deliberate attempt to maintain anarchy and unrest in this part of the world.[42]

The Free Officers of Egypt quickly demonstrated that the concern for order expressed by el-Barawy was not mere rhetoric: within a month of taking power, they brutally suppressed a strike that had broken out at the Kafr al-Dawwar textile works, arrested 545 workers, and staged a show trial after which two workers were hanged to prevent, in the words of the titular head of the Free Officers, Muhammad Naguib, "the possibility of the spread of these strikes."[43] Military regimes in Syria and Iraq displayed a similar intolerance for what they commonly referred to as "anarchy" by repressing political opponents and dealing harshly with movements advocating ethnic or religious autonomy.

Whether or not it is true, as some scholars have maintained, that "the dominant, normative orientation within the Free Officers' inner core at the time of the coup was a pro-authoritarian one,"[44] the triumph of the principle of order over promises to restore a "cleansed" pluralistic democracy among military rulers cannot be attributed to the authoritarian proclivities of those rulers alone (if, indeed, such proclivities existed at all). As el-Barawy's allusion to the "interference on the part of [foreign] Powers" indicates, the military conspirators were attuned to and profited from the designs of foreign powers—first Great Britain, then the United States—in the region and planned their strategies accordingly.

As early as 1949 the British government had begun to distance itself from the very regimes it had created and had supported for years. Worried lest American capital become dominant in what had been an exclusively British economic sphere of influence, the British foreign secretary Ernest Bevin called for "a bold development plan," warning,

> The old regimes, which we were forced to support, would not stand up to revolutionary conditions and would be swept away. These regimes were greedy and selfish and had not allowed any of the wealth which they have made out of the war and out of oil to benefit the poorer classes. If we continued to support them we should be blamed in the event of the Communists succeeding in turning the peoples of the Middle East against us.[45]

While British policy-makers pushed developmentalist programs to make the *ancien régime* governments more palatable to their peoples, the American government adopted a very different strategy in the postwar Arab East. Because American policymakers were enticed by visions of newly opened markets and haunted by the fear that colonial withdrawal would lead to chaos, communism, and Soviet expansion into the region, the quest for stability and the fear of revolutionary change appeared as refrains in American diplomatic parlance almost as frequently as they appeared in the communiqués of Free Officers. So did "corruption," an accusation which had often been lodged by those waiting in the wings for their chance at power but which, when used by American diplomats, was construed by military officers as a conspiratorial wink and nod. Until the second half of the 1950s, American policymakers contemplating the future of the Arab East looked to those officers in much the same way as would their successors when contemplating the future of Iraq after Operation Desert Storm: for the Americans, military officers represented a "progressive" yet stabilizing force in a region not ready for democracy. The assistance American governments provided military conspirators through the mid-1950s—from cues for action and political guidance to the more colorful (but perhaps fanciful) suitcases filled with money—was critical for their successful assumption and consolidation of power. Furthermore, American interference in domestic political processes calls into question the teleological presumption that the transition from "corrupt" civilian regimes to authoritarian military regimes in the Arab East was an inevitable consequence of "Arab political culture" or world system dynamics.

The economic strategies initially followed by the military officers were comparable to, if not directly derived from, those that had been scripted in the West. The wide circulation of such works as Doreen Warriner's 1948 appeal for land reform, *Land and Poverty in the Middle East* (a major influence on, among others, Nasser's first advisor on land reform),[46] the reports of the International Bank for Reconstruction and Development (World Bank) which sent missions to Iraq in 1951 and to Syria in 1954,[47] and other publications likewise informed by assumptions of modernization theory reinforced the developmentalist impulses of the officers and provided them with policy recommendations and ideological ammunition that might be aimed at their "corrupt" and "feudalist" predecessors and domestic opponents. It should not be surprising, therefore, that military regimes in Egypt, Syria, and even Iraq initially acted with regard to domestic policy as American policymakers had anticipated.

With the exception of land reform in Egypt and Iraq—which was, at first, applied more tentatively than onerously—the policies promulgated by the military regimes projected a populist orientation but did so while accommodating the needs and concerns of the private sector. Gamal Salim, the Egyptian minister of national guidance, put it succinctly: in an ironic contrast to the Wafdist Fuʾad Sirag al-Din, Salim stated: "We are not socialists: I think our economy can only prosper under free enterprise."[48] Lest it be thought that Salim's words were spoken merely to mollify onlookers from the West, the regime undertook a series of measures that lent them credence: the regime purged leftists from the inner circle of Free Officers, enacted policies long advocated by the Egyptian Federation of Industries, boosted the holdings of the industrial bank, and eased restrictions on foreign investment. Similar accommodationist policies were enacted in Syria and in Iraq where, after the 1961 nationalization of territories unexploited by the Iraq Petroleum Company, increased oil wealth expanded the government's capacity to provide an environment for private sector growth.[49]

The attempt by military regimes to foster a developmental alliance with the private sector was a logical outgrowth of their political fragility, narrow base of support, and unformed political agenda. Rather than providing the foundation for a correspondent liberalization in the political sphere, however, no "democratic bargain" emerged from this experiment. The policies of accommodation initiated by the incipient military regimes not only failed to secure what the regimes deemed an appropriate level of cooperation from the private sector, they reinforced the mutual suspicions held by the military officers and private sector capitalists. Capitalists were wary of regimes that spoke in a populist idiom, restricted avenues of investment and capital accumulation, and enervated or destroyed the old parties that not only had provided them with their primary link to the political process, but had accorded them remuneration for entrepreneurial risk in the form of privileged access to political spoils.[50] For their part, the military governments were suspicious of the ties that had bound capitalists with the *ancien régime* and foreign capital, particularly in the context of their disinvestment, profit-taking, and capital transfers abroad. As viewed through the anxious eyes of the political parvenus who now held power, these actions were not taken as a logical and correctable response to uncertain conditions, but instead were evidence of obstructionism, if not out-and-out treachery.

≺ III ≻

From Revolts to Revolutions

By the early 1960s all military regimes had abandoned policies of accommodation and replaced them with programs that gave the state an inordinate control over the economy. The event that precipitated this change was the Suez War (the "Tripartite Aggression"), the ill-conceived 1956 invasion of Egypt by British, French, and Israeli forces. Although launched to topple Nasser's government in the wake of the nationalization of the Suez Canal Company, the invasion had the opposite effect: it not only energized Egyptian nationalist sentiment, it raised Nasser's political stock both at home and throughout the region. Taking advantage of his newfound popularity, Nasser eliminated a potentially disruptive foreign presence from the Egyptian economy and broke the regime's dependence on the private sector by expanding the wartime sequestration of alien resident- and foreign-owned assets into a full-scale program of nationalization and centralized planning. By the mid-1960s, the Egyptian government found itself in control of banks, insurance companies, textile mills, sugar-refining and food-processing facilities, air and sea transport, public utilities, urban mass transit, cinemas, theaters, department stores, agricultural credit institutions, fertilizer production, and construction companies. To assure state dominance of both the economic and the political process, the Egyptian regime harnessed what remained of the devitalized private sector in service of the public sector.[51]

The shockwaves of the Suez War were felt not only in Egypt, but in Syria and Iraq as well. In addition to creating a political atmosphere in Iraq conducive to the overthrow of the monarchy, Nasser's anti-imperialist stance incited select political groupings in both countries to demand unification with Egypt. Because of the magnitude of Egyptian power and prestige, the short-lived union of Egypt and Syria (1958–1961) was carried out in accordance with the stipulations of the Egyptian benefactor, not the Syrian petitioner. The Egyptian model was transferred to Syria and Egyptian-style land reform, nationalizations, and political structures were imposed on the junior partner. Military rulers in Iraq also bowed to Egyptian conditions in preparation for political union, adopting policies similar to those adopted in Syria. Although plans for Egyptian-Iraqi union never reached fruition, and although etatist policies were briefly relaxed in Syria after the union with Egypt dissolved, the widely-heralded promise of the Egyptian "revolution" and the transformative impact of an activist state conditioned popular expectations from governments throughout the region. The accession of Baᶜthist regimes in Syria (1963) and Iraq (briefly in 1963, then again in 1966) solidified the gains made by the state in the immediate aftermath of the Suez War.

The shift from accommodationism to "state socialism" (or, as viewed from the left, "state capitalism") in the economic realm was accompanied by a corresponding shift in official political discourse, particularly as it pertained to democracy. As described above, in the immediate aftermath of the first military coups the officers who had seized power presented developmentalism and the establishment of a (true) pluralist-democratic system as two legitimizing pillars of their movements. On the eve of the first anniversary of the Free Officers' coup, Gamal Abdul Nasser affirmed that

> The kind of government best suited to modern Egypt is one that is based upon true democratic principles. This government should be directed solely to the public good, and not to private ambitions and interests. Why should we want to have a single-party constitution and establish a dictatorial power now, when the countries which have tried such a system are having to revert to democratic rule and a multiplicity of parties? Why should we not leave a free field for every doctrine which is put forward by a group with goodwill, whose aim is to serve the public good? The present period should therefore be regarded as one of transition only, while we prepare the way for a return to normal, democratic life.[52]

Notwithstanding his early pronouncements such as this in favor of political pluralism and his protestations that the Free Officers were merely engaged in political housecleaning and not out to establish a new political system, by 1955 the Egyptian president began to act as if he believed that party politics as they had existed under the *ancien régime* were beyond redemption. Publicly expressing disgust at the recalcitrance of the established parties to "cleanse" themselves of "corrupt" elements and at the resistance of extraparliamentary groupings to the blandishments of the regime, Nasser announced in May of 1955 that military rule would end in eight months—but with a catch: "associations" (*hay'at*) would replace political parties as the medium of representation within the reopened parliament.[53]

By the end of the Suez War, promises made by the Egyptian Free Officers to relinquish control had been laid to rest alongside the attempts made to reach an accommodation with purged political parties and the private sector. While democracy continued to play a legitimating role in official discourse, the Egyptian government invested the term with new meanings apposite to the altered circumstances and the state's expanded responsibilities. In speech after speech Nasser differentiated between the "reactionary democracy" (*al-dimuqratiyya al-raj*ᶜ*iyya*) practiced under the old regime, in which the formal trappings of political pluralism masked oligarchic rule and economic exploitation, and "integral (socialist) democracy" (*al-dimuqratiyya al-salima, al-dimuqratiyya al-ishtirakiyya*) which conflated political rights and economic justice and made the state—the repository of the "popular will"—the guarantor of the latter.[54] The official discourse of democracy, which had once embraced political pluralism, now vilified it as incompatible with the developmentalist and social justice goals of an activist Egyptian state.

A similar shift in official discourse as it pertained to democracy can be found in the pronouncements of the Baᶜth Party. At its inception, the Baᶜth Party resembled other ideologically-inspired political groupings whose roots can be traced to the economic crisis of the 1930s and the social transformation it induced. Indeed, although its founders were two Sorbonne-trained Syrian secondary-school teachers, Michel Aflaq and Salah al-Din al-Bitar, who recruited the initial cadres from among their students, the party came to incorporate as leaders and members many who had received their political training in Syrian political parties of the Depression era, including the Communist Party, the Arab Socialist Party, the League of National Action, and the Syrian Social Nationalist Party. The party thus retained a front-like character, its members divided between left and right wings, between scientific and utopian socialists, and, more significantly, between experienced agitators who spoke to bread-

and-butter issues and romantic nationalists who waxed poetic about the "Arab fatherland." While all factions were committed to the cause of developmentalism and "socialism," party ranks divided on a variety of tactical issues, including the role of the state in the economy and political pluralism.

In its early days, the oft-repressed Baᶜth Party publicly advocated the principles of political pluralism. Indeed, for its public debut the party challenged the validity of the 1947 Syrian parliamentary elections and called for reforms to make parliament more representative.[55] Furthermore, the party inscribed its commitment to individual rights and political pluralism in its constitution, written under the supervision of Michel Aflaq:

> The Arab nation is characterized by virtues which are the result of its successive rebirths. These virtues are characterized by vitality and creativeness and by an ability for transformation and renewal. Its renewal is always linked to growth in personal freedom, and harmony between its evolution and the national interest . . . Freedom of speech, freedom of assembly, freedom of belief, as well as artistic freedom are sacred. No authority can diminish them . . . The regime of the [future] Arab state will be a constitutional parliamentary regime. Executive power is responsible before the legislative, which is directly elected by the people.[56]

But as had occurred in Egypt, the events of the mid-1950s reduced the appeal of individual rights and political pluralism among Baᶜthists. In addition to the recalcitrance of the former political and economic elites who refused to subordinate their interests to those of the Syrian and Iraqi regimes, the example of Egyptian "socialism," persistent regime instability, and a political atmosphere in which the furtherance of political interests depended upon the formation of clandestine cells and conspiratorial intrigue rather than parliamentary debate strengthened the position of those within the party who advocated an authoritarian approach to achieve party goals. The concluding statement of the sixth national convention of the Baᶜth Party, held in the aftermath of Baᶜthist seizure of power in both Syria and Iraq, reflected their ascension within the party. Gone from this document were the conciliatory pledges of 1947 made to private sector capitalists to respect private ownership of immovable property and the right of inheritance; in their place was a blanket condemnation of the bourgeoisie as an "ally to the new colonialism" which "is unable to carry out any positive task in the economic sphere." The dominant wing of the Baᶜth Party now charged the state with the historic mission socialist doctrine usually conferred on the bourgeoisie. Gone from this document, too, were the references to the sacred nature of individual liberties and the inviolability of democratic rights; although recognizing the singular right of the working class to form parties, the sixth national convention contended that political participation should be restricted solely to "associations that are within the national political line."[57]

While coercion, foreign assistance, and a constant state of war mobilization facilitated the imposition of a political regimen in post-Suez Egypt and Baᶜthist Syria and Iraq to which the notion of integral democracy was germane, three other factors enabled the regimes to garner support for their political precepts. First, since none of the regimes was anomalous with respect to the populations it governed, the developmentalist goals they articulated reflected attitudes held by a large proportion of their compatriots as well. The Egyptian regime and the Baᶜthist regimes of Syria and Iraq embedded the adjunctive concept of integral democracy within an official discourse that not only gave pride of place to developmentalist goals, but melded developmentalism with the reinvigorated post-Suez slogans of anti-imperialism, Arab unity, and social justice. Second, the regimes matched their populist rhetoric with a host of programs—from rural electrification to food and commodity subsidies, rent control, and expansive educational and employment opportunities in the civil service and state-run industries—that lent credence to their rhetoric and provided those from whom they were attempting to fashion an "Arab socialist" coalition with a vested interest in upholding the new order regardless of their true attitude toward integral democracy. Finally, the embodiment of integral democracy through the institutionalization of a corporatist apparatus induced structural changes in society which further reinforced regime capabilities.

Corporatism, to borrow Phillipe C. Schmitter's definition, refers to

> a system of interest representation in which the constituent units are organized into a limited number of singular, compulsory, noncompetitive, hierarchically ordered and functionally differentiated categories, recognized or licensed (if not created) by the state and granted a deliberate representational monopoly within their respective categories in exchange for

observing certain controls on their selection of leaders and articulation of demands and supports.[58]

While commonly associated with right-wing regimes in southern Europe and Latin America, corporatism is, in fact, ideologically neutral; Nasser, for example, borrowed his ideas for corporatist instrumentalities from both Salazar's Portugal and Tito's Yugoslavia.[59] Corporatism was appealing in the post-Suez Arab East because it provided a suitable structural foundation for regime consolidation and etatism consistent with the eclectic philosophy of "Arab socialism."

The roots of corporatism in the Arab East stretch back at least as far as the interwar period when Egyptian governments, confronted by the power of unregulated and uncontrollable extraparliamentary groupings and searching for a means to tighten controls over the political process, began to adapt and/or co-opt pre-existing institutional forms (guilds, chambers of commerce, professional syndicates) to ensure their compliance with state objectives. The regulatory and administrative edicts of the Middle East Supply Center reinforced and expanded corporatist structures in Egypt and spread the prototypes for these structures to Syria and Iraq during World War II.[60] Until the consolidation of military regimes, however, corporatist initiatives affected almost exclusively the organization of professional and business interests which had to share political space with a number of less-submissive pluralist formations among the lower and working classes, such as independent trade unions. It was not until the aftermath of the Suez War that regimes in Egypt, Syria, and Iraq could mobilize the necessary combination of prestige, system of rewards, and instruments of coercion to institute a comprehensive corporatist system correspondent to the imperatives of integral democracy.[61]

The power of the state to recognize certain functional categories of association, to repudiate others, and to allocate resources accordingly endowed the state with a capacity for oversight and social engineering commonly lacking in pluralist democracies. In Egypt, for example, the peasantry was one of five categories recognized as making up the "alliance of working forces" which the state called upon to ratify the 1961 "Charter for National Action." Because the peasantry was a recognized category of society, its organization received special attention from the state and the state's mobilizational and ideological arm, the Arab Socialist Union (whose role in Egypt was analogous to that enjoyed by the Baᶜth Party in Syria and Iraq). Although the state's efforts to bring about a comprehensive transformation in agrarian relations ultimately fell short,[62] the union used a carrot (agricultural credits, the deployment of agronomists to the field, health clinics, social services) and stick (monopolization of marketing, coerced participation in cooperatives, surveillance) approach to construct vertical linkages connecting the state, the village unit, and the peasants who inhabited the villages and to crush once and for all large landowners whose position was not recognized in categorical terms.

Interestingly, while the institutionalization of corporatism in Nasserist Egypt and Baᶜthist Syria and Iraq diminished the rights enjoyed by members of some incorporated groups, it had the opposite effect on the rights enjoyed by members of others. For example, the rights of workers were substantially curtailed by labor's incorporation into the corporatist structure. In all three countries the state destroyed the organizational independence of trade unions, first by purging potentially dissident elements (liberals, leftists, Islamists[63]) from leadership positions, then by integrating unions into broader labor confederations which held the exclusive right to represent their members. Other groups that had organized themselves before the onset of the revolutionary period—the press, professional and trade associations—similarly lost the independence they had fought to acquire or maintain since the interwar period.

But while the state rescinded the privileges that had been enjoyed by some groups, others—particularly those whose organization had never previously been officially sanctioned—profited from official recognition. By recognizing women as a distinct category of society worthy of representation, for example, the state delineated and guaranteed social rights for women that were new or withheld in the West during the same period. The Egyptian constitutions of 1956 and 1963 guaranteed equal opportunities to all Egyptians regardless of gender. These constitutional provisions were discharged through a series of laws that enfranchised women (like their Syrian sisters, who were enfranchised soon after the Zaᶜim coup in 1949) and guaranteed equality of opportunity in the public sector, paid maternity leave, and the right to child care if employed at a large facility.[64] The Baᶜthist regimes of Hafiz al-Asad in Syria and Saddam Husayn in Iraq legislated similar measures in the 1970s and, like the Egyptian government during the same period, amended laws regulating personal status to expand women's conjugal rights and protect their right of inheritance. Notwithstanding their stated commitment to social justice and their faithfulness to the egalitarian and secular "spirit of the age," the regimes stepped into this social minefield and promoted "state feminism" for a number of reasons: not only did they aspire to co-opt the middle classes and to displace feminist organizations which had been active in the region since the 1920s and which might have provided the nucleus for liberal challenges to their rule, they sought to undermine "private patriarchy" as an underregulated zone of freedom with a state-defined "public patriarchy."

As might be expected, the sanctioning of representational groups by the state and their integration into the state apparatus further attenuated political life already debilitated by the dissolution of political parties independent of the state. Deputies to the "people's assemblies" and "party congresses" that convened to debate public policy did not use public fora to contest the policy implications of divergent political philosophies. Rather, because the state defined the parameters for both political representation and ideological disputation, and because economic development and social welfare played a central role in the official ideology, the officially-sanctioned politics which functioned under the rubric of "integral democracy" devolved into little more than attempts by various sectors of society to appropriate for themselves larger shares of the political and economic pie.

Two of the categories represented in the Egyptian "alliance of working forces," for example, comprised professionals and civil servants who had benefited from the expanded educational opportunities provided by the state, and the weakened remnant of the indigenous bourgeoisie (the "productive capitalists") which survived on the fringes of the public sector and at the sufferance of its managers. Under ordinary circumstances these groups might have been the most vocal advocates of political and economic liberalization (as they have been in other countries).[65] But regardless of the private feelings held by members of these groups toward the policies of the regimes that governed them, their economic dependence on the government and the lack of independent organizational channels through which they might express dissent sapped both the incentive and the capacity to win political concessions from the state. Because the Egyptian regime held fast to the levers of control and provided more than adequate compensation for compliance with its designs—"middle class welfare" policies in the case of the first category, access to the financial resources of the state in the case of the second—members of both groups in the main acquiesced to the stipulations of the state.[66]

Nevertheless, while the imposition of corporatist structures did narrow the domain of permissible politics and fundamentally strengthen the intrusive capabilities of the central state apparatus, two factors mitigated this strengthening. First, since the state assumed a central position in the reallocation of resources, the stability of the state was inextricably tied to maintaining benefits provided to the recognized constituent groups. State planners could only curtail those benefits—even in times of dearth—at the risk of alienating the very constituencies they had mobilized. Second, while the state did expand its reach, it was hardly able to stifle political dissent in toto; instead, rather than curtailing political dissent, the political restructuring undertaken by the revolutionary regimes merely fostered an alteration in its form.

Regimes that had governed Egypt, Syria, and Iraq before the period of military takeovers faced domestic opposition from two organized sources: popular-based political parties and associations, on the one hand, and conspiratorial groupings within the military, on the other. The revolutionary regimes confronted these threats to their authority by adopting a two-pronged strategy. First, they outlawed and repressed those parties and associations they could not co-opt. Second, to guard themselves against the possibility of conspiracy, the regimes increasingly concentrated power in the hands of a few core members who, in turn, solidified political support through informal vertical ties to select "clients" (in all three cases) and/or informal vertical ties to a reliable religious/ethnic/ geographic base (in the cases of Syria and Iraq) which paralleled the formal vertical ties of corporatism. On one level this two-pronged strategy worked surprisingly well: even in notoriously unstable Syria and Iraq, ruling elites who applied it in the 1970s have successfully maintained power for more than a quarter of a century. But this strategy was not risk free: taken in the broader context of the policies followed by Egypt, Syria, and Iraq, it opened up cleavages in society that had not previously existed (*pace* those who cite the transhistorical role of "primordial" attachments in the political process or who use a "mosaic" society framework to analyze Middle Eastern states) and facilitated the emergence of political Islam as the main challenger to the regimes governing those states.

While political Islam is not new to the region—the first modern Islamist group, the Egyptian Muslim Brotherhood, was founded in the 1920s—it thrived in an atmosphere in which the state not only broadcast its commitment to "social justice through development," but made that commitment the foundation for political legitimacy: although Islamism is hardly monolithic, social justice is an issue upon which all Islamists agree. As early as the 1950s and 1960s, Islamist groups in Egypt and Syria successfully used their programmatic association with the cause of social justice to recruit not only from the petite-bourgeoisie whose livelihood was threatened by the "socialist" decrees of the two governments, but from sympathetic professionals as well.[67] In the 1980s, when financially-strapped regimes attempted to renegotiate responsibilities they had assumed when their revolutionary fervor was in full flower, Islamism's appeal touched those who were hardest hit by that renegotiation, as well as those who simply viewed the state's attempted retreat as an abnegation of its charge.

The co-option or destruction of popular-based parties and associations gave Islamist groups a virtual monopoly on organized resistance to policies of the regimes in all three countries. In the aftermath of the Iranian Revolution, for example, it was not uncommon for politically-active Iraqi Shi^cis who had previously been associated with the hard-hit Communist Party to give vent to their political aspirations by joining Islamist groups, many of whose social policies closely resembled those advocated by the party they had been forced to abandon.[68] Along with the regimes' practice of granting privileges to groups of trustworthy clients, which gave credence to the familiar charge of "corruption," the fact that the security-conscious ruling elites of Syria and Iraq had become too closely associated with specific clusters of religious minorities—Alawites from Latakia in the case of Syria, Sunni Muslims from the village of Takrit in the case of Iraq—enabled Islamists to define themselves as the true representatives of the nation in opposition to a sectarian "other." Ironically, when combined with a discourse focused on social justice, a fixation on the regulation of individual behavior, and the constraints imposed by existing political conditions, their self-definition as the representatives of the true "Islamic essence" of the nation makes it unlikely that upon attaining power in Syria or Iraq Islamists would abandon the precepts of integral democracy promoted by the very regimes they currently oppose.

≺ IV ≻

"Liberalization," "Democratization," and the Legacy of the Developmentalist Past

The heyday of revolutionary regimes in the Arab East was short lived. Although the economies of Egypt, Syria, and Iraq had been buoyed from their inception through the 1970s by a combination of primitive accumulation, foreign assistance, and oil revenues—both direct (Iraq) and indirect (in the form of subsidies to Syria and Egypt from oil-producing countries)—by the early 1980s all three were compelled by a variety of factors to undertake structural adjustments. While none was so foolish as to attempt to abandon the goal of economic development as a legitimizing norm, all adopted policies of limited economic liberalization.

Egypt was the first to experiment with such policies, initiating them only three years after the death of Gamal Abdul Nasser and the ascension of Anwar al-Sadat to the presidency in 1970. Forced into action by the need to stimulate a stagnant Egyptian economy, to build a base of political support independent of Nasserist "centers of power," and to redress the staggering economic costs of defeat in the June War of 1967 and the subsequent War of Attrition against Israel, al-Sadat launched a program of economic liberalization known as the *infitah* ("opening"), an idiosyncratic amalgam of "Arab socialist" and free-market economics which combined a strong state sector and the continuation of state welfare programs with incentives for foreign investment and private enterprise. Al-Sadat learned through bitter experience that any attempt to revitalize the Egyptian economy could not be undertaken at the expense of the broad range of welfare guarantees provided to the population: the brief flirtation with policies that would curtail those guarantees ended disastrously with widespread strikes by industrial workers in 1975–76, regime-threatening bread riots throughout the country in 1977, and a surge in support for the Islamist opposition.

Syria and Iraq began their programs of economic "liberalization" somewhat later. While Hafiz al-Asad, who assumed power in Syria in 1970 in what he called a "corrective revolution," initially strengthened the corporatist structures put in place by his predecessors, his policy of allowing select businessmen to contract with the public sector terminated the war his adversaries within the Baᶜth Party had waged against private commercial interests and opened the door a crack for economic liberalization. Only after the post-1979 collapse in oil prices reduced aid from Arab oil producers and civil disorder—sparked by a sluggish economy, unemployment, and the distress felt by small merchants and artisans—erupted in Aleppo (1979) and Hama (1982)[69] did the government attempt a more extensive economic opening. In Iraq, it was the exigencies generated by the Iran-Iraq War which prompted Saddam Husayn's ephemeral "pragmatic revolution" and the extension of an olive branch to private sector businessmen whom the regime needed to provide expertise and funding for reconstruction. As in Egypt, however, economic liberalization in Syria and Iraq did not entail a weakening of the public sector or a politically-dangerous withdrawal of subsidies, employment guarantees, or social security benefits from the population:[70] instead, both states attempted to reinvigorate the economy by applying private initiative to support a languid public sector.

It should not be surprising, therefore, that the economic liberalization of the 1980s did not foster an analogous liberalization in the political sphere. Indeed, with the exception of Egypt, the limited economic openings might be seen as conscious efforts to buy time for regimes that had, if anything, grown more narrow and authoritarian. Even in Egypt, the regimes of al-Sadat and his successor, Husni Mubarak, balked at linking economic and political liberalization; indeed, in the 1974 *October Paper* which laid out the blueprint for the *infitah*, al-Sadat warned that the social progress realized since the Free Officers' revolution could be protected only if the government maintained a firm control over the political process. Since the announcement of the *October Paper*, Egyptian governments have parried foreign pressure and domestic (mostly Islamist) threats by adopting the formal trappings of pluralist democracy, all the while ensuring regime survival by applying a variety of tactics, from repression (as prescribed in the notorious "Law of Shame" of 1980, for example) and the manipulation of the electoral system to maintaining the wide-ranging subventions initiated under Nasser and the balancing of corporatist divisions against each other.

Although the regimes that govern Egypt, Syria, and Iraq may continue or even expand their experiments with limited economic liberalization in the future, their policies will most likely also continue to have little impact on the political sphere. As a number of scholars have observed, so long as the power of states and the power of those seeking expanded economic privileges remain asymmetrical, so long as economic liberalization and political democratization remain incommensurable except to the states which reserve the right to define the permissible terms for their equation, so long as a population fragmented by corporatist structures retains a stake in regime survival, and so long as the Islamist "cure" seems for so many far worse than the authoritarian "disease," no "democratic bargain" is likely to be struck.[71] In the meantime, the ardor with which broad segments of the population first greeted the revolutionary regimes in the early post-Suez period may have dissipated as a result of chronic repression, unfulfilled promises, and, in Egypt and Syria, the regular substitution in official discourse of *raison d'état* and the ostensibly non-ideological, "scientific" rhetoric of free-market capitalism for the populist appeals of their predecessors. The structures and norms institutionalized by these regimes, however, continue to regulate the relationship binding the inhabitants of Egypt, Syria, and Iraq not only with the regimes that govern them, but with the movements that oppose them as well.

≺ 4 ≻

Ideas of Freedom in Modern India

SUDIPTA KAVIRAJ

IN HIS ESSAY on two concepts of liberty, Isaiah Berlin warned against conceptual conflation between two ideas about freedom. The first idea of freedom referred to the liberty of the individual, the different institutional arrangements which led to its expansion or contraction. The second, with which the first was never to be confused, was the very different meaning of the "freedom" of a collectivity such as a class or a nation.[1] While acknowledging that in real historical contexts, it was difficult to prevent groups from speaking a language of freedom, Berlin thought it was analytically essential to show that these were not ideas of freedom proper, but more of injustice. In studying the history of ideas in a colonial context like India, however, it is impossible to separate these two concerns, except analytically. This chapter tries to follow the story of the ideas of modern freedom in India in both senses, as liberty of individuals to choose their lives, but also the freedom of specific social groups like castes and the nation to follow what they regard as their "destiny." In studying intellectual history in India, the central organizing principle is not the distinction between negative and positive liberty, but the liberty of individuals and communities.[2]

≺ I ≻

Methodological Choices: Two Forms of Intellectual History

There is general agreement that in doing history of ideas it is essential to follow historically reliable "contextualist" methods.[3] On closer inspection, there can be some further problems of finer methodological choice involved in this type of intellectual history. In contemporary discussions about contextualism, it is possible to discern two analytical styles. Although they share fundamental historicist principles of interpretation, their actual analytical and interpretative practices contain somewhat different emphases.

The first form of contextualism is represented by the Cambridge school, which focuses on the study of "intellectual" or *theoretical* texts to find their correct historical meanings by recovering authorial intentions.[4] The meanings of concepts fundamental to theoretical arguments are established by studying linguistic conventions of a particular time from a wider study of "small texts."[5] It is the circulation of concepts within a general political discourse that gives them particular common meanings. Even when major thinkers introduce innovative inflections of the current meanings, these can be precisely established by measuring their difference from norms of common linguistic practice. Although these contextual studies use at times a vast repertoire of "small" texts, the object of study is usually the "great texts" of social theory. The humbler texts are usually the means to an understanding of the great ones. At times however this form of intellectual history transcends its focus on exemplary theoretical texts, and its purpose shifts to an illumination of an historical "structure of thought" of which great and small texts are illustrations.[6] A second feature of this interpretative style is a certain hesitancy about the "political." Its insatiable curiosity about how people talk about politics, its "language" in the wider sense, is usually not matched by its interest in politics, what this language talks about. The context it considers methodologically relevant is primarily linguistic and intellectual.

By contrast, the *begriffsgeschichte*[7] produced by Reinhart Koselleck and his collaborators in German intellectual history follows a somewhat different strategy, focusing less on theoretical constructs, more on practical meanings of individual concepts which are central to the successful operation of modern social practices. For engaging in modern economic practices successfully, social agents have to acquire an abstract concept of a "market," altering the traditional connotations of the idea. Concepts like these—market, state, society, law, others—are practical concepts in a double sense. They are required for the successful conduct of social practices central to modern existence; but, conversely, they are real or correspond to something substantial in social life, only as long as social practices animate them. When social practice moves away, they become hollow.[8] Usually these new concepts[9] are set in something like a new conceptual field, like the idea of an "economy," an abstract conception that combines the totality of all practices of a particular kind. The two other concepts of a similar kind are obviously "society" and the field of public exchanges that constitute "the political."[10] This form of conceptual history seeks to establish the meaning of these concepts (of both the small and large types, that is, market and economy) by looking at the slow evolution of their historical relation with determinate practices. Often there are no privileged texts associated with individual concepts like these; their historical evolution has to be read through texts and other types of documents. This method involves more attention to humbler forms of writing like journals, newspapers, or other pieces of utterly ordinary discourse, rather than intellectual construction of theoretical arguments.

Evidently, the difference between the two styles is in their emphasis, not in methodological principles, and actual studies usually combine them. Yet this is not an insignificant question of methodological choice. In the Indian case, there are some obvious advantages in either following the second method, or combining the two, since there is no self-conscious tradition of social theorizing in the Western sense until the twentieth century.[11] But the fact that there is no "theory" of freedom developed by recognizably specialized political thinkers does not mean there were not enormous shifts in mentalities on the question of freedom. Nor does it imply that ideas of freedom in civil society and public domains of politics did not fundamentally alter everyday operations of power. In the Indian case, it might be most fruitful to combine the two approaches.

≺ II ≻

Translation of Ideas and Translations of Practice

In any case, historical semantics in the modern Indian context would require a procedure different in some obvious respects from the standard methods of studying European political thought.[12] In the European cases, the transformation of concepts they are trying to analyze is internal to the Western tradition, within a larger framework of cultural and intellectual continuity.[13] The clashes and conceptual transformations in colonial India were of a vastly different kind. Indian societies had fairly developed and institutionally entrenched intellectual traditions at the time of entry of European colonialism. The process by which European concepts entered this cultural world and the structures of semantic transactions that ensued had a specific pattern of complexity. A successful project of historical semantics here would involve three successive steps.

The first is to look for a practical concept or a cluster in earlier intellectual traditions.[14] Second, we must establish the precise form in which a particular European concept enters the discourses of colonial India: after all, concepts like freedom, or property, or law differed a great deal in their particular semantic connotation, theoretical inflection, and institutional purchase between distinctive European traditions.[15] It is therefore important to understand precisely which particular concept is introduced, or indeed, if it is a single or homogeneous one at all. Third, we must look at how the presence of each concept affects the practical and conceptual shape of the other. Often the traditional concept, discredited, displaced, or undermined by the modern European one, continues a shadowy existence of subterranean influence, subtly refracting the meanings of the modern term. This is particularly likely in cases in which the European concept enters and works through a translating term in the vernacular. The European term then has to be converted to a vernacular term by literal translation. Sometimes, this is not an easy transition of signification as the new meaning has to work through and gradually displace a stubborn older meaning.[16]

Because ideas like freedom are practical concepts which exist as constituents of a conceptual field, they raise problems of translation—not merely the linguistic translation of straight intellectual terms, but "translation" of practices.[17] There is an odd, implausible, but widespread implication that when new practical concepts like "privacy" or "publicity" come into colonial society they get written as it were on a clean slate. The historical process of translation is far more complex and untidy. In most cases, there existed premodern social practices and concepts necessary to them, over which new, different institutions came to be placed. In many cases, this led to the apparent establishment of a new practice, though, if one looked at the actual daily routines within the formal institutions, traditional forms continued to shape the understandings and behavior of actors.[18] The first step in the history of modern freedom in India, then, is to ask if there were similar concepts in pre-colonial intellectual traditions. Or were there ideas sufficiently similar, so that these could form an indigenous substratum of thinking on which modern Western ideas could be grafted.

≺ III ≻

Were There Traditional Concepts of Freedom?

Is there then an earlier story of "freedom"? Does the modern Western ideal of freedom come as an entirely unfamiliar, unsettling idea, or as one that had traditional equivalents, though differently inflected? It is a curious fact of intellectual history, that India had highly developed traditions of philosophical reflection, but none of these took "society" or social principles, like justice, as a serious object of analytical attention. Although classical Indian philosophy developed highly sophisticated and intricate traditions of thinking on logic, metaphysics, epistemology, and aesthetics, there is hardly any application of these skills of distinction, analysis, elaboration, or critical debate to social problems in a narrower sense: like the justification of the caste system. The two great traditional texts which deal with problems surrounding political power, the *Arthasastra*[19] and the *Manusmrti*,[20] have the character of compendia, rather than of philosophical justification, which, by its very discursive form, admits of the theoretical possibility of skepticism. Some of the most powerful reflections on the justifiability of social restrictions can be found instead in the great narrative texts.[21] But despite the great moral complexities portrayed in the epics, and sometimes direct invitations to reflect on the undecidability of the good (*dharma*),[22] they did not generate a tradition of critical debate on the justifiability of social arrangements.

A curious feature, often noted, of the complex architecture of Hindu culture was its strange combination of enforcement of social orthodoxy and tolerance for intellectual difference. Not only were the six systems of philosophy allowed within the general framework of trust in the Vedas; there could be an immense variety in the imagination of God's nature and his manifestations in the world. God could be worshipped in any of the canonical forms—Visnu, Shiva, Shakti, and others—each one having sub-forms according to the mood or disposition that predominated. By contrast, the actual social life of Hindus was bound to strictest details by rules of caste which governed the most significant aspects of social relations—the choice of an individual's occupation, marriage, sociability. The Hindu system, therefore, was a strange combination of considerable freedom of purely intellectual enquiry and the strictest observance of social rules.

The classical tradition of pluralism of religious imagination was given a more elective bent by the medieval religious movements of bhakti (devotion) which swept through most parts of India and introduced a deeply emotional, voluntaristic conception of religiosity. Most of these bhakti movements were anti-brahminical and, significantly, preached an elective conception of religious life. Individuals decided consciously to adopt these new ways of finding God in preference to orthodox brahminism with its emphasis on ritualistic observance. It is this strand of traditional Indian thought which is most similar to an ideal of choosing one's life as opposed to living it as given by rules of caste. Not surprisingly, most of these bhakti movements were strongly critical of the brahminical intellectual dominance and social practices of caste. In the longer term, however, after an initial period of social rebelliousness, most of these traditions were re-integrated into Hindu caste society while retaining their distinctiveness in the fields of religious ideas. As long as caste rules controlled the details of social lives of individuals, there could be no pre-figuration of the modern conception of freedom.

Caste was the primary grid of social relations in traditional Indian society: both the actual social relations that governed conduct and a set of values, which justified them.[23] Intricately devised and detailed rules of individual behavior not merely restricted room for maneuver in the negative sense, but actually commanded specific courses of action. The *Manusmrti* is the classical example of a moral text that produced a grid of moral commands arranged on two axes. One provided an intricately detailed biographical line of activities, specifying a set of general principles and details for obligatory ceremonies from the individual's birth to death. The other axis, of relation with other people, was equally significant, since without that there could not be a complete system of moral conduct encompassing the entire society. The *Smrtis*[24] consequently laid down in equally painstaking detail how an individual belonging to caste A should behave with other castes B to Z. The moral order can thus be seen, for all individuals of a particular type, as an intricate grid in which responsibilities and right ways of conduct are set down so minutely that there is little room for maneuver or innovation. Hindu individuals thus lived socially standardized lives in which freedom of choice in vital matters was not just limited, but conceptually absent.[25] Only the renouncer (*sannyasi*) could leave the life of a householder and not be bound by caste rules: the price that the renouncer had to pay was as radical as the freedom he was allowed to enjoy. The doctrine of the renouncer could not be considered an archaic or inchoate version of a theory of freedom, for freedom makes sense only in the context of society and an amplitude of social actions; the terrible freedom of the *sannyasi* was predicated on his being out of society's demands and comforts.

Hindu doctrine spent considerable time to reflect on the nature and forms of *mukti* within the mundane, everyday, householder's world. It was a concept closely connected, in original religious philosophies, to more cosmic ideas of disentanglement—*moksa* in the Hindu tradition or *nirvana* in the neighboring Buddhist one. And, in both traditions, the search for *mukti* or deliverance goes on in the framework of a predominantly pessimistic picture of ordinary human existence—condemned to social prohibitions, vulnerability to death and disease, the insatiability of desires. The original ideal of *mukti* was, to use a Weberian conceptual distinction, entirely otherworldly.[26] It suggested an impossibility of freedom in mundane social terms; true freedom meant disentanglement from the unending predicaments of daily human life, and was to be sought outside it.[27] This "outside" could be interpreted in several ways: it could mean going outside the circle of the ordinary householder's life by accepting renunciation; or going outside the succession of lives in which souls are trapped by winning deliverance from the chain of rebirths.

Some religious doctrines, like the famous schools of Advaita and Buddhism, offered more complex and subtle forms of such renunciation, by advising non-attachment to desires and persons within worldly life. This could be interpreted to say that achieving a form of high indifference was possible while accepting the fetters of ordinary life. But none of these forms referred to the question of freedom from social restrictions, and thus could not qualify, without a fundamental conceptual re-inflection, as a translation of the modern concept.

Their principal characteristic was that they suggested ingenious ways of enlarging an internal "freedom" of the mind, taking social restrictions as given—unlike modern freedom, which turns the principle of freedom of action itself into a force which determines forms of social life.

However, one of the more interesting questions of comparative history of ideas is the technical nature of translation. Because the vocabulary of the traditional culture lacks an exact equivalent, the new ideas have to find awkward translations and slowly work their way into the semantic structure. After repetitive and consistent use, the older term is often invested with the new meaning, erasing the conventional one, or the two meanings exist side by side, differentiated by native users by the use-context. In the Bengali language, the early search for a semantic equivalent for the modern idea of freedom led to this type of linguistic displacement. An excellent example of such semantic operation on the term *mukti* can be found in a group of poems by Rabindranath Tagore. Tagore insisted that intellectual modernity must be accessible through the resources of the vernacular but felt at the same time the conceptual inappropriateness of traditional terms like *mukti*. His solution was to argue for a re-conceptualization of *mukti* in distinctly this-worldly terms. Directly addressing the traditional form of alienating religiosity, one of his poems suggests the impossibility of such deliverance, since the creator himself is tied to every part of the universe by his acceptance of the bonds of creation.[28] True deliverance (*mukti*), therefore, must have a this-worldly, mundane, sensuous meaningfulness. In another poem, he declares directly "my *mukti* does not lie in cultivating detachment. I want the joyous taste of freedom within innumerable bonds. Again and again, You will fill this earthen cup with Your nectar of colours and fragrance."[29] Though this is a poetic reflection, it shows the precise difficulties with the older concept of *mukti*—its otherworldliness, and the implicit belief in the cycle of rebirth, both unacceptable to a modern consciousness. The kind of semantic and conceptual shifts that Tagore proposed in his poems became fairly general by the end of the nineteenth century; and in modern language, the term came to carry increasingly modern connotations of freedom. Eventually, *mukti* would come to stand, at least in Bengali writing, for not merely social freedom, but also the new all-encompassing desire of the people-nation for freedom from colonial rule.[30]

< IV >

Colonial Influences: Liberty and Modern Institutions

Ideas of modern liberty entered colonial Indian society through three different routes; and the peculiarity of the route by which an idea came in influenced its reception, its precise meaning inside the Indian conceptual structure, and its eventual fate. Some institutions of colonial rule, like the legal arrangements of property, required a tacit understanding of the rights or freedoms of individuals to acquire and dispose of wealth. Any approach to the new colonial government also implied, however minimally, a vague right of a subject to the British rule of law.[31] A second institutional influence, of inestimable significance, was the new educational culture, produced by the establishment of institutions for the spread of modern, Western education. These were established primarily through the initiative of modern Bengalis, though with ample encouragement from the British administration. A third kind of influence, which depended on the success of the second, institutional spread of Western-style education, was the more direct intellectual influence of Western social thinking. Rousseau and John Stuart Mill became required reading for aspiring intellectuals in Calcutta, which also boasted quite early an energetic Positivist Society.[32]

Colonial rule, once settled, brought in several types of administrative practices that required, because they conceptually presupposed, conceptions of modern freedom. One of the first was the freedom to possess and dispose of private property, an idea involving huge silent shifts of conceptual understandings about ownership. Traditional forms of ownership were legally revised and fitted increasingly into modern conceptions of private property and administrative rules formulated for its protection. When the colonial administration created new types of secondary rights over property through the Permanent Settlement, a new land revenue arrangement introduced by Lord Cornwallis, disputants had to make their way through the new, intricate legal system of property rights. Besides property, other legal practices under colonial rule similarly implied the existence of the right to freedom—from the publication of newspapers to the marriage of minor girls.

In all these fields of changing social practice, frequently complex and difficult cases occurred which led to either highly publicized court cases or considerable agitation in the vernacular press. In both contexts there had to be discussions about the nature of these rights and two types of justifications: justifiability of individual acts involved in these cases, but, through them, more indirectly, also justifiability of the larger, interconnected system of individual rights themselves.[33] In highly significant cases of reform, like the abolition of sati, the advocacy of remarriage of widows, or legal prevention of marriage of girls considered too young, the arguments invariably moved from the dispute about the specific rule of conduct to a larger one of choosing between two moral orders. In the traditional one the primary appeal was to performance of duty or social responsibility by actors according to the rules of their caste/community, while the modern moral culture rested on giving individuals "civilized" treatment, because of their intrinsic moral worth.

In actual disputes often the lines between these two types of moral arguments were fudged for practical reasons. Ram Mohan Roy, the first significant modern thinker and social reformer, for instance, used both types of arguments to persuade the Bengali Hindus to abandon widow-burning. He deployed his considerable erudition in the *sastras* (Hindu scriptures) to point out that in earlier, "purer" stages of Hindu thought, women were treated with respect, if not accorded equality; it was only in more recent degraded times that Bengali moral codes placed severe and unjust restrictions on them. But the major part of the argument had to appeal to reason, in asking the educated middle classes to choose the first part of their tradition over the second. Although traditional material or evidence was used in the argument, the decisive element was an appeal to a liberal rationality.[34]

Born in a traditional Brahmin family employed in administrative offices of the Islamic rulers, entirely fluent in Sanskrit, Persian, and English, Ray acquired an English education and eventually concluded that Europeans were "generally more intelligent, more steady and more moderate in their conduct." "I gave up my prejudice against them, and became inclined in their favour, feeling persuaded that their rule, though a foreign yoke, would lead more speedily and surely to the amelioration of the native inhabitants."[35] By the end of the nineteenth century, English-educated professional classes were deeply attracted by an alternate style of social life outlined by Western ideas and vaguely encouraged by the colonial regime.[36] This segment of the new, English-educated elite was already intensely active in reforming Hindu society. They demanded the legal abolition of sati, formed societies like the Brahmo Samaj, fiercely advocating a rationalistic and anti-ritualistic Hinduism, and supported re-marriage of Hindu widows. The curricula followed in the first colleges, like the Hindu College in Calcutta[37] and later the Calcutta University,[38] were of course imitative of the contemporary regimes of knowledge in the West.[39] Students in these establishments absorbed a highly celebratory narrative of Western modernity which systematically neglected the internal contradictions and complexities of the rise of modern society in the West. To attend these institutions itself was at times an act of courage, an assertion of an individual's or a family's freedom in face of the disapproval and ostracism of surrounding Hindu society. By the end of the eighteenth century, the battle of education and cultural instruction had been decisively lost by the Hindu traditionalist forces. Inside half a century, the Bengali enthusiasm for a critical ingestion of modernity completely restructured the curricular structure, personnel, social purposes, and sociological arrangements associated with education.

Once modern education became widespread, creating a substantial intelligentsia that could read Western texts in the original, the Bengalis developed an insatiable curiosity about literature and social theory. In the field of moral and social reflection, European social theory entirely replaced traditional Hindu scriptures. Not surprisingly, of the dominant social theories current in contemporary Britain, individualist liberalism had the deepest influence in colonial Bengal. Young people eagerly learned the arguments and often the texts of modern British political theory, particularly Mill and Spencer.[40] Acquaintance with other cultures of European theory, especially the very different theoretical inflections of German thought, was naturally more limited.[41]

However, the assessment of Western civilization with its offer of a new liberal moral order was subjected to critical reflection. Reformist authors emphasized that rules of Hindu social conduct should be evaluated by rational arguments, not accepted simply because of their scriptural authority. This emphasis made it easy for more skeptical intellectuals to argue that identical evaluative principles should be applied to Western practices as well. Otherwise, this kind of thinking constituted an invidious suspension of rational criticism; and Western practices could be adopted by Indians not because they were rationally defensible, but on the basis of authority—because these were the ways of the colonizer. This would merely substitute for the social power of tradition the coercive power of colonial rule. Western forms of sociality and conduct needed to be subjected to rational critical analysis as much as Hindu ones. As a consequence, three types of dissenting ideas emerged in the second half of the nineteenth century.[42] First, because of an emerging concern that Western thought is endemically atomistic, some writers took interest in European traditions or thinkers critical of individualism—like Rousseau[43] and later Hegel.[44] Second, discomfort about inequality attracted some writers toward early ideas of socialism. Third, from the middle of the century, some more original thinkers began to ask if the task of social thinking is best served by simply an imitative discussion about the merits of various Western modes of thought; or if it was, in fact, the task of social thinkers to develop less materialistic and individualist arguments which suited Indian (Hindu) society more closely.[45]

The pre-eminent Bengali writer of that generation, Bankimchandra Chattopadhyay, a novelist, humorist, and essayist, evinced all these tendencies in his writings. An early convert to positivist certainties, he came to question Mill's combination of utilitarianism and positivism and wrote an enormously influential essay on "Equality," hailing Rousseau as the third great apostle of equality (samyavatara) after the Buddha and Christ.[46] However, in his humorous essays, he used a cat which has been converted to socialism to question humanity's exclusive possession of milk and other goods which ought to be, in an ideal world, more equitably distributed between various species on earth.[47] The most systematic exploration of the third question was done by Bhudev Mukhopadhyay, who compared *pascatya bhav* (Westernness) with Indian civilization, offering a cogent summary of its essential features: "What are generally referred to as Western attitudes/dispositions are among the following: (1) selfishness (2) belief in progress (3) equality (4) this-worldliness (5) independence/autonomy (6) scientificity (7) the state's representativeness of society."[48]

Bhudev believed that the major conflict in India was between two different civilizations:

> The nature of Hindu society is its pacific quality, of the British a constant effort in search of prosperity. Hindu society is primarily agricultural, the English predominantly industrial and commercial. Hindu society recognises collective property and ownership; the English recognise primogeniture and has intense preference for private property. In Hindu society child marriage is customary, in the English marriage at a later age is normal. Hindus are in favour of internal governance of society; the English strive to make the jurisdiction of the state paramount in preserving rights. In India a conflict between these two different societies has arisen. The English are energetic, efficient, arrogant and greedy. Hindus are diligent, peaceable, submissive and easily contented. On considering these things carefully it becomes apparent that Hindus should learn efficiency from the English, nothing more; indeed, it is better that they learn nothing else.

Most writers held a less self-confident view about the strength of their civilization and were less extreme in their rejection of Western practices. Most significantly, even thinkers like Bhudev had to present their arguments in a new rationalistic form which immediately undermined the idea that scriptural citation was proof or justification. Clearly, this form of reasoning could eventually subvert not merely an intellectual style, but also major parts of the Brahminical social system resting on that intellectual basis. In all these spheres, the idea of freedom and autonomous decision was central. Appeal to rational arguments and intellectual freedom undermined scriptural authority and asserted the cognitive autonomy of the rational individual. Subsequently, the arguments about freedom spread from this highly abstract cognitive form to more substantive social areas and were expressed in claims to the freedom of individuals from parental or communal authority and of women from traditional social repression. In literature, there was sometimes a general romantic celebration of artistic individuality.

≺ V ≻

Realms of Freedom: Individuals and Family Life

Ram Mohan Roy's life illustrates in some respects the paradigmatic forms of the struggle for personal liberty. He came from an ambidextrous Brahminical background; his father's family taught him Persian to prepare for administrative service for Muslim rulers, and his mother's family of priests introduced him to scholastic Sanskrit. But Roy wrote an early tract in Persian rejecting Brahmin practices of idolatry and accusing Brahmins of causing the degeneracy of modern Bengali society by imposing irrational customs. Even in this early tract, a crucial factor is the appeal not only to the ancient Hindu scriptures, but also to reason for justification of doctrinal arguments. Roy's later education in English, association with Europeans, and evident study of Western ideas naturally strengthened his rationalistic beliefs and led him to defy orthodoxy and establish a debating society for members of all religions who believed in monotheism. Later this turned into a separate strand of reformed Hinduism around the Brahmo Samaj. Roy spent the last three years of his life in England, coming into contact with British intellectuals and visiting France. With utter libertarian consistency he remonstrated with Talleyrand, French ambassador in London, about the legal requirement for a passport to enter the land of the free.

Although Ram Mohan Roy's celebrated heterodoxies started in the purely intellectual sphere of doctrinal disputation about whether the ancient Hindu scriptures sanctioned idolatry, the attack on Brahminical authority soon spread to social issues. Roy played a major role in persuading the colonial government to legally ban the performance of sati, and debate around that question forced him to assert with greater vehemence and clarity two principles of liberty. First, the liberty of conscience and of religious practice and observance implied the prior intellectual freedom of rational disputation and unforced judgment. Second, the argument about sati, as it went along, brought out more undisguised declarations of the dignity of women as human beings and objects of civilized treatment.

Once ideas of freedom were introduced in their intellectual forms, these considerations tended to snowball and extend into interconnected spheres. Initially, driven by a humanistic argument about stopping cruelty to women, intellectuals justified their position by asserting the moral rule of humane treatment of persons, irrespective of gender—which already involved a liberal conception of abstract individuality. Next the debate extended to remarriage of widows, where again the primary argument was to stop wasting human lives. Additionally, in deciding to marry widows, Hindu males were inevitably involved in questions of moral autonomy. They had to assert the moral right of individual young men to decide whom they wished to marry rather than allow their families to arrange their marriages. Such arguments slowly became more generalized and went on to assert the superiority of marriage based on personal attraction and love rather than customary considerations of caste compatibility and mercenary gain.[49] Literature played an immensely significant role in disseminating the new culture of family life and celebrating its superior values. Romantic love thus came to acquire astonishingly radical associations in Bengali culture, and the tradition of Bengali novels and short stories never ceased to celebrate the ideals of love and, less directly, a companionate marriage. While in actual life Bengali middle-class individuals might generally acquiesce in arranged matrimony, they read romantic novels insatiably and tried to adjust the realities of an arranged union retrospectively to the ideals of romantic love.

This did not mean that the trajectory of the Bengali family followed closely on the social history of Europe. Social changes were not accompanied by massive industrialization which could destroy traditional large families. Bengali society remained primarily rural, although the expansion of the British Empire in India created a large market for Bengali professionals who generally supported moderately modern social forms. The forms that this social change took were sometimes surprisingly mixed. Modern men often had to marry child wives, but many who had the means got them privately educated so that they could give their husbands company in all spheres of life, and fit in with the social circle of their colleagues and friends. Some of these women became writers and poets of standing. The altered social context in which women could come out of the *antahpur* (inner part of the house) into the society of strange men required not merely acquiring education, but also more mundane changes like invention of a proper social dress, which continued with the much later stage of women joining professional work.[50] The famous Tagore family experimented with various combinations until it devised a combination of a Western-style blouse to be worn under a traditional sari—which became the emblematic dress for the modern Indian woman. In an understandable transposition, at times wearing this dress itself became a declaration of freedom.[51]

Yet this acceptance of the principle of individuality of men and women, and the legitimacy of a domain where its traits could be allowed to flower, did not immediately spell the end of the joint family. Even individuals committed to reform remained part of large joint-family households and accepted the responsibilities, often splitting their lives between traditional village and modernist Calcutta, juggling as best they could their very different social habits. Instead of an eruption of nuclear families, there was a new kind of moral legitimacy to the conjugal relationship within the larger joint family. Although women's subordination was not ended, its forms were changed and degradation of women reduced.

Traditionally, the wife was mainly the "producer of sons,"[52] and the relation with the wife was regarded as far inferior to other familial relationships with father, mother, or brothers. The relation of the wife to the husband was of such complete subordination that it precluded companionship, often additionally for reasons of substantial difference in age. Under new conditions, successful professionals were often obliged to live outside their ancestral household, in considerable official opulence with only the company of their wives. Differentiation of professions encouraged this trend, as family labor in a common occupation was slowly antiquated in the middle class, with individual males occupying well-paid non-ancestral jobs. Eventually, the moral hierarchy of relationships was completely reordered and the middle-class professional learned to look upon his wife as his closest relation; and because she partook of his professional life and its very different demands of sociability, it was essential for her to acquire equal education and cultivation.

This new conception of intimacy came to be celebrated in modern literary forms. Romance based on elective affinity came to be the staple of Bengali novels, stories, songs, and eventually in a different age, films. Most often the narrative structure would follow either a trajectory of the European *bildungsroman* where the hero would slowly, through character-forming adventures, find himself; or it would be a story of adventures constituting tests of romantic loyalty through which the protagonists would eventually come together. It became a convention to portray the families and their authority figures as the obstacles in their path: but love would always win. Winning had two predominant forms: either directly in the course of the narrative (in Bengali classification, *milananta*, ending in union), or by a narrative resolution where they might be forcibly separated by family, fortune, or death, which was another way of showing the triumph of their love over everything (in Bengali, again, *viyoganta*, ending in loss). Such romantic unions or separations were vastly different in theoretical terms from traditional narratives of transgressive love like the famous narrative of Radha and Krsna. Bengali lovers, with the assistance of the Bengali romantic novel, came to engage in an activity that was recognized, however grudgingly, as socially legitimate. In both types of narratives, the formation of the hero, his slowly finding himself, discovering who he was, or finding himself through love, the underlying theme was an endorsement of ethical individuality. The distinctive contribution of the novel to the grand narrative of the birth of human freedom is not to be underestimated.

Another novelistic theme that confirmed this cultural trend was the astonishing emphasis on friendship. Decline of the ties with the family led to the inevitable exploration of alternative forms of sociability. Traditionally, an individual's social energies were entirely absorbed inside the circle of intense and intricate family relationships. The altered circumstances of urban life in colonial Bengal, when successful professional men had to live away from the family home, forced them to seek relations of sociability with others, often without consideration for caste or kinship affiliation. In deliberative processes of everyday life, when individuals or couples had to decide about significant questions, since family advice was not available, they tended to depend on friends, making these relationships more intense and valuable.

A new kind of sociality developed, understandably much portrayed and valued in novels; intellectual elaboration of its principles emphasized the elective principle. Family relationships were a matter of accident: one could not choose one's brothers; and there was no guarantee that when they became adults siblings would have common inclinations. In a startling inversion of literary values, family relationships with parents in romantic plots, or with brothers or sisters in social novels, were often described as oppressive, obstacles in the untrammelled search for one's self. Friends were found through common entanglements of occupation, common intellectual pursuits, or simply a sympathy of temperament. The sociability of friendship was therefore elective, based on rational choice, a considered judgment about one's own temperament and of someone else's, and compatible with the freedom of development of personality of the new individual.

Unsurprisingly, the modern Bengali novel, particularly in its early phase, represented by the works of Rabindranath Tagore and Saratchandra Chattopadhyay, is full of friendship relations and a counter-position of the two principles of sociability—of the family and friends. What is significant for a story of the concept of freedom is that initially the caste-based Hindu family was seen as a primary obstacle to a modern form of self-realization. Gradually, the change in the climate of ideas and underlying structural changes in the economy transform the family. At least for the educated upper middle classes, the new family provided a framework conducive to development of individuality of the person. From a social institution in which he was smothered by responsibilities toward others, it became, in its altered form, the individual person's fortress, where he could find emotional refuge. Although these developments began in colonial Bengal, as colonial modernity spread to other parts of India, similar cultural patterns emerged. By the middle of the twentieth century, the intimate companionate marriage, the family, and the private individual were increasingly common in the social life of the Indian middle classes—although subject to regional variations.

≺ VI ≻

Re-conceptualization of Society

Schematically, it is possible to argue that the ideas of freedom first entered Indian society through the rationalist disputations about the grounding of religious beliefs. As religion, particularly Hinduism, is composed of theological beliefs and interconnected social practices, the rejection of the purely intellectual aspects of religion cannot be without serious social consequences. Because social practices like caste are grounded in the metaphysics of Brahminical Hinduism, the decline of its intellectual authority leads necessarily to challenges to its social conduct. It is hardly surprising therefore that the rationalistic ideas of intellectual and cognitive freedom led not merely to a re-structuring of the forms of intimacy in elite circles, but also to larger upheavals of the caste order itself. When ideas of freedom moved into the field of social practices, the bearers of freedom were not primarily individuals, but communities, especially caste groups. But the re-structuring of families and the larger demands for freedom from caste practices are impelled by the same intellectual and social forces.

Moving outside the boundaries of the affinal sociability of the family immediately places the individual in a different kind of social field. Accumulated effects of these exploratory practices slowly led to a discernible change in the conceptualization of the idea of society (*samaj*). One commentator remarked that from the mid-nineteenth century, the Bengali term "*samaj*" came to be used exclusively as the equivalent of the English word "society," and not in its traditional, indeterminate meaning.[53] Several scholars have argued persuasively that the modern conception of society emerged in the West around the time of the French enlightenment and replaced earlier usages.[54] A similar case can be made for colonial Bengal and later for all of India. The term for society, *samaja* in original Sanskrit, meant a group of things/beings who are not clustered accidentally, but exist together habitually. In social discourse it referred to individuals who lived inside the normal entanglements of social/domestic life.[55]

In ordinary usage of premodern vernaculars, particularly in Bengali, the term *samaj* was commonly used, but not to mean what it connotes in modern social discourse—an abstract field, or combination of all possible groups and individuals—probably because there was no practical need to think of an abstract entity of that kind. The connotation of the traditional term was quite precise, but in important ways different from the modern one. A reference to one's *samaj* meant one's community in an indeterminate, context-dependent sense—to indicate the relevant form of community in a particular context of use. Thus it was wrong to marry outside one's caste, because the "community" would not accept it, referring here to kinship groups. But it could similarly refer to the village, the religious sect, or other specific forms of sociability which were relevant in the case of each social practice. Usually the reference would be to a local, normally face-to-face community in which, by such an act of infraction, individuals could lose face. To speak of the brahman-*samaj*, or the vaishnava *samaj* of a town or a locality would have made perfect sense, but to speak of something like the Bengali *samaj*, or still better, the *samaj* in Bengal—such an inescapable staple of modern discourse, would, to traditional users of language, have appeared linguistically awkward and referentially opaque. References to society indicated primary groups composed of dense, local, everyday concrete relationships. The idea of something like a second-order, or abstract field of relations in which such primary groups all existed, and which could be known by rational analysis, was difficult to articulate in the grammar of traditional concepts. This was, I would like to suggest, because the conception of a reflexive relation to the social self, which this abstract conception of society presupposes, was difficult to conceive.[56]

The first significant change is the rapid emergence of the abstract idea of a society in the modern sense—a society made up of communities (a *samaj* or *samaj*-es in Bengali, since the same word has to work as two concepts)—the idea of a field, a secondary order of reality, a plane on which all communities of the first type existed. But there was also a second, highly significant semantic alteration implicit in the new usage.[57] The central Brahminical strand of Hindu religion had always emphasized orthopraxy, but significant religious sects, like the Vaishnavas, admitted considerable degrees of voluntarism in the choice of religious beliefs. Vaishnavism, for example, could be adopted by an individual through a process similar to conversion, and it therefore implicitly accepted choice in matters of religious worship. Yet it would be misleading to see this as equivalent to modern voluntarism and associationism.

After the introduction of Western education, progressive groups began to set up associations for religious reform like Ram Mohan Roy's Brahmo Samaj. Brahmo Samaj uses the same term, *samaj*, in its name, but its denotation is quite different from the earlier *given* communities; this was, by contrast, a *chosen* community of individuals brought together by a religion of their *choice*, and on a fellowship of spirit based on rational reflection on religious matters. Freedom of the new type expresses itself, in colonial Bengali society, as the freedom to practice religion as individuals wanted. Implicitly included are freedom of thought on religious matters, critical application of rational principles to the doctrines and practices of one's community, and the right to reject them and to follow radically new forms of worship.

Religious freedom included within itself the freedom of individuals and groups of similarly inclined individuals to form associations. Naturally, this led to disputes on religious questions among Hindus and between Hindus, Brahmos, and Christian missionaries.

These disputes could not be prosecuted without freedom of expression and, once a public sphere of discussions emerged, freedom of the press. Indeed, when colonial authorities sought to close a journal and deport its English editor on grounds of fomenting trouble, Roy petitioned the viceroy with an interesting analysis of colonial control. American colonies rebelled against English dominion because they were denied representation and expression of their grievances; Canada remained within the empire because its demands were heard. Entirely unrestricted freedom of the press was necessary if India was to remain within the empire, like Canada, and not take a resentful American way.[58]

Associations based on a common purpose began for religious pursuits, but soon spread to other, mundane fields of enterprise. Soon upper middle-class and elite society in colonial India saw an astonishing growth of associations of all kinds—for pursuit of knowledge and science, religious worship, worthy social causes like upliftment of women—but most significant were associations of various castes to present their demands to the colonial government. Implicitly, these caste associations realized a most important difference in the colonial context. Political authorities in Hindu society were always culturally precommitted to a preservation of the caste order—continuity of closed occupations and an inflexible hierarchy among them. With the British government, for the first time, a new kind of political authority existed which was either indifferent or skeptical about the caste system. Caste associations could therefore present their demands and petitions for favorable treatment to this government.

The new definition of *samaj* (as used in Brahmo Samaj) referred to something important in the relation of a group of people to themselves: the individuals' inclusion in this group was out of rationally grounded choice, not mere ascription. The new domain of a restricted colonial civil society was created by an extraordinary proliferation of associations.[59] Two types of associations became increasingly common in urban India: voluntary associations for the establishment of educational projects, of literary committees, of projects for the advancement of women, and of sports clubs in a process likely to delight liberal theorists; and curiously, other, equally effective and influential ones, based on caste or religion, whose relation to liberal principles was more ambiguous.

Caste associations are particularly significant as they demonstrate a strange combination of apparently contradictory principles: the universality of modern liberal associations and the particularity characteristic of traditional groups. A *kayastha sabha* for instance was in principle open to all *kayasthas*, but closed to others: a strange form of segmentary universality. This acceleration of the associational principle led to greater articulation of a concept of "interest" of the individuals formed into these groups; and in some cases, the more these particular groups organized themselves, the more their interests clashed with others. The creation of this restricted domain of "colonial civil society" was seen by commentators as both liberating and dangerous. The logic of segmentation of caste society ensured that goods were available segmentarily: Brahmins could not hope to amass great wealth; merchants could not acquire political power. In a modern social context such "goods"—wealth, political influence—were in principle universally accessible, and therefore could be coveted by all; and the chances of getting these goods increased in proportion to the extent these groups were numerically large, organized, and internally coherent. Principles of freedom and self-determination for individuals and groups were evidently undermining Hindu caste society, and it was hardly surprising that Hindu conservative groups tried to provide reasoned criticisms against these trends. Paradoxically, however, the more sophisticated defense of Hindu orthodoxy had to appeal increasingly to the same principles of reason and human dignity. Although religious groups might have fierce differences on doctrines and practices, increasingly a common alphabet of rational reasoning was accepted as general intellectual currency.

Indian social thought shows, not surprisingly, great variety across its different cultural regions. Different cultural regions of India—Bengal, Oudh and northern Gangetic plains, the Punjab, Gujarat, and Maharashtra; entire South India—formed distinct regional cultures, with highly specific language-based cultures of thought and historically established forms of political rule. British rule reached these areas at different points in its colonial expansion, and made adjustments with regional circumstances. What was selected out of British influences depended partly on these regional histories. Thus the intellectual or social history of Bengali modernity is not repeated in other regions; each develops its own encounter with what colonial modernity offered.

One significant difference lies in the centrality of the debates about caste and Brahminical privilege. In Bengal, the initial attack on traditional society was led by groups who came from the upper-caste elite. In other parts of India, in the west, south, and north the question of social freedom became increasingly focused on the dominance of Brahmins and upper castes. In Maharashtra, initial opportunities offered by colonial administration and English education were secured by Brahmins and upper castes. Thus, although liberal ideas about the economy, education, and politics created an active public sphere in which questions of public interest and public policy were intensely discussed, opportunities of entry into this charmed sphere were restricted to upper-caste elites. It was only a section of the traditional elite, more alert to opportunities, which came to form the new elite. Modern ideas of freedom circulated among these groups with intellectual consequences similar to the Bengali example. Social reform was introduced. Western education was embraced on a wide scale. Rationalist thinking undermined traditional Hindu orthodoxy.

However, cultural transformation in western India showed a distinctive feature, absent from the Bengali precedents. Soon after the emergence of the new education and social effects of modernity, intellectuals from lower-caste groups pointed out the restrictive logic of this modernity and used ideas of social freedom to mount a fierce attack on caste hierarchy. Jyotirao Phule, the most significant figure of the lower-caste argument for social liberation, published a powerful tract called *Ghulamgiri*, literally meaning slavery, a searing indictment of the Hindu social order.[60] He compared it to European and particularly American practices of slavery, and dedicated the book to Abraham Lincoln.[61] Phule's actual writing relied on a kind of speculative, radical reinterpretation of classical Hindu scriptures, taking them primarily through an inversionist reading. Partly appropriating colonial orientalist arguments, he regarded the Brahmins as descendants of the invading Aryans who defeated an indigenous people and imposed the degrading caste system on them. In Phule's reading, the Brahminical system punished social groups according to the intensity of their defiance, and the lowest groups were therefore those that resisted Aryan-Brahmanical domination the longest and most fiercely. The main divide in Hindu society was the line separating the Brahmins from all the other castes below them, who formed a single radical bloc. Phule's publicistic writings and practical efforts were directed at convincing this social bloc to come together and see itself, against Brahminical ideology, as a single community of social interest, and to persuade the colonial government to shift benefits to them, against the Brahminical conspiracy.

Several interesting points come out of this early movement for lower-caste assertion against high Hindu orthodoxy. It put the question of "social reform," that is, transformation of inequalities internal to Hindu society, at the center of the arguments on freedom, implying that the ideals of freedom were unreal if they were confined only to the inchoate, emerging "public sphere" of administrative and political questions. The meaning of freedom was located in the tiny, unobserved, incessant transactions of everyday life, governed by caste exclusions and indignities. Freedom therefore meant the emancipation of lower-caste groups from upper-caste domination; but this emancipation was supplemented by an additional demand for preferment and reservation in new modes of advancement opened by colonial government. However, this demand had interesting implications. The mode of argument placed the caste groups at the center of the emancipatory process, and made them, rather than the individual, the main protagonist of social change. It also showed a possible conflict between the strand of social reform, seeking an end to social domination of upper castes, and political emancipation, which was to be concerned primarily with the conflict between Indians and the British government. Several movements for radical social reform in different parts of India saw the colonial government as a potential ally in their fight against upper-caste domination and supported colonial authorities, accusing political nationalists of creating distraction by calling for national independence from British rule.

Eventually, these two meanings of freedom—social freedom from caste domination and political freedom from colonial rule—remained in a state of potential conflict in Indian thinking of the twentieth century, producing three alternative strands of thinking about how this tension could be resolved. First, writers most intent on social inequality at times saw pan-Indian nationalism as an essentially upper-caste and class movement, unlikely to deliver radical social reform. For them, the British were more likely to behave as impartial authorities, probably even inclining in favor of the lower castes. These groups at times supported British authorities against early nationalism. A second strand was a direct response by upper-class groups in Indian nationalism to this line of attack. Arguing that fight against colonialism required complete unity among all sections of Indians, these nationalists sometimes used nationalism as a means to deflect attention from issues of social inequality, suggesting that raising issues of lower-caste indignity or untouchability was a betrayal of the national struggle against imperial rulers. Generally, however, the broad mainstream of Indian nationalists adopted a third position—that there must be some subsumption of the demands for social equality within the overarching political demands of Indian nationalism—although there were large variations inside the Congress on this point. However, the most well-known nationalist writers in the twentieth century—Rabindranath Tagore, Gandhi, and Nehru—all recognized in their own ways the inextricable link between the questions of social and of national freedom.

≺ VII ≻

Freedom of the Nation

One of the most interesting questions in the history of British colonialism in India is how the structure of thought and practice of the modern Indian elite, which initially inclined rationalistic ideas about freedom toward loyalty to the European empire, turned into a very different structure directed against colonial dominion. Usual histories of colonialism and nationalism slide over this problem by offering a plausible teleological account of Indian nationalism. It is true that, chronologically, movements of rationalist thinking demanded social reform, then encouraged energetic efforts at commercial and economic improvement, and finally evolved into political nationalism. Yet the actual direction of rationalistic modern thinking and the precise structure of alignment of arguments are radically different between different historical epochs. To understand this historical movement it is essential to go against the logic of the history that nationalism gives to itself. That account is not merely uncritically celebratory, but also technically teleological. It assumes the function of each stage of patriotism in modern Indian history is to "produce" the next stage, thus overstressing the genetic logic of evolution at the expense of the structural differences between discrete stages.[62] This history can be presented more realistically if we attend to the ruptures between these structures of thinking at the expense of their genetic connection. Only that can explain how the style of thinking encapsulated by Ram Mohan Roy's demonstrative loyalty, which pleaded with the British for European settlement on a large scale and hoped that British rule should continue for three centuries, could turn in the course of a century into Gandhi's characterization of British rule in India as Satanic.

The coming of colonial modernity forced various communities to reflect on their suddenly altered historical situation since all were affected deeply by astonishingly rapid social transformation. In some cases, like Bengalis, especially the middle class, the unmixed beneficiaries of colonial settlement and expansion, it produces an instant sense of self-regard, of cultural preciousness. As the Bengalis absorbed Western education and were rewarded by instant and unprecedented economic prosperity, they naturally thought of themselves as an elite. This gave rise to an intense but odd sense of patriotism. This sense of patriotic pride cannot be unproblematically regarded as an early stage of Indian nationalism, for two clear reasons. First it is regional: the more the Bengalis feel special and superior to others, the more they find it difficult to make common cause with more "backward" peoples of the Indian empire; second, it is inextricably linked to a deep sense of gratitude to the Empire and the civilizing benefits it had brought to them. So it is not nationalist either in spatial spread, or in its critical attitude toward colonialism. In early Bengali literary productions effusive expressions of loyalty to Britain were common; and some of the early lyricism about the specialness of Bengalis also contained deep attachment to Mother Britannia. It took some time for this beneficent, protecting, all-powerful mother to change her personality radically, to turn from Britannia into the more recognizable shape of Bharatmata (Mother India). Loyal Bengali middle classes thus saw the early stage of British rule as a period of expansion of their freedom in social terms, although within a benevolent framework of British dominance. But in a certain sense, their freedoms and their secure enjoyment depended on continuation of British rule. Not surprisingly, the new Bengali middle class extended their complete loyalty to the East India Company's side in the great conflict of 1857, when British rule was seriously challenged for the first time.

Patriotism naturally took a form and flavor derived from the distinctive history of regions and communities. Muslims constituted one of the most politically powerful and culturally eminent communities in precolonial India. Although internally heterogeneous in terms of regions, languages, and status, they had an identifiable elite based in northern India. Apart from the Mughal emperor, ruling families in many of the north Indian kingdoms were Muslim, and they constituted much of the ruling elite and landed nobility. As a result of Islamic domination of political authority for several centuries, the high culture of northern India had a predominantly Islamic character.

Initially, the Muslim community in north India did not respond enthusiastically to establishment of British rule. Unlike as in Bengal, British authority did not come stealthily, through a series of almost imperceptible steps, but rather as conquering power; and with the establishment of British control, the Muslim ruling elite were the immediate losers in terms of political eminence. After the annexation of the important northern Nawabi of Oudh a rebellion broke out in northern India in 1857, when large sections of the army mutinied and installed the old Mughal emperor on the throne of Delhi for a brief interlude. The Muslim nobility and minor royalty were sympathetic toward the rebels and their advocacy of the emperor of Delhi.[63] After the defeat of 1857, the traditional Muslim elite retreated in sullen resentment against British power; the traditional religious leaders were alienated by educational reform and advances of rationalistic thought, and the political leadership alienated by their sense of defeat. Their alienation from British rule was intensified by the perception that Hindu elite groups were making rapid progress by adopting Western education and taking up professional jobs created by colonial rule.

The sense of community pride and patriotism took a different character among the north Indian Muslims. By the middle of the century a small elite emerged which received Western education and abandoned the traditional attitude of sullen rejection of British ways. Sir Sayyid Ahmad Khan (1817–98), the first modern leader of the north Indian Islamic community, argued, against the religious and political traditionalism of the Islamic elite, that the Indian Muslims must accept the offer of modernity by adopting Western education and affiliating themselves to British power. However, this was not just an argument in favor of political loyalty to the empire; the British should be emulated for cultural reasons as well. "The natives of India, when contrasted with the English in education, manners and uprightness, are like them as a dirty animal is to an able and handsome man."[64] Consequently, Sayyid Ahmad Khan "felt that some of the characteristics of English society—its discipline, order, efficiency and high levels of education, along with science and technology—must be adopted by the Muslim community."[65]

Limited acceptance of rationalist arguments involved Sayyid Ahmad Khan in bitter controversies with the traditional Ulema, who feared the long-term consequences of such religious reform. He asserted that "the Quran contained ultimate truths, and existed prior to the knowledge of science"; but science and laws of nature which it discovered were also true, and did not conflict with the truths of religious beliefs. But Muslim orthodox opinion could be incensed by his suggestion that "it was all right to wear shoes for prayer in the mosque, to participate in Hindu and Christian celebrations, and to eat at a European style table."[66] Thus, the reforms advocated by Khan were in some respects parallel to Ram Mohan Roy's defiance of Brahminical orthodoxy. However, Khan and his associates among the Muslim notables of north India established the Muhammadan Anglo-Oriental College at Aligarh, which was to turn into one of the major centers of Islamic opinion in modern India. Parallel to his ideas about cultural and educational reform of the Islamic community, Sayyid Ahmad Khan's writing showed increasing concern about the political fate of Muslims as a social group, and the anxiety that under British rule, this group, which was once the ruling elite of north India, would fall behind the Hindus and come under their domination. He therefore saw the future of Indian Muslims in unfailing loyalty to the British and laid down a trajectory of Islamic politics that led to religious nationalism by opposing the establishment of the Indian National Congress for its openly political objectives; he also set up the United Indian Patriotic Association in direct opposition to the Congress, giving the term "patriotic" a most ironic twist.

Admiration for modern rationalistic ways of Europe took a third, distinct form in western India. Here a Maratha regional empire had grown after the decline of the Mughals from the mid-seventeenth century. This period of highly successful rule of the Peshwas was a fairly immediate political memory for the military and Brahminical groups of western India. But several social groups responded positively to the opportunities opened by British victory. Using their traditional literacy skills, Brahmins and other upper castes, earlier engaged in administration, acquired Western education and professional posts in the modern sector. Western India traditionally had an energetic commercial culture, centered on famous trading ports like Surat, and Gujarati merchants were renowned for their commercial skills. Gujarati and Parsi merchants welcomed the entry of British control and benefited by the opening of new commercial opportunities, particularly in the new port city of Bombay. The first effects of Western education and acquaintance with European ways were similar to those in Bengal and northern India. They led to the rise of a new professional elite, intent on the expansion of Western style education.[67] One of the peculiarities of the western Indian reception of rationalist ideas was an intense criticism of caste privileges of the Brahmins.

However, the logic of associationism for social welfare mixed with the commercial spirit of western Indian society to lend to its intellectual discourse a distinctive character which played a crucial role in the formation of Indian nationalism. Of the rationalistic doctrines coming from the West, some intellectuals placed a peculiar emphasis on the teachings of the new science of political economy.[68] In the discourses of modernity in western India, improvement was not only social and intellectual, it meant not merely emancipation from traditional customs; "improvement" in the economic sense came to occupy a primary place. Social reformers engaged in discussing means for the "improvement" of Indian social life came to place far greater emphasis on the question of material prosperity and reduction of poverty of the common people—a strand of thought hardly significant in the Bengali or north India reflection on colonial modernity.[69] Major intellectual figures of the western Indian modernity gave to the question of economic prosperity a far more central place in their general reflections.[70]

Ironically, some of these dissenting ideas evolved through piecemeal transactions with elements of British colonial ideology and administrative thinking. At the peak of British power in India it became a principal article of administrative claim and academic writing that British rule had brought unprecedented prosperity to India and brought it out of a barbaric civilization. The first generation of reformers did not argue against these claims particularly strenuously, but careful study of political economy put the claims into some doubt. Certainly, British rule and associated economic changes had brought unprecedented prosperity to a small modern stratum of Indian society, but study of political economy forced them to calculate the "wealth of the nation" in less selfish ways. It appeared, on more critical economic reflection, that under British rule India was going through a phase of de-industrialization, as competition from English textile mills ruined domestic artisanal craft. Ironically, debates about the claims of colonialism's "civilizing mission" led, in surprising ways, to the first steps toward a nationalistic argument, by authors who entirely sincerely declared their undying loyalty to the Empire.

Familiarity with European capitalist societies was accentuated by study of modern science and political economy, selected, as we have seen, by Indian writers as the two subjects from the West really worth emulating. In the general literature about colonialism there was an implicit belief that European colonialism was justified precisely because governments should be judged consequentially—not in terms of who ruled, but what resulted from their rule. The fact that Indians were ruled by a foreign power was outweighed by the modernizing consequences of their administration. However, there was an interesting twist in this argument. Justifying colonial power by its modernizing consequence immediately brought into play comparisons with the social and political conditions in England, because the purpose of colonial rule was presumably to create similar conditions in India in economic and political terms. Comparisons with England brought out stark contrasts between the two countries: England's prosperity with India's poverty, England's scientific advance with India's backwardness, and the most awkward contrast of all, England's freedom and India's colonization. Some counterarguments were advanced on behalf of colonial ideology. Lack of prosperity was at times attributed to the different geographic and climatic conditions, a vestigial influence of Montesquieu and Buckle, and the incurable sloth of natives. Absence of free institutions was similarly explained/justified, often by libertarian writers like Mill, by lack of education and a backward stage of civilization. "Despotism is a legitimate mode of government in dealing with barbarians, provided the end be their improvement and the means justified by actually effecting that end." Mill stated in *On Liberty*, "Liberty, as a principle, has no application to any state of things anterior to the time when mankind have become capable of being improved by free and equal discussion. Until then, there is nothing for them but implicit obedience to an Akbar or a Charlemagne, if they are so fortunate as to find one."[71] Indians, in this view, were fortunate in finding the British to rule over them during their period of slow growth into historical maturity. Additionally, this lack of self-government was the condition for steady improvement of the economic condition of the country.

Study of political economy by entirely loyalist politicians cast doubt on this view. Early economic studies by British radical writers and Indians claimed, on the contrary, that India had declined economically as a result of British rule; and these students of political economy detected a damning trend toward ruralization of Indian society.[72] Classical authors like Adam Smith extolled the virtues of the commercial impulses of the city in the transformation of modern economies. Ruralization, if true, thus showed the falsity of the claims of colonial ideology: instead of progressing economically, India was languishing or slipping back. Readers of John Stuart Mill were not slow to point out that in such matters it is only those affected who can represent their interests; no one else can, not even a paternalistic colonial government. Arguments famously marshalled by Mill in advocating the enfranchisement of the working classes in Britain could, with slight adaptation, be used with great force to demand self-government for economic improvement.[73]

Ironically, the first writers of this school could be called "economic nationalists" only retrospectively; they began, in reality, as economic loyalists. This was the first genuine school of Indian liberals, because they extended the arguments about intellectual rationalism in the direction of a celebration of commerce and material prosperity—the classic arguments of liberal bourgeoisie. One of the clearest and most concise statements of this mode of thought came from M. G. Ranade, a principal figure in Western Indian social thought. In a lecture in 1892, later published as a highly influential essay, Ranade quoted Mill's *Political Economy* to argue that "purely economic questions" do not always have "purely economic" solutions.[74] While claiming at the start of one of his essays that "here we eschew politics altogether, for there is really no conflict of interests between rulers and the ruled, who all alike desire to promote the industrial and economic progress of this country,"[75] Ranade's argument slowly but surely moves toward a complaint about industrial decline: "India, fifty years ago, clothed herself with her own manufactures, and now she is clothed by her distant masters."[76] From this he concluded: "Political ascendancy is not the only particular vantage ground which we have lost. Commercial and manufacturing predominance naturally transfers political ascendancy and in this our collapse has been even far more complete."[77]

By strange pathways, the entirely loyal concerns about harmless associationism for the welfare and upliftment of society, and its corollary, a search for development of manufacture and industry, had brought social thought in western India to the brink of economic nationalism. The intellectual associationism of Bengal, its spread of education, and the exclusively intellectualist and literary emphasis of Bengali rationalist thought had led to the first uncertain stages of political demands for limited autonomy and self-government; yet, paradoxically, it was strangely uninterested in the economic questions of industrial development and capitalism. The more economic and commercial emphasis of social thought in the works of the significant writers of western India brought an essential element into the pre-history of Indian nationalism.

Dadabhai Naoroji, the first serious exponent of a theory of a drain of wealth from the colony, wholeheartedly accepted the idea that the ultimate objective of British rule was to produce conditions similar to those in Britain and thought the evidence of widespread poverty proved the un-British character of colonial government.[78] His lectures and public writings argued with passion and consistency that Indian poverty was linked to the exploitative nature of colonial rule and the systematic drain of wealth from India.[79] This line of argument became increasingly important in Indian public life, as authors like R. C. Dutt, in his large *Economic History of India*, sought to make it more systematic and academically undeniable. However, this line of thought accomplished two important tasks for the growth of Indian nationalism. First, it introduced a powerful theme of economic exploitation alongside the growing sense of the purely political indignity of colonial rule. Second, the centrality of the theme of development of manufacturing and industry ensured the staunch support of the emerging Indian capitalist class for the movement of political nationalism. It was the liberal writers of western India like M. G. Ranade, Gopal Krishna Gokhale, and Dadabhai Naoroji who were the closest in intellectual spirit and rigorous political argument to the liberal strand of Western political thought,[80] though their emphasis on loyalty kept them firmly inside purely constitutional criticism of British rule, thus allowing succeeding generations to accuse them, with some justification, of an attitude of mendicancy rather than self-respect.

≺ VIII ≻

Freedom of the Nation: Stages and Forms of Indian Nationalism

By the first decade of the twentieth century, Indian intellectual discourse had gone through an irreversible transformation: all other concerns get slowly connected to and dominated by the problem of nationalism—the demand for the end of British rule. That does not mean that earlier concerns in this intellectual story—demands for the liberty of conscience, to shape individual lives electively, for the freedom of lower castes from Brahminical oppression; or the question of unrestrained pursuit of commercial growth free of governmental control and British monopolies—disappeared. Some of these concerns continued, but were less noted—for two reasons. They were not equally novel and therefore caused less comment; and in some cases they were linked to colonial rule. For example, the question of freedom of expression or thought became increasingly political. Formerly, the threat to freedom of thought and conduct came from Hindu social orthodoxy; now increasingly from curbs imposed by colonial authorities. Freedom of expression remained significant, but it became subsumed within the more general question of national independence. However, the struggle of the person to be free from social control remained an important theme. Gandhi and Nehru, for instance, wrote highly influential autobiographies in which there was an intense concern about the discovery of the self. Clearly, however, this self-discovery was in the context of the growing political movement, and inevitably, as Nehru's book showed, the story of the individual man was submerged and subordinated to the story of the movement of the nation. Considerations on the nature of freedom in the twentieth century became inextricably connected to the question of freedom of the nation.

Nationalism proper, when it emerged at the turn of the century, gradually divided into several strands, each giving its particular spin to the idea of freedom. As a political movement, it developed in some clearly identifiable stages. Generally the current history of Indian nationalism identifies four clear stages. In a first stage from the late nineteenth century, ideas of political liberalism get transformed into a cautious, constitutional, almost mendicant movement for self-government. However, the earlier tradition of social reform, critiques of religion, and intellectual rationalism are dominant, and political writers develop compelling arguments about freedom for individuals, groups, and the whole society. A second stage is represented by more radical petit-bourgeois constructions of the freedom of the nation, which is more politically adventurous and populist, and is inclined toward support for extremism. The third stage is represented by Gandhi's popular movements; and a fourth by the startlingly modernist reinterpretation given to Indian nationalism by Nehru's rather fortunate rise to power in the 1950s. The question of freedom in all these stages is rendered complex by the ways in which the claims of the individual and the community are reconciled by various strands.

As nationalist sentiment began to gain strength, it gave rise to a feeling that the "nation," its people, is special. But in a heterogeneous society like India, this sense of special quality or favor could move in several different, at times contradictory, ways. The precise sense in which the nation was "special" depended on which exact group of people constituted it. Those who regarded the nation as Hindu naturally constructed a history which saw the ancient past of India as particularly glorious, followed by subsequent decline through loss of freedom to Islamic conquerors. The iconic repertoire this strand developed naturally depended heavily on the use of the Sanskrit language and Hindu iconic systems, in particular the imaginative merging of the idea of a beneficent, protective mother goddess and the idea of India. The famous song *Vande Mataram* displayed all the distinctive features of this iconic mode of representation—use of direct Sanskrit words, the feminization of the land, and the transfer of the religious iconicity of the mother goddess to a secular image of the nation. This iconic structure had contradictory effects; by giving the idea of the nation a visual, feminine representation, combining the Hindu ideas of her vulnerability and irresistibility, it produced an image which became a focus of intense nationalistic emotion. At the same time, Muslims would find this iconic construction alienating, and impossible to accept. Rise of Hindu nationalism was paralleled by similar growth of Islamic patriotism which saw the Muslims as the basis of a rival nation with appropriate cultural structures.

Hindu nationalism itself was in some ways a complex intellectual tradition, with considerable internal diversity. Some early Hindu reformers, like Swami Vivekananda, clearly saw the agenda of nationalism as containing within itself all the demands of rationalist religious reform. Vivekananda distinguished social practices like caste and patriarchy from the philosophical beliefs of Hinduism and associated its philosophical core with the Vedantic tradition in particular. Given this definition of what was Hinduism and what was central to its self-recognition, it was not difficult for him to continue crusading against caste inequality while defending Hindu culture against Christian and rationalistic criticisms. Vivekananda's attitude toward the Muslims varied considerably, and according to some interpreters he could not be accused of communal hostility toward Muslims.[81] Some recognizably communal writers, like V. D. Savarkar, who coined the term "Hindutva," argued that Indian nationalism could include only those for whom India was not merely a place of mundane dwelling, but also a holy land. This obviously excluded Muslims from the true people of India; but Savarkar continued to recognize that practicing caste would make Hindu nationalism impossible.[82] However, Hindu nationalists more commonly asserted that defense of India meant the defense of Hindu culture, which was inextricably associated with caste and patriarchy, and used arguments of cultural relativism to defend them.

Gandhi's views on questions of nationalism were highly complex and idiosyncratic. His classic early statement on the content of Indian freedom and the preferred mode of winning it was written in

Gujarati and used the vernacular word for freedom in its title, *Hind Swaraj*.[83] Although translated as Indian Home Rule in the English version, the term *swaraj* came to stand for national freedom in many north Indian languages.[84] Gandhi's construction of an argument for *swaraj* was ingenious and used ideas of self-rule of individuals in a highly idiosyncratic fashion. Gandhi famously argued in the *Hind Swaraj* that, contrary to common belief, "the English had not taken India, we (Indians) have given it to them."[85] Yet this was not the usual argument about dissension among Indian princes or social groups, making it possible for militarily advanced and institutionally well-organized British to rule India. Gandhi's argument went in a startlingly different direction. The British were in India because Indians wanted the modern civilization in which the British were more advanced.

But Western civilization for Gandhi was not true civilization, as its only object was to extend man's material comfort.[86] In a famous diatribe, reminiscent of Rousseau, he denounced those aspects of modern civilization most vaunted by Indian modernists—railways, modern medicine, the legal system—as contributing to India's misery. True civilization consisted in peoples' gaining control over their minds and their passions.[87] "The tendency of Indian civilization was to elevate the moral being, that of the western civilization is to propagate immorality."[88] *Swaraj* or freedom would mean Indians learning to rule themselves in terms of their civilization: if Indians did not want Western civilization, the cultural authority of the West, and consequently British rule, would become redundant. The method of driving the British out, Gandhi held, in another famous argument, was not through the use of force, for that would turn Indians into images of the British, and those groups who would muster the greatest amount of brute force to destroy British domination would subsequently establish their own domination over ordinary people. The only secure way of making India free, thus, was to use methods of passive resistance: to disobey British laws, but accept the punishments associated with sedition. Not to return force against force required a superior, moral strength, and could only be practiced by those who have conquered fear. Passive resistance, in Gandhi's brilliant inversion, was the method of the brave; terrorism, of the cowardly.

This is not the place to expatiate on Gandhi's political thinking.[89]

It is clear that Gandhi is an advocate of an intense sense of freedom of the individual—to hold onto and practice his beliefs, and to be different from others, ideas central for instance to Mill's advocacy of liberty.[90] Yet Gandhi's emphasis and specific inflection take his construction of individual freedom in a different direction from common liberal thought. Human beings must search for *their* truth, true self, or true nature (*svabhava*), with a strong, uncompromising moral emphasis that makes it closer to Kant's ethics than to Mill's.[91] At least the ideas about individual liberty strongly emphasized the need not to live by either custom or authority,[92] but they placed equal emphasis, like Kant, on individuals learning to control their passions and interests by a higher moral sense, though Gandhi does this by using the standard Hindu idea of bringing the senses (*indriya*) under control. This is *swaraj* for the individual: rule over himself; and clearly, in his thinking, it is only an individual who has established self-mastery (*swaraj*) in this sense, who can, without inconsistency, desire or demand *swaraj* (self-rule) from British dominion over India. The second sense of *swaraj*, or self-rule, applies to daily lives of common people. In a powerful passage in the *Hind Swaraj*, Gandhi states, for him, true *swaraj* does not mean simply the end of British rule: "My patriotism does not teach me that I am to allow people to be crushed under the heel of Indian princes, if only the English retire . . . If I have the power, I should resist tyranny of Indian princes just as much as that of the English. By patriotism I mean the welfare of the whole people."[93]

By these arguments *swaraj* stretches from individual moral self-determination to larger areas of collective freedom from want and indignity. It goes some way in the direction of social and economic freedom, although ultimately what he made of this aspect of freedom remained vague. The third and final aspect of freedom, which was true freedom for India, the real meaning of *swaraj*, was of course freedom not from British rule, but from Western civilization. India's freedom was meant to be free not to be like Europe, not to choose European modernity as the ineluctable future of mankind.

Modernist radicals in Congress, communists and socialists, differed with Gandhi principally on this point. Gandhi saw freedom as an opportunity for India to be unlike modern Western societies, to retain her traditional social forms, because that was true civilization. For Jawaharlal Nehru, the most eloquent radical in the 1930s and 1940s, the purpose of freedom was exactly the opposite. Nehru and the radicals continued the tradition of economic nationalist critique of British rule. They saw colonialism as the primary obstacle to the achievement of true modernity, which consisted in industrialization, establishment of democracy, and general development similar to modern Western forms, although they had a strong preference for a socialist organization of modern society. In opposition to Gandhi, they saw welfare of society to consist in industrial growth, urbanization, parliamentary democracy; Gandhi saw in each of these fundamental deficiencies and real degeneration of civilizing values. Curiously, in India communism established itself as an ideology earlier than socialism,[94] but communists' early efforts, cocoordinated long-distance from Europe by the intellectual leader M. N. Roy, met with sporadic success in organizing trade unions and the peasantry. It was a communist sympathizer who moved the first, unsuccessful resolution demanding "full independence" in the Indian National Congress, an unpardonable extremism in 1921 in the eyes of more reformist Congress leaders. Within eight years of this, however, in 1929, Nehru was to move a successful resolution for full independence.[95]

But the real influence of the radicals within the Congress consisted in emphasizing that real pressure on the British Raj to move out of India required the wholehearted involvement of the poorer classes, the peasantry and the proletariat. They were unlikely to find much enthusiasm for the Congress if it did not take up their economic demands more seriously. From the 1930s, the Congress party's ideology acknowledged a link between political and economic freedom, and extended support, often lukewarm or divided, to trade union or peasant struggles over economic demands. The tardiness of British response to demands for independence steadily radicalized the Congress, and the influence of the radical strands increased spectacularly during the 1940s, with the socialists playing a major role in the Quit India movement in 1942.

The clearest exposition of this extension of the meaning of the idea of freedom from a narrowly political to a wider economic one came in the works of Jawaharlal Nehru. In two presidential addresses to the Indian National Congress, in 1929 and 1936, Nehru outlined this construction of the idea of Indian freedom, especially what it meant for common people to be free, and for India to be independent. Nehru had a complex intellectual biography, starting with immense fascination for "scientific socialism," being disillusioned about Soviet communism after Stalin's show trials, and eventually adopting a much milder social democratic approach to social revolution, when it really mattered—when he came to power in 1947. Ironically, he was very radical when he did not have real power; when he actually did, he had abandoned much of his early radicalism. Even so, his arguments retain great significance for the clarity and passion with which a particular case about freedom was made.

Although the principal question in the 1929 Congress session, which overshadowed everything else, was Congress's demand for "full independence," and his task as the president was to argue for it, Nehru subtly bent the interpretation of the fullness of freedom in a radical direction. Admitting that his view was a minority in the Congress, he asserted:

> I must frankly confess that I am a socialist and a republican, and am no believer in kings and princes, or in the order which produces the modern kings of industry, who have greater power over the lives and fortunes of men than even the kings of old, and whose methods are as predatory as those of the old feudal aristocracy. I recognise, however, that it may not be possible for a body constituted as is this National Congress, and in the present circumstances of the country, to adopt a fully Socialistic programme. But we must realise that the philosophy of Socialism has gradually permeated the entire structure of society the world over, and almost the only points in dispute are the pace and methods of its full realisation. India will have to go that way too, if she seeks to end her poverty and inequality.[96]

In a famous article, "Whither India?," Nehru showed the structure of the socialist argument and its major disagreements with others with sharp clarity. "What are we driving at," the article asked, "Freedom? *Swaraj*? Independence? Dominion Status? Words which may mean much, or little or nothing at all. Again whose freedom are we particularly striving for, for nationalism covers many sins and includes many conflicting elements."[97] "Being essentially a middle-class movement, nationalism works chiefly in the interests of that class."[98] The nation does not have concrete enough interests in the abstract; at every step of real political decisions, some interests have to be sacrificed for others.[99] "A more vital conflict of interests arises between these possessing classes as a whole and the others: between the haves and have-nots . . . We cannot escape having to answer the question, now or later, for the freedom of which class or classes is

India especially striving? Do we place the masses, the peasantry and workers, first, or some other small class at the head of our list? . . . To say that we shall not answer that question now is itself an answer and taking of sides, for it means that we stand by the existing order, the status quo."[100] There could be no clearer presentation of the socialist case within and against Indian nationalism. "India's struggle today is part of the great struggle which is going on all over the world for the emancipation of the oppressed. Essentially, this is an economic struggle, with hunger and want as its driving forces, although it puts on nationalist and other dresses."[101]

Nehru's presentation of the socialist interpretation of the objectives of the nationalist movement, however, contained several ambiguities, or potential contradictions which were yet undeveloped. First, he was simply urging nationalists to acknowledge and incorporate within nationalism the legitimate demands of the peasants and workers. This merely made the list of freedoms longer, adding economic freedoms to the usual list of individual and national freedom; it did not say what should be done in case a conflict arose between them. As Nehru's political experience grew, and his disillusionment with the Soviet Union increased, he inclined toward a less radical, at least a less impatient presentation of the socialist idea. By the time independence was won, he clearly believed that political democracy was too valuable to be sacrificed for rapid achievement of economic equality and reduction of poverty. Clearly, he also felt that the constitution and its formal arrangements of democracy were vital for a democratic future for free India. This subtle turn in Nehru's thinking also caused a serious rift between him and the Indian communists who attempted, for a short period (1948–1951), to destroy his government through armed insurrection.

The evolution of Indian nationalism over the twentieth century shows an interesting feature of collective reflection on the nature of modern freedom. By the beginning of the century, two important developments had taken place. First, through the discussions of the English-speaking intelligentsia, a recognizable liberal doctrine started taking shape in the works of the moderates in the early stages of the Indian National Congress. Second, in vernaculars, a new conceptual language for the expression of the demand for modern liberty takes shape, although in the vernacular writings the modern European civilization is assessed more negatively from the mid-nineteenth century, particularly for its exclusive emphasis on this-worldliness, usually seen as crass materialism, and individualism, seen similarly as a license to unbridled selfishness. However, the emphasis on individualism, the freedom of the autonomous individual, increasingly comes under serious scrutiny and criticism. Individualism, often celebrated in a romantic conception of artistic creativity, is condemned in social conduct as egotistic behavior.

The criticisms of individualistic thought and behavior ground their argument in very different premises, but their conclusions have a strange convergence. First, a section of the modern intelligentsia revised their opinion about Europe and its rationalism as a liberating force and criticized its tendency to dissolve communities and turn toward militaristic nationalism. Second, Gandhi continued this tradition of criticism against the modern European civilization and gave it a new, highly individual, form. Finally, the rise of the left inside the national movement began an assault on the economic individualistic premises of modern European civilization and urged socialist solutions.

Liberal individualism, in its most uncompromising forms, never became immensely popular or prestigious in India's intellectual life. But the map of intellectual ideas, the relation between individual and collectivist conceptions of freedom, remained a complex matter. The fundamental argument about the expansion of autonomy of individuals continued unobtrusively, at times through these ideologies, at others, despite their conscious decisions. Often, joining the nationalist movement or playing an active role in political life itself involved individual self-assertion against family and parental authority. Ironically, all these trends welcomed and applauded women's participation in the political struggles, which could not be done without a certain relaxation of patriarchy. Participation in political movements itself was to bring traditional individuals into a field of social mixing and miscegenation where caste and community identities were put into question, and people had to develop trust among strangers. Independent of the ideological self-understanding of political groups, the relentless sociology of a mass movement surreptitiously widened the conditions for individual assertiveness.

≺ IX ≻

Freedom after Independence

In 1936 the young Nehru wrote with characteristic radical impatience, "We have got into the extraordinary habit of thinking of freedom in terms of paper constitutions."[102] Yet after independence, he recognized the significance of establishing a permanent framework for political and social life and devoted most of his intellectual energies to this task for about three years. Congress, in a display of remarkable generosity and foresight, invited into the Constituent Assembly legal figures like B. R. Ambedkar whose relations with it were not entirely trouble-free. As a consequence, India received a constitution which, with the important shortcoming of being excessively detailed and legalistic, was exceptionally sensitive to emergent problems of a new nation-state, and which strenuously abjured over-simplifications. Consequently, the legal structure of democratic politics was constructed in great detail with enormous technical care, and after exhaustive, often extremely subtle, theoretical debates in the Constituent Assembly.[103]

In some ways, the nature of political discourse was significantly altered after independence—not in its ideological positions, but in its medium. Before independence, as real power was not in the hands of nationalists, political positions could be articulated only as ideas, in a theoretical form. Traditionalists, communalists, conservatives, Gandhians, liberals, socialists, communists—all presented their views to a political public audience in the form of theoretical arguments about future social arrangements and political possibilities. After independence, this suddenly stopped. Except for Nehru's occasional attempts to argue his positions theoretically and the communists' inertial adherence to Marxist doctrine, large theoretical arguments became less common. Political discourse focused understandably on more mundane and pressing issues of quotidian politics. But the most powerful influence, which acted silently and unseen, was from the structure of constitutional arrangements adopted after independence: the particular inflection given to the ideas of nationalism, federalism, social reform, individual liberty. The constitution, astonishingly, was a primarily liberal document.[104] For various reasons, more radical political aspirations like the communalists' desire for a Hindu state, or Nehru's for a more redistributive commitment were either defeated or bartered away in the service of reaching compromise.

What was left, and therefore set firmly into the basic structure of government and its commitment to citizens' rights, was a solid, internally coherent structure of liberal principles centered on a section on fundamental rights. Its configuration of rights was centered in its turn on a right to freedom conceived in a primarily negative liberal manner: of speech, association, belief, faith, acquisition of property—an unsurprising recitation of liberal freedoms. Critically significant was the translation of the right to equality into a liberal conception of political, and in the peculiar Indian context, *social* equality rather than economic. The juridical structure established to defend this pattern of liberties followed equally liberal principles, based on the independence of the judiciary, a formalistic legalistic system of judicial defense of freedom rather than a reliance on popular activism. If we accept a simple distinction between procedural and participatory aspects of democracy, this will imply that there are two distinct ways of securing freedom. The first, the procedural way, advocates relying on the liberal state and the rules of procedure for equal treatment it put in place. The second, participatory, trend often concentrates on opposing the state and forcing it through political mobilization, to recognize demands for justice. The nationalist movement was based on vast participatory impulses: its primary target was after all the colonial state. Despite the powerful participatory rhetoric in nationalist thought, and in spite of the historical fact that the new state was created by a period of strong mobilization, the nation, when it came to decide its institutional fate, opted for a broadly individualist liberal conception of parliamentary government.

The political history of independent India can be divided into two distinct historical periods to date. The first extended to the end of the 1960s, over four general elections. Political life in these two decades appeared to fit unproblematically into the liberal-individualist format of the constitutional arrangements. Constitutional disputes, reflected in the judgments of the Supreme Court, involved personal liberties of expression or the sanctity of the right to property.[105] Debates in Indian political life were carried on primarily in the language of familiar Western democratic discourses, in terms of conflicts between political ideals of laissez faire and state intervention, mainly capitalist freedom and socialist redistribution.[106] The underlying sociology of these ideological conflicts saw the movement of social classes like the industrialists, managerial elites, and proletariat as central to political life. What is remarkable, in retrospect, is less the contents of the debate, than their implicit sociology. On all sides—from Nehru's centrist socialism, the advocacy of unrestricted capitalism by the Swatantra (Free) party, the strident egalitarianism of the Communists—there is a calm indifference toward the discourses of caste and religious identity which were to break with massive fury into the political domain within a decade.

Within ten years, Indians would be forced to recognize that these discourses were the vernacular of Indian politics, as opposed to the rationalist English discourse of the first two decades, which imparted a strange unity to the combatants. From the 1970s, Indian political discourse began to speak a kind of political vernacular, and it was the inequalities of caste, region, and religion which would completely dominate political demands, entirely erasing the earlier language of class interests, capitalism, and socialism.[107] Indira Gandhi's victory in the elections of 1971 on the basis of the slogan *Garibi Hatao* (remove poverty) was the last, and already disingenuous, recourse to the discourse of socialism. By the mid-1970s, communists had lost their intellectual significance at the national level, being effectively reduced to regional parties, too engrossed in winning elections to care much about high principles.

The historical movement of political ideas in India shows that there can be two different ways ideas of collective freedom from oppression and individual liberty from interference can be related to each other. Many analyses in political theory have concentrated on cases in which the ideal of collective freedom of a group suffocates and eventually abrogates liberty of the individual. Intense demands for freedom or self-assertion of a religious community might restrict the freedom of individuals by interpreting all aspiration for individuation as disruptive of the community's identity. The ideals of the freedom of a community and of individuals are certainly not the same, as Berlin argued in the context of the Cold War; indeed the two can be opposed to each other in specific contexts. The relation between these two aspects of freedom in India has followed a peculiar trajectory. After independence, the overt, dramatic, explicit political conflicts centered around group rights of various kinds. Since the

1970s, the conflicts have occurred especially around the assertion of the lower castes, former untouchables, and the strata immediately above them in traditional caste hierarchy. These strata make their claims on the state and other social groups in the liberal language of rights, but obviously their focus is the assertion of the right of their groups in the political arena. Yet, neither in caste-based electoral mobilizations nor in the Hindu communal politics can one detect a simple conflict between group identity and expression of individual freedoms.

In the case of lower castes, this assertion of group rights and a heightened public sensitivity toward caste inequality has created greater space for lower-caste individuals. Because of their collective numerical power, political parties can hardly ignore them. It has been a peculiarity of the Indian social debates of the past century that although conservatives have occasionally tried to defend their practices in the name of continuity of culture, there have been no serious, straightforward arguments defending practices like untouchability or explicit indignity of lower castes. Some sections of the upper-caste groups have voluntarily abandoned practices of separation and hierarchy through their conversion to modern beliefs and indeed have been major agents of reform. Less progressive elements among them, who would like to practice caste inequality, have in effect accepted the formal directions of the state, and have resorted to the freedom of private belief and private behavior to practice such conduct where possible. Their hostility to the, albeit slow, uplift of the lower castes has to be expressed in the mendacious form of an acute concern for merit. Traditional forms of conduct have been sent decisively into the defensive; they are forced to seek respectable subterfuges.[108] The historical result is that although the attention of political movements and mobilization is rarely directed toward questions of personal liberty, for lower classes at least, there is a slow but perceptible expansion of personal freedom, at least in the negative form of the lesser likelihood of insults, indignity, and formal discrimination within state institutions. In recent decades, however, Indian politics has seen a new form of danger to freedom of minorities through the rise of Hindu nationalism.

Thus the story of modern India since independence can be seen as a story of freedom, although its form and movements have been different from European precedents and somewhat strange. The three domains of freedom we identified in accordance with nineteenth-century social thought—the domains of freedom of the individual, of freedom of association and forming groups to pursue collective ends, and of the freedom of large collectivities, particularly colonized nations—have all been affected by the movement of freedom in modern Indian political imagination. The relations between these aspects have never been simply linear, or simply encompassing. Rather there has been occasional restructuring of their hierarchy of significance for specific social groups, and consequently, in the domain of public discussions. Yet all three have slowly moved forward and expanded in a complex historical movement. The history of modern India tells us a complex, surprising, captivating, and yet unconcluded story of freedom. It is appropriate to express a Tocquevillesque astonishment at this historical phenomenon. If we look from age to age, from the earliest antiquity to the present day, we can agree with Tocqueville that nothing like this has ever happened before.[109] We have not yet seen the end of this unprecedented historical process; it is still puzzling because it is certainly not concluded. It is also true that "the past has ceased to throw light on the future," but on one point at least, the mind of man does not wander in darkness. For the eventual shape of the destination of this process might be unclear, but the movement toward greater expansion of freedom is irreversible.[110]

≺ 5 ≻

Freedom in Burma and Thailand: Inside or Outside the State?

ROBERT H. TAYLOR

THERE ARE a number of apparent paradoxes when one examines freedom in Southeast Asia today. The questions of freedom for whom and freedom from what have to be asked here as anywhere else. If freedom is defined as the ability of relatively autonomous individuals to effectively pursue individual rights vis-à-vis the state and the current rulers, including the right to publicly criticize the authorities as well as to have at least an indirect and largely passive role in the choice of those rulers, then freedom is relatively constrained to a greater or lesser extent in all of the countries of the region. But Southeast Asian societies are far from unique in this respect. All polities place limits on individual rights as a condition of maintaining an orderly society. The degree to which this limiting is done, and the level of public awareness and acceptance of these constraints, are often contested, however, both inside and outside the legal institutions of the state.

Another concept of freedom, found in variations of theories of political pluralism, involves the idea of autonomy for the leaders of groups or institutions, who can operate largely outside the constraints of the state. This autonomy often requires the apparent subordination of the freedom of individuals in the name of a larger cause, while simultaneously denying the legitimacy of the state to constrain the rights of these same individuals. In the ethnic, linguistic, and cultural diversity which exists in all Southeast Asian societies, the demand for freedom for the group, whether aspiring to nationhood or to recognized minority group rights, is often heard as an argument for independence or autonomy in the name of a good larger than the individual but a rather different collectivity than the internationally recognized state.

Thus constraints on freedom can occur both inside and outside the confines of the state. Not only are these constraints often contested, but also much of the politics of the region in recent years has centered on issues about the degree to which they can be allowed to operate in an orderly society. When they are contested in the first sense of individual rights vis-à-vis the state, we see the emergence of usually peaceful "democracy movements," demands for civil rights, and most recently, the recognition of civil society by the state. When in the sense of collective or group rights against the state, there often emerge armed movements seeking secession or autonomy from the laws of the state.

Changing economic and social structures through recent historical periods have encouraged redefinitions of earlier indigenous concepts of freedom. Changing gender relationships, different modes of agricultural and industrial production and organization, the growth of surplus-generating economies linked to external markets and trade, have all reshaped contested notions of freedom in Southeast Asian societies during the past two centuries. Perhaps the most important change has been in the reach of the state. The emergence of tightly-drawn borders and the capacity within those borders of the state to regulate many aspects of life have redefined people's sense of self and of society. Such wide-ranging effects have all had a role in shaping the ways in which ideas of freedom have been constructed and contested in Southeast Asian polities, from the precolonial period through the colonial period to the present era. They provide a background to the more narrowly defined discussion of the concepts of freedom and their implementation in this chapter.

≺ I ≻

The Common Political Roots

I propose in this chapter to consider one of the paradoxical dualities of Southeast Asia—Burma (or Myanmar[1]) and Thailand. Thailand today is a constitutional monarchy with a relatively free press, an open economy, an elected parliament, an established stock market, and a lively political life, whose citizens have a relatively high degree of freedom within the law. Despite the political aftershocks of a major economic crisis in 1997, the governing institutions have remained remarkably effective. While the country is not without its critics, most observers would say that it has developed a democratic political system with institutions of governance within the law which bestow a large degree of legitimacy on the acts of the government and corporate entities and of individuals in civil society and the economy. Moreover, Thailand has managed to assimilate a large immigrant Chinese population into the polity and also resolve tensions arising from the existence of previously rebellious indigenous minority hill tribes in the north of the country.

Burma, on the other hand, is widely regarded as one of the most autocratic and authoritarian military regimes in Asia and Africa. It is a country riven with ethnic separatism, allegations of human rights abuses, and the denial of electoral outcomes. The state and the military dominate the economy, and much of what occurs in other areas of economic life takes place in a semi-legal environment. Rather than being assimilated into Burmese society, many of the South Asian immigrants who arrived in the country during the first half of the twentieth century had fled by the mid-1960s. The stark contrast between the two countries' conditions today is of significant comparative interest when it is recalled that two hundred years ago they were remarkably similar in all of the characteristics by which ideas of freedom and individual rights in the modern industrialized and urbanized societies are contrasted with those of pre-industrial peasant societies. If Locke and Mill prevail in Thailand, Hobbes won out in Burma.

Notions of individual freedom and liberty, like ideas of the public and community, were essentially non-existent in Thailand and Burma two hundred years ago. Also absent were contemporary notions of oppression and the denial of liberty. But it is fair to say that persons located at various places in the elaborate structure of patron-client relations, which was the basis of the hierarchical social structure which existed, had different perceptions of appropriate behavior and appropriate opportunities for the expression of self-interest. Where people were in the social order, and what their social, economic, and cultural roles were, determined their notions of rights and freedom. Appropriate behavior for a king would not have been appropriate behavior for a village headman, a regional tax collector, or a village monk. F. H. Bradley's Hegelian notion of "my station and its duties" would not have been inapt in such circumstances. The "flat" concept of every man and woman having equal rights and equal opportunities to express those rights, including an equal say in government, at least periodically, played no role in this world view.

We will take the rise of the Konbaung Dynasty in Burma (1752) and of the Chakri Dynasty in Thailand (1782) as comparable points of departure to trace the evolution of both countries until the present. The years following the second decade of the nineteenth century were a watershed in the history of both countries. Following the arrival of British and French imperial ambitions in the region, each polity, under new and reinvigorated dynasties, marked the beginning of the unforeseen end of the old order and the advent of the reforms which led to the formation of the new order. But the pace and agency of these transitions were very different, as were the ultimate outcomes in terms of freedom and liberty.

Thailand during this period has been described by S. J. Tambiah as a "galactic polity."[2] Burma could be described similarly. The galactic polity model is that of a state which arrayed itself around the king like a galaxy of mini- and sub-states, each with its own hereditary or semi-hereditary rulers. The morally appropriate special order on earth was conceived of as a material representation of the cosmos. Political power and the force of custom gained their authority and legitimacy from their link with the cosmic order. The power of subordinate governors through to the central monarch both stemmed from and replicated the authority the cosmos had bestowed on the king as the self-fulfilling consequence of the king's just rule. The order that resulted was proof of the legitimacy of the moral order which had been created. Seen from the center, from the perspective of the monarch, this description was apt. In broad outline, Tambiah's description of the form and purpose of the premodern state in Siam is equally apt for all of the major states of precolonial Southeast Asia, from the mainland to what is now Indonesia.

Michael Adas, however, looking less at the underlying Buddhist rationale of these polities and more at the conditions of governing them and the methods available for doing so, describes the nature of authority relations in these monarchies as those of a "contest state."[3] In the precolonial order, while formally there was a clear line of command and control from the center to the periphery, in reality there was a continual struggle for the generation and then the retention of resources at whatever level. This struggle led to a contest for power and authority, with the king sometimes siding with the villagers against rapacious intermediary governors, and sometimes with his intermediate agents against the peasantry. But there was always a third option in addition to compliance or resistance. That was avoidance. The low level of coercive capacity, and the abundance of land and nature, meant that the alternative of exit was always available and this in itself tempered the levels of demands the agents of the state felt they could impose on their subjects. Freedom emerged unseen in the interstices of what looked to be an order which did not recognize liberty as an option.

The point of these descriptions is that in terms of a definition of freedom which assumes a greater degree of autonomy for the individual vis-à-vis the state, the further from the protection of the state one was, the freer she became. As Edmund Leach made clear in his description of the parallel political worlds of the "frontier areas" of Burma,[4] the "democratic" Kachin social order was much more egalitarian, and much poorer, than the high Buddhist culture of the Shan hereditary rulers who replicated the amalgam of secular power buttressed by cosmic sanction of the former Burmese kings. Kachin and Shan were not then immutable ethnic categories but ways in which societies organized production and consumption. An individual could, and did, move between one category and another in the course of a lifetime. There was a stark choice between freedom and security. Inclusion in the state meant a diminution of autonomy and liberty and an assumption of obligations. Self-exclusion meant an increase in freedom but a diminution in comfort and culture.

Nonetheless, during the precolonial period the activities of the central state would have seemed less obvious and obtrusive to the populace than would be the case today, for far more of the regulatory aspects of people's everyday lives were controlled by the patron-client system in the cellular organization of traditional society. Members of different population categories—*ahmudan*, *athi*, slave, Tai, or swidden agriculturalists in Burma, *phrai*, *lek*,[5] slave, Muslim in Thailand—knew what the state expected of them. Their patrons' tasks were normally carried out without the need to invoke the structures of the state or the use of physical coercion. As a consequence of the low population density of the precolonial world, the need to maintain a contingent of people to work the land required the rulers to restrain their tax collecting proclivities, whether in kind or in the form of corvee labor.

Both the Burmese and the Thai kings drew their ideas of legitimacy and authority from concepts derived from Theravada Buddhism. The monarchs were *deva rajas*, or god-kings, who by their sumptuous displays of wealth demonstrated the power they derived from the cosmos. In a world that assumed that disorder was the normal condition of man, the god-kings existed to create order. They enforced sumptuary laws and conducted ceremonial and other acts to impress upon their subjects their dominance and authority. Custom defined social practices and behavior for the population. Respect and deference defined relations between superiors and inferiors. Society was constructed in a series of patron-client relationships from the monarch to the lowest slave.

Institutions such as slavery were not seen as immutable, or unusual. Everyone had his or her role and status and responded to them accordingly. Freedom meant getting free from attachments to life, not controlling life. Law was seen as not a set of rules which constrained the behavior of others in order to protect one's liberty and property, but as a set of customs which were malleable and continually negotiable, seeking a sense of fairness and equity in a world of compromises, not justice and retribution in a world of sharp distinctions between right and wrong. The reach of the state, moreover, was limited and was a function of the transitory power of any given monarch. As the monarch increased or decreased his sway and territorial control, the ability of the state to impose its definitions and customs, rights and demands, increased or decreased. The ill defined, traditional, and negotiable demands of the state became weaker and weaker the further in a spatial sense from the capital and the monarch one went. And because the state had few functions, its exactions were in modern terms light.

Freedom in this world was a negative freedom in the sense that the absence of the state defined how free a person was. There were state areas and non-state areas. To move from the state area to the non-state area was what determined the degree of individual rights one had. Mobility was the key to freedom, in fact it was the primary positive freedom. Therefore kings and their institutions devoted a great deal of effort to attempting to limit mobility because any diminution in population meant a weakening of the state's power and territorial reach.

Seeking freedom by moving outside the reach of the monarchical state had its price. One moved away from "civilization" as defined by the religion and culture of the monarch's court and its ostentatious displays. One moved away from a steady and stable supply of food and sustenance in wet rice-producing regions of the country. One, in a sense, moved from an economy of comfort, culture, and surplus to one of mobility, agility, and scarcity. In an area of low population density, with a pre-market economy, the choices were stark, but perhaps less stark than they would seem today.

Linguistically the Thai and Burmese languages expressed these attitudes toward ideas of freedom and liberty. Words for freedom had connected with a concept almost of license and abandon. *Lutlatyei* or *lutlathmu*, the contemporary terms for liberty in Burmese, *seriphap* and *itsaraphat* in Thai, are rooted in concepts of exemption from the rules and from restraints. Words for authority and right, *sitthi* in Thai and *awza* or *a-na* in Burmese, have much more positive nuances attached to them. These are connected with the personal greatness and power possessed in an individual person because of status and rank, not because of office or position. Equality and individualism were not meaningful concepts in societies which defined order through hierarchy rather than legal structures.

≺ II ≻

Burma—Forced to be Free

The arrival of European colonialism and imperialism undermined this world and attempted to replace it with rules and principles antithetical to these traditions. Required in turn was a redefinition of the individual vis-à-vis the state and political authority. The speed of and the method by which changes were introduced would appear to have had a significant impact on the degree to which new ideas and concepts became accepted and ingrained into the societies of Burma and Thailand. Where these new conceptualizations of freedom were forced upon a society as part of the achievements of imperialism and foreign rule, as in the case of Burma, they were rejected in the name of a modernized concept of "tradition." Where they were introduced by an indigenous monarchy in the name of state-strengthening and the maintenance of independence, new ideas of freedom have been more readily accepted.

The political, social, and economic consequences of foreign rule and imperialist economics came more quickly and more thoroughly to Burma than perhaps to any other Asian society. The incorporation of the ideas of freedom which lay behind them came perhaps the most slowly, however, because of their apparent arbitrariness and unjust imposition by a foreign force without any legitimacy rooted in traditional concepts of power and authority.[6] The British Indian Empire colonized Burma in three wars between 1825 and 1886 and annexed the country in 1886; in 1937 it was established as a separate colony under the Secretary of State for India and Burma. The attempts the Burmese had been making to come to terms with the force of European imperialism were cut in 1886 with the nearly instant eradication of the power of the indigenous state and its replacement with a British-Indian army of occupation. At the time, the British argued that by this action they were freeing the Burmese people from a form of oriental despotism.[7]

How rulers perceive their roles within the manifold forces which have shaped the societies they govern is an important indicator of what kind of state they wish to create and perpetuate. Their concepts of the state's duties provide them with the reasons for administering the institutions of social control and economic production in the particular manner they decide on. For the kings and ministers of the precolonial state in Burma, the maintenance of order and security required them to be involved intimately with the symbolic, spiritual, and customary life of society and the regulation of economic affairs. Any distinction between the public and private spheres of life was alien to their conception of the relationship of state to society.

The colonial rulers, however, viewed their roles and obligations very differently. They were detached from society not merely because they were foreigners but because their ideas of rule presumed a distinction between the public and the private aspects of life. The rationality of the modern state was a force separate from the liberty of personal choice, even though it was its guarantor. The ideological justification of nineteenth-century European liberalism not only provided them with a moral justification for colonialism, but also allowed them to interpret the political and social consequences of the policies they implemented and the institutions they created to carry these out as integral to and a necessary consequence of the evolution of the modern world.

From the arrival of the first British officials to govern Arakan and Tenasserim in 1825 until the last of them walked out of the country before the advancing Japanese imperial army in 1942, they believed that the colonial state was "a benevolent but impartial umpire" which freed the economy of Burma from the precolonial state's restrictions on trade and commerce, and thus liberated the individual from the fetters of custom and the extortion of an exploitative ruling class. The nineteenth- and twentieth-century elite of the imperial bureaucracy, the officers of the Indian Civil Service (ICS), saw themselves as "holding the ring" for the political and economic life of Burma in order that the people who resided there, indigenous and foreign, might conduct their political and economic affairs in a safe and peaceful manner.

As the ultimate arbiters and guides of Burma, the British civil servants saw no contradiction between their powers to rule an alien land and their preachments about creating self-government in that country. Recognizing no form of self-government in existence upon their arrival, but only an outdated form of oriental despotism, they saw themselves as the midwives of the modern freedom in reactionary Asia. If there was any contradiction between the freedom and prosperity of Burma, which they governed, and that of Britain, for whom they governed, it could and would be resolved by their own abilities to see the "true" interests of all sides and to govern in the name of fairness, efficiency, and the long-term welfare of all concerned. If the people they governed did not view the state they created and the policies they pursued in this way, this was because they did not as yet understand the intricacies of statecraft in the modern world. In that sense the British who managed the colonial state were like their indigenous predecessors who also believed that their methods of rule were the most appropriate for the maintenance of society, even if occasionally resisted by those they governed.

The mature Indian empire had at its disposal instruments of government which were modern and powerful. The legal system was well established and the armed forces well equipped compared to their foes. When the British came to establish their administration in all of Burma finally in 1886, they did not have to look for a model of administration. Rather they had in their possession a model which was perceived as rational and effective. And they had a cadre of British and Indian officials to staff it. In the eyes of the Burmese, they were not colonized once but rather twice, once by the British, once by the Indians, for not only were the armed forces and civilian bureaucracy of the new rulers staffed by Indians, but Indian capital soon dominated the modern economy of the country.

At the end of the third war, the Burmese monarchy was dethroned, British-Indian bureaucratic codes and laws were introduced and replaced traditional Theravada Buddhism codes and customary laws, and capitalism replaced economic subsistence. Rangoon, in the 1880s a minor commercial center, became in 40 years the world's busiest port for immigration and the rice trade. The country also had a murder rate which only Chicago in the 1920s could rival. Litigation was widespread and peasant unrest endemic as the previously largely subsistence peasants were turned into a rural proletariat. The pace and thoroughness of change was, however, unevenly imposed by the colonial state.

In contrast to the changes in central Burma, in the frontier regions of the colonially defined borders of Burma custom and tradition were preserved and indeed reinforced by the might of colonial protectors. No longer defined as non-state populations, the peoples of these areas became reconceptualized as previously oppressed tribal and linguistic minority groups, in the language of nineteenth-century British anthropology. And the seeds of a subsequent conflict between two concepts of freedom arose. On the one hand, radical nationalists who had inculcated modern egalitarian ideas and viewed freedom as the quest for equal rights within the state saw the perpetuation of the tribal rulers and tribal customs, based on ascribed principles of order, as an anachronism. They sought to end this order by the inclusion of the minority communities into the wider society on the terms of the new definitions of rights and freedoms of the modern state. However, those who sought to preserve this order argued the reverse in the name of pluralism and preserving traditional social values.

The response of the indigenous population in Burma to the imposition of colonial rule varied over time and in response to the application of different policies in different areas. In the upland, minority areas, little changed as power was ceded from the king at Ava to the queen in London other than that the authority of those rulers recognized by the British was greatly strengthened. In the majority parts of the country, however, there were catastrophic consequences, initially for the Burmese kings, subsequently for their British supplanters.

The introduction of free trade and commercial freedom in those areas of Burma governed by the British after the wars of 1824–26 and 1856 was remarkably successful. The ease of making a profit proved attractive and many people migrated from the king's territories south to the new opportunities created by access to the world economy. But the dethronement of King Thibaw in 1885 and the annexation of the country to India resulted in widespread revolts led by former officials and beneficiaries of the defeated order. As their powers were no longer respected and their rank in society was denied by the new rulers, they organized armed resistance which required nearly ten years of military campaigns, referred to by the new administration as the "pacification of Burma," to subdue. Indian troops were positioned throughout the country and civilian rule, albeit with a new governing cadre, was not reestablished for a decade. Only then could British ideas of freedom, which paid little or no heed to Burmese customs and practices, begin to be formally introduced. No one asked whether freedom could be imposed on a people.

At the end of World War I, British policy toward India, and therefore Burma, began a new chapter, as the institutions of parliamentary democracy were gradually introduced into the Indian political order. Aware of the need to involve the Indian people in the political process, in the mistaken belief that they would then naturally wish to remain part of the empire, the British introduced elections for provincial assemblies. Burma was initially not included among those involved in this experiment in colonial democracy; however, in 1922 elections were held for a provincial legislature in Rangoon. Only the central areas of Burma were included in the election, as the frontier areas where indirect rule prevailed under indigenous chiefs were excluded from the reforms. The elections encouraged the development of political parties; and among the small educated elite made up largely of lawyers and journalists, an interest in party politics quickly emerged. Though the authority of the legislature was severely limited and the British governor's ability to rule was not affected in any major way by this change, the existence of elections and a legislative forum provided outlets for political views not previously available.

The response of the wider public, however, was much less enthusiastic than that of the urban elites. The voter turnout was very small, 7 percent of eligible voters in 1922, 16 percent in 1925, and 18 percent in 1928.[8] While voting had little appeal, a new political term entered the Burmese vocabulary for freedom—boycott. Aware of the tactics of Sinn Fein in wresting the independence of the Republic of Ireland from the British at about the same time, Burmese nationalists latched on to the boycott as a way of mobilizing support for the ending of British rule. Moreover, the boycott tactic spread from merely nonparticipation in elections to the nonpayment of taxes and rents. The popularity of those who led the boycott campaigns was overwhelming, especially as they provided a way of directly addressing the economic and political grievances of the majority of the population at the time of the depression which began in 1929. The Saya San peasant revolt, which occurred in 1930, was in part a consequence of organization of the peasantry in resistance to economic conditions, but also evidence of the ability of the peasantry in Burmese politics to take action separate from the formal institutions of democracy as practiced by the Rangoon elite. The lessons of the Saya San revolt, during which more than 1,300 people died, were not lost on future governments of Burma once independence was regained in 1948.

As previously noted, in the border areas institutions of democratic government were not introduced in the British period. Not only were institutions to protect political rights and liberties not instituted among the indigenous minority populations in these areas, but the institutions of the free market and the commodization of land were limited as well in order to preserve the existing social order. Here, and to the British they were a welcome contrast to nationalist politicians and fiery student agitators, traditional chiefs were honored. In many cases, the effect of colonialism was to strengthen their powers over their subjects. Shan Sawbwas and Kachin Duwas (the traditional leaders) became not only wealthier, but also entrenched in power in the poorest parts of the country. Little was to change in these areas until the 1950s, following independence.

≺ III ≻

Thailand—Modernization for Preservation

The creation of modern capitalist and democratic Thailand from the former royal Siam of old took place during the same period as the more traumatic transformation of Burma from a Buddhist monarchy to a fractured colonial dependency. Why then the dramatically different outcome? The initial materials were much the same and the external pressures were remarkably similar. It is the thesis of this chapter that the difference fundamentally was the consequence of the agents of change and the purpose of the changes which were introduced. In the case of Thailand, the fact that the Thai monarchy was not deposed and the country not ruled by a powerful foreign bureaucracy created political conditions which required change to be tempered by the court's need to maintain its position and at the same time create the resources to maintain the country's independence. Nineteenth-century monarchical preservation created the conditions for the democratic Thailand of the twenty-first century.

Both before and after the military coup of 1932 which ended the absolutist period in Thai history, Thailand has been ruled by a relatively small, self-defining and self-regulating elite. In a remarkable adaptation to new economic and political pressures, the old elite, composed of the royal family and lesser nobility and court officials of the Buddhist monarchy described above, were able to graft onto themselves the economic power of foreign entrepreneurs and agents. As the modern state developed out of its monarchical predecessor, there emerged new social categories made up of professionals, mainly civil servants and military officers who, despite their different social origins, remained attached to the same values and interests as their predecessors thanks to their loyalty to their monarchical benefactors. And equally importantly, their economic interests were seen to be compatible with the state and its modernization.

In contrast to Burma, where opposition to the process of modernization emerged simultaneously with the imposition of colonial rule, few rival bases of power and protest in mass movements and religious organizations emerged in Thailand. The state was able to use popular political sentiments to strengthen itself, rather than have its ability to govern weakened. One of the chief paradoxes of the emergence of the modern institutions of freedom is that it was the strength of the Thai state, rather than its weakness, which allowed for the successful transition to democracy and elected government.

The social and economic attitudes of the Thai political elite have remained remarkably traditional and conservative in the face of change. And they have managed to inculcate their values through education and example into the overwhelming majority of the Thai population. Patrimonial attitudes originating in a society of passive, submissive peasantry were undermined in new market-oriented, urban conditions hugely different from their agrarian origins. Judicious reform, sometimes forced by events and relatively minor public protests, has resulted in a remarkable degree of political and social stability.

Unlike the Burmese monarchy, which when threatened by the superior power of the British Indian Empire was unable to compromise and reach a modus vivendi with its opponents, the Thai kings from Mongkut (1851–68) on saw the need to compromise in the present in order to be strong in the future. Preservation of the monarchy became the first order of the day. Only if the throne retained its basic integrity could the economic development and national power required to provide Thailand and the monarchy with the strength to resist foreign domination be generated. The balancing of internal and external allies and opponents became essential in this long-term strategy. Thus foreign capital and entrepreneurship were grafted onto Thai political power in a marriage of mutual convenience.

Seeking the source of the power of British and other European threats to its security, the monarchy increasingly realized the need to utilize Western enterprise and organizational acumen. King Mongkut, who himself experimented with Western scientific methods mixed with Buddhist cosmological theories, hired foreign advisers in order to reorganize and modernize the administration of the kingdom.[9] Thailand was perhaps fortunate during this time as the pressure from Britain and France to colonize the country was not as intense as that experienced by the neighboring Burmese and also Vietnamese, Lao, and Khmer kingdoms.

The Bowring Treaty reached with Britain in 1856 opened the country to trade and established the principle of extra-territoriality for foreigners doing business in Siam. Import and export tariffs were set at very low rates, which limited the government's revenue; thus the king's administration was required to improve its efficiency and limit its ambitions. More thorough changes were introduced by Mongkut's successor, King Chulalongkorn (1868–1910). Chulalongkorn set out to bring Thailand to a position of equality with Western nations while strengthening the power and independence of both the Crown and the state. Continuing an external policy which posed no threat to the powerful neighboring European empires, Thailand conceded all authority over what became Laos and Cambodia to France in 1873 and 1907 respectively, while ceding four Malay states in the south to Britain in 1890. At the same time, the remaining outlying regions of the kingdom were brought more directly under the control of Bangkok, with the traditional indirect methods of control gradually being replaced by more modern, bureaucratic methods. By the beginning of the twentieth century, the last residual powers of various princes and nobility had been curtailed and then finally eliminated, thus strengthening the grip of the center on the entire kingdom.

Because of the limitations on import tariffs imposed by the Bowring Treaty, the government was denied a usual source of revenue for weak and inefficient governments. Having an underdeveloped domestic taxation system on land and agricultural produce, it was forced to develop alternative means of generating income. Perhaps the most significant, and not only in the short term, was the development of tax farming arrangements with Chinese entrepreneurs. By the turn of the century the royal licenses granted to powerful leaders in the Chinese community to tax on behalf of the state the consumption of opium and liquor as well as gambling and lotteries, all popular with the immigrant Chinese working population, produced nearly half of the state's revenues. The modernization of the Thai state was being funded in a manner which generated little resistance from the majority of the indigenous population but benefited Western enterprise, thus keeping both the major threats to the security of the king at bay.

The pace and extent of the reorganization of the government increased in the 1890s in the face of a perception of renewed imperialist threats to Thailand's independence, most notably the rivalry that existed between Britain and France for influence in the country.

This rivalry resulted in the 1896 Anglo-French convention which neutralized the Chao Phraya basin. The heightened reform program comprised several stages, beginning with the replacement of traditional territorial government departments with ministries charged with specific functions on a "national" basis. At the same time a central treasury was created separate from the Crown's privy purse. But Chulalongkorn was an astute ruler and he proceeded slowly as he centralized power in Bangkok so as to avoid antagonizing older princes who until their powers atrophied had the capacity to thwart his plans. In order to get administrative support that would be loyal only to him and his modernizing schemes, the king's government hired more foreign advisers from a variety of European countries.

Aware of the military strength of Western nations, Chulalongkorn set out to develop a modern, bureaucratic army for Thailand. However, the purpose of the army was not to challenge Britain and France as they sought to encroach on Thai territory. The futility of that was demonstrated by the fate of the Burmese and Vietnamese kings. Rather, it was to create a powerful instrument for internal control. In 1884 a military academy was established and in 1904 universal conscription was adopted, abolishing the old corvee system of military manpower recruitment. Modern nationhood was thus bestowed on the Thais without their needing to organize a revolution to get it. Further to this end, legal changes were introduced in an attempt to end the extra-territoriality principle which held Thai law to have no jurisdiction over foreigners. These reforms allowed for Thai law to be in accord with Western legal norms, establishing the principle of individual property rights guaranteed by the state. Chulalongkorn's gradualist policy served to allow these reforms to occur with remarkably little opposition, in contrast to the need for the British to militarily "pacify" Burma during the same period.

Indeed, there was little change in the conditions of the mass of the rural population during this time. The creation of a modern state around an existing Buddhist monarchy took place with the use of resources generated from external sources and manpower, European and Chinese. Visible change could be seen in Bangkok, the capital, but elsewhere life proceeded much as before. Nothing had occurred to upset the principles of the legitimacy of the Thai monarchy, and the government's discreet introduction of changes during the following decades was rarely questioned.

Chulalongkorn's successors began to change the political culture of Thailand in the 1910s and 1920s, much in keeping with political changes taking place around the world at that time. Wachirawut (Rama VI, 1910–25) introduced nationalism into Thai political discourse. A royal pamphleteer with some European prejudices picked up during his education abroad, he attempted to defend Thai culture and wrote nationalistic and anti-Chinese essays. Arguing that the strength of the West came from the nature of social and family structures found there, he introduced surnames into Thailand, as well as Western sports and organizations such as the Boy Scouts, and the principle of compulsory primary education. While in practice his changes had little immediate effect, the course for creating modern Thailand had been set. His successor, Rama VII (1925–35), dallied with the idea of introducing Western-style democracy and constitutionalism but was overtaken by events.

Opposition to absolute monarchy among the Bangkok elite circles developed in the late 1920s and early 1930s because Rama VII, who believed in constitutional government, was reluctant to act the autocrat. At the same time there was growing unhappiness among many young commoners who had been trained for the new roles in government and administration but whose ambitions were thwarted by the king's continued reliance on princes and other members of the royal family for top civil and military appointments. As the government's revenues shrank in the early 1930s as a result of the world economic depression, many of the commoners who had been brought into the government feared they would lose their new privileged positions. The result was a coup in 1932 which ended the absolute powers of the king but had no impact on the country at large. Thailand became a constitutional monarchy without a revolutionary shot being fired. The republican moment came as the result of bureaucratic intrigue, not of a strident call from the oppressed masses demanding their democratic rights. While the world economic depression of the early 1930s resulted in a peasant revolt in Burma, it precipitated another step toward freedom in Thailand.

≺ IV ≻

Thailand and Burma—The Contrasting Fates of Immigrant Communities

Paradoxically, in an age which has been riven with nationalism, one of the criteria for judging the degree to which a society was free in the twentieth century has been the way it has treated immigrant communities in its midst. The nineteenth and twentieth centuries saw widespread immigration across Asia. However, immigrant labor and immigrant capital have played very contrasting roles in Thailand and Burma. Chinese and Indians immigrated to both countries; but because of Burma's link with British India, Indians far outnumbered all other immigrants there, amounting by the 1930s to 7 percent of the population. More than half the population of Rangoon, the capital, were of Indian ethnic descent. By contrast, the long links between Chinese traders and the Thai court, and the ease of immigration to the south, meant that Chinese immigrants to Thailand amounted to over 12 percent of the population by the same time, again with a large concentration in the capital city. But the political responses of the indigenous populations to the presence of such a large number of immigrants in their midst were markedly different.

The relatively low rate of economic growth in Thailand prior to the 1960s meant that Chinese economic penetration of the countryside was relatively slow and unobtrusive. In Burma, on the other hand, there was a demand for capital to expand agricultural production and only Indian moneylenders provided enough to meet demands. Indigenous moneylenders were soon squeezed out by their better capitalized foreign competitors. At each agrarian depression from the 1890s to the 1930s, more land fell into the hands of foreign moneylenders; by the early 1930s more than half of the best agricultural land in the country was controlled by them. The Burmese peasantry was being turned into a foreign-employed agricultural proletariat. And when Burmese migrated to the cities and modern industries in search of work, they were in competition with Indian laborers, as evidenced by the dockworker riots and oil field strikes of the 1930s. This was fertile ground for nationalist politicians and from the 1920s onward demands for land reform and the expulsion of Indian capitalists and laborers grew. Local organizations organized campaigns to boycott the payment of taxes and rent and large amounts of land were confiscated by the armed Indian police, called the "punitive police," which the British used to control the countryside. Thailand was never to see such a phenomenon until the 1960s and then nothing on the scale that occurred in Burma.

The Chinese in Thailand tended to assimilate more readily than the Indian population in Burma which, because of their protected legal status under the colonial regime, lived outside the jurisdiction of Burmese Buddhist law. Not having a powerful external protector, the Chinese in Thailand accommodated themselves to their new hosts more quickly. Also, the Chinese immigrants to Thailand did not compete for land and employment with the indigenous population but took urban jobs which developed with the growth of trade. The abolition of the old system of corvee labor also opened new opportunities for labor which the indigenous population did not seek. Whereas the growth of the foreign population in Thailand might have been interpreted as a blessing as it relieved tax pressures on the indigenous population and generated surpluses for the Thai state, in Burma the population came to feel displaced in their own country.

The extra-territorial rights of the Chinese population ended by the beginning of the century; and as the wealthiest Chinese had become so useful to the Thai king, they were ennobled and brought into the ranks of the new elite, often as government officials. In Burma, the Indian elite remained dependent on the British and while useful to the colonial state, were perceived by the indigenous population as part of the oppressive regime they sought to eliminate. The fate of the Indian community in Burma was sealed at independence; and by the time of the military coup of 1962 and the wholesale nationalization of the economy, Indian wealth in Burma had no protectors.

Despite the rise of Chinese nationalism in the twentieth century and the growth of a more politically and economically aware population, the modus vivendi which had been worked out between the Thai state and the Chinese population survived so sturdily that by the 1990s one could easily talk of the Sino-Thai elite in Bangkok. And though racial stereotypes adopted from the West were sometimes crudely deployed, such as when Rama VI published a tract entitled *Jews of the East* in 1914, the Thai political institutions provided no effective vent to such sentiments and these ideas did not land on fertile soil. The conditions for the race riots and religious attacks that became prevalent in Rangoon and other Burmese cities during the depths of the depression in the 1930s did not exist in Bangkok or in the countryside.

The growth of Thai nationalism in the 1930s did produce pressure on the Chinese community to assimilate into Thai society. The pro-Japanese military governments of Field Marshall Pibun, especially after 1938, attempted to break the Chinese hold on the economy. Businesses were for a time expected to take Thai names and an ineffectually backed government cooperative scheme attempted to supplant Chinese traders in rural areas. But these problems seem to have concerned the elite more than the mass of the population and there was relatively little friction between ethnic groups throughout the twentieth century. Only during World War II did Pibun's Japanese-allied government take more drastic measures to control the Chinese population, including limiting the right to reside anywhere; but the fall of his government in 1944 brought an end to this policy. The war years were much harsher on the Indian community in Burma, and many Indians fled with the British following the Japanese invasion.

Pibun's return to power in 1947 once more saw the government adopt policies intended to limit Chinese control of the economy. These were now portrayed, however, as limiting the growth of Communism among the Chinese community following the successful taking of power by the Communist Party in Beijing, rather than as being anti-Chinese. They did not prove to be a serious impediment to the continued development of a political economy of mutual convenience for Thai army officers and bureaucrats and Chinese business leaders. Protection and assistance from the state became essential for doing business and Thai cabinet ministers and generals were in the 1950s brought onto the boards of major Chinese-owned organizations in large numbers. The growth of the economy and the development of a Thai form of capitalism thus became mutually convenient. Without the political pressures which militant peasant movements generated elsewhere in Southeast Asia at this time, Thai politics adopted the conservative cast which allowed for the emergence of institutions of bourgeois democracy in subsequent years.

The contrasting fortunes of the Indian minority in Burma and the

Chinese minority in Thailand underline the theme of the differing fates of modern freedom in the two societies. By the 1990s, Thailand lived easily with the idea of a Sino-Thai business elite with great political power. Even a provincial businessman of Chinese descent could be elected prime minister in the mid-1990s. But the Indian minority in Burma was effectively ousted from any political or major economic role by the early 1960s. Though the reasons are complex and the process less sudden than this description may convey, the granting of independence in 1948 had sealed the fate of the remaining Indian population. Capitalism and bourgeois democracy to many older Burmese still means foreign domination and serves as a prop to continued autarkic authoritarianism.

V

Thailand—Post-Monarchical Dictators for Capitalism

At the time that the remaining countries of Southeast Asia were experiencing mass mobilization movements in the name of nationalism as well as economic redistribution in favor of the majority peasantry, often with disastrous economic consequences and the creation of the authoritarian political systems necessary to extract the resources of the society to mount grandiose socialist development projects, Thailand was gradually evolving from absolute monarchy through military dictatorship to democracy. There emerged by the 1950s a political elite and a political culture which were distinctly less radical than those characterizing any of its previously colonized neighbors. The bureaucratic polity that Fred Riggs described in the 1960s[10] may not have been democratic, but it produced a remarkably stable political order, possible only through the absence of politicization in the majority of the Thai population. Their acceptance until the 1970s of their rulers being unconstrained by electoral politics permitted the continuance of gradual social and economic change, which, in turn, established the conditions for eventual political evolution toward democratic institutions. Freedom within the state became possible because of the state's overwhelming control of Thai society. This control was consolidated during these years of military rule.

The army was clearly the dominant political institution from the time of the 1932 coup. Following a brief period of civilian government after the war, Field Marshal Pibun returned to power as prime minister in 1947. His eventual fall from office in a coup led by his former subordinates is illustrative of the elite politics which persisted in Thailand, unhindered by serious regard for ideological trends or popular opinion. The heads of the army and the border police, Generals Sarit Thanarat and Phao Siyanon, were both jockeying for Pibun's post, but Pibun, to strengthen his position as he was no longer directly in command of troops, sought to open the political system to popular forces. His efforts led to victory for him in elections held early in 1957. These were followed later that year by a military coup led by General Sarit Thanarat, which the army justified because the "situation got out of hand." The elected parliament provided an arena for criticism of the government and the army, which, coupled with demands from representatives of the poverty-stricken northeast of the country for economic redistribution and administrative decentralization, raised in the minds of the Bangkok elite the specter of revolutionary change.

This was but one of the more than eighteen coups or attempted coups which Thailand experienced after 1932. Unlike the governments formed after most of these, however, Sarit's regime lasted for fifteen years with strong backing from the United States, especially during the Vietnam War era when Thailand became a major base for U.S. forces fighting in neighboring Indochina. The close ties between Thailand and the United States, which generated massive aid flows from the U.S. and Japan, as well as significant levels of foreign investment, commenced the industrialization of the Thai economy. By the 1980s Thailand had become one of the new economic tigers of Asia. At the time Sarit took office, it was the prevailing view that peasant-based Asian economies such as Thailand were incapable of industrialization; but that was a Western conceit soon proved to be wrong.

Sarit was in many ways the archetypical "third world" dictator. Lacking the foreign experience of his predecessors, he was much more rooted in Thai intellectual traditions which regarded correct behavior and social stability to be paramount goals for the government. The government existed to protect the people, and politics as practiced in Western societies was to be eschewed because it would lead to divisions in society. His paternalistic view of government ensured that power was used to control society, not to create space for democratic institutions. For Sarit, the people should remain agrarian in outlook and condition while the government, as represented by civil servants, would look after their interests. Social mobilization should be minimized so as not to cause disintegration of traditional institutions and values.

As Thak Chaloemtiarana argues,[11] Sarit's views should not be considered merely as those of a political reactionary, for he saw these traditional goals as part of the road to the further modernization of Thailand. He referred to his seizure of power as not a crude coup d'etat but rather a revolution. He wanted to make Thailand a modern nation around traditional Thai concepts of king, religion, and nation, the three symbols that had come to encapsulate the established version of Thai national feelings. As a consequence, he saw Communism as a threat to king and religion; hence his Cold War alliance with the United States was not motivated purely for the economic rewards it brought. Believing in simple virtues such that national well-being could be defined in terms of environmental cleanliness, the appropriateness of arrangements, and material well-being, Sarit explicitly limited freedom as a political aspiration.

But as with so many political blueprints created to achieve a predetermined goal, the results of Sarit's policies were very different. The social changes which occurred and were sometimes even encouraged made the goals of proper social order and behavior on the part of the people more difficult to achieve. This difficulty was seen outwardly in changes growing out of the rapid urbanization of first Bangkok and then other Thai cities as a result of economic growth and the injection of large amounts of foreign capital into the economy. Thailand was opened to American and other foreign cultural influences, which led to the deterioration of traditional social attitudes and practices. The rapid expansion of education created a large, politically aware, and vocal student population which did not share the values of their conservative rulers but were in tune with American anti-Vietnam war protesters at the American universities to which many young Thais were sent to study.

In the late 1960s, following Sarit's death, the Thai military government installed a new constitution under which a parliament with no powers to unseat the government was created. But even this largely powerless body displayed too much independence for the generals. The government conducted a coup against itself in 1971, dissolved the parliament, and increased political controls. Like those of the parliament that existed briefly in the 1950s, the representatives made attempts to gain more authority for themselves. Doing so was perceived as a legislative threat to bureaucratic privilege and carried the risk that younger army officers' routes to power and wealth would be cut off before their turn had arrived. The phony coup of 1971, like those which preceded it, was justified by the army in terms of the need to limit crime, excessive criticism, and economic deterioration and of the necessity for a strong government in the uncertain international environment of the early 1970s.

Aware of the need to provide some form of ostensibly democratic trappings for the regime, the army created in 1972 a legislature, every member of which was, however, appointed. This legislature merely provided a forum for factional politics within the army to play themselves out in another, and more public, arena. The sham, however, angered the thousands of university students who were now studying in Bangkok and they began to support civilian politicians' demands for increased participation in government. Factionalism within the armed forces allowed civilian politicians, backed by the increasingly influential and vocal business community which had developed leverage over the government because of its crucial role in national prosperity, to form alliances with rival army camps and thus establish links to the very center of power.

During 1973 thousands of Thai university students, perhaps emboldened by the models of American students demonstrating against the Vietnam War, took to the streets in Bangkok to demand the return to civilian rule. The severe factionalism in the army made their protests possible, for the army was split on how to respond. Following the 1971 spurious coup, the military government had put itself in a difficult position. It could not put together a tame partially-elected parliament to serve it. Infighting over position and power made the government appear without purpose and without unity. The administration of the country was becoming increasingly militarized, making the regime even more isolated from public opinion. Meanwhile, the middle class from which the students mostly came had grown as a consequence of the growth of the Thai economy and the development of large banking, manufacturing, and trading firms, often with links with the United States, Japan, and beyond.

Opposition political groups had become better organized. While students provided a catalyst for political change, it was the political power generated by other groups such as the foreign-oriented English-language press and the growing business community which forced the army to stand down in 1973. The end of the Vietnam War in the eyes of many undermined the military's rationale for continued military rule. Crucial to this result was the role of the king, who as a consequence of the army's own anti-communist campaigns had greater power and prestige than ever before, despite his nominal position in the constitutional order. When the king publicly backed the students, the last shred of legitimacy of the military regime dissolved in front of the public. The events of 1973 at first bred euphoric expectations that the role of the military in Thai politics was now over and that a new regime predicated on modern ideas of democratic freedom would inevitably emerge.

But the patterns of Thai politics of 1932 or 1958 had not yet been erased. What occurred in 1973 was the first of several similar episodes during the next two decades until the balance of power finally swung apparently decisively in favor of civilian political parties and electoral politics and the era of military-run governments ended. As was to reoccur again and again until the early 1990s, a civilian head of government emerged who promised reform and a new constitution. Elections were held and it appeared that a new bourgeois democratic order had been established. Freedom of the press blossomed and trade unions and peasant organizations began to urge their members' interests. A constitutional convention, which was appointed by the king, produced a conservative document that kept ultimate political power firmly in the hands of the government. Finally elections were held in January 1975. Though the freest and most fiercely contested campaign in Thai political history up to then, it clearly was affected by money and violence in the electoral process. The government formed after the elections was forced to call new elections within a year and a similarly unstable situation emerged.

Soon another military coup took place which brought back once more a full-blown military government, equally as repressive as that ousted three years earlier. Though the immediate catalyst to this coup was student protests at the return from exile in Taiwan of one of the key dictators ousted in 1973, giving rise to rhetoric emotionally charged with claims of acts of *lèse majesté*, the underlying issue was a contest between the army and civilian political forces over control of the government. In particular, the army was concerned about attempts by parliament to limit its control of the military budget, the running down of the military's close alliance with the United States, and the intervention of other groups representing new demands in politics and administration which made bribery difficult and undermined the economic role of the bureaucratic elite in favor of rising business groups. The political atmosphere in the country was now very different from what it had been a decade earlier. Peasant unrest had become widespread, trade unions had by now organized in key industries, and almost daily there were protests and demonstrations on the streets of the increasingly crowded capital. Control of the economy had passed from the state to the private sector and political freedom reemerged in the space thus created.

Initially, however, the atmosphere following this coup was very repressive. Many students and leaders of the minuscule political left fled the capital and joined with the out-of-date, largely Chinese-led Thai Communist Party until they became disillusioned with its illiberal and antiquated policies. Though a civilian façade was created by the military in an attempt to soften the government's image, the harshly authoritarian regime had a chilling effect which soon earned it the enmity and non-cooperation of large segments of the increasingly prosperous and progressive urban middle classes. Within two years the army had intervened again and installed a new government which pursued much more moderate policies; in retrospect, this installation can be seen to be the beginning of attempts by the military to learn to share power with civilian political classes. In 1979 new elections took place under a conservative constitution which allowed for half the membership of Parliament to be elected.

The successive governments of the 1980s were composed of a mixture of army leaders and moderate politicians who worked together to develop a modus vivendi that allowed for a degree of power sharing while addressing some of the major issues which had emerged in the Thai polity during the boom years of the 1960s and 1970s. One was rural armed insurgency which had been swelled by the students who had fled the cities after the 1976 coup. The governments of General Prem Tinsulanonda, the astute unelected prime minister for many years, worked with the elected civilians in the parliament to pursue a moderate program of political inducements designed to entice students and others back from the jungle and it succeeded. Former guerrilla fighters were granted amnesties and many were provided land on which they could settle. Similarly, the government adopted wealth redistribution policies of the kind resisted by the military in previous decades. In particular more attention was paid to the development of the poorer rural areas of the country well away from the prosperous Bangkok municipal area and the central plains but increasingly politically important with the development of national electoral institutions.

Put in a political language which became popular only subsequently, the army had seen the need to provide democratic space for other autonomous political forces in civil society to emerge. Recognizing that political power and financial security could be achieved in a contest which was not a zero sum game, the army came to share power, sometimes reluctantly and certainly with many misunderstandings along the way, with technocrats and urban specialists as well as provincial business people and politicians. The tight bureaucratic control of the central Bangkok bureaucracy which Chulalongkorn had constructed a century before began to be loosened, with elections being permitted and local bosses of great influence emerging to head financially powerful political machines.

The opening up of the Thai political system also provided openings for money politics and new forms of manipulation.[12] Strikes by trade unionists in government-owned industries over privatization plans and the like were often orchestrated to embarrass ministers and protect privileged positions. Wealthy individuals came to dominate party politics as creating incentives to get out the vote became widespread. But the locus of power had shifted from the military-bureaucratic polity that Riggs described so convincingly in the 1960s to a new, if sometimes unstable, parliamentary order. The monarchy remained a stabilizing institution during this period of transition. And the Thai commercial economy had evolved from being a noticeably Chinese-dominated phenomenon to being effectively indigenized through intermarriage and acculturation.

Rural politics, as suggested above, has come to be controlled by powerful bosses with wealth to control election outcomes. As the majority of the population remains, as Sarit had hoped, rural in outlook and occupied with agriculture, there is great potential for provincial business people to mobilize voters for their parties and take control. But this leads to a form of corruption and nepotism in politics which the Bangkok middle-class sophisticates who seek "clean" governments find distasteful. In a wonderful paradox, the demand for "clean" government led in February 1991 to a brief alliance of the Bangkok civilian elite with the military in the last successful coup which ousted a government dominated by rural interests. In less than a year, however, the army was forced to abandon power as students took to the streets demanding the restoration of democracy. A kind of democracy has been established in Thailand, which has now experienced its longest period of civilian government since the coup of 1932 ended the absolute monarchy.[13]

This transformation has taken place in the context of remarkably stable social and political attitudes. As power has been redistributed in Thailand, the constitutional monarch and the established institutions of Thai society, most especially the Buddhist faith, have remained largely unaffected, if not actually more secure than before. The development of a kind of pluralism, in which urban classes are allowed to enjoy their wealth and international links, the rural population gets minor rewards and benefits through the political system, and the bureaucracy, including the army, still maintains its position among the institutions of prestige, has resulted in a strikingly successful, if unusual, democracy. Even the collapse of the national economy in 1997 did not prompt another coup, and party politics has managed what could have been a major national crisis without the legitimacy of ruling institutions being severely challenged. The evolution of freedom in Thailand during the second half of the last century stands in marked contrast to the experience of neighboring Burma during the same period.

≺ VI ≻

Burma—Dictatorship for the Working People

The course of freedom in Burma took a very different and many would say unexpected route from that of Thailand during the twentieth century. By the end of the 1930s, Burma was formally one of the most advanced democratic colonies in the world, even though the British-appointed governor had powerful residual powers. The

1935 Government of Burma Act had created a constitutional order which allowed for an elected premier and cabinet with responsibility for all government powers other than foreign affairs and the currency. While this system excluded the frontier areas and heavily over-represented urban areas, the overwhelming majority of the population was eligible to be involved in electoral politics. The franchise had been made as wide as it was in England. The participation rate had increased by 1936, the year of the last election before World War II, to over 50 percent. Political parties were well organized and had auxiliary organizations as young men and women were recruited into politics with spirited patriotic calls. Rangoon and Mandalay had a lively, independent press; political debate was widespread; university students were politically engaged; and Burmese politicians, Indian and Chinese businessmen, and British civil servants were learning how to manage a political system which British policy intended to evolve into a stable, conservative democratic order.[14]

But two forces combined to upset those plans. One was the catastrophic destruction of World War II and the other was the growing support for Burmese nationalist politicians who demanded more than a role in government for themselves and sought a massive redistribution of social and economic power to put the Burmese economy back into the hands of the indigenous population. The mass mobilization of radical nationalism flourished during the chaos of war. While the Japanese invasion of Thailand was not resisted, and was indeed perhaps initially welcomed by the government, in Burma the British adopted a scorched earth policy as they retreated in the face of overwhelming Japanese armed forces. Four years later, as the Japanese retreated, this destruction was compounded. The economy was seriously dislocated and economic production did not return to pre-war levels until the end of the 1950s. Thousands of Indian immigrant workers fled back to India during the war years, which became a time of great privation for the remaining population.

The war years also saw the rising power of a new political class which had resisted the attractions of the British-created democracy of the 1930s. In the mid-1930s, a new nationalist organization, the *Dobama Asiayon* (We Burmans Association), founded by a traditionally educated novelist, poet, and Buddhist philosopher, Thakin

Kodaw Hmaing, but soon taken over by students at Rangoon University, demanded non-cooperation with the British and immediate independence. The movement was led by those who became the political elite of the country after independence, many of whom saw in World War II an opportunity to strike for Burma's independence. Marxism and Communist ideology derived from both the Soviet and the Chinese Communist Parties as described in the writings of Western journalists, as well as Fabian Socialist tracts, provided their political models. But Fascist Japan provided the first opportunity to seize power.

The so-called "Thirty Comrades," who became legends in Burmese nationalist historiography, marched in with the invading Japanese in 1941 as the nucleus of a new Burma army which in the name of freedom would wrest independence from the British. Led by General Aung San, and including many of the major figures in Burmese military and Communist circles after the war, the Burma Independence Army, as it became known, four years later entered into an alliance with the returning British in conjunction with political organizers from the Burma Communist Party. While the details of all the political groups and interests involved in this heady period need not detain us here, what was clearly the case was that during the wartime period, when arms were liberally distributed across the country, there was a great mobilization of popular political energy. The defeat of the Japanese had lifted the lid on political quietism and in 1945 a myriad of political groups emerged and came together, in first the Anti-Fascist Organization, and later the Anti-Fascist People's Freedom League (AFPFL), to demand immediate independence.

Arms and politics became intimately mixed. In the negotiations which emerged after the war with first the British military administration and subsequently the restored civilian government of the British governor, the AFPFL, despite the ideological differences of the many groups which composed it, remained united in the demand for independence. Moreover, General Aung San, who had resigned from the army to lead the AFPFL, had behind him a number of independent private "pocket armies" of formally demobilized but still armed troops which could be mobilized in armed support of the nationalist forces should negotiations fail. When Lord Mountbatten, the governor general of India, made it clear to the British government that if armed revolt broke out in Burma there would be no Indian troops available to put down a widespread peasant revolt as had happened in the 1930s, Burma's independence was assured. At that point, the British merely aspired to leave Burma in the hands of a government which would be friendly to remaining British and Indian interests. This meant, in those early days of the Cold War, insuring that the Burmese Communist Party and its allies did not take power.

Negotiations ensued between the AFPFL and the British government, which resulted in independence on January 4, 1948. Six months earlier, however, Aung San and other members of the putative government had been assassinated by political rivals. The independent government, which excluded the Communist Party earlier expelled from the AFPFL for its opposition to the independence treaty and for its demands for revolutionary land reform and the nationalization of British-owned industries, immediately faced severe tests. Despite its having won a national election in 1947, its legitimacy was in doubt because of the low voter turnout, barely a third in the most politicized parts of the country including Rangoon. The success of the government and the governing parties in encouraging support for the government was balanced, if not overwhelmed, by the support for an election boycott and tax and rent strikes on the part of the peasant majority led by the Communists and other left-wing anti-government groups.

Within months of independence, the government was surrounded by armed enemies on all sides. The Burma Communist movement, itself split into two factions, had become during the war years a major political force in the country. In the organizing of peasant support for the nationalist movement, and the maintaining of political uncertainty and revolutionary fervor, the Communists were the most visible political force in the three years between the end of the war and the formal grant of independence. However, the leaders of the Communists were not the beneficiaries of independence, the fruits of which fell to their former allies in student and anti-Japanese politics of the previous decade. Though one small faction of the Communists had threatened to take up arms against the government, the situation remained largely peaceful (except for Muslim separatists in Arakan Province) until three months after independence, when the government ordered the arrest of the Communist leadership.

From their friends in the government, of course, the Communists knew what was about to transpire and immediately went underground where they organized a guerrilla campaign against the government. Moreover, the armed forces of the government soon split, with a sizable number marching off, with their arms, to become the nucleus of a Communist liberation force along with units of the AFPFL's pocket armies which had not been demobilized at independence. Burma in 1948 not only achieved independence, but also had a civil war.

Though the government attempted from time to time to open negotiations with the rebel Communists, agreement could never be achieved. As long as the parliamentary system of government existed, much of the legal opposition to the government maintained links with their armed compatriots, making serious bargaining the more difficult. Meanwhile, the security forces felt justified in using both authorized and extrajudicial measures to try to keep their armed opponents in check. The Burma Communist Party did not surrender for more than 40 years, though its widespread popularity soon waned as the population wearied of continual political unrest and bloodshed. Cynicism and apathy followed quickly on from euphoria and hope as ambitions were dashed and life did not become better because the colonial authorities and their exactions had ended. Indeed, the tax collectors still came round and, if anything, conditions deteriorated. Years after independence, the structure of the economy had not changed; the only difference was that now most of it was owned and inefficiently operated by a Burmese nationalist government rather than Indian and British capitalists.

Many postcolonial administrations in Asia and Africa faced challenges from their domestic lefts which had been mobilized by nationalist enthusiasms for a brave new postwar world. The government of Burma faced as well both a severe challenge from its right and an external invader. As part of the process of British withdrawal and the establishment of a new constitutional order, most of the leaders of the minority groups living in the frontier areas came to an agreement with the Burmese government which permitted them and their societies a degree of autonomy from central government control, thus maintaining the differential administrative and political arrangements which the British had introduced between the majority and minority areas. However, leaders of one community, those of the minority Christian Karen population, which felt particularly loyal to the British, refused to enter into an agreement with the AFPFL. Though the Christians were themselves a minority of the Karen population in the country, their power and influence was disproportionate because of their mastery of English and close links with British institutions and foreign missionaries.

Karens had been one of the beneficiaries of the inversion of social order that occurred at the time of the dethronement of King Thibaw. From being a marginalized social group living in the hills, as a result of the work of British and American missionaries they became stalwarts of the indigenous armed forces and police. The first commander of the Burmese army was himself a Karen Christian, trained by the British. Karen troops remained loyal to the British during the Japanese occupation, thus putting them at odds and out of sympathy with their Burmese nationalist compatriots. Moreover, the Karen National Union (KNU), the oldest political organization in Burma, with its origins tracing back to the 1880s, believed that Karens had been promised separate status by the British, a form of Karenistan. Irresponsible politicians in Britain and British veterans of the war in Burma provided this view with some credence.

Soon Karen units of the armed forces also went into revolt against the government. The Karen National Defence Organisation, the armed front of the KNU, proved to be a powerful opponent. Within a year of gaining independence, the government had control of little more than the capital city and one or two other towns. While fighting armed opponents of this magnitude, the government incurred an additional challenge in the form of the incursion of Chinese Nationalist (Kuomintang or KMT) troops fleeing the victorious People's Liberation Army from Yunnan Province. Backed by the government of the Republic of China on Taiwan and the U.S. Central Intelligence Agency, and receiving the cooperation of the Thai border authorities, the KMT troops posed two threats to Burma. One was the possibility of a Chinese Communist invasion to drive the KMT out; the other, not yet apparent to the outside world, was the establishment of the opium and heroin trades which have subsequently thrived in the area as a result of the initial protection the KMT troops provided. While the first threat was forestalled, largely due to the forebearance of the Chinese authorities, the latter has now become a major international issue.

The unpropitious circumstances of the launch of the post-independence democratic constitution of Burma could hardly have been greater. The AFPFL, itself composed of a variety of factions, some armed and supporting the government when successfully appeased, was a weak coalition on which to build a new state.[15] Many of the most experienced administrators resigned at independence, just when the government was launching programs to nationalize large parts of the economy. This rickety machine could not produce much in the way of resources to finance a successful state or to satisfy a military which felt justified in its demands for resources as it was the only loyal instrument the civilian government of bickering politicians had by which to cling to power.

Despite conditions in the country, there was a degree of democratic life in Burma during the 1950s. The English-language press was remarkably critical of the government from time to time and the Burmese-language press, which had its foreign ideological backers, nearly equally so. Student politics were exuberant and almost always anti-government as they were often linked with the underground Communist Party. And elections were held, even following an eighteen-month period when the army governed after a serious split in the ruling coalition which once more threatened serious armed conflict among forces supporting different factions in the cabinet. The 1960 election, the last multi-party election held until 1990, generated more popular participation than those held in 1951 and 1956. But beneath the facade of elections were two poorly hidden realities. One was that the armed forces had established themselves during the previous decades as a parallel government in large parts of the country such as the northern Shan States, where the KMT had invaded and martial law had been declared in the early 1950s. The other was that the party system was not rooted in commercial or industrial interests separate from the government. Controlling government office was the only route to wealth and security in Burma but still involved a very small number of people and interests.

In terms of political principles and institutions, constitutionally post-independence Burma looked remarkably like pre-independence Burma, except for the minority hill tribe areas along the northern borders. Here notions of egalitarian rights under a national regime had not been introduced by the British; but the postcolonial administration, fired by the ideals of egalitarian nationalism, wished to see these areas and their peoples integrated into the larger polity. The constitutional compromises of 1947 which had preserved the powers of the Shan Sawbwas and other traditional rulers were seriously questioned by the socialist politicians of the majority, who viewed these as feudal anachronisms. The government sought to negotiate the end of these rights in the mid-1950s and this process was completed in 1958 under a temporary military caretaker government. When in 1962 the civilian government of Prime Minister U Nu offered to negotiate a degree of greater autonomy for the leaders of the Shan States, the army viewed this offer as a threat to the unity of the country and used it to justify the military coup of that year.

The senior officer corps of the Burma army eventually drew two lessons from their experiences at the time of independence and subsequently. The first was that it was necessary to keep party factionalism out of the army, and perhaps out of the administration, because it was the disunity generated by ideological and ethnic rivalries within the armed forces in the early months of independence which could have resulted in the country once more losing its independence. The other was that civilian politicians, often with their own foreign allies, were a threat to the unity and stability of the country.

In March, 1962, the Burma army, under its commander, General Ne Win, launched a coup against the government of Prime Minister U Nu. The army soon set about creating a new political order in Burma similar to that attempted in many other newly independent countries in Asia and Africa. A one party, socialist state, one which would mobilize public support through authoritarian political institutions and strongly nationalistic economic policies, would overcome, in the army's view, the country's weaknesses. The result was a 26-year period of joint rule by the army and its creation, the Burma Socialist Programme Party; the suppression of the independent press and independent political and social organizations; the nationalization and impoverishment of the educational system; and eventual human disaster as economic growth failed to keep pace with population growth. During the period Thailand was economically growing and politically evolving away from military government while engaging with the larger world, Burma became increasingly isolated and stagnant. As the institutions of bourgeois democracy were stifled and repressed, the military became by default the only powerful institution in the society.

Despite the government's aspiration to create a unified political and administrative system linking all parts together as one nation, the absence of economic growth and development during the 1960s and 1970s sapped the state's ability to incorporate the frontier areas into the national economy. As a result a form of freedom outside the state, in the grey areas of contested control along the country's long borders with Thailand, Laos, and China, emerged in the form of smuggling and insurgency. Here, beyond the reach of the state, freedom for the group was championed over the freedom of the individual as a plethora of separatist groups contested with each other and with the central government's army for control of land and resources.

The failure of the military-led socialist one-party order in Burma was revealed to the world in the upheavals that occurred in the country in 1988 as minor student disturbances turned into major popular demands for a change in regime.[16] But the outcome of those pro-democracy demonstrations has been a great disappointment to advocates of democracy around the world. Coming soon after the fall of the Marcos regime in the Philippines, but prior to the wave of change in Eastern Europe and the former Soviet Union that followed the collapse of the Berlin wall, the repressive socialist order in Burma, having demonstrated its bankruptcy and even admitted its failure, would, it was felt, be replaced by a new democratic order. This has not happened. Rather, even though elections were held in 1990, the civilian politicians elected were denied their claim to power. The army has held on to power, ignoring calls from the National League for Democracy, student groups, and others within the country, and ignoring the economic sanctions of many Western governments.

Which is not to say that there has been no political change in Burma since 1988. Prior to that time, the army failed to enter into negotiations not only with the former Communists but also with the plethora of ethnic minorities in the border areas who were also in armed revolt against the central government. Since then, however, the Communists have surrendered and all but three of the armed ethnic insurgents have entered into a cease-fire with the government. These changes have allowed for the opening up of the economies of the border areas, which while limiting the capacity of the government to formally control these territories, in reality has created a more effective means of supervising political developments and economic life.

≺ VII ≻

Freedom in Thailand and Burma: Contrasting Institutional Fates

This chapter has tried to suggest some of the reasons for the different fates of concepts and institutions of freedom in Thailand and Burma during the past two centuries. The idea of freedom has been present in both countries throughout the period being assessed. But the results have been strikingly different. Thailand, in the name of conservative monarchical self-preservation and anti-communism, has evolved as the formally freer of two societies which started from similar conditions. Burma, in the name of modern capitalism and imperialism, and their even more modern antitheses, socialism and nationalism, has created a society which remains under the control of an unelected, unrepresentative military government. During the first half of the twentieth century, the call for freedom and democracy, and the demand for social justice and change, was heard repeatedly in Burma, but was nearly mute in Thailand. In the second half, the demand for freedom was raised in Thailand but thwarted in Burma.

One can explain the differences partially as a result of contingent circumstances. Geography helped ensure that Thailand in the nineteenth century could more easily maintain its independence from European imperialism because it was not a sizable market, it was not perceived as a route to the fabled markets of China, and it posed no threat to anyone as long as it remained autonomous. Burma, with its long borders with both China and India, would always have been seen as a potential source of threat to the security of either. And similar circumstances continued to produce similar results in the next century. While Thailand saw Communist China and perhaps Communist Vietnam as a threat which needed to be balanced by a powerful ally, the United States, Burma saw that its position between rivals India and China required that it antagonize neither. Neutrality made sense for one; alliances for the other.

But it was the internal configuration of political power which was the more important for determining the outcome of the past two centuries in terms of freedom. The transition from military authoritarianism in Thailand resulted from a number of factors which generated powerful political forces with the economic and organizational capacity not only to challenge the political power of the government, but also to share their wealth and prestige with the military. The demand for democracy in Thailand has been based on more than a demand for a change of regime. It has been rooted in powerful, established classes and institutions which enhanced the capacity of the state to govern the country for mutual benefit. As a result, the institutions of a democratic state emerged inclusive of a multiplicity of interests as the alternative of fleeing the state's coercive machinery disappeared. It was the long shadow of the bureaucratic centralization of Thailand by the absolute monarchs of the nineteenth century which created the conditions for the political opening of the twentieth.

But in Burma, there has since independence been no development of independent social classes and economic interests to challenge the power of the armed bureaucracy. Indeed, the effect of socialist policies has been to undermine independent economic power. Such power had once existed only because of the support it received from an illegitimate colonial ruler. In an age of nationalism, arguments about the need for balanced democratic institutions and the rule of law were easily lost in the strident demands for justice for the indigenous majority and the end of the unequal distribution of resources in favor of aliens. In such circumstances, seeking freedom outside the state, in the black market and through separatist movements and insurgency, becomes the modern equivalent of the older form of freedom which existed outside the reach of the king when freedom was not available within the confines of the state. Once power had become monopolized, it was much harder to find a way of granting freedom without having the entire edifice of the state appear to be threatened.

Ironically, only powerful, self-confident governments can permit their populations freedom within the state. The sapping of the strength of the state in Burma since World War II has made governing the country through institutions which encourage freedom seem to those in power to be too difficult. The contrasting strength of the Thai state to control events within that country has encouraged the rulers there to compromise and eventually encourage ideas of freedom to emerge. If it is indeed the case that "when all else fails, clubs are trumps," the way to encourage freedom to grow is to ensure that all else does not fail.

≺ 6 ≻

Reverberations of Freedom in the Philippines and Vietnam

BENEDICT J. TRIA KERKVLIET

THIS CHAPTER analyzes political struggles in the Philippines and Vietnam about the meaning and practice of freedom. In neither country is "freedom" a singular idea. Each country has several and frequently contending discourses about it. I shall concentrate on three highly pronounced ones. They are also similar to discourses in other countries, including many Western ones. The three are national freedom, personal and civic freedom, and socio-economic freedom.

The political histories of the Philippines and Vietnam during the last one hundred or so years have some broad similarities. In the nineteenth century, both were colonies of Western powers. In each, anti-colonial movements emerged that eventually became a revolution for national independence. In each case the revolution was interrupted, leaving inconclusive results for several years before the country obtained independence. Vibrant debates about freedom during anti-colonial movements (beginning in the late nineteenth century in both countries) and revolutions for independence (1896-early 1900s in the Philippines; 1945–54 in Vietnam) reverberated in the subsequent period when the results of revolution were inconclusive (Philippines 1900–1946; Vietnam 1954–75) and then again after each country achieved political independence under one national government (post-1946 in the Philippines; post-1975 in Vietnam). The three discourses about freedom have frequently been in contention with each other, but in different ways in the two countries. Since the period of anti-colonial struggles, the most contentious discourses in Vietnam have concerned national and civic freedoms. In the Philippines, however, debates over national and civic freedoms have been relatively subdued; more intense have been struggles over socio-economic freedom. Helping to explain these different patterns are the contrasts between how the two countries became independent and between the regimes that have ruled since.

≺ I ≻

Possible Roots of "Freedom" as an Idea

The principal elements of Philippine and Vietnamese societies had long been families and small communities, typically built on kinship and lineage. They remained so on the eve of anti-colonial struggles in the late nineteenth century. In most areas families and communities were patriarchal, although women generally had more standing in the Philippine archipelago and southern Vietnam than they did in much of central and northern Vietnam.[1] Social hierarchy and authority were often determined by wealth and power measured in land, material goods, and especially personal followings, as much as by gender.

Overlaying the thousands of communities, most of them rural with inhabitants relying on agriculture and fishing for a meager living, was a governmental administration that was considerably more centralized in Vietnam than in the Philippines. For centuries, Vietnam had had dynastic rule extending from the emperor's court down to villages. The rule was based on Confucian beliefs and a strong sense of Vietnamese independence, especially from its northern neighbor, China. By the time France started to take over the country in the 1850s, Vietnam was "the paramount bureaucratic society in Southeast Asia."[2] After appropriating this apparatus, French rulers began to bend, then break it to their needs, undermining Confucianism and dividing the country into smaller administrative units. The Philippines had been nominally ruled by Spain since the 1600s but the governing infrastructure of the archipelago in the nineteenth century remained thin beyond Manila and other urban areas where the Spanish officials were concentrated. Villages and municipalities were typically rather autonomous from Manila so long as their local leaders paid tribute to the central authorities. More extensive was the Catholic church, whose Spanish religious orders had divided the archipelago among themselves and whose friars' power and ambitions often went far beyond religious matters.

How "freedom" and such related ideas as "liberty" or "independence" emerged in this nineteenth century social and political context is not well understood. The most that can be said from the evidence available is that concepts, drawing on words that previously had somewhat different meanings, evolved due to internal and external influences. In Western countries, according to Orlando Patterson's influential argument, the idea of "freedom" is traceable back to struggles against "slavery" in one or more of its several forms.[3] Societies in the Philippine archipelago and in Vietnam had social institutions involving bondage and forms of slavery, but whether those were the source of people coming to value freedom or liberty is unclear.

Precolonial and colonial societies in the Philippines typically had three, sometimes four, social groups. In Tagalog-speaking areas, for instance, the *alipin* were slaves, bonded people, and others attached to village heads (*maginoo, dato*) and to people, less powerful than those heads, called *timawa* (also *timaua*) or *maharlika* (also *maharlica*).[4] Translated into Spanish, *timawa* meant *esclavonía,* without servitude, that is, not being a bonded or an enslaved *alipin.* The Tagalog verb *timawain* meant "to set free," such as to set a person free from bondage or slavery, a common act because people often moved into and out of servitude.[5]

But these terms apparently were not commonly used in discussions of freedom during the late nineteenth century. Although the Tagalog word in the 1860s for the Spanish *libertad* (liberty, freedom) was *camaharlicaan,* based on the root word *maharlica* or free person, it does not appear in surviving Tagalog texts of the late nineteenth century, nor does it have any currency today.[6] *Matimawa* was sometimes used late in the century, such as in Marcelo del Pilar's 1889 polemical poem against Spanish rule with a stanza about "one's native land" being "free from suffering."[7] The more commonly used word for freedom, however, was *kalayaan.* It remains so to this day. Del Pilar himself used it in 1882 to convey *libertad* in his Tagalog translation of a patriotic essay written in Spanish by his compatriot José Rizal.[8] *Kalayaan* was also used during the 1880s to convey in Tagalog the European ideas of "liberty, fraternity, equality."[9] Why Filipinos used *kalayaan* rather than *katimawaan* or *kamaharlikan* is not yet well understood. But the fact suggests that the origins for ideas about "freedom" were not necessarily the antithesis of slavery, even though Filipinos since the late nineteenth century have often associated lack of *kalayaan* with enslavement. Rather, the reference point seems to have been a more positive condition about the "self" or "individual."

The origins of the word *kalayaan* are uncertain. The closest term in surviving Tagalog dictionaries from the eighteenth or nineteenth century seems to be *layao*, meaning "bodily pleasure," "gratifying or entertaining oneself," "assisting someone with her/his needs or wants," and "separating oneself from the company of others."[10] But the connection between it and *kalayaan* or the root word *laya* is hazy. The earliest recorded usage of *kalayaan* (then spelled *calayaan*) was 1864 when a Catholic priest in the Philippines, Padre Sevilla, modified the word *layao* to convey what awaits people who accept Jesus Christ and enter the kingdom of God.[11] In Manila during the early 1870s, Sevilla and del Pilar reportedly discussed the word and its meanings. For del Pilar, it took on political dimensions and referred to the "great happiness and prosperity" that would be enjoyed once Spanish oppression had ended. By the 1890s, *kalayaan* involved for many rank and file revolutionaries against Spain a "leap from the 'familial' to the 'national'," suggests Reynaldo Ileto. It combined emotions of contentment resulting from being pampered by parents and the contentment people believed their forebears had enjoyed before Spanish conquest and would be revived after Spanish rule was overthrown.[12]

In Vietnam, too, the modern idea of freedom appears to have evolved from notions involving the self. The usual Vietnamese word for freedom is *tu do*, which literally means "self-originating," "self-causing," perhaps "self-directing." It is probably connected to classical Confucian, Buddhist, and Taoist concepts of "self" and "self-strengthening."[13] By the second half of the eighteenth century, *tu do* referred to notions regarding the place of the self or the individual in the overall order of human affairs and the cosmos. It had positive connotations to those who held that individuals could bring about change rather than being at the mercy of higher authority, spiritual beings, or destiny. For others, writes Alexander Woodside, the "belief that the 'self' could 'originate' its own destiny" was frightening and "pernicious" because it could lead to lawlessness, abuse of power in human political affairs, and "a rejection of the cosmological unity of humankind with nature."[14]

Another strand in the evolution of the concept of freedom in Vietnam is the examination system by which individual men (never women) could, on their own intellectual merit, despite in some cases being poor, gain coveted positions in the bureaucracy. Underlying this system was the idea that education is a means to bringing out the good in human beings. To many Vietnamese, education involved developing one's mind and heart ("the path of inner transcendentalism"), and bureaucracy was an institutionalized version of that quest, not merely a way to use power effectively. "To the degree that the civil service examinations provided access to such forms of self-development, within government service, to people without great wealth, they did maximize freedom."[15]

Tu do and *kalayaan* and other related concepts in Vietnam and the Philippines (such as *doc lap* and *kasarinlan*, "independence") acquired new meanings in the last decades of the nineteenth century in the context of widening exposure to debates about freedom, liberty, and equality among reformers and anti-colonialists in both countries, in China, Japan, and India, as well as in Western countries. In the Philippine archipelago, claims to freedom of association, belief, and letter writing were sometimes factors in discontent and protest against colonial and Catholic church authorities even before the 1870s, the decade those assertions merged with widening demands for political and economic reforms and expressions of Philippine nationalism.[16] Beginning in the 1870s, a small but vocal and soon influential group of Filipinos studied in Madrid and other Spanish cities where they became conversant in debates in continental Europe about liberty, democracy, republicanism, among other ideas. From Spanish books and articles these and other Filipinos learned about the French and American revolutions and about such influential writers as Rousseau, Montesquieu, and Jefferson. The ideas pulsating in those revolutions and those writers' works probably first reached Vietnam indirectly through translations and other writings in Japanese and Chinese read by a handful of Vietnamese living in Japan and China from 1890 to 1910. In the 1910s to 1930s, a more direct avenue opened from France itself as more Vietnamese studied in French-speaking schools in both Vietnam and France. Meanwhile, beginning in the early 1900s, Vietnamese intellectuals and activists were also exposed to reformist ideas of Chinese, Japanese, and Indian intellectuals and activists such as Liang Qichao, Sun Yat-sen, Fukuzawa Yukichi, and Tagore. Through written and oral commentaries, literate Filipinos and Vietnamese conveyed these ideas and their interpretations of them to others in their countries.[17]

Another major influence on the evolving meaning of "freedom" to Vietnamese and Filipinos was colonialism itself.[18] People often lived in misery under colonial rule: critics commonly said they were forced to live like slaves or like animals. There was a stark contradiction between this miserable reality and the high-minded claims of colonialism: like colonial rulers elsewhere, French and Spanish authorities and (especially in the Philippines) the Catholic clergy preached morality and humanity and praised the good they were supposedly doing for Vietnamese and Filipinos—claims that rarely corresponded to what people experienced. And people could imagine life without colonial rule: for some Filipinos and Vietnamese, the ideals preached but not practiced by colonial secular and religious rulers were themselves inspirations; others idealized a pre-colonial past as superior to what Spanish and French rule had brought. Thus many Filipinos and Vietnamese, literate or not, came to contemplate how to escape, to "be free" from the colonial system and situation they found themselves in, as individuals, as families, as communities, and as whole nations.

≺ II ≻

Freedom Discourses in Anti-colonial Struggles and Revolutions

A prominent theme in writings and speeches of Filipinos and Vietnamese opposing colonial rule was freedom from foreign domination and the right to self-rule. In Vietnam, this theme was pronounced from the outset of colonial occupation. In the Philippines it evolved during the anti-colonial struggle itself.

For many Vietnamese, freeing their nation from foreign domination was imperative in order to retrieve their culture and civilization. The idea of "Vietnam" and being "Vietnamese," distinct from other countries and cultures, was well entrenched long before French troops started to seize the country in the mid-nineteenth century. Foreign rule was, as poets in the 1890s wrote, "unnatural," like a time when "water flowed upward."[19] It meant to many Vietnamese not only the loss of sovereignty but the loss of national identity and potentially even the end of their ethnicity. The desire for national freedom, therefore, was rooted both in *re*instating an independent government and *re*asserting Vietnamese distinctiveness.

For Filipinos, on the other hand, there had been no nation, hence none to *re*claim. Rather, they were *pro*claiming the freedom of a new nation and asserting their new national identity. A Philippine national identity had only recently emerged. Indeed, many who had opposed Spain sought not a free Philippines but a free *Katagalugan*—Land of the Tagalogs—or some other linguistic-based nation within the archipelago. But gradually during the 1880s and 1890s an awareness developed about being Filipino, different from Spaniards and having rights as a people to their own nation, independent from Spain.[20] Thus, Emilio Aguinaldo, a revolutionary leader, said in 1898 that compatriots should "struggle as long as the breath of life remains, in defense of our national integrity" and against any foreign power attempting "to deprive us of any part of this Archipelago."[21]

A second discourse in anti-colonialism concerned personal and civic freedom.[22] Prominent themes included individual and organizational freedom from coercive and abusive rules and rulers; freedom to develop one's potential and that of one's family and community; and freedom to criticize authorities, engage in public affairs, and participate in governance—matters that people in other Asian countries were also debating at the turn of the century.[23]

Aspects of these concerns were expressed in objections to colonial rulers' behavior. In the 1870s to 1890s, Filipino criticisms of Spanish rule bristled with condemnations of colonial rulers and Catholic friars who arbitrarily raised land rents, swindled illiterate villagers, and treated subjects with contempt.[24] Ho Chi Minh and other Vietnamese in the 1920s and 1930s wrote scathing critiques of French colonial authorities who took villagers' lands and other properties and inflicted wanton violence and other abuses on people.[25] Vietnamese villagers in the 1920s and 1930s frequently rebelled against colonial officials' excessive taxes and demands on their labor.[26]

Filipinos and Vietnamese also sought religious freedom. Cao Dai believers in Vietnam, for example, wanted to stay as far beyond the reach of French rule as possible in order to live in peace among themselves, without interference.[27] In the Philippines, when some anti-colonialists, despite their antipathy to Spanish friars, wanted Catholicism to be the official religion, they encountered vigorous counter arguments in favor of religious liberty. Those counter arguments prevailed when creators of the country's first republican constitution in 1899 approved the provision for "freedom and equality of religious worships, as well as the separation of the Church and State."[28]

Many Filipinos and Vietnamese anti-colonialists celebrated the freedom to develop one's potential. For some advocates, this was intrinsically valuable. Others emphasized its importance for national modernization and the republican state they envisioned in which "the people" would be sovereign. Individuals in such a system needed to be able to think for themselves in order to be responsible citizens and guard against tyranny. The absence of such development, many argued, was due to colonialism itself. By subjugating people to their rule, the French and Spanish had turned Vietnamese and Filipinos into servants and caused their self-confidence, consciousness, and minds to deteriorate or die.

Many Vietnamese also blamed traditions and customs—particularly Confucian values and practices regarding the family, gender relations, and authority—for stifling personal awareness and creativity. Writers like Nguyen An Ninh in the 1920s exhorted Vietnamese to merge their quest for personal freedom from such oppressive Vietnamese customs with their struggle for national independence.[29] The effort to emancipate women from male domination was one of many arenas in which struggles for individual freedom and against colonialism were joined, although not all anti-colonialists embraced ideas such as women picking their own spouses and being as educated as men.[30] Some intellectuals, like Phan Chu Trinh, argued that Confucianism per se was not the problem but rather its misapplication by those who had twisted it to subjugate people. A truly Confucian society, Phan Chu Trinh argued, would be characterized not by tyranny and backwardness but by equality and democracy. Nguyen An Ninh, among others, disagreed, calling instead for replacing Confucianism and other old beliefs with new ideas and values, often learned from other parts of the world and adapted to Vietnam's circumstances.[31]

Filipino anti-colonialists, too, often linked personal development and freedom to new ideas and education. Emilio Jacinto, Jose

Rizal, and Apolinario Mabini, for instance, believed that by nature people are free and equal. But there are periods, Jacinto wrote, "when Liberty is smothered by errors, by the blind worship of ancient bad practices, and laws suggested by crafty henchmen."[32] To retrieve liberty, he and others argued, requires the development of each person's intellectual and moral faculties, especially through education. Then people would be free and tyranny could not survive.

Individual rights to freedom of press, freedom of association, and having a voice in government were also prominent claims of many Filipinos and Vietnamese. In *La Solidaridad* and other publications during the 1880s and 1890s, Filipinos pressing for reforms in the colonial system insisted on freedom of expression, association, and religion.[33] Similar views were widespread in Vietnam among reformers and budding revolutionaries alike. Phan Boi Chau, a prominent nationalist at the turn of the century, wrote in 1907 that, after being liberated from French rule, "the door of freedom" in Vietnam will be "wide open"—newspapers and magazines will "flood the streets," people will freely "discuss and debate domestic and foreign matters," and literary people will be permitted a "wide avenue" to say what they want.[34] Similarly, in 1938, among the demands for change published by intellectuals in Hanoi were freedom of assembly, speech, publication, and travel.[35]

While some Filipinos and Vietnamese demanded these civic freedoms as inherent rights, probably more believed that they deserved what citizens in France and Spain already had. For example, a 1926 protest rally in Saigon involving three thousand people, among them many workers and students, voted to demand that the "Rights of Man and the Citizen" be observed in Vietnam as they were in France and that Vietnamese be permitted freedom of education, assembly, and movement, among other civil rights. Despite risks of harsh reprisals, a thousand people also signed petitions supporting these claims.[36]

The constitution written when each nation's revolutionary leaders asserted its independence protected many of these individual and civic liberties. The Philippine Republic's 1899 constitution provided for freedom of association, of press, of petition, and of other ways to express views about public issues and governance. These and other political rights, such as voting for national assembly delegates, applied to both men and women.[37] In Vietnam, a 1945 publication of the revolutionary organization Viet Minh promised "personal freedom," which included among other provisions the right to live peacefully, own property, and be protected from government harassment. The publication also espoused the "political freedoms" of speech, press, assembly, and belief, among others. A year later, after the Viet Minh had established the Democratic Republic of Vietnam, these rights and freedoms were written into the nation's constitution.[38]

Writers and activists in both countries wrestled with the universal problem of finding a suitable balance between individual rights and freedoms and the need for community peace and order. Several Filipino advocates cautioned that, carried too far, individual pursuits of freedom could undermine society and lead to chaos. "Liberty does not mean we should not obey anyone," Mabini said. He talked about "true freedom" existing in a civil society in which citizens obeyed laws made by a legitimate government, meaning one that expressed the will of the people.[39] In Vietnam, a "collectivist" approach to this problem of balance emphasized the role of government and leaders, as representatives of the people, to assure justice and equality for all individuals. A "libertarian" approach, more skeptical of authority and organization, emphasized individual freedom, which would lead to self-perfection and thereby a moral order. Yet even advocates of this way of thinking, such as influential writer Nguyen An Ninh, did not "extol individual freedom at the expense of the people." He believed that individual liberation and self-realization also required dedication to society.[40]

In a third discourse, visions of better living conditions were embedded in opposition to colonial rule generally or to specific colonial policies and practices. Rid of colonial policies and foreign rule, many Filipinos and Vietnamese expected to live free from hostility, envy, hunger, and poverty. For some anti-colonialists, national independence was a means of reaching these economic and social goals. For others, such goals were central to their understanding of what freedom meant. Such views resonate with Western philosophical arguments that to be free requires a sufficient degree of material well-being.[41]

Major complaints against Spanish rule were hunger, exploitation, and deep social divisions. A large majority of the people were mired in poverty while a tiny minority, composed of colonial officials and indigenous elites, lived in splendor. Rectifying this situation was a major theme for many who supported and participated in the revolution against Spain and for national independence. To many Filipinos, social inversion, an equitable redistribution of property, and social unity would be the fruit of freedom from foreign rule. For these people, Ileto finds by closely reading Tagalog texts, freedom would bring "a condition of brotherhood, equality, contentment (*kaginhawaan*) and material abundance (*kasaganaan*)."[42] For many rebelling against Spain and the United States between 1896 and 1905, "true freedom" was "not mere political autonomy, but the attainment of certain possibilities of existence. Politics could not be divorced from all other aspects of life, like morality and economics."[43]

Similar aspirations surfaced in Vietnam, particularly in uprisings dotting the countryside during the 1930s that often combined opposition to the colonial regime with demands for better living conditions. Vietnamese participants wanted to be rid of numerous taxes and other colonial impositions that impoverished and starved millions of villagers. They also often sought to redistribute land and to reduce inequalities. During a wave of uprisings in 1930, villagers in Nghe An and Ha Tinh provinces managed to establish temporarily (until colonial soldiers smashed them) their own local governments. Freed from their colonial regime's officials, villagers quickly abolished all colonial taxes, redistributed funds that the ousted officials had accumulated, seized rice from the rich and gave it to the neediest households, confiscated and redistributed to poor peasants land that previously had been communally owned but under the French had been accumulated by a few households, and reduced the rents and debts that peasants owed to landowners and creditors.[44] This "new life," according to a history of one such locality, was the "meaning of 'liberation,' 'equality,' and 'freedom'."[45]

These three discourses on freedom were variously emphasized by anti-colonialists, who frequently disagreed sharply over numerous issues, among them which freedoms had priority. For many Vietnamese, overthrowing the French was essential before anything else by way of personal freedom, modernization, or self-government could occur.[46] In the Philippines, Apolinario Mabini and several other nationalists had concluded by the 1890s that national independence was a fundamental prerequisite for individual freedom and progress.[47] For some anti-colonialists, however, national independence was not necessarily so intimately connected to other freedoms. Several influential writers and critics of colonial rule, most notably Jose Rizal and Phan Chu Trinh, were even prepared to have their respective countries remain under Spain and France provided such a government would, among other major reforms, assure Filipinos and Vietnamese their civil liberties.[48] National independence was not necessarily the same as individual freedom nor the means to achieving it. Indeed, independence might bring worse repression of other freedoms. Rizal asked, "What is the use of independence if the slaves of today will be tyrants of tomorrow?"[49]

A profound tension within the Philippine revolution against Spain concerned the place of socio-economic freedom. For those revolutionaries who sought a more equitable distribution of wealth and a society in which people lived in harmony, breaking down the class society and removing divisions between the propertied elite and the propertyless were at the heart of the struggle. Such visions were widely shared in the Katipunan, an underground organization formed in 1892 that initiated the revolutionary uprising in 1896.[50] Most Katipunan members were from working and peasant classes. Early leaders like Andres Bonifacio and Apolinario Mabini were also from those humble backgrounds, although they had managed to become more educated and live more comfortably than average members.

By 1897, however, the Katipunan and also the fledgling revolutionary government were dominated by people who rarely shared those visions. For these people, many from privileged classes, an end to Spanish rule would mean independence for a new nation, which they would lead. With few exceptions, they paid little attention to socio-economic reforms. To them the chasm between their classes and the masses was natural and unquestioned.[51] Redistributing land to the landless was not on their agenda. Indeed, some of these men took advantage of their elite status and their high positions in the revolutionary movement to claim more land for themselves. Even in language there was often a gap. Many of these revolutionaries spoke and wrote, especially among themselves, in Spanish. Only a few disseminated ideas in Tagalog and other local vernaculars so as to communicate to the majority of people who spoke no Spanish.

While the discourse regarding socio-economic freedom was sidelined during the Philippine revolution in the late 1890s, it remained prominent during Vietnam's armed resistance against France in 1945–54.[52] Vietnam's primary revolutionary movement was the Viet Minh (formed in 1941).[53] Although different from the Katipunan in many other respects, it too sought major reforms in Vietnamese society along with national independence. Liberating the peasantry from poverty and redistributing wealth were very much part of what overthrowing the French was all about. Unlike what happened to the Katipunan a half century earlier, however, the Viet Minh's leadership remained firmly oriented to the lower classes, especially the peasantry, even though some leaders were from relatively privileged backgrounds. Viet Minh leaders benefited from communist and socialist movements and governments elsewhere in the world, which did not exist during Bonifacio and Mabini's time. Often Viet Minh leaders were influenced by Marxist, Leninist, and socialist writers and activists. Many joined Vietnam's Communist Party. Leaders, exemplified by Ho Chi Minh, also spoke and wrote among themselves and to the masses in the Vietnamese language (even though many leaders knew Sino-Vietnamese and French). In this and other ways, they sought to bring down barriers between classes, not maintain or enhance them. No Viet Minh leaders are known to have used their positions after defeating the French to grab huge chunks of real estate for themselves. Instead, the Viet Minh began land redistribution in the early 1950s as a way to bolster peasant support for major armed offenses against French military forces.[54]

During Vietnam's anti-colonial movement, tensions emerged between the socio-economic and the personal-civic discourses. People emphasizing the former included communists. They dwelled on liberation from economic impoverishment as well as national independence, stressed social justice more than civil liberties, and focused on class more than individuals as both the target and source of change. Those accenting personal and civic freedom included many writers and artists who entwined individualism, individual freedoms, and self-emancipation with national independence.[55] Individuals and groups emphasizing one of these orientations toward freedom were frequently at odds with those who gave higher priority to the other. But many of both orientations also joined together as opposition against France intensified in the late 1930s and escalated into war after 1945. Many artists, writers, and other intellectuals accepted the Communist Party's leadership of the armed struggle, believing the party had an effective nationalist agenda and was in the best position to assure Vietnam's independence. Often such people compromised or put on hold some of their ideals and beliefs in individual rights and civil liberties. Perhaps they anticipated that these could be revived later, after independence was secure. Meanwhile, the relationship between the discourse of personal and civic freedom and that of socio-economic freedom remained uneasy.

≺ III ≻

Interrupted Revolutions

The Spanish were ousted from the Philippines in 1898; the French were driven from Vietnam in 1954. Despite these victories over colonial powers, neither the Philippines nor Vietnam immediately achieved full national independence. The United States government played a major role in the interruption of both revolutions. In 1898 the United States, as part of its war with Spain elsewhere, sent a naval fleet to Manila Bay. Its subsequent battles against Spanish forces, already weakened by the Filipino revolutionary army, convinced Spain to surrender—to the Americans, not to the Filipinos. The U.S. government then decided, for a panoply of reasons including "manifest destiny" and economic gain, to annex the Philippines rather than leave it to the government recently established by Filipino revolutionaries. Guerrilla warfare soon ensued as thousands of people across the archipelago resisted the U.S. troops arriving to impose the new colonial government's law and order. The United States claimed victory in 1902 and the Philippines remained under American colonial rule until 1946, except for the period 1942–45 when Japanese forces during World War II occupied (though never completely ruled) the country.

Japanese forces also occupied Vietnam during World War II. In early September 1945, in the wake of Japan's capitulation to the Allied forces, the Viet Minh and associated groups declared the country independent from both the French and the Japanese and established the Democratic Republic of Vietnam (DRV). To make that declaration stick, however, the new Communist Party government, with extensive popular support, especially among the peasantry, had to fight the French army, which attempted to repossess the country. The French together with other Vietnamese who opposed the DRV also set up a government, headquartered in Saigon with the Emperor Bao Dai its titular head, that claimed it, not the DRV, represented the entire country.

Unlike what had happened in the Philippines a half century earlier, in Vietnam, the revolutionary government, the DRV, ultimately won its war. By this time—1954—however, the U.S. government was leading the "Cold War" against "international communism" and since about 1950 had been financially supporting France's hot war in Vietnam and its Saigon-based government. Determined not to let Vietnam "fall to the Communists," the United States and its allies insisted on a temporary division of Vietnam into a northern "zone" governed by the DRV and a southern "zone" under the Saigon government. DRV leaders were also under considerable pressure from their Soviet and Chinese allies to agree to this measure. The temporary demarcation was supposed to end in 1956 with a national election to determine which government would rule a united and independent Vietnam. The United States, however, together with the new government it had helped to establish in the south, headed now by Ngo Dinh Diem, never let that election occur, despite protests by many people in the south. War began a few years later and raged until 1975. Vietnamese fought Vietnamese and Vietnamese fought Americans (and about 30,000 other foreign troops allied with the United States).

These events in the Philippines and Vietnam significantly affected politics in both countries, including struggles regarding freedom. Let us look at the three freedom discourses during this period, beginning with the national one.

In the Philippines, the United States from the outset encouraged Filipino participation in the new colonial government and said it intended to rule only long enough to "educate" Filipinos to govern themselves in an independent republic. Numerous Filipinos quickly collaborated, among them many from propertied classes who had joined the revolution against Spain but who saw the Americans not as spoilers of their revolution but as liberators. One, for example, said in 1906 that the national assembly then being established by Americans to give Filipinos a say in governing the country was the "Gate of Freedom."[56] Consequently, U.S. colonial rule affected the discourse on national freedom in two major ways. First, it created legal forums in which Filipinos could debate national independence and even pressure U.S. policy makers on the matter. Second, much of the discourse dwelled not on *whether* but on *when*, exactly, would the Philippines become independent. By 1934, the date 1946 was fixed as the year that independence would be granted, which indeed it was.

Notable exceptions to these two impacts of U.S. rule on the national freedom discourse periodically surfaced. One, there was sporadic armed resistance and the threat of other uprisings against U.S. rule and for complete and immediate independence. Second, some Filipinos opposed independence, preferring instead that the Philippines become a state within the United States—somewhat akin to what anti-colonial reformists had wanted with Spain in the 1880s. Third, some groups wanted a completely different nation, independent from both the Philippines and the United States. Most vocal here were many Muslims, who had no affinity with Philippine nationalism. During the American period, many repeatedly petitioned, sometimes on behalf of a particular cultural-linguistic group (for instance, Maguindanao, Sulu, or Maranao) and sometimes on behalf of an inclusive "Moro Nation," for a free and independent country of their own.[57]

Vietnam was an entirely different situation. After 1956, when national elections that were supposed to have been held were not, no Vietnamese knew for sure when full national independence would occur—or even if it would. The country was divided and fighting a civil war. One of the major issues for which Vietnamese were killing and dying was the meaning and substance of their nation's freedom.

"Nothing is more precious than independence and freedom," Ho Chi Minh said in July 1966 as he vowed that his country would never surrender even though U.S. bombs rained down on the country and the number of American soldiers there multiplied daily.[58] These words, later emblazoned for posterity on public buildings throughout the country, underscored the resolve of the DRV government and Vietnamese supporting it to "save the country"—meaning, to reunite it and defeat U.S. imperialists who were trying to keep it divided and rule the southern half with what Ho Chi Minh and his followers regarded as a colonial puppet and illegitimate government based in Saigon.

Ho Chi Minh's supporters included many nationalists living in the south who opposed the Saigon-based Republic of Vietnam government and U.S. involvement. Many of these people assisted and some joined the National Front to Liberate the South (NLF, *Mat Tran Dan Toc Giai Phong Mien Nam*), which was formed in 1960 and worked clandestinely with the DRV. The more U.S. soldiers came, the bigger the war became and the more Vietnamese in the south supported the NLF. To them, the NLF offered both attractive socio-economic reforms and the best hope for national independence and liberation from this new colonial power.[59]

Among those supporting the Republic of Vietnam government between 1954 and its final collapse in 1975 were other nationalists who sought the same national freedom and independence from colonial rule that Ho Chi Minh was espousing but without any communist involvement. To be "free," many said, Vietnam must not only be independent of colonialism but be free of communism. Most leaders in the Saigon-based government, beginning with Ngo Dinh Diem, claimed to be defending Vietnam's territorial unity and the entire country's independence against both foreign rule and "Vietnamese Communism."[60] By the 1960s, some Vietnamese, however, had come to see "South Vietnam" as a separate nation fighting for its independence against a foreign invader, "North Vietnam."[61]

The arguments of the Saigon government and its defenders for national freedom faced major obstacles, which were never overcome. Because the government in south Vietnam was largely created, financed, and militarily sustained by the United States, it was not a credible advocate for national independence. It had only modest popular support, partly because its claims to being a defender of Vietnam's national freedom were unbelievable but also because it was usually incompetent, despotic, and riddled with corruption.[62] The idea of South Vietnam being a separate nation had an additional obstacle: it flew in the face of a centuries-old understanding among most Vietnamese that "Vietnam" was one.[63]

Personal and civic freedom issues also animated political activity during the interrupted revolution in each country. The basic laws in the Philippines and Vietnam during these periods theoretically assured citizens very similar liberties, including freedom of speech, press, assembly, religion, privacy, and travel, as well as freedom from unjust punishment and government abuses.[64] In practice, such liberties were far more evident in the Philippines than in Vietnam.

Filipinos could and did readily publish journals and newspapers which criticized public policies and officials (including Americans); used courts for legal redress; formed organizations that advocated the interests of particular sectors of society; and espoused different religions. They also had numerous political organizations, including political parties that competed in local and national elections. Indicative of this general consensus inside and outside the government favoring personal and civic freedom is that not only did Filipinos establish associations like the Civil Liberties Union (CLU) in 1937 but the High Commissioner, the top American official in the government, commended the CLU for its work defending free speech and other civil liberties.[65]

This consensus is partly explained by U.S. colonial government policy to allow Filipinos liberties similar to those in the United States. Another part of the explanation is that, with the national independence question having been largely settled, authorities could afford to be more tolerant of free and open political debate than would have been the case had national independence continued to be highly contentious, pitting Filipino political activists against American colonial rulers. Also contributing to this political atmosphere is that, after the last of the armed revolutionaries had been put down in the early 1900s, the country was essentially at peace. Additionally, Filipinos enthusiastically embraced free press, competitive elections, and other such institutions. Most Filipino political leaders and organizations were also largely in agreement with each other and with American authorities on how the country should be governed and where it was headed.

Indeed, violations against personal and civic liberties often occurred when authorities and powerful individuals and groups dealt with others who strenuously criticized the prevailing order, particularly those who demanded major social and economic reforms. To many peasants, peddlers, workers, and others from lower classes, U.S. rule fell far short of the social or economic changes they had envisioned. According to this view, apart from removing Spanish officials and friars and creating a public school system, the Americans had preserved most of the previous socio-economic order characterized by huge inequalities and a political system dominated by the wealthy landed elite. The "true freedom" lower classes had aspired to in the revolution had yet to come because economic and social oppression continued, property ownership was still concentrated among a few people, and society was profoundly divided by inequality. Moreover, those elite Filipinos collaborating with the Americans, instead of being humble servants of the people, were often serving themselves.

In the early 1900s, there were people like Macario Sakay, Ruperto Rios, and Felipe Salvador whom American and Filipino authorities saw as bandits and outlaws but whom their many rural followers regarded as spiritual and political leaders because they preached real freedom. They sought a redistribution of wealth and a unity among people of different backgrounds based on a morality that stressed love, compassion, and virtue. They opposed a society in which the gentry maintained and dominated a hierarchical order.[66] Felipe Salvador's religious political movement, called the Santa Iglesia, which flourished in central Luzon in 1900–1910, was "an army of liberation, a legion to free the poor people and stop their suffering," said Pedro Calosa, a man who more than a decade later was active in subsequent groups with similar aspirations.[67]

Freedom from socio-economic injustices was a theme in such peasant and worker organizations during the 1920s and 1930s as *Tanggulan* (Defense), *Sakdalista* (Advocates), *Kalipunang Pambansa ng mga Magsasaka sa Pilipinas* (National Society of Peasants in the Philippines), *Anak Pawis* (Children of Sweat), and *Aguman ding Malding Talapagobra* (General Workers' Union). Similar to the Katipunan four decades earlier, these groups sought an end to burdensome taxes, usurious interest rates, poverty, and, as a Sakdalista publication summed it up, "oppression of the poor by the rich."[68] In essence, one Sakdalista leader said, they wanted a Philippines in which those collaborating with the Americans "would cease to be powerful. Instead, it would be the people who were powerful. The people would have their freedom. We would have our own lands; they would no longer be the monopoly of the *propietarios* [large landowners] and of the government officials."[69]

To silence or destroy such organizations, government authorities, business owners, and landowners often used illegal methods. Consequently, workers and peasants added to their demands that their rights to freedom of assembly, organization, and speech must be protected. When suppressing the *Partido Komunista ng Pilipinas* (PKP, Communist Party of the Philippines) authorities first tried to curtail members' freedom of speech and assembly; later the Supreme Court (composed of Filipino judges) outlawed it as a subversive group.[70] In an effort to quell waves of strikes and protests by peasants and workers in central Luzon, local officials teamed up with landlords' hired gunmen to threaten activists, disrupt meetings, and kill leaders, whom they dismissed as "anarchists," "Communists," "Bolsheviks," and "revolutionaries." The violent uprisings that occasionally occurred in the 1930s were often triggered by local and national government officials persistently violating people's civil liberties and legal rights.[71]

In Vietnam different conditions contributed to much less personal and civic freedom during its interrupted revolution. National independence was both unresolved and a central issue in the civil war, which for many leaders, north and south, justified severe restrictions on what people could say or do and swift repression against anyone deemed an "enemy." Moreover, each part had a government that probably would have been wary of extensive civic freedom even had there been no war.

The Communist Party government in the north emphasized class struggle against feudal and colonial elites. It took decisive measures to improve living conditions of peasants and workers, often at the expense of upper classes who were allowed little opportunity to object, constitutional provisions notwithstanding. By 1956, the government had redistributed nearly all land more or less equally, allowing no compensation to previous owners but benefiting nearly three-fourths of the north's rural population.[72] Mass literacy campaigns, health programs, laws about gender equality, together with other measures during the 1950s and 1960s went a long way toward earning the government considerable popular support and liberating villagers from the inequalities and deep poverty they had resented during French colonial rule.[73]

The Saigon-based government was different. It showed little commitment to addressing grievances of poor villagers. After reversing the land reform carried out in the south by the Viet Minh before 1954, it did not seriously begin one of its own until 1970, a few years before its defeat. Instead, the government's orientation in south

Vietnam was primarily to landlords, former colonial officials, and urban upper classes—and to its American benefactors, who only half-heartedly attempted to alter the leaders' authoritarian and militaristic approach to governing.[74]

Despite these circumstances, voices for personal and civic freedom surfaced. In the south, groups advocating freedom of press and other civil rights ran opposition candidates for elected offices when they dared and from time to time demonstrated openly in the streets of Hue, Saigon, and other cities. Free elections and other democratic features of government were said to be the objectives of some military officers involved in coups d'etat during the 1960s.[75] Perhaps the most sustained voice grew from Buddhists' ongoing protests. In 1962–63, when Ngo Dinh Diem was still president, many people openly objected to the government's discrimination against Buddhism and for Catholicism. Later, Buddhists' and their supporters' demands, which they expressed in demonstrations and publications (produced despite government prohibitions), broadened beyond freedom of religion to include freedom of press and assembly and a democratic political system.[76]

In the north, many Catholics fled to the south for fear that the Communist Party government would persecute them for their religious beliefs. Many other conflicts over civic and personal freedom probably occurred after 1954 but remained hidden due to tremendous constraints and pressures imposed by the government on public discourse. One revealing episode, however, did come to light when many writers, artists, social scientists, natural scientists, and others loosely referred to as intellectuals, mainly in Hanoi, had concluded that the Communist Party government was trying to dictate what was appropriate literature, art, commentary, and research. In early 1956, emboldened by the "hundred flowers" movement in China and public criticisms of Stalinism in the USSR, they expressed their concerns in essays, poems, and short stories published in independent magazines, particularly *Nhan Van* (Humanism) and *Giai Pham* (Masterpieces).[77]

One theme in these writings concerns freedom of thought and creativity. The intellectual community, writers argued, must have more autonomy from the state and the Communist Party. Without "freedom of thought" (*tu do tu tuong*), "artistic freedom" (*tu do sang tac*), and "freedom of discussion" (*tu do thao luan*), writers and researchers cannot be creative or do scientific research. Moreover, in order for intellectuals to help the country to develop, they must have the freedom to conduct research, study, and write.[78] If forced to follow a government-imposed standard of art or scholarship, they would become useless.[79] Artists, said one writer, must live "not as slaves in any form" but as people who "search for freedom . . . and fight against the loss of any freedom of thought."[80]

Numerous writers stressed freedom to publish; to speak out on cultural, social, and political issues; and to criticize public officials. Such liberties, they said, are affirmed in the constitution, are essential to Vietnam's hard-won democracy, and will help the political system to correct itself.[81] In particular, several writers said, the mistakes and abuses that occurred when land was redistributed could have been avoided and certainly minimized had people been freer to complain. A "concrete matter concerning freedom facing people of the north [Vietnam] today," wrote Tran Duc Thao, is the serious threat posed by authoritarian, dogmatic, and self-centered officials. Essential, in order to counter them, is the "freedom to criticize publicly," including in print.[82]

Communist Party officials and others had several counter arguments.[83] First, creativity springs not, as the intellectuals claimed, from "inner freedom" but from one's class background. Art relates to class struggle, and to rid society of class behavior, the Communist Party must fight for revolutionary change on various fronts, including cultural ones. Second, artists, poets, and others should serve the people, advance the socialist revolution, and preserve national independence. Intellectual work unconnected to those purposes, officials argued, undermines the regime and the nation and helps to revive capitalism and all its oppression. "Art for art's sake" is unacceptable. Everyone is free to criticize, but criticisms must be "constructive in character," not hostile to the revolution and socialism. Third, the intellectuals who were complaining are excessively individualist and demand "absolute freedom." Claims to "artistic freedom," said one official, really only amount to "freedom to create poison and rot," which threatens the country.[84] Enemies in south Vietnam and the United States, they said, will use what these intellectuals say against Vietnam's struggle for full independence and reunification. Some party officials said these writers were even using "freedom" as a smokescreen to hide their real intent to topple the Communist Party and the political system.

Many intellectuals rejected these characterizations. No one, wrote Phan Khoi, was demanding "indiscriminate freedom."[85] Writers and artists readily acknowledged freedoms were not absolute. They were not seeking to overthrow the regime nor oppose the Communist Party. Indeed, many were members of the party; many had fought against the French. They continued to have, as one said, "confidence in the leadership of the Central Committee of the Party."[86]

In late 1956, the government began to silence these claims to wider civic and personal freedom. Authorities shut publications deemed excessively critical and dangerous, arrested some writers, removed others from their jobs, and intimidated many more. New regulations further restricted which magazines, newspapers, and other public media could operate and what they could say. A decree signed by President Ho Chi Minh endorsed "people's freedom of expression in the press" but spelled out measures aimed at "preventing any misuse of this freedom to harm the struggle for peace, national unity, independence, and democracy of the country."[87] Two years later, during discussions about revising the nation's constitution, Ho Chi Minh said that all citizens have the right to "freedom of speech, press, assembly, organization." But the constitution forbids the use of these freedoms to "transgress" the interests of "the state and the people." Those interests, he added, were "of one mind."[88] And the state, he intimated, would determine what those interests were, a stance that permeated the north for years to come.

≺ IV ≻

Independence and Contested Freedoms

In July 1946, as scheduled since 1934 but following an unanticipated war in which Filipino guerrilla groups fought for liberation from the Japanese army (1942–45), the Philippines became independent from the U.S. In May 1975, immediately after the military defeat and collapse of the Saigon-based government, Vietnam for the first time in more than a century was again under one government run by Vietnamese. Ending colonial rule did not, of course, end political problems and debate in either nation. Prominent in ensuing political struggles were familiar discourses about freedom.

Even national independence continued to be debatable, especially in the Philippines. Numerous Filipinos argued that their country was still excessively influenced by the United States and by foreign, especially American, capitalists. This view figured to some extent in two armed uprisings, the Huk rebellion (1946-mid 1950s) and the New People's Army (1969-early 1990s). U.S. military bases in the country, parity that American businesses had with Filipinos, and persistent U.S. government meddling in Philippine domestic politics were among the facts substantiating these contentions.[89] Only after parity for U.S. businesses ended (1974) and the U.S. bases left (1991) did the arguments significantly subside. Meanwhile, in another dimension of national independence, many Muslims in the southern Philippines continued to press, sometimes violently, for their own nation, completely separate from the Philippines. In Vietnam, the country's complete independence from colonial rule was not questioned and no significant secessionist voice was heard from its minority populations. But demands for "national freedom" and a "free Vietnam" continued to be voiced, primarily by Vietnamese who had left their homeland after 1975. To them the nation had been engulfed by another foreign and sinister "ism"—not colonialism but communism. Hence, they continued to speak of "overthrowing the Communist Party regime" and "freeing Vietnam from Communism."

Inside Vietnam the discourse on civic and personal freedom has continued, resonating with the brief public debate in the north during the mid-1950s and the concerns of many anti-colonialists earlier in the century. Almost immediately after reunification in 1975–76, the Communist Party government imposed on the south the same tight restrictions on speech, publications, assembly, and other public expression that existed in the north, often over the objections of NLF members who favored a more liberal political system.[90] The state allows, even encourages, public criticism but only on certain topics and in limited ways. Going beyond those bounds can result in severe punishment, including years of imprisonment. Consequently, usually only the government-sanctioned side to the discourse about what constitutes civil liberties is publicized. Contrary views and wide-ranging criticisms are usually hidden from the authorities. On occasion, however, such as occurred in the 1990s, alternative views do surface.

The Communist Party government and its vocal supporters argue that the political system is democratic and freedoms such as those of speech, press, assembly, and religion are provided for in the constitution. But, according to this position, the government must assure that these freedoms are used responsibly. The government must also guard the nation against hostile domestic and international forces that often hide behind a pretense of "human rights" and "democracy" to threaten peace and order and the country's hard-won social and economic improvements achieved since the end of colonial rule.[91] Those advances include much greater freedom from exploitation and deprivation. In order to continue economic improvement the government has embraced certain economic and political reforms. But drastic changes in the political system, the government argues, such as allowing several political parties, will result in chaos, similar to what happened to the Soviet Union.

Numerous other Vietnamese within the country, however, favor a more open political system. They include many former supporters of the Saigon-based government, former NLF members, current and former Communist Party members, among others. They advocate freedom to speak, assemble, and organize, as well as freedom from state domination in the media, arts, and research. Many insist on practicing their religious convictions without interference from the state.[92] Some want the freedom to form political parties. Many favor elections in which voters can freely choose among candidates advocating different programs and policies.[93] To support their views, they often invoke the country's own constitution and official pronouncements. Some cite Ho Chi Minh's writings decades ago that lambasted the French for depriving Vietnamese of these very freedoms.[94]

Such "democracy and freedom," writes Nguyen Ho, "has permeated the bones and blood of Vietnamese people."[95] These ideas and values, he and others write, are not foreign and were among the aspirations around which the Communist Party mobilized peasants, workers, and intellectuals to fight against colonialism. During wars for independence and reunification, writes Tran Do, "people restricted and even sacrificed their rights to freedom and democracy" in the interest of winning those wars. Now the regime owes them an "over-due debt," which must be paid by assuring their freedoms, such as those of speech and assembly.[96]

Many writers emphasize that democracy in Vietnam, just as in the West, need not be "boundless" or "excessive," but to be real it must have freedom of thought, speech, and press.[97] Absent that freedom, they say, people are virtually powerless to protect themselves against abuses by authorities and the state generally. Civil liberties are also essential to national independence. Alluding to the official national motto, one critic writes that "Independence without freedom and happiness is meaningless."[98]

Advocates also argue that civic freedom is a means to other important ends. Some, for instance, contend that without it, the country cannot use well its intellectual resources and develop economically and politically.[99] Duong Thu Huong, among others, believes that without "human rights," creativity is stunted, morality decays, corruption flourishes, and leaders become self serving.[100] Others emphasize that personal and civic freedom is necessary in order to avoid chaos and deep social unrest. They contend, contrary to what Communist Party leaders argue, that such freedom is not a threat to stability and national unity but a means to assuring those conditions. Some even recommend it as means for the Communist Party government to fight corruption, regain public confidence, and remain politically powerful.[101]

Outbursts of rural unrest in 1997 gave government authorities and critics alike substantiation for their positions in the ongoing struggle over personal and civic freedom. The principal causes of protests, involving thousands of villagers in Thai Binh province and elsewhere, appear to have been rampant corruption, arrogance, heavy taxation, and illegal accumulation of land and other wealth by local government and party officials. The national government defended the political system, which encourages citizens to report their criticisms. The problem got out of hand, they said, because local officials ignored villagers' legitimate complaints and because "bad elements" incited otherwise well-meaning villagers to take extreme and illegal action. Critics, however, emphasized that until freedoms of speech, assembly, and press are allowed, the political system will continue to deteriorate and unrest will become worse.[102]

In the Philippines, civil liberties since independence have not been greatly disputed, with two significant exceptions. Expanding on the trend set during American colonial rule, the country since independence has had numerous political parties and competitive elections, public debate over government programs, privately owned and robust news media, numerous religious groups, freedom of movement within and beyond the country, and thousands of nongovernment organizations that routinely criticize public officials.[103]

One exception to this situation resonates with what occurred during the American colonial period: frequent repression of organized workers, peasants, and others seeking a fairer distribution of wealth and land. That repression and severe economic and social inequalities have been among the principal causes of the unrest and rebellion that have erupted several times in the Philippines since 1946.[104] Government authorities and their defenders have justified or excused their behavior on the grounds of preserving peace and order and countering communism and subversion. The other major exception was the "martial law" that President Ferdinand Marcos imposed in 1972. This included, among other measures, abolishing the national legislature, militarizing the state, eliminating independent newspapers and other mass media, and arresting thousands of suspected subversives and opponents. Among those imprisoned were politicians, journalists, student leaders, peasant and labor organization activists, writers, and professors. Although martial law was "lifted" in 1981, Marcos and the military continued the authoritarian regime until 1986 when several factors brought together a nonviolent "people's power revolution" to overthrow it.

Marcos and his supporters offered two main justifications for imposing martial law; ideas about freedom figured in both. One was to build a "new society," which I will return to. The second was to counter subversion. The Marcos government argued that two rebellions in the early 1970s threatened to destroy the Philippine nation. A Muslim separatist rebellion in the south wanted to create a new country. Elsewhere in the archipelago, the Philippine Communist Party and its New People's Army, which Marcos claimed was aided by foreign powers, sought to take over the Philippines and impose communism. To crush these rebellions, Marcos insisted, martial law was necessary.

Many Filipinos did not believe that the rebellions were nearly this serious. Marcos, they said, was using the unrest as a pretext for remaining president beyond the constitutional limit and for concentrating power. Numerous Filipinos defied the severe restrictions on press, speech, assembly, and other public expression of opinions. Often such people were imprisoned.[105] Some people went underground, joining the New People's Army, the Communist Party, and other organizations. Many more Filipinos participated in less daring forms of resistance. Word-of-mouth commentary, songs, and jokes as well as one-off or low-profiled skits and plays became popular ways to take swipes at the regime while minimizing detection and arrest. Organized opposition gradually grew, at first mainly clandestinely but by the early 1980s also more openly, despite decrees banning such activities. Government enforcement could not keep up with widening public discontent.

Two arguments against martial law bear on freedom issues. One was that the Marcos government was further compromising Philippine national independence because it depended on the U.S. government, transnational corporations, the World Bank, and the International Monetary Fund to remain in power despite its low credibility and legitimacy within the country.[106] A second was that the government was vicious, murderous, and arbitrary. "End the repression" and "restore civil liberties" were prevalent messages in satirical remarks, music, and literature, and eventually in waves of demonstrations against the government. A play about political prisoners performed in 1979 suggested that the entire country was imprisoned.[107] The popular novel *Dekada '70*, released in the early 1980s, depicts how spreading repression affected a middle-class urban family when a teenage son failed to return home one evening after going out with friends. His parents discover that the police had mutilated him to death and then discarded his body. The parents got nowhere when they attempted to hold authorities accountable.[108] The song "*Balita*" (News), recorded in 1979, laments a "bloodstained" country hit by some unspeakable force that has left "trees without leaves," "parrots without wings," and "hearts that cannot talk about what has engulfed a land of promise."[109]

Many Filipinos wanted free elections, not the "sham" and "phony" ones that the martial law regime occasionally held to give the appearance of democracy. And they wanted freedom of press and speech. Workers wanted restored their right to form their own unions and go on strike. Church groups, students, and parents condemned the police and military for waves of torture, arbitrary arrests, murder, and other violations of personal freedom. Civil liberties were prominent among the demands shouted, written on placards, and printed in leaflets during the 1983–85 "parliament of the streets" when tens of thousands of people in Metro-Manila and elsewhere marched in hundreds of demonstrations against the Marcos government. They were hauntingly brought out in the song "*Bayan Ko*" (My Homeland), which became a unifying anthem for the expanding anti-martial law, pro-democracy movement.[110] They were also high on the list of aspirations during the 1986 presidential election and uprising that toppled the government.[111]

Marcos's other major public justification for martial law was to carry out "a revolution from the center" that would create a "New Society" featuring the "democratization of wealth."[112] For too long, Marcos and his supporters argued, Philippine society had endured corruption, opportunism, and gross inequality. These conditions had evolved in part from a narrow view of "political liberty" inherited from Americans and from European philosophers like John Locke. Seeing government as a major threat to liberty, that view in effect protects the few who are economically well-off—what Marcos called the "oligarchy." These wealthy few were taking advantage of a free press and other political liberties to advance their own interests and put down the poor. Meanwhile, the poor majority lacked the material and intellectual means to use those same liberties. Only when "free from . . . bodily infirmity, intellectual ignorance, and moral depravity," argued O. D. Corpuz, one of Marcos's advisers, could people actually enjoy freedom of speech, fair trials, and other "political liberties." In the New Society, he said, the government would redistribute wealth and take other measures to free people from "poverty, ill health, and lack of opportunity."[113] The argument was similar to what Egypt's Gamal Abdul Nasser had advocated in the mid-1950s when he and his followers rejected political pluralism and contended that the state's job was to bring about social and economic justice.[114]

Some Filipinos rejected the separation between freedom from economic deprivation, on one hand, and civic freedom, on the other. To obtain the former, these critics argued, people must have the latter.[115] Marcos's and Corpuz's arguments were powerfully attractive, however, to many Filipinos who had been pressing for a more just distribution of wealth. They fit well within the discourse on socio-economic freedom going back to the Katipunan and the revolution against Spain. More recently, from 1946 to the mid-1950s, such ideas had been major claims of the *Huk* rebellion. Composed mainly of peasants and agricultural workers in central Luzon, that rebellion had sought land tenure reform and an end to political repression, economic insecurity, and poverty. After the rebellion died down, due in part to the national government making some reforms and waging an effective military campaign against it, demands for economic reforms and an end to poverty were repeated by various worker and peasant organizations in the 1960s. Redistributing wealth was also one of the main objectives of the New People's Army rebellion in the 1970s and 1980s.

The Marcos government never delivered economic and social development for the masses. That and other broken promises became themes in mounting criticisms against it.[116] Economic inequalities in fact worsened. The oligarchy remained. A new super-rich class emerged, which included Marcos himself, his family, and his "cronies." Under martial law, in other words, the Philippines ended up losing civil liberties, suffering more repression, and having no economic benefits for the majority to show for these costs.

≺ V ≻

Summary

This chapter has developed three main themes. One is that three discourses on freedom, which were pronounced during anti-colonial struggles against Spain and France, have reverberated in Philippine and Vietnam politics. All three are similar to ideas and debates over the meanings of freedom found in many western countries. One of the discourses concerns arguments for national freedom from foreign domination and for Vietnamese and Filipinos to govern themselves. Clearest during anti-colonial struggles and revolutions for national independence, claims for national independence continued in some measure after colonialism because some Filipinos and Vietnamese argued that, although formally independent, neither country was free from foreign powers. The Philippines also has had Muslim groups seeking a separate nation of their own. Another discourse is freedom from coercion and freedom to speak, organize, and in other ways participate freely in public affairs. Although the post-colonial governments of both countries have formally endorsed these and other personal and civic freedoms, there has been considerable debate and conflict about the extent to which those freedoms may actually be exercised. The final discourse is freedom from impoverishment and gross socio-economic injustice. This understanding of freedom in the struggle against colonialism has been emphasized by the Communist Party government in Vietnam but minimized or opposed by governments in the Philippines.

A second theme is that these discourses have often been in contention with one another. During anti-colonial struggles, many Filipinos and Vietnamese gave national independence priority over other freedoms but some were willing to forego that if they could have the freedoms enjoyed by Spanish and French citizens to develop their talents, speak their minds, and participate in government. For some anti-colonialists, national independence and self-rule was an end in itself; for others it was a step to higher goals, particularly to liberate people from poverty and elite domination. Since independence in the Philippines, individuals and organizations pressing to give high priority to socio-economic freedom have frequently been at odds with the political-economic elite who insist on preserving the status quo even at the expense of denying to others the very civil liberties they claim to uphold. Numerous authorities in both countries have justified putting civic freedom secondary to vigilantly guarding against subversion and preserving national independence.

The third theme is that differences in how the two countries became independent and in the regimes that have since ruled in each help to explain different patterns in the three discourses. National independence in Vietnam came only after the country had been divided in two, had been ruled by opposing governments, and had fought a horrendous civil war. In these conditions, which stretched from the early 1950s to 1975, personal and civil liberties were sidelined, although some Vietnamese struggled to keep that discourse alive. Meanwhile, the Communist Party government in the north redistributed wealth and carried out other programs compatible with the socio-economic freedom aspirations expressed during the earlier anti-colonial struggle. Since national reunification and full independence in 1975, that Communist Party government has continued to justify severe restrictions on civil liberties on the grounds of preventing the nation from becoming again irreconcilably divided and losing its independence and its socio-economic achievements. Nevertheless, voices pressing for the personal and civic freedom ideals of the anti-colonial era continue to surface.

In the Philippines, on the other hand, the issue of national independence was resolved peacefully early in the twentieth century when the country was still under U.S. colonial rule. That condition plus American encouragement of Filipino self-governance and the compatibility between the Filipino elite and U.S. authorities contributed to institutionalizing free speech and other civil liberties so long as they were not used to threaten the upper classes' domination. Since self-government in 1946, there has been considerable scope for and consensus around civic and personal freedom. But there has also been considerable repression against those seeking liberation from socio-economic injustice and impoverishment.

Japan: State, Society, and Collective Goods versus the Individual

SHELDON GARON

IN MODERN HISTORY, Japan stands out as the first non-Western nation to become a military and economic power. Among the peoples of Asia and Africa, Japanese may also claim to be the first to widely embrace discourses of freedom at the levels of society and state alike. Within a few years of the birth of Japan's modern nation-state in 1868, dynamic movements surfaced to demand greater freedoms. Liberal-minded opponents of the ruling oligarchy founded political parties and campaigned for political freedom and civil liberties. The European-inspired constitution of 1889 extended various freedoms to all Japanese. The following year saw the inauguration of Asia's first parliament, complete with a popularly elected lower house and opposition parties. Vibrant intellectual discussions of "freedom" not only influenced Japanese politics, but also provided liberal Chinese thinkers with a new vocabulary in the late nineteenth and early twentieth centuries.[1]

Yet throughout this long history, Japanese attitudes toward freedom have been ambivalent in the best of times and outright hostile in the worst. Many Japanese remained dubious of the virtues of individual liberties, as opposed to the collective good of the nation, community, workplace, or family. Like many other Asians, Japanese leaders and ordinary citizens have often critiqued the very concept of freedom, associating it with the libertarianism and social breakdown they claim to see in the West.

The cause of freedom suffered its greatest setbacks under the authoritarianism prevailing in Japan during the 1930s and the era of World War II. In the wake of imperial Japan's crushing defeat in 1945, postwar scholars in both the West and Japan commonly spoke of the "failure" of freedom and democracy to take root in Japanese soil during the prewar decades.[2] Many remark upon the flowering of freedom-seeking movements during the last three decades of the nineteenth century, sadly concluding that the promise of Japanese liberalism was not to be fulfilled. How was it, they ask, that the prewar liberals and parties proved so weak, failing ultimately to prevent the rise of the authoritarian rule and militarism that culminated in Japan's disastrous "Fifteen Years' War" against China and the Anglo-American powers (1931–45)?

Their explanations of the failure of freedom are in part cultural. Unlike many European societies, Japan had few traditions of individualism, Magna Carta-like limitations on government, and equal rights. Nor did Japanese towns or religious institutions retain various "liberties" vis-à-vis sovereigns, as had happened in medieval and early modern Europe. Under the Tokugawa shogunate (1600–1868), observes Robert Scalapino, the dominant philosophy of Confucianism sanctioned inequality as natural, and it stigmatized groups that offered alternatives to the orthodoxy as dangerous "factions" or "heretical sects."[3] Others discuss the weight of "tradition al ideas such as communal conformity and indigenous, family-centered orientation," and the constraints these ideas placed on the early advocates of freedom.[4]

Though they consider ideological and cultural constraints, progressive Japanese scholars generally highlight the modern state's systematic efforts to obstruct the growth of freedom. During the 1870s and early 1880s, they argue, the discourse of freedom was vibrant in intellectual salons and village societies alike; it would have continued to flourish had the oligarchic government not constructed an "emperor-system state" in the 1890s. By this the scholars mean the establishment of a rigid emperor-centered orthodoxy, a bureaucracy and military independent of parliamentary control, and a highly intrusive police force. They further point to the regime's use of the schools and semiofficial associations to inculcate ultranationalism and loyalty to the emperor. To many Japanese scholars, the imperial state's capacity to control thought and curb popular freedoms was nearly total before 1945. Writing of the freedom of religion, one historian insists: "all religions quest for the Absolute. Thus, in a nation like prewar Japan, *where the emperor system was the source of all values*, any true religion inevitably came in conflict with the emperor system."[5]

There is merit to both the cultural and "emperor system" analyses of the impediments to freedom in prewar Japan, but they are inadequate on three counts. At the most obvious level, Japanese "culture"—if by that we mean enduring norms—did not prevent a great many Japanese from pressing for more freedom. Second, despite the government's stepped-up efforts to manage society after 1890, discourses on freedom remained key elements in many political questions prior to World War II. Their content would, however, change. Whereas the earlier advocates spoke of freedom as an abstract *idea* or sought to expand freedoms across the board, after 1900 the issue of freedom frequently arose in the context of specific policies and legislation. Accordingly, this chapter examines the evolution of the idea of freedom with respect to a selected set of policy debates in the following areas: freedom of religion, freedom of the press, freedom of association (including labor organization and women's political rights), and the liberation of unfree persons (especially prostitutes).

Lastly, "emperor system" theories are flawed by their insistence that the restraints on freedoms were imposed on the populace solely from above. Instead the following cases suggest that popular groups often demanded greater freedom for themselves while calling on the state to regulate the activities of rival groups. Moreover, in some cases, self-styled "liberals" and social democrats campaigned for considerable state intervention into people's lives. They did not necessarily hark back to an essentialized Japanese tradition or culture. Rather, as modern-thinking men and women, they commonly supported state intrusions in the name of civilizing the masses, achieving a just society, or protecting the nation against perceived foreign threats. In short, the discourses *against* freedom and individual rights must be sought within society as well as the state.

≺ I ≻

The Birth of Japanese Liberalism

Under the rule of the Tokugawa shogun and the domainal lords (daimyo), few conceived of freedom as a natural state. The sociopolitical order was based on a hereditary status system. In principle, people were born, worked, and died within a given status—be it samurai, peasant, artisan, merchant, outcaste, or ethnic minority. With each status subject to different laws, neither the concept of a citizen's rights nor equality before the law had meaning. Nor did the freedom of occupation. The military ruling class (samurai) strictly prohibited commoners from banding together or distributing circulars. The authorities vigorously proscribed Christianity and required all Japanese to be registered at Buddhist temples. The shogun and lords did permit village headmen to present petitions about local concerns, although peaceful protests and the submission of improper petitions could be punished harshly.[6]

The Tokugawa order collapsed in 1868 when a coalition of powerful domains defeated shogunal forces and installed a government that ruled in the name of the emperor. The fall of the shogunate set in motion remarkable changes in the concept of a proper polity. Within a few short years of the "Meiji Restoration" of 1868, Japanese—from urban publicists to village notables—were campaigning for the thoroughgoing liberalization of society and politics. While indigenous transformations inclined many to promote greater freedom, unquestionably the chief stimulus was the introduction of the liberal thought then influential in European political debates. Forced by Commodore Matthew Perry's famed mission in 1853–54, Japan's rapid opening to the outside world gave rise to a new generation of men and some women who learned Western languages, consulted the newly resident foreigners, or at the very least sought out translations of Western political tracts. In 1871, John Stuart Mill's *On Liberty* was translated into Japanese, followed by widely read translations of John Locke, Herbert Spencer, Jeremy Bentham, and other British thinkers. Rousseau's *Social Contract* was equally influential, appearing in translation in 1877 and again in 1885.

The novelty of the term "liberty" or "freedom" was apparent to Japanese at the time. Mill's translator, Nakamura Masanao, observed that "liberty" had "no equivalent in either Chinese or Japanese."[7] Indeed, in 1866 when the noted publicist of things Western, Fukuzawa Yukichi, introduced the Japanese to the American Declaration of Independence, he drew on an obscure two-character compound from ancient Chinese texts to translate liberty and freedom. Pronounced *jiyū* in Japanese and *ziyou* in Chinese, the compound lacked a clearly established meaning in classical Chinese—aside from connoting behavior of a self-centered nature. *Jiyū* soon became standard Japanese for freedom, following Nakamura's best-selling translation of *On Liberty* in 1871. The Chinese thereupon adopted the nineteenth-century Japanese reformulation of the ancient Chinese term as their own translation of freedom, as did the Vietnamese (reading the characters as *tu do* in Vietnamese).[8]

The process of disseminating and refining the concept of freedom began at the elite level. In 1873, several students of Western learning organized the *Meirokusha* (Sixth Year of Meiji Society). The club dedicated itself to debating important contemporary issues and enlightening the public. Members included not only the independent scholars Fukuzawa Yukichi and Nakamura Masanao, but also several bureaucratic specialists within the new regime. Its magazine reached hundreds in the government and intelligentsia in Tokyo, Osaka, and beyond. Meirokusha thinkers introduced mid-nineteenth-century Western liberal theory in terms that were readily understandable to the literate public. They commonly defined freedom in opposition to slavery and to oppression by monarchs and aristocrats. Mitsukuri Rinshō recited the history of liberty in the West, starting with the Roman distinction between free men and slaves who lacked all liberties. Linking liberty to democracy, he further expounded that "the people of a country are like servants enslaved by their masters when they are oppressed by their ruler." If the people were to live in a state of liberty, he concluded, all (or at least, a majority) of the people must "participate in ruling the country," so as to avoid depending on the whims of the monarch. The society's essayists repeatedly identified freedom and individualism as major sources of the Western nations' power and efficiency. In the words of Nakamura, "no longer silenced by useless restrictions, individuals may expand their aspirations and plan alike for public benefits."[9]

The Meirokusha also debated more specific questions of freedom. In his best-selling book, *Gakumon no susume* (The Encouragement of Learning), 1872, Fukuzawa Yukichi warned of official encroachments on the autonomy of individuals. Advising scholars against working for the government, Fukuzawa declared: "independent individuals make for an independent country."[10] Concerning the freedom of religion, the "enlightenment" thinkers opposed both the establishment of a national religion and any infringement on the freedom of religious beliefs. However, they divided over the degree to which the government should supervise religious activities that might threaten the state and the rest of society.[11]

The Meirokusha intellectuals generally championed the individual's freedom from the state, but some, as had J. S. Mill, aimed to liberate individuals from subjugation by other members of society. Several—Fukuzawa, Nakamura, and Mori Arinori—wished to protect wives from husbands, the patriarchal household, and concubines. They proposed to outlaw polygamy and establish the principle of contractual marriage by the mutual consent of the man and the woman. A few, notably the government official Tsuda Mamichi, likened the widespread phenomenon of prostitution to slavery itself, for brothel keepers severely curtailed the women's liberties. In 1872, Tsuda authored the government's "Ordinance Liberating Prostitutes," although the measure proved ineffectual.[12]

Intellectuals and middle-ranking officials were not the only advocates of freedom. Top leaders of the new regime evinced sympathy for certain aspects of Western liberalism. Their support undoubtedly contributed to its diffusion. In a series of measures during the 1870s, the state removed the old regime's most egregious barriers to individual freedom. The modern government systematically obliterated the Tokugawa order's status system. Samurai lost their privileges and monopolies as the military and administrative elite. The introduction of universal military conscription and universal education further eroded their political dominance. Individuals became legally free to choose their occupations, as well as to travel freely throughout Japan (a tremendous boon to commerce, as it turned out). Above all, a new legal regime recognized all Japanese as equal before the law. The reforms of the 1870s undoubtedly introduced greater freedom into the everyday lives of the Japanese people than any subsequent change introduced.

Why would the decidedly statist Meiji oligarchy do so much to extend freedom? Fiscal considerations were part of the story. Leaders confronted the enormous costs of paying stipends to hundreds of thousands of samurai by virtue of the military aristocracy's hereditary status. Equally if not more important, the oligarchs took an instrumental approach, recognizing that greater freedom and equality of opportunity would strengthen the nation. Several had toured America and Europe as part of the Iwakura Mission in 1872–73. Like the Meirokusha scholars, they became convinced that economic freedoms, universal education, and universal conscription lay at the heart of Western strength; Japan would never catch up, unless it, too, harnessed the talents of the entire nation.

When it came to expanding political freedom, however, neither the oligarchs nor the Meirokusha intellectuals were eager to introduce the institutions of parliamentary democracy. Yet the government soon confronted an outpouring of political opposition, which drew heavily on the new rhetoric of freedom. Though diffuse in organization, these forces became known as the Freedom and Popular Rights movement. In 1874, the former government leader Itagaki Taisuke organized the *Aikoku-kōtō* (Public Party of Patriots), centered on disgruntled samurai from his domain of Tọsa. Declaring that heaven endows men with rights (*kenri*), the Aikoku-kōtō promptly petitioned the government for the establishment of a popularly elected national assembly. Itagaki himself faced criticism, at the time and subsequently, for his shallow commitment to liberalism and democracy. He appeared to be using the language of freedom primarily to return to power; and in demanding popular rights, he and his followers restricted the "people" to samurai and well-to-do commoners. The early political opponents were also prone to popular chauvinism. They attacked the cautious regime for its reluctance to extend Japanese influence into Korea or to press the Western powers to revise the "unequal treaties" which had been imposed on Japan in the 1850s.[13]

Nonetheless, by the late 1870s the Popular Rights movement had expanded beyond the former samurai to include liberal journalists, merchants, and rural notables throughout the nation. Together they spearheaded some 60 petition drives for a national assembly and garnered a quarter-million signatures by 1880. The following year, unabashed in their admiration for British and French liberalism, Itagaki and his disciples founded the *Jiyūtō* ("Liberal Party" or "party of freedom"). The Liberal Party's chief theorists, Ueki Emori and Nakae Chōmin, popularized Western ideas of freedom, drawing heavily on Rousseau's concepts of natural rights and government by social contract. The party's opening manifesto declared: "Liberty is the natural state of man and the preservation of liberty is man's greatest duty."[14] That same year Ueki wrote and disseminated the most liberal draft constitution of the era. He unequivocally placed sovereignty in the people, even granting them the right to overthrow unresponsive governments. His proposed constitution would guarantee freedoms in a number of areas, including thought, speech, publication, assembly, and protection of self and property. Most remarkable, Ueki advocated equal civil and political rights for men and women.[15]

Popular Rights activists debated questions of freedom at the village and town level, as well. Typically these were headmen, landlords, priests, school officials, and other men of stature. Some went so far as to write their own draft constitutions.[16]

How was freedom understood locally? For many advocates, imported ideas of freedom merged with Tokugawa-era visions of village self-government and Confucian (or Mencian) concepts of the right to rebel against corrupt rule. Local leaders often resented the Meiji state's intrusions into communal life. Tokyo had conscripted their sons and forced the populace to pay for new schools and roads. Rustic discourses on freedom focused heavily on entrepreneurs' resistance to centrally imposed taxes. At the inaugural meeting of the Liberal Party in 1881, *sake* brewers turned out in force to protest excise taxes levied to finance vessels for the new Imperial Navy. "Freedom of industry" was their battle cry.[17] As in Western societies at comparable stages of democratization, these "rural bourgeoisie" demanded political representation commensurate with their rising economic power. They desired the right to decide on policies that affected their prosperity. Moreover, during the 1880s, the gospel of economic individualism penetrated to the grass roots, spurred by translations of Samuel Smiles's *Self-Help* and other tracts. In prefectural assemblies, local representatives vociferously opposed the government's poor-relief measures, contending that aiding the "idle" poor unjustly punished diligent taxpayers.[18]

The Meiji leaders did not hesitate to use their extensive police powers to suppress Popular Rights activists, yet they soon recognized the futility of antagonizing the local elites who were emerging as the basis of national administration and the economy. In 1881, the oligarchs announced plans to introduce a constitution and national assembly in the future, even as they endeavored to manage the process of democratization. Pointedly ignoring proposals from below, officials surveyed European constitutions. In 1889, the Meiji Constitution was promulgated as a "gift" from the emperor. The following year the emperor opened the first session of Japan's parliament or Imperial Diet. Suffrage was initially limited to a small percentage of adult males based on property, but all members of the lower house were nonetheless popularly elected. Although the constitution vested sovereignty solely in the emperor, most laws required the approval of both houses of the Diet.

If the institution of parliament was strikingly new, so too was the Meiji Constitution's codification of a wide array of civil liberties. In the section "Rights and Duties of Subjects," the government guaranteed Japanese subjects freedom of residence, property rights, equal opportunity in recruitment for all public offices, and the right to petition the government. However, in no case did the constitution offer freedom on absolute terms, as seen in the key clauses below:

> Art. 28. Japanese subjects shall, *within limits not prejudicial to peace and order, and not antagonistic to their duties as subjects*, enjoy freedom of religious belief.
>
> Art. 29. Japanese subjects shall, *within the limits of law*, enjoy liberty in regard to speech, writing, publication, public meetings and associations.[19]

Such restrictions on freedoms may strike Americans as retrograde, but they were commonplace in continental European constitutions of the time, notes Gregory Kasza. The French Revolution's Declaration of the Rights of Man and of the Citizen guaranteed freedom of speech and press "except as prohibited by law." Several contemporary European constitutions made no mention of civil liberties whatsoever.[20] If anything, the contemporary European press—including the British—judged the Meiji Constitution to be too liberal for a people just emerging from "feudalism." In the words of the *Morning Post* of London in 1889, "it is impossible not to see that Japan is progressing so fast it seems very likely to trip in its hurry."[21]

Far from foreclosing the debate over freedom, the Meiji Constitution invigorated the Popular Rights camp to press for comprehensive liberalization from the floor of the new Diet. In the first parliamentary election in 1890, the "popular parties" (those opposed to the government) secured a majority in the lower house. The quest for greater liberty figured prominently in the opposition's spirited attacks on the oligarchic cabinets. Indeed, the popular parties regarded the extension of freedoms as crucial to their political survival against an autocratic regime. At issue were a series of ordinances that the government had previously effected to restrict newspapers, books, public assembly, and the formation of political associations.

Promulgated in the 1870s and 1880s, most of the ordinances had specifically targeted the Popular Rights movement. During the 1890s, the opposition in the Diet introduced nineteen bills to liberalize provisions of the Newspaper Ordinance of 1887, only to see each fail in either the lower house or the House of Peers.[22]

Another bone of contention was the Law on Assembly and Political Association of 1890. The government had hurriedly effected this measure, without parliamentary approval, on the eve of the first Diet. Authorities gained the sweeping powers to suspend and disband political meetings, dissolve political associations, and prohibit all outdoor political rallies and the organization of branch political associations. Other provisions categorically banned the following persons from joining political associations, or sponsoring or even attending political meetings: military personnel, police officers, teachers, students, minors, and women. In the Diet sessions of the early 1890s, the lower house defiantly passed several revision bills that would relax or eliminate various constraints in the original law. A measure of the popular parties' commitment to liberty can be seen in the lower house's approval of a revision bill in 1892. Under the legislation, women would have gained the freedom to join political associations and sponsor and attend political meetings. However, all but one of the lower house's revisions died in the House of Peers (and that amendment legalized only outdoor political rallies and the act of founding branch associations).[23]

≺ II ≻

Freedom Marginalized

In retrospect, the popular parties' protests against state controls during the early 1890s marked the end of an era. Rarely again in the decades before World War II would proponents be as united in their defense of freedom as an absolute principle, or as eager to expand freedom in so many realms. To be sure, impassioned activists continued to press for more freedom, yet they concentrated on narrower sets of issues than before.

Take the case of women's political rights. During the first two decades of the twentieth century, a small circle of stalwart liberals, socialists, and women's groups maintained the drive to eliminate the prohibitions on women joining political associations and sponsoring or attending political meetings. Remarkably, the entire lower house had voted to do just that in 1892. Thereafter, however, the mainstream of the parties lost interest in the cause.

Efforts to abolish state-licensed prostitution similarly suffered from marginalization. The abolitionist movement derived its energy from the fervent efforts of Japanese Protestants. Constituting less than one half of one percent of the population, Protestants nonetheless exerted political influence because of their ties to governments and moral reformers in Britain and North America. In the mid-1880s, the Japanese chapter of the Women's Christian Temperance Union launched the antiprostitution drive, and it was soon joined by the Japanese headquarters of the Salvation Army.

Although Christian social reformers worked to improve conditions among prison inmates and the nation's large outcaste community (the Burakumin), the treatment of prostitutes politicized Japanese Christians as the plight of no other group of unfree persons had.[24] Inspired by the contemporary British campaign against state-regulated prostitution, the abolitionists attacked the license system from a decidedly liberal perspective. Prostitution was, in their words, a "system of slavery" and a "violation of human rights." Supported by the state, brothel keepers denied the prostitute such basic liberties as the freedoms to cease her trade, to leave the licensed quarters at will, and even to communicate with the outside world.

To be sure, a few non-Christian liberals and social democrats joined the abolitionist movement, yet the cause failed to attract support from most erstwhile champions of freedom in the Diet and elsewhere. On the contrary, many politicians sympathized with the government's defense of licensed prostitution. The license system, they concurred, served to curb the spread of venereal disease and protect the "daughters of good families." Defenders also agreed with a leading bureaucratic specialist, who in the 1920s chided abolitionists for judging the Japanese system by the standards of Western liberalism. Westerners, he argued, "put the freedom of the individual first and regard the maintenance of public morals [regulating unlicensed prostitution] as of secondary importance."[25]

How do we explain the declining enthusiasm for freedom as an ideal after the mid-1890s? One answer is that the early political opponents had in large measure achieved key freedoms for themselves, and they were less inclined to extend these freedoms to others. The Meiji Constitution introduced unprecedented guarantees of rights. Moreover, the new representative assemblies at the national, prefectural, and municipal levels offered men of property a voice in budget-making and taxation. After clashing repeatedly with the government in the first half of the 1890s, the popular parties gradually entered into cooperative relationships with the oligarchs. Prime ministers invited party leaders to serve as ministers of state, in exchange for their party's approval of the government's budgets. Between 1918 and 1932, imperial advisors regularly appointed the leader of one of the two major parties to serve as prime minister and form his own party cabinet. The once-cantankerous "popular parties" became known as the "established parties." Also, during the early twentieth century, the established parties increasingly represented the interests of big business, shedding their identity as groups of back-country philosophers and notables who regarded the central state with suspicion.[26]

As representatives of the propertied classes, Diet members began allying with the government to enact repressive legislation of the type that they had adamantly opposed a decade earlier. Veterans of the Popular Rights movement were no longer considered dangerous rebels. That distinction now applied to activists in Japan's nascent labor and socialist movements. In 1900, the lower house overwhelmingly passed the Police Law (*Chian Keisatsuhō*), with little debate and one minor revision. The statute incorporated several provisions of the 1890 Law on Assembly and Political Association (including the bans on women's political activities). The Police Law further established sweeping controls over collective action by workers and socialists. The state gained new powers to disband their organizations, and Article 17 effectively outlawed the act of "instigating" or "inciting" others to strike, join unions, or engage in collective bargaining.[27]

The Diet's enactment of the Newspaper Law of 1909 followed a similar course. The popular parties and newspaper owners had fought hard to weaken the government's press controls in the 1890s. Ironically, a lower house subcommittee of five—all of them active in the newspaper business—now voted to *increase* police powers to ban offensive newspaper and magazine editions and summarily seize all copies. The bill passed the lower house with little opposition. Nor did the mainstream press offer criticism. Once again, the former champions of liberalism endorsed controls that appeared aimed not at the respectable press, but rather at pornographers and political radicals.[28]

If changing class structure lessened the commitment to thoroughgoing liberalization, so, too, did the erstwhile liberals' growing identification with the nation-state and the collective good. Scholars conventionally highlight the role of emperor-centered orthodoxy in silencing the voices of freedom. There is much to this argument. Of the 30-some extant constitutions drafted by Popular Rights figures around 1880, only one—that by Ueki Emori—explicitly placed sovereignty in the people. More typical, as stated in one petition to the emperor in 1881, political societies eschewed demands for changes that would give "free play to the menace of a Western type of revolution which would strip [your majesty] of sovereignty and give it to the people"; rather they envisioned a national assembly as a means of strengthening "cooperation between those high and low."[29] From the start, the Popular Rights movement denied itself the possibility of constituting government as the creation of a naturally free people. This stance made it easier for government leaders to conflate in the public's mind a sacrosanct emperor and the "state," placing both above society and political debate.

The aura surrounding the emperor did not necessarily stop his subjects from pursuing self-interest. As long as they tactically blamed inept officials while revering the emperor himself, demonstrates Carol Gluck, villagers might even litigate against the imperial household's confiscation of their lands. Likewise, Andrew Gordon describes the phenomenon of "imperial democracy" during the early twentieth century. Champions of popular participation often demanded rights for working-class people on the grounds that they, too, were subjects of the emperor and therefore equal to the propertied classes.[30]

Still, the problem for liberalism was not so much the cult of the emperor, but the nation-state itself. Many liberals so valued this collective expression of the Japanese people that they self-consciously muted their calls for individual freedom. In the late nineteenth century, nationalism profoundly influenced the discourse on freedom. This reformulation arose amid widespread concerns about Japan's vulnerability vis-à-vis the Western powers. From the 1870s to the 1890s, at the high point of "new imperialism" in Asia, the West seemed to be closing in on Japan. The Russians moved into Chinese Turkestan and Manchuria and sought influence in Korea, while the British expanded into the Malay Peninsula and Burma. The French colonized Indochina, and the Americans established a presence in Hawaii. Meanwhile, Japanese themselves envisioned control of Korea after the mid-1870s. Referring to Korea as a "dagger pointed at the heart of Japan," military men sought Japanese domination of their neighbor lest a foreign takeover place the imperialists on Japan's doorstep. Journalists and opposition politicians tended to espouse a more liberal imperialism, looking to a modernizing Japan to bring the benefits of "Western civilization" to the rest of East Asia.[31]

Japan's liberal nationalists were also inspired by the contemporary Western doctrine of Social Darwinism. To preserve Japan's independence, a former foreign minister, Soejima Taneomi, justified Japan's quest for territory in Korea and China in the following terms in 1885: "What kind of world do you think we live in? I call it a world where there is a struggle for power. Strong countries make it their business to conquer weak ones . . . If life is a struggle, then our country must have adequate military strength to cope with this reality."[32]

Alarmed at Japan's vulnerability, several of Japan's outspoken liberals concluded that the independence and freedom of the individual must take second place to the independence and freedom of the nation as a whole. Fukuzawa Yukichi, once the foremost proponent of the autonomy of the individual, by 1881 feared that Japan would fall victim to the new wave of Western imperialist expansion. For Fukuzawa, true freedom depended on a strong state that could preserve national independence and the happiness of its people. Without such a state, he warned, Japan would end up as contemporary China, where English merchants sold opium with impunity, and the Chinese people accordingly "lose money, injure their health, and year by year their national strength is sapped."[33] Japan's resounding victory over China in 1895 reinforced this message among many progressive thinkers, observes Kenneth Pyle. Liberals, who had previously disparaged Japanese tradition and urged total emulation of the West, now discovered their national identity and pride in Japan's military power. In coming years and with more victories, liberals found it harder and harder to argue with the efficacy of national mobilization and individual sacrifice in the name of the collective good.[34]

The state's remarkably positive valence among late-nineteenth-century liberals also emerged out of the distinctive relations between Japan's new middle class and the state. As in other societies, the growing urban middle class offered the greatest potential for advancing the cause of freedom. Its members were products of the newly established universities and colleges. They included journalists, educators, lawyers, and white-collar employees, and they were disproportionately drawn to Christianity and other Western influences. Their stratum furnished the leadership of liberal movements for universal suffrage, women's rights, and the abolition of licensed prostitution.

Nonetheless, while middle-class activists criticized the regime for particular infringements on freedom, they generally regarded the state as an indispensable agent of modernization and even liberation. Indeed, the new middle class owed its existence to the Meiji regime's elimination of the old status system, its establishment of institutions of higher learning, and the official encouragement of Western studies. In the world of nineteenth-century imperialism, the intelligentsia and the state commonly found themselves in agreement on the urgent need to modernize the people's thought and habits from above. They shared the mission of inculcating a "sense of nation" in the masses, as well as eliminating the embarrassing "evil customs of the past." To do so, middle-class reformers actively supported the use of the emperor, the national education system, and myriad semi-official associations to socialize the people. Japanese Christian educators and social workers, in particular, worked closely with the authorities, despite their reservations about the state's other policies concerning prostitution and freedom of religion. Beginning in the early twentieth century and increasingly in the 1920s and 1930s, men and women of the new middle class enthusiastically assisted the government in many "moral suasion" campaigns to promote household thrift, improve hygiene, and eradicate popular "superstition." In the process, would-be critics became enmeshed in relationships with the state that inhibited them from resisting intrusions into everyday life.[35]

No discussion of the limits on the idea of individual freedom would be complete without mentioning the emergence of a powerful family ideology. The Civil Code of 1898 legally subordinated family members to the authority of the three-generation household. The household head (usually a male) was granted extensive powers to control property and decide on such matters as whom his children married. In the absence of an elaborate system of state welfare, households were further obligated to care for indigent and elderly members, including fairly distant and non-resident relatives. By the early twentieth century, this "family system" had become a core feature of Japanese identity. In 1910, a senior Home Ministry official, Tokonami Takejirō, explained that in Western societies where "individualism" flourished, costly welfare programs treated family members as individuals, whereas

> in Japan, the family is the unit of society. A parent must raise a child, and a child must help his parent . . . It is a family shame to send one of its own out to bother outsiders and to depend on others for assistance. This has been the social organization of our country since ancient times.[36]

Advocates of women's rights questioned the woman's subordinate place within the household, and many sought to elevate her to the central figure in maintaining the family system. However, few—either before or after World War II—fundamentally contested Tokonami's formulation that in Japan, the individual should be secondary to the household or group.

≺ III ≻

Interwar Liberalization

The Japanese discourse on freedom entered a new phase following World War I. As in the previous two decades, the various movements for freedom continued to campaign independently on behalf of their respective constituencies. Yet their demands carried greater weight than before because of changes in the international environment, as well as major social transformations at home. Rapid industrialization during World War I gave rise to an assertive labor union movement. Union membership quadrupled between 1921 and 1936, from 103,000 to 421,000. The proportion of industrial workers in unions rose to nearly 8 percent. Tenant farmers also formed unions and pressed landlords for rent reductions. During the first half of the 1920s, well over 100,000 tenants took part in such dispute actions annually. The expanding new middle class had grievances of its own. Though a central force in economic and cultural life, many middle-class men remained politically disenfranchised. Significant numbers of educated women made their mark in the professions and public life, challenging the existing prohibitions on political activity. "Democracy" became the watchword of the era, as popular movements insisted that their disenfranchised and marginalized members be allowed to participate fully in politics and the economy.

To achieve truly democratic participation, the new activists recognized that the majority of the Japanese people must gain greater freedom from state control. Thus the labor movement struggled to secure not only universal manhood suffrage, but also the rights to strike, organize unions, and collectively bargain—demanding first and foremost, the enactment of a labor union law. Labor further demanded the abolition of the 1900 Police Law and other measures that had given the authorities a free hand in crushing collective labor action, dissolving left-wing associations, and even suspending labor and socialist meetings at the mention of objectionable phrases. Liberal and radical publishers, for their part, lobbied for the relaxation of the Newspaper Law and Publication Law. Together with male allies, women's groups vigorously campaigned for the repeal of the Police Law's provisions that denied them the freedom to join political associations (that is, parties) and to sponsor and attend political discussion meetings. They soon agitated for women's rights to vote and to hold office.

Previously such demands had fallen on deaf ears among the governing elites. This time, influential elements within the major political parties and bureaucracy took the calls seriously—particularly within the Kenseikai party and the powerful Home Ministry. The result was an elite discourse on liberty that colored many of the policy debates of the 1920s and early 1930s. Gone was the late-nineteenth-century idea of freedom, in which the Popular Rights theorist Ueki Emori, citing Herbert Spencer, equated progress with "less government."[37] Japan's liberal visionaries of the 1920s, much like British proponents of "New Liberalism" one or two decades earlier, welcomed state intervention of two types. Government, they believed, was obligated to reduce the insecurity of working people's lives by means of factory legislation, social insurance, and other measures. At the same time, these politicians and "social bureaucrats" looked to the state to guarantee the right of workers and tenant farmers to organize themselves into unions and socialist parties. In principle, the state would play the referee on a field of freely competing political parties and interest groups, enabling, say, labor unions and employers to negotiate with each other. Needless to say, the Kenseikai party and the Home Ministry approached the task in an instrumental fashion. Rather than proclaiming freedom as an absolute end, they recommended measured amounts of liberalization as a key means of relieving pressures from below and restoring social stability.[38]

This liberal vision emerged in response to international and domestic developments in the wake of World War I. Many in the Kenseikai party and the Home Ministry regarded freedom and democracy as inevitable "trends of the world." They represented the war as a triumph of the forces of "liberty and equality"—Britain, France, and the United States—over the autocratic regimes of Germany and Austria-Hungary.[39] Likewise, younger officials in the Home Ministry—which commanded the national police—concluded that if the Japanese government continued to rely solely on repression, it, too, would suffer the fate of Europe's despotic regimes. The surge in popular dissatisfaction threatened to overwhelm the nation's relatively small police force. Although urban crowds had taken part in some politically-charged demonstrations during the early years of the century, the authorities had not confronted serious mass disorder since the early 1880s. Yet in 1918 and again in 1919, more than 60,000 workers went on strike. When the price of rice skyrocketed in 1918, a previously unimaginable one to two million Japanese took part in "rice riots" throughout the country. Many sacked the warehouses of rice merchants or battled the police.

In an effort to mollify workers and the general populace, state officials responded to these disturbances with a comprehensive campaign to curb abusive police practices. Returning from study tours abroad, influential bureaucrats remarked upon how deftly English police defused radical discontent by permitting full freedom of expression at socialist and Bolshevik rallies. The leading police reformer Matsui Shigeru contrasted such displays of English tolerance with the Japanese police, whose "excessive role as a political police" called to mind the self-destructive practices of the Czarist police before the Russian Revolution.[40]

After coming to power in 1924, the Kenseikai allied with reformist Home Ministry officials to advance their program of liberalization. The program's dual nature was explicit. Rights and freedoms would be extended to "sound" unions and social democratic parties, while the state would continue to isolate and suppress popular movements associated with the underground Communist Party. With respect to extending freedom, in 1925 the Kenseikai-led coalition enacted universal manhood suffrage. The electorate instantly quadrupled, and a number of socialist parties formed to capture the new working-class, middle-class, and tenant-farmer votes. The following year the Diet passed government-sponsored bills that abolished the anti-strike provisions of the Police Law of 1900. Other legislation established a liberal mechanism for the voluntary conciliation of labor disputes. The Kenseikai cabinet introduced its longstanding labor union legislation, which would recognize and protect workers' right to organize unions. However, the labor union bills failed twice in the face of opposition from rival parties.

The program's repressive side is better known. The Kenseikai-led cabinet that spearheaded universal manhood suffrage simultaneously sponsored the infamous Peace Preservation Law, which the Diet passed with little opposition in 1925. The law imposed a maximum ten-year sentence on anyone who organized or joined an association with the objective of "radically altering the national polity or denying the system of private property." Although later governments indiscriminately enforced the law against liberal critics and new religions, the Kenseikai's home minister in 1925 did his best to assure unions that anarchism and Communism were the sole targets: "As long as workers do not call for anarchism or Communism, this bill will not, in the least, inhibit their participation in the labor movement."[41]

In the end, the interwar liberal agenda failed. The Kenseikai's chief rival, the Seiyūkai party, never accepted the validity of trade unionism and socialist parties, whether "sound" or radical. In 1928, a Seiyūkai government dissolved the far-left socialist party, an affiliated labor federation, and the leading tenant-farmer organization—all of which the preceding Kenseikai cabinet had tolerated. Whereas the Kenseikai regarded social conflict as inevitable and looked to freely competing groups to resolve discords, Seiyūkai spokesmen condemned class conflict as antithetical to traditional Japanese norms of "harmony." Allying with conservative bureaucrats, members of the House of Peers, and much of the business community, the Seiyūkai repeatedly blocked passage of labor union legislation. Attempts at liberalization came to a crashing halt in 1931, when the Kenseikai's successor, the Minseitō, again failed to secure the Diet's approval of a liberal labor union bill and a farm tenancy bill. The latter measure would have recognized tenants' rights to form unions and negotiate rent reductions.

The interwar debate over women's rights followed a somewhat different trajectory. In 1922, both houses of the Diet, including the conservative House of Peers, repealed the Police Law's provisions that prohibited women from sponsoring or attending political meetings (but maintained the ban on their joining political parties). The breakthrough occurred in part due to lobbying efforts by one women's organization, but also because the bureaucracy and most politicians had come to recognize the benefits of granting women the freedom to learn more about politics and government. Here, too, the lessons of World War I were critical. Japan's political elites expressed admiration for the active role played by women in supporting the war efforts of Western nations. In the words of one liberal politician, women must be given the freedom to hear political discussion, if they were to be taught to be "members of the State" and instill in their children the "sense to work for the State."[42] By 1930, the two major parties supported suffrage for women in local (but not parliamentary) elections. One year later the relatively liberal Minseitō cabinet sponsored a measure that would enable women to vote and hold office at the municipal level. The supporters' logic was, as ever, pragmatic. Enfranchised and office-holding women would "purify" local politics in their capacities as "good wives and wise mothers"; their innate conservatism, moreover, would weaken the hold of radical parties. France, noted the sponsoring home minister, was one of the few Western countries that denied women the freedom to vote, and "it is, after all, a revolutionary nation." Despite bipartisan support, the local women's suffrage bill of 1931 failed in the House of Peers, where it ran up against an extremely conservative gender ideology. Peers warned of a slippery slope. Enfranchised women would break "away from the family system" and, as individuals, insist on "right after right."[43]

Although liberal-minded forces did not succeed in significantly extending rights to workers, tenant farmers, and women, they had at least defended the utility of freedom with vigor. Nonetheless, their aversion to other forms of freedom is equally striking, and surely ominous in view of the illiberal era that followed the 1920s. Democratization, Kasza reminds us, need not result in greater freedom for all. In the Japan of the 1920s, manhood suffrage and the rise of new social forces may have conversely *broadened* popular support for suppressing Communists and other elements deemed beyond the boundaries of the expanding political community.[44] Ideas of modernity, I would add, similarly prompted many self-styled Japanese "progressives" to deny freedom to groups they considered irrational, backward, or superstitious.[45]

Consider the question of religious freedom during the interwar era. In 1927, the government sponsored a Religions Bill, which would give it extensive controls over the activities and internal operations of the nation's religious bodies. The bill empowered the authorities to restrict or prohibit the propagation of any teachings, or the conduct of any ceremony that they "feared might be prejudicial to peace and order, corrupt morals, or be antagonistic to one's duties as a subject." The appointment of the head and manager of each religious group required the approval of the minister of education. The minister of education was also charged with taking "necessary steps to maintain its rules and order" in cases of disputes within the religion.

Coming at the high point of prewar liberalism, the Religions Bill encountered surprisingly little opposition. Excepting several Christian spokesmen and a small group of liberal Buddhists, the nation's religious organizations generally supported the measure. In exchange for giving up substantial freedom, religious bodies obtained tax-exempt status. Buddhist orders were effectively silenced by a provision that would have returned some of the temple lands seized by the state in the 1870s. Above all, many established Buddhist, Shinto, and Christian groups looked to state intervention to bolster their leaderships against breakaway factions and their archrivals, the "new religions." Ironically the Religions Bill and a similar measure in 1929 might well have passed the Diet, had it not been for principled opposition from some legally minded members within the conservative House of Peers. They, almost alone, invoked the constitution's Article 28 to kill the legislation in the name of freedom of religious belief.

The established religions were not the only ones to turn to the state to control the new religions during the interwar era. A host of modern-thinking men and women crusaded for the regulation and outright elimination of these newly arisen sects. Even before the government staged its first raids on the enormous Ōmotokyō sect in 1921, leading socialists, liberals, and psychologists were warning the public of the "superstitious" tendencies of the new religions. In 1935, the Home Ministry commenced a "campaign to eradicate the evil cults." The authorities systematically destroyed Ōmotokyō and several other sects, imprisoning their leaders. Far from protesting this brutal repudiation of religious freedom, many intellectuals applauded the police. Responded Takashima Beihō, a liberal Buddhist layman and champion of the rights of women and prostitutes, "I fervently hope that the Home Ministry will not stop at the arrests of Ōmotokyō alone, but will stage one massive roundup, concentrating its fire on those groups possessed of quackery."[46] Intolerant of divergent creeds, progressive intellectuals and the established religions unwittingly paved the way for the oppressive controls over *all* religions at the height of World War II.

≺ IV ≻

Demonizing Freedom

Historians debate what to term Japan's authoritarian rule from 1932 to 1945. Was it fascism, Japanese nativism, or something else? Whatever the label, the era's leaders united in their total rejection of liberalism and individual freedom. Japan confronted the dual crises of the Great Depression and the international tensions resulting from the Imperial Army's occupation of Manchuria in 1931–32. Officials and the media declared the nation to be in a "state of emergency." Few Japanese remained confident that a liberal system of freely competing groups—whether political parties, labor unions, or employers' associations—would ultimately result in what was best for the country. Matsuoka Yōsuke, a former Seiyūkai member of parliament and a future foreign minister, spoke for many in 1933. He denounced party politics as "blind to everything but party interests." Referring to organized labor and socialism, he called on his countrymen to "renounce consciousness of class war, halt rivalry among economic units and, in short, wipe out antagonism of every sort in favor of co-operation."[47] The last party-led cabinet in prewar Japan fell from power in May 1932, after young naval officers assassinated the prime minister. Thereafter cabinets were dominated by military men and higher civil servants, who were widely thought to transcend partisan bickering and operate in the true interests of the nation-state.

The rise of European fascism significantly shaped the contours of Japanese illiberalism. To be sure, Japan did not experience a broadly based fascist movement or party. Moreover, the authoritarian politics of the era contained distinctive elements of Japanese nativism, whose adherents wished to return Japan to its premodern past—before the Meiji Restoration and the nation's adoption of Western institutions. Nonetheless, most bureaucrats and political leaders prided themselves on being modern-thinking men who studied the latest "trends of the world," which invariably meant the Western world. In the 1930s, the latest trends assumed the form of Italian Fascism and German National Socialism. While insisting on Japan's uniqueness under its ostensibly incomparable imperial rule, Japanese officials identified with Italy and Germany in their common struggle against "individualism, liberalism, utilitarianism, and materialism."[48]

Practice closely followed rhetoric. Censorship reached levels of thoroughness and severity not seen under the oligarchic rule of the late nineteenth century. In addition, the regime methodically stamped out groups associated with left-wing socialists and the outlawed Communist Party. In 1933, moving to circumscribe overall academic freedom, the minister of education forced the resignation of Takigawa Yukitoshi of Kyoto Imperial University. The moderate law professor's only crime, it appears, had been to critique existing judicial practices. Takigawa's ouster signaled a new offensive against heretofore accepted liberal ideas, which were now deemed incompatible with the imperial orthodoxy.[49]

Nazi Germany's radical reorganization of liberal market relations profoundly influenced Japanese officials as they searched for new mechanisms to regulate the workplace in lieu of independent labor unions. The reformist "social bureaucrats," who in the 1920s had advanced a liberal labor policy, no longer accepted labor-management conflict as natural. They envisioned a new order that rested on the total "unity of Labor and Capital." They further pointed to the world-wide ascendancy of "ideologies of statism and control that have superseded past ideas of socialism and liberalism."[50] In 1940, the bureaucrats coaxed and coerced the remaining unions into dissolving themselves. In their stead, workers and managers were to cooperate in plant-level "industrial patriotic" units and the national-level Industrial Patriotic Association. The political parties, too, disbanded that year. They and myriad groups—from farmers' organizations to writers' guilds—lost their autonomy and were absorbed into the state-run Imperial Rule Assistance Association.

This blistering assault on freedom formerly was regarded as solely the product of a police state. Recent work, however, suggests that the government's intrusions into the autonomy of individuals and groups might not have been so total but for the active support of many elements within society, including those often identified as "progressive" or "liberal." Impassioned public support for the suppression of new religions in the 1930s has already been described. In addition, a number of left-wing intellectuals played vital roles in introducing ideas of European fascism. Several served in cabinet-level research bureaus or in semi-official think tanks. When they recommended the formation of a Nazi-like single mass party that would integrate state and society, they provided a critical philosophical basis for the later Imperial Rule Assistance Association. Like their allies in the military and bureaucracy, these intellectuals condemned the evils of liberalism, party politics, and individualism. As socialists or former socialists, they tended to equate the principle of individual freedom with the self-interests of capitalists.

Individual freedom thus ran contrary to the collective good of the "national community" (*kokumin kyōdōtai*, or *Volksgemeinschaft* in German). In an influential report written for the government in 1938, prominent thinkers spoke of the need to sacrifice individual rights for the "whole": "In contrast to individualism, which considered the individual first and society second, cooperativism [the principle of community] considers society first and the individual second."[51] The good of society, the national community, and the state had become one.

Similarly, within the labor movement, key socialist leaders appreciated the weak position of unions vis-à-vis employers, and they increasingly turned to state officials and military men to protect labor from "capitalists" and promote "socialism from above." Socialist politicians eagerly cooperated with governments to pass wartime social policies, notably national health insurance. Eventually one group of labor leaders collaborated with the bureaucracy to disband the nation's unions and form the Industrial Patriotic Association in their place.[52]

Progressive thinkers did not entirely abandon the language of freedom. However, like contemporary German and Italian ideologues and Japanese liberal nationalists of the late nineteenth century, they now spoke of freedom with respect to the nation-state, rather than the individual. In the words of Royama Masamichi, a well-known political scientist active in government think tanks, "the freedom of the [individual] personality consists in recognizing by oneself the higher necessity of the cooperative body [*kyōdōtai*], entering into it, and being placed under it."[53] Like most Japanese in the late 1930s, these progressives believed their nation to be locked in a struggle to preserve its independence and way of life against "encirclement" by hostile powers—the Americans, British, and Soviets. Many intellectuals also worked on behalf of the wartime propaganda effort, portraying Japan as the "liberator" of the rest of Asia from subjugation by Western imperialists. One of the more surprising reinterpretations of "liberation" was put forward by prominent women's leaders who enthusiastically cooperated with the wartime regime after 1937. Ichikawa Fusae, the nation's best-known suffragist, lauded the state's mobilization of women for the war effort. These activities, she declared, achieved "women's liberation," for they freed wives from the fetters of the households that oppressed women.[54]

Then there was the interesting odyssey of the opponents of licensed prostitution. Throughout most of the prewar era, they had been courageous critics of a system that rendered large numbers of young women unfree. Abolitionists had long insisted that they did not seek to eradicate prostitution itself, but simply to remove the state from the business of managing and exploiting the licensed prostitute. Yet there existed within the abolitionists a tension between the desire to grant the prostitute more freedom, and the moral crusade to eliminate all forms of extramarital sex. In the illiberal atmosphere of the 1930s, their suppressive tendencies won out.

When the police stepped up campaigns to stamp out dance halls and arrest cafe waitresses and their customers, abolitionists not only applauded the crusade, but demanded more state suppression. Well-known abolitionists greeted the outbreak of war against the Western powers in 1941 as a "fine opportunity" for "a great sweep-up" of immorality.[55] They ignored the exploitation of tens of thousands of Japanese and Asian "comfort women" (military prostitutes), while enthusiastically assisting the regime to preach the virtues of sexual continence, temperance, and wartime austerity.

≺ V ≻

"A Gift from Heaven": Freedom in Postwar Japan

Ideas of freedom did not advance along a unilineal path before 1945, to say the least. As such, they bequeathed a complex legacy to postwar Japan. In the aftermath of the country's defeat in World War II, few Japanese wished to return to the excessive illiberalism of wartime. But did many wish to liberalize their society beyond where it had been in the interwar era, when the state possessed considerable powers to censor publications, harass religious groups, and prosecute political radicals? We shall never know definitively. Within two weeks of the Japanese decision to surrender on August 15, 1945, Allied forces arrived to occupy the vanquished nation. They remained until 1952, dominated by the Americans under the supreme command initially of General Douglas MacArthur. The Potsdam Declaration of July 1945 required the Japanese government to "remove all obstacles to the revival and strengthening of democratic tendencies among the Japanese people. Freedom of speech, of religion, and of thought, as well as respect for fundamental human rights, shall be established." The Occupation proceeded to impose a constitutional-legal structure of nearly unconditional freedoms and rights, which awestruck Japanese at the time termed a "democratic revolution" and a "gift from heaven."[56]

Once in Japan, the Allies moved with alacrity to eliminate the presurrender order's formidable impediments to freedom. On October 4, 1945, MacArthur issued the revolutionary "civil-liberties directive." The Japanese government was instructed to abrogate the core laws and ordinances used to repress free expression, assembly, and association. These included the Peace Preservation Law (1925), the Police Law (1900), and the censorship provisions of the Newspaper Law (1909) and Publications Law (1893). To the horror of Japanese elites, all political prisoners—including several Communist leaders—were ordered released. To curb state abuses of popular freedoms in the future, the directive further mandated the dissolution of the Special Higher Police (the so-called thought police) and "all secret police" organs. In 1947, the Occupation finished the job by dismantling the Home Ministry itself and, with it, the central government's capacity to command a national police force.

Among other momentous reforms, the Diet in December 1945 enacted Japan's first Trade Union Law. After having several legislative setbacks in the interwar era, workers finally gained the rights to organize unions and collectively bargain. That same month the government was directed to cease all support and supervision of Shinto shrines. So ended the institution of State Shinto. The presurrender cult had legally subordinated other religions and compelled all Japanese subjects to worship the emperor in state-sponsored rituals at the shrines. The Americans also took aim at another of the prewar emperor system's potent weapons against democratic thought and religious freedom: the criminal charge of *lèse majesté*, or insulting the dignity of the imperial household. In 1947, the Occupation forced the removal of the *lèse majesté* provision from the Criminal Code, over the conservative cabinet's vociferous protests.[57]

The capstone of the Occupation's liberal reforms was the postwar constitution (effected in 1947). The Americans desired the nearly unconditional protection of popular freedoms, and they initially looked to the Japanese to revise the Meiji Constitution accordingly. The prewar constitution, it will be recalled, had granted freedoms only "within the limits of the law," or "within limits not prejudicial to peace and order, and not antagonistic to their duties as subjects." Although parties and groups on the Left responded to the Americans' call with impressively liberal draft constitutions, the nation's conservative leaders firmly resisted any meaningful revisions. Speaking for the cabinet's Constitutional Problem Investigation Commission, the chairman Matsumoto Jōji uttered the curious promise that the rights and freedoms of Japanese subjects would be made inviolate, except "as otherwise prescribed by law." Outraged by the Japanese government's intransigence, MacArthur and his staff delegated the task of drafting the postwar constitution to an all-American team of 24. In less than one week in February, 1946, the Americans produced a strikingly new constitution that, with minor revisions, was approved by an unhappy Japanese cabinet and later the Diet.[58]

In the chapter on "Rights and Duties of the People," the postwar constitution guarantees an array of liberties in terms that are close to absolute. Gone are the Meiji Constitution's debilitating limitations. The protected freedoms cover—among others—religion, thought, speech, press, assembly and association, and the right to petition peacefully. Also, in contrast to the U.S. Constitution, then or now, the Japanese Constitution stipulates the "essential equality of the sexes," applying the principle to the choice of spouses, property rights, education, and other areas. Overall, as John Dower notes, Japan's postwar constitution guarantees "a more extensive range of human rights than even the U.S. Constitution."[59]

In its protections of freedom, the postwar constitution has proved an enduring document. In more than 50 years of operation, the constitution has yet to be amended. As a result, postwar Japanese have enjoyed fairly high levels of civil liberties. Since the end of the Occupation, the media has functioned freely without official censorship.[60] To be sure, the press is still subject to informal constraints. Right-wing groups have employed intimidation and even violence against journalists and media owners who appear overly critical of the emperor. The government, for its part, has blunted press criticism by granting more access to privileged media outlets, through such arrangements as the notorious "reporters' clubs" attached to each ministry.[61] Nonetheless, these constraints are a far cry from the overt censorship of the prewar and war eras.

The postwar constitutional order likewise expanded the freedoms of assembly and association significantly. The permit system covering public assembly was simplified and vastly liberalized. Whereas the pre-1945 state held sweeping powers to dissolve popular organizations, postwar governments have been severely constrained. The most egregious exceptions to overall liberalization occurred under the Occupation and its immediate aftermath. The Occupation initially disbanded many ultra-nationalist groups and temporarily "purged," or removed, their leaders from public life. In the later "Red Purge" of the early 1950s, the Americans and the conservative government removed all members of the Communist Party's central committee from office. They also supported the dismissal of Communist members and sympathizers in public and private enterprises. Another repressive measure, the Subversive Activities Prevention Law, enacted by conservatives in 1952, empowers the state to restrict and even dissolve organizations engaging in "violent, subversive activities." However, as fears of a Communist insurrection subsided, few arrests actually occurred under the law. Moreover, no government has successfully used the law to disband an organization outright.[62]

Postwar guarantees of the freedom of association played a central role in elevating the position of labor and the political left. The Trade Union Law of December 1945 firmly protected workers' right to organize. Employers were prohibited from discriminating against union members, and the law immunized unions from claims for damages arising out of properly conducted dispute actions. Emboldened by the Trade Union Law, workers joined unions by the millions. By the end of 1949, unions had organized 56 percent of Japan's industrial work force—one of the highest organizational rates in the world. However, the Occupation moved to weaken some of labor's freedoms in 1948 and 1949. Following the left-wing labor movement's attempt at a general strike on February 1, 1947, American and Japanese officials grew concerned about the prevalence of militant unions in such public enterprises as the national railways and postal service. New legislation prevented workers in the national public enterprises from striking, and civil servants lost the rights to strike and to bargain collectively.

Despite these restrictions, workers in postwar Japan enjoy impressive rights. The legislative revisions of the late 1940s did not reverse postwar guarantees of the freedom to organize unions, nor did they did significantly harm private-sector workers. In subsequent adjudication, observes Anthony Woodiwiss, labor relations commissions and the courts have taken the postwar constitution and Trade Union Law quite seriously. Judges and commissioners insist on "very literal readings of what are very unambiguous prohibitions" of discrimination against workers because of union activities.[63]

The case of labor illustrates the two-step process that has enabled the early postwar freedoms to endure, notwithstanding their imposition by foreign occupiers. Although most Japanese remain uneasy about the unbridled exercise of freedom, the Occupation's guarantees fueled the growth of potent constituencies that became able to defend the freedoms of direct benefit to them. In the case of labor, the workers' new rights permitted the rise of a sizable labor movement and socialist parties, which in turn opposed conservative attempts to revise labor legislation and the postwar constitution.

A similar dynamic developed as the result of the Occupation's unequivocal guarantees of religious freedom. The American-imposed constitution not only extended the freedom of religion to all, it also barred the state from granting privileges or financial support to any religious organizations. Clearly, few of Japan's established religious groups, on their own accord, would have promoted such sweeping freedoms or the strict separation of state and religion. Indeed, following defeat in 1945, most Buddhist and popular Shinto sects continued to look to the government to regulate religious bodies and especially to protect their hierarchies from secessionist groups. Moreover, a number of religious organizations—including several Christian denominations—demanded a prewar-style ordinance that would control and even prohibit "unhealthy or injurious" sects—that is, the rival new religions. Nevertheless, the Americans stood firm against the enactment of new repressive legislation.

In addition to the postwar constitution, the Religious Corporation Law of 1951—formulated with the blessings of Occupation authorities—effectively barred the state from intervening in religious matters. The law further granted religious groups broad rights to sue government agencies that interfered with the "freedom of faith." Just as the unions benefited from the Occupation's expanded freedoms, the previously persecuted new religions have flourished under the postwar constitutional-legal structure, enrolling millions of members. Like the workers, the new religions and other more established religions have organized themselves politically to defend their postwar rights. Notably they have successfully prevented conservative governments from financially supporting Shinto shrines. Most vocal in this regard has been the *Kōmeitō* (Clean Government Party), the political arm of Japan's largest new religion, the Sōka Gakkai.[64]

The Occupation's expansion of liberty thus empowered forces that indigenized the postwar debate over freedom. By the same to-ken, the American occupiers may have instituted constitutional-legal guarantees of freedom, but their efforts did not necessarily result in an American-style regard for individual freedom among Japanese. Although few Japanese any longer talk about the "state" in transcendent terms, most continue to value the collective units of society, community, family, and workplace over individual interests, which retain the connotation of selfishness.

The postwar constitution itself contains several statements of a collectivist approach to freedom that noticeably differ from mainstream American norms. Growing evidence suggests that the constitution's American authors—many of them New Dealers—were influenced by both the Weimar German Constitution and the drafts put forward by Japanese socialists and Communists. One Austrian-born participant in the drafting process recalls that the American staff closely consulted European constitutions, notably the Weimar Constitution.[65] Rather than simply guarantee freedom *from* the state, the Weimar Constitution and the Japanese left's proposals spelled out the government's responsibility to insure the people's economic freedoms from want. Similarly the Japanese Constitution's Article 25 establishes the people's "right to maintain the minimum standards of wholesome and cultured living," and it obligates the state to extend social welfare and public health to all. Article 27 stipulates that "all people shall have the right and the obligation to work." Article 28, a cornerstone of postwar labor law, firmly guarantees the "right of workers to organize and to bargain and act collectively." None of these guarantees of socio-economic rights exists in the U.S. Constitution.[66]

Reflecting both conservative and social democratic concerns for the collective good, Japan's postwar constitution also places limits on individual liberties that conflict with the interests of the whole. Article 12 pointedly requires the people to "refrain from any abuse of these [all of the constitutionally guaranteed] freedoms and rights" and to "always be responsible for utilizing them for the public welfare." Article 13 is emphatic on the boundaries of individual freedom: "All of the people shall be respected as individuals. Their right to life, liberty, and the pursuit of happiness shall, *to the extent that it does not interfere with the public welfare*, be the supreme consideration in legislation and in other governmental affairs."[67]

Moreover, in their preoccupation with overall social stability, postwar Japanese often prefer to locate rights and freedom in society's constituent groups, rather than in individuals. Workers' collective rights have endured in large part because the public regards them as the primary means of maintaining high employment and income equality, against putatively self-interested capitalists. Small retailers and farmers similarly enjoy an array of legal and informal guarantees of their way of life, in the face of competition from large stores and market forces. In terms of the political economy, the focus on collective rights tends to favor well-organized producer groups, at the expense of unconnected individuals, notably consumers.[68]

One of the most remarkable examples of vesting groups, not individuals, with rights was government policy toward the outcaste minority known as the Burakumin. As Frank Upham explains, the state encouraged local governments to funnel large payments for welfare and public projects to Burakumin communities, as represented by the assertive Buraku Liberation League. At the same time, the government did nothing to prohibit discrimination against individual Burakumin, nor did legislation in 1969 enable Burakumin to use the courts to pursue equality. The system lasted well into the 1980s with the collusion of the Buraku Liberation League. Such policies dramatically improved people's lives within the Burakumin ghettos, while inhibiting individuals from achieving freedom from discrimination in mainstream society.[69]

The local police constitute another impediment to individual freedom. Along with the postwar constitution and the rise of the political left, the Occupation did much to end the presurrender police's worst abuses. The Americans radically decentralized the national police into municipal forces, though conservatives in 1954 partially recentralized the police into prefectural units under the looser supervision of the National Police Agency. In fact, vestiges of prewar and wartime police behavior survive at the grass roots. Through a system of one- or two-man "police boxes," patrolmen maintain much closer surveillance over neighborhoods than in most societies. They do so with the active collaboration of informer households, as well as the neighborhood and women's associations that exist in each locale. Foreign observers frequently laud these networks as the source of Japan's low crime rates. Yet pervasive mutual surveillance also encourages residents to inform the police of their neighbors' "suspicious" activities or to report on families of "undesirable backgrounds."[70]

Finally, continuities between the prewar and postwar discourses appear in the ambivalence toward certain freedoms among some of Japan's most politically progressive and left-wing elements. The postwar campaign against licensed prostitution is one such case. Aided by the Socialist Party, feminist and other women's groups forced the ruling conservatives to pass the Antiprostitution Law in 1956. One might have expected this progressive movement, whose leaders vociferously defended civil liberties in general, to seek to outlaw only brothels and pimps from exploiting the prostitute, while permitting the woman to ply her trade. Instead socialists and leading feminists pressed for the arrest, investigation, and "punishment" of the prostitutes themselves. When two male labor organizers helped prostitutes form a union in 1956, the Socialist Party summarily expelled them. In its final form, the Antiprostitution Law was a liberal measure. It recognized the act of prostitution itself as legal—to the consternation of the socialists and feminists. Ironically, the liberal legislation passed with the support of conservatives and bureaucrats who expressed an aversion to infringing on the "human rights" of the postwar era.[71]

At the beginning of the twenty-first century, public doubts persist in Japan about the nearly unconditional nature of the postwar constitution's guarantees of freedom. These concerns resurfaced dramatically in 1995, when the new religion *Aum Shinrikyō* (Aum Supreme Truth) staged a deadly nerve-gas attack in the Tokyo subways. Aum's murderous nature distinguished it from other new religions and made it subject to a battery of criminal laws. Yet most Japanese concluded that Aum became a dangerous force, first and foremost, because the constitution's freedom of religion clause handcuffed the authorities from protecting society. Many further considered the new religions, in general, as a significant threat. In a public opinion poll taken shortly after the subway incident, fully 85 percent favored revising the Religious Corporation Law of 1951 so as to grant the government greater powers to supervise all religious bodies. Despite opposition and reservations voiced by several leading religious organizations, the Diet toughened the Religious Corporation Law late in 1995. The authorities gained new powers to investigate financial improprieties and other irregularities within religious bodies. The measure passed with surprisingly strong support from the Socialist Party and the Communist Party. These self-professed champions of postwar freedom continue to regard the new religions as political rivals and irrational, premodern cults that must be controlled.[72]

These episodes remind us that discussions of freedom in contemporary Japan remain influenced by discourses of the nation's not so distant past. Still, the Occupation-imposed expansion of freedom has not been rolled back to any significant degree, and indeed has gained potent indigenous supporters. It is all too easy to examine freedom in Japan in absolute terms—whether it exists, whether it "failed," or how it measures up against American ideals of individualistic freedom. Such inquiries overlook ample evidence that the Japanese have accepted the need for freedom, in some measure, for more than a century. For just as long, they have seriously debated where to draw the line between freedom and the collective good (variously defined by state, society, community, or family). Relative to the rest of Asia, Japan has permitted the exercise of freedom to a considerable extent—before and after World War II. Relative to the United States, Japan often favors the interests of the whole or of powerful groups, at the expense of individuals.

Japanese ideas of freedom, this chapter suggests, may most resemble those of continental European nations, whose theories of the state, constitutionalism, and social democracy profoundly influenced Japanese before and after 1945. As in many European societies, Japan's conservatives and social democrats generally agree on a collectivist approach to freedom. Although both camps in postwar Japan endorse the state's obligation to guarantee the people's freedoms from economic dislocation and social instability, neither is as impassioned as most Americans about promoting the freedom of the individual as an absolute principle. Historically and presently, Japanese and Europeans have embraced ideas of freedom. Yet both peoples have tended to be far more explicit than Americans in their quest to balance the needs of individuals against the good of state and society.

Redefinitions of Freedom in China

ANDREW J. NATHAN

A CONTEMPORARY CHINESE liberal thinker in exile, Hu Ping, defines the essence of Western liberalism as the belief that "the freedoms and rights of the individual have the highest value" and that "government power should be limited so as to protect the freedoms of the individual."[1] His definition provides a good focal point around which to explore evolving Chinese conceptions of freedom. We can compare various Chinese ideas of freedom against this core Western-liberal conception. The definition licenses such comparison, by showing that the central Western-liberal idea of freedom, for all its particularity, is not cross-culturally ineffable. Hu expresses the idea quite clearly and does so in the Chinese language.

It is, however, immediately clear, as Hu goes on to argue, that liberalism in this sense has never been well established in China. Our task therefore is to identify and characterize the most influential, widely-held conceptions of freedom in historical and contemporary China and then to inspect some recent statements to see whether and how the concept is being redefined. Considering the vastness of the topic, I have chosen to focus more heavily on the recent period; and considering the comparative focus of the series in which this chapter appears, on the ways in which some leading Chinese conceptions of freedom in the political realm resemble or depart from certain conceptions influential in the modern West.

Two hypotheses are possible. Given the spread of democracy around the world, China's domestic economic liberalization and economic growth, the rise of a Chinese middle class, and the reemergence in China of debates over political reform, one might hypothesize that Chinese ideas of freedom would now be converging with those of the West. If such convergence is occurring, it could be due either to the diffusion of ideas from the West through cultural contact, or to the functional compatibility between Western-style ideas of freedom and China's emerging market economy and consumer society. On the other hand, the persistence of Chinese tradition and the assertion that "Asian values" are different from and as viable as those of the West suggest that Chinese ideas of freedom might continue indefinitely to be different from those of the liberal West. Which view does the contemporary record support?

Clarity on this issue is worth having for several reasons. Since the nineteenth century a common political vocabulary has swept the world. Ideals like democracy, freedom, and human rights have become universal, but perhaps only as terminology. The problem is that these concepts are given differing meanings in different contexts. For example, "democracy" in modern China has for most thinkers meant not limited government but popular participation to strengthen the state; "human rights" has meant not a barrier to certain government actions against the individual but a set of long-term governmental goals aiming at human welfare.[2] The idea of freedom of course is linked to the ideas of democracy and human rights. In Western thought it is perhaps more central than the other two, being less exclusively linked to the political and legal realms and invoking central values of the Greek, Roman, Jewish, and Christian traditions as well as of modern political thought. But precisely because of its religious and philosophical connotations the idea of freedom may be even more susceptible to cross-cultural variation than those of democracy and rights, which are linked to specific political institutions and legal documents.

Much misunderstanding arises if one assumes that these valence terms have the same meaning across cultures or even across individual thinkers within a given culture. Some argue that cultural values set limits to the political possibilities of a civilization. Others believe that values adapt to new economic and political institutions. In either case, understanding one another's cultures is important, because culture is a window on political actors' and the public's current priorities and intentions. In a shrinking world, the rise of "soft power" and human rights diplomacy, the "clash of civilizations" and "Asian values" debates, and the increasing political and economic interdependence of societies, make it important that we sharpen our tools of communication across cultures and refrain from misleading one another through the use of different ideas disguised in common terminology.

Culture, of course, is contested territory not only between nations but within them. We will use the orienting notion of Western and Chinese mainstream conceptions to open an inquiry into areas of ambiguity and axes of debate in China as seen in comparison to similar issues of contention in the West. We will rely mainly on a careful reading of texts whose significance we will establish by placing them in political and polemical contexts. Besides a dominant Chinese view of freedom as a value enhancing the individual's ability to contribute to the group, we will discover a less frequently invoked Chinese concept of freedom as something necessary to the full development of human potential. Neither is the same as the dominant Western liberal view which sets individual freedom against the state; but both have points of contact with ideals that are valued in the West.

≺ I ≻

Ideas of Freedom in the Chinese Tradition

There were, as Wm. Theodore de Bary has argued, a number of protoliberal strands in the Chinese tradition, which he characterizes as "Confucian communitarianism."[3] Chinese ideas of good government favored humane or virtuous rule (*renzheng, dezheng*) that would neither torment nor exploit the populace but would "love" and "protect" them (*aimin, baomin*). The hand of government should be light so that society could go about its own, natural business; but this did not mean that government could not interfere whenever it wished, to seize property, compel service, or punish any challenge to its rule.[4] In this spirit the early Qing scholar Huang Zongxi criticized the late Ming rulers for exploiting the people to the point where the natural bond of sympathy and common interest between ruler and subjects was broken.

Similar to the situation in traditional Southeast Asia described in chapter 5, people could gain relative freedom by moving to the edge of the reach of the state. The classical philosophers did not recommend that people should exercise this option. Rather, they directed their advice at the rulers and suggested benevolent government as a way of reducing the population's incentives to flee.

Classical philosophy and religion entertained other conceptions of freedom as well. For Confucius, the wise adviser has the responsibility to speak the truth and to refrain from serving an unethical ruler. Neither political loyalty nor physical force intrudes on the autonomy of his conscience. This is freedom of a sort; yet the sage's conscience and will are bent not on self-assertion but on service—to the ruler and to the ruler's higher interest, which is seen as identical with the higher interest of the community. For the Daoist philosopher Zhuangzi, the enlightened mind is unfettered by conventional logical and ethical categories. It roams freely. But it is detached from society and places little value on the right to express itself socially. Freedom from suffering was a prominent goal of Buddhism, popular in China from the fourth century on, but this was to be achieved by detachment from rather than engagement in the life of society and politics.

In these respects the Chinese tradition was similar to other Asian traditions described in this book. Freedom took many forms. All encompassed a sense of the human personality as capable of full development only through the exercise of moral autonomy. To be a full human being (*zuoren* or *weiren*) in Chinese thinking entailed moral choice, and choice meant freedom, although it was seldom conceptualized as such. But freedom could be valuable only when it was exercised correctly—in the Confucian tradition, to social ends; in the Daoist, to asocial ones.

The premodern Chinese state tolerated such ideas of freedom as well as other forms of diversity and independence in religion, art, literature, and philosophy, but it did so only so long as there was no direct challenge to the authority of the regime. It tried to repress Daoist- or Buddhist-inspired political movements like the Nian or White Lotus rebellions, fought against the power of the Buddhist clergy, punished the individual Confucian remonstrator, and wiped out Confucian schools that tried to set themselves up as autonomous organizations, like the Donglin Academy of the late Ming.

What was entirely absent in the Chinese tradition, so far as I know, was a liberal conception of freedom in the sense defined by Hu Ping, that placed the individual against and above the state. If traditional Chinese government was in fact quite limited in its exercise of power on the ground, it was not by virtue of legal restrictions but owing to lack of ambition and reach. And if government authorities were supposed to refrain from abusing their power it was not because the liberties of individual citizens were considered to be matters of ultimate importance but because government was thought to be more effective when it did not abuse the populace.[5]

≺ II ≻

Freedom at the Turn of the Century

The gap between mainstream Chinese and mainstream Western conceptions of freedom is manifest first at the level of language. The modern Chinese word for freedom is a two-character compound, *ziyou*, which literally means "from oneself." (This is the same pair of characters pronounced *tu do* in Vietnamese and *jiyū* in Japanese, terms which are discussed in chapters 6 and 7.) It appears in a number of ancient works not as a fixed lexical compound, but as an ad hoc combination of words conveying the idea of doing something as one wishes, without regard to the social constraints that should be observed.[6] In the nineteenth century, Japanese modernizers chose hundreds of such two- and three-character combinations from the Chinese classics to serve as equivalents for Western terms. Many of these terms were then transported back into modern vernacular Chinese with the same meanings they had acquired in Japanese. *Ziyou* was one of these neologisms, assigned to stand for the Western concepts of "freedom" and "liberty" and, with the suffix *zhuyi* ("main idea"), for liberalism.[7] A negative connotation of selfishness has continued to shadow the term up to the present.

Late-nineteenth and early-twentieth-century discourse fixed on a conception of freedom that has remained dominant in Chinese political thought ever since. Perhaps the most influential political writer of the first half of the twentieth century was Liang Qichao (1873–1929). Liang wrote against the background of a crisis in Chinese consciousness, in the middle of the "century of humiliation" during which weak governments signed away chunks of territory and sovereign rights to imperialist powers. His and his colleagues' central concern—like that of writers elsewhere in Asia at the same time—was the weakness of the national state. Most of the ideas

Liang imported from the West (via Japan) were those he believed were secrets of Western and Japanese success in producing a strong state.

For Liang and his successors, a strong state was one that stood out in the international system because of the ability of its people to unite in the national interest, that is, because of its cohesiveness (*ningjuli*). Liang did not conceive of such a state as being authoritarian, because in his idealized view the Western liberal state demonstrated an ability to mobilize popular support that rendered repression superfluous. Such a state achieves growth and modernity, eliminates civil disorder, and keeps foreigners at bay through the well-geared, voluntary cooperation of all its citizens in the national project.

In his influential book-length essay *The New Citizen*, Liang opens the chapter on freedom with the phrase "Give me liberty or give me death." But as he continues it becomes clear that his interpretation of this injunction is rather different from Patrick Henry's. Two problems of liberty, Liang argues, are most important for modern China in the social Darwinian world which threatened its very survival:

> [First,] the problem of the right to political participation. When all who live within a country are considered to be citizens when they reach a certain age, and can participate in the nation's governance, then this is the liberty which the citizenry as a whole has achieved vis-à-vis the government, through struggle . . . [Second,] the problem of nation-building. When the people of a nation gather together with those of the same race to establish their own state, and do not allow other races or states to exercise sovereignty over them or to interfere in the slightest way in their internal affairs, or to seize an inch of their territory, this is the liberty achieved through struggle by the people of this state vis-à-vis the people of other states . . .
>
> In China today, the most urgent issues [of freedom] are these two, the issue of participation and the issue of nation-building. The two are aspects of the same problem. If you manage to win one, the other will also be achieved . . .
>
> [True] freedom is the freedom of the group, not the freedom of the individual. In the savage era the freedom of the individual was dominant and the freedom of the group was destroyed. In the era of civilization the freedom of the group is stronger and that of the individual is superseded . . . If individuals [within the group] abuse their freedom to invade the freedoms of other individuals [within the group] and thus to invade the freedoms of the group as a whole, then this collectivity cannot survive and will become

the slaves of another social group, and then what freedom will it have? Thus, true freedom requires obedience—to the laws which the group itself has set to preserve its freedoms as well as to restrict its freedoms.

In short, Liang concludes, "the freedom of the group is the sum of the freedoms of its individual members."[8]

Liang thus viewed democracy as a way to strengthen the state rather than as a way to protect the individual from the state. It was in the context of such ideas that he expressed his appreciation for Rousseau's perception that a man may be forced to be free in order to serve the needs of the group and hence his own needs. Liang borrowed the authority not only of Rousseau, but of Hobbes, Locke, and a host of other Western thinkers to promote a conception of freedom that was different from the liberal conception most of them adhered to. Scholars of Liang's thought believe that he did so not out of bad faith, but because of the power exerted on his reading of Western texts by the language in which he wrote and the concepts he used.[9] In addition, Liang's misreadings of Western texts derived from his structural situation as citizen of a strong state gone weak. As Sheldon Garon shows in the case of Japan, similar misreadings were promoted by Westernizers elsewhere in Asia.

III

Orthodox and Dissident Ideas of Freedom in Early-Twentieth-Century China

The subordination of individual freedom to national freedom became the orthodoxy of twentieth-century China as soon as the weak multi-party and multi-faction government of the early republic, which was liberal on paper, gave way to the authoritarian dominant-party regime of the Kuomintang (or Guomindang), the Nationalist Party. For the Kuomintang, *ziyou* still carried negative connotations. The party's founder, Sun Yat-sen, advocated Three Principles of the People—nationalism, people's power, and people's livelihood. But his target in doing so was the Qing imperial regime, seen as alien, autocratic, and exploitative. His goal was not a liberal state-society relationship, but a nativist modernizing autocracy.

Sun had famously written of the Chinese as having so much liberty that they were like a sheet of loose sand. As Edmund S. K. Fung points out, in this remark Sun "equated liberty with permissiveness and excessive individualism. In his view, traditionally Chinese had enjoyed a great deal of personal freedoms since imperial times without knowing it. China's youth, he feared, had become increasingly decadent and permissive in recent times."[10]

When the Nationalist Party came to power in 1927, Sun's successor, Chiang Kai-shek, founded the new regime on Sun's theory of "tutelage." This meant that the ruling party would impose order and implement modernization until the people had learned enough about self-government to be given the freedoms in practice to which they were entitled in principle.[11] Under the twin challenges of communist rebellion and Japanese invasion, however, the devolution of power never came.[12] Instead, citing the crisis of the nation, the regime adopted increasingly dictatorial measures—illegal arrests, forced conscription, assassinations, closings of newspapers and magazines, suppression of political parties, de facto military rule, and suspension of progress toward constitutional democracy. Yet it remained normatively democratic. Official rhetoric stressed "the compatibility of democracy with strong government" and the "subordination of the individual to the collectivity."[13]

Even in China's darkest national hours, there were a number of liberal thinkers who held to an idea of freedom as even more important than the urgent needs of state-building. Perhaps the best known was Luo Longji (1896–1965), an American- and British-educated political science professor and newspaper editorialist, who was a leading critic of the Kuomintang and who ended his life as a "rightist" because of criticisms which he voiced against the Chinese Communist Party in the Hundred Flowers movement of 1957. For all his Western training, Luo echoed traditional Chinese values when he argued that freedom is a necessary condition for the development of the human personality. In his contribution to the influential book *Renquan lunji* (Essays on Human Rights), 1930, Luo wrote:

> Where there is man, there is thought. Where there is thought, there is the desire to express the thought. If there is the desire to speak one's mind, it cannot be denied. A man wants to say what is on his mind, not what others want him to say . . . If freedom of speech is proscribed, not just speech but thought is proscribed; and not just thought but the [development of] personality and character as well. To proscribe the [development of] personality and character is to terminate life for the individual man and to destroy life for the mass of men.[14]

Freedom, moreover, for Luo must be absolute—"if there is not absolute freedom, there is absolutely no freedom"—and must be understood as prior to law and more important than the interests of the state.[15]

However, Luo followed his mentor Harold Laski in supplementing his commitment to freedom as an end in itself with an instrumentalist argument for its social utility.[16] He argued that the full development of the human personality through freedom is a requirement for a flourishing community. Freedom of speech, for example, would enable the individual to contribute more fully to the welfare of society. Contrary to his rivals, Luo used the thesis of freedom's utility to argue not for limiting freedoms but for expanding them. As society develops, he contended, new rights would become socially necessary. The attraction of such a utilitarian argument for liberalism was that it could appeal to those whose overriding concern was for the fate of the nation rather than that of the individual. Its weakness was that it would fail to persuade those who were skeptical about the value of individual liberty for strengthening the state.

Luo's strong defense of freedom remained a minority position in the stream of oppositionalist or "third force" politics of the Nationalist era, whose participants spanned a wide ideological band, from anarchism to a Chinese version of fascism.[17] The Nationalist government had the grudging approval even of many Chinese liberals in restricting freedom to meet the national emergency. Throughout the 1930s and 1940s the liberals conducted a series of debates over the relative desirability of dictatorship or democracy for China.[18] Most came out in favor of dictatorship because, in their view, the very purpose of liberalism is to create a strong state. Thus the debate pivoted on the issue of which system was more efficient and effective in achieving this end, rather than on the issues of protecting citizens from government. This was due not only to the exigencies of nation-building and, later, the Japanese invasion, but also to the sense, similar to Liang Qichao's, that the contradiction between freedom and the strong state was not a real contradiction. As Edmund Fung writes, the wartime liberals "were more inclined toward democracy [than toward liberalism], taking a greater interest in the insertion of popular power into the state than in the technique of limiting the state's power."[19]

In seeking a solution to the national crisis, Chinese liberals could entertain what might seem to a Western liberal to be contradictory ideas because they carried down from the neo-Confucian tradition a kind of transformative optimism, an ideal of a perfect political-social system, which could combine freedom and order, democracy and authority. They could tolerate intellectual elitism and political authoritarianism in pursuit of individual freedom not so much because they were willing to sacrifice liberty for some other goal, as because they did not contemplate the relationship as a necessary tradeoff. This may at root have been because they had an optimistic rather than a pessimistic view of human nature. On such a view of humanity, the exercise of liberty can serve and not contradict the collective or national interest; while on the other hand the exercise of authority need not lead to corruption and abuse. If human nature is good, neither liberty nor authority will be used selfishly or corruptly and the two can be achieved together in harmony. By thus eliding a conflict central to Western liberalism the Chinese liberals were again the heirs of Liang Qichao, as well as being precursors of the liberal Chinese intellectuals of the 1980s and 1990s.[20]

≺ IV ≻

Mao and His Successors

With the victory of the Communist revolution in 1949, the Chinese got the strong state they had been hoping for. The ruler of that state from 1949 to his death in 1976, Mao Zedong, knew what Hegel called "the freedom of one." His power was so great that no one could contradict his will either in politics or in personal life. He ate and slept when he wanted to, summoned and purged people at will from his private household, moved about the country from villa to villa, called colleagues to meetings at any hour of the day or night in any part of the country, reversed major policies on personal inspiration and re-reversed them when he chose, and summoned up both civil turmoil and the troops to repress it.[21]

The complement of Mao's perfect freedom was unfreedom of his intimates, colleagues, and subjects. It often pleased Mao to urge others to exercise freedom under his rule. He challenged intellectuals, non-Communist political figures, and intra-party rivals frankly to criticize his policies, promising that he would listen patiently to their ideas. The worst that could happen to those who spoke up, he pointed out, was dismissal from one's job, expulsion from the Party, divorce, imprisonment, or death—things not so fearful to a Marxist, he claimed, and therefore popularly labeled the "five fear-nots."

"Comrades, we are revolutionaries," Mao famously announced in one conference of Party cadres in 1962.

> If we have really committed mistakes of the kind which are harmful to the people's cause, then we should seek the opinions of the masses and of comrades and carry out a self-examination . . . Those of you who . . . do not allow people to speak, who think you are tigers, and that nobody will dare to touch your arse, whoever has this attitude, ten out of ten of you will fail. People will talk anyway. You think that nobody will really dare to touch the arse of tigers like you? They damn well will! . . . Let everybody criticize us. As for me, I will not go out during the day; I will not go to the theater at night. Please come and criticize me day and night.[22]

But those who accepted Mao's invitations to think for themselves[23]—during the "new democratic" period of the early 1950s, the Hundred Flowers period of "blooming and contending" in the late 1950s, and the Great Proletarian Cultural Revolution of the 1960s—indeed ended up in internal exile, in prison, or dead. What Mao offered in fact was only the freedom to be right. Because the standards of right and wrong were set down retroactively by Mao—as in the case of the famous six criteria for permitted speech introduced into the Hundred Flowers campaign after hundreds of thousands of intellectuals had already spoken out in ways that were deemed after the fact to have been unconstructive[24]—the freedom he offered was more precisely the freedom to agree with him.

In a less paradoxical mood Mao gave a more straightforward account of his ideas on freedom in a 1937 essay entitled "Combat Liberalism." "Liberalism" in this title is literally "freedom-ism," where freedom is again the two-character term *ziyou*, with its connotation of acting from a primary concern with self. Mao's essay belongs to an abundant genre of Communist Party literature which explains to Party members the need to subordinate themselves absolutely to the organization. In this essay Mao criticizes the tendency of some Party members to opt out of ideological struggles against friends within the Party or to preserve comfortable social relations with those around them instead of making strict demands for conformity with the revolutionary project—in short, the tendency to prefer one's own ideas or values to those of the party organization.

> [These ways of acting] are all manifestations of freedom-ism. Freedom-ism is extremely harmful in a revolutionary collective. It is a corrosive which eats away unity, undermines cohesion, causes apathy and creates dissension. It robs the revolutionary ranks of compact organization and strict discipline, prevents policies from being carried through and alienates the Party organizations from the masses which the Party leads . . . Freedom-ism stems from petty-bourgeois selfishness, it places personal interests first and the interests of the revolution second, and this gives rise to ideological, political and organizational freedom-ism.[25]

For Mao, the correct resolution of the dyad organization-versus-self is based on the familiar assumption that the true interests of the individual are identical with higher interests of the group. This is the premise that makes freedom in its individualistic form not only inconvenient for the organization but a damaging delusion for the self. As Mao puts it elsewhere, "The individual is an element of the collective. When collective interests are increased, personal interests will subsequently be improved."[26] Thus, as for many earlier thinkers, for Mao the possible contradiction between freedom and authority is dissolved, and the individual achieves his only true freedom by obeying the collective's orders.

The Communist Party leaders who followed Mao in power held to his illiberal conception of freedom, even as they carried out a series of liberalizing reforms in the economy, society, and the legal system. Freedom, in other words, expanded in practice but not (in the political realm, at least) in theory. The leaders of the Chinese reform era were Deng Xiaoping (in power, 1978–92, died 1997) and Jiang Zemin (Deng's presumptive successor from 1989 onwards, still in power as this is written). By dissolving the agricultural communes, opening the economy to private investment, and permitting private entrepreneurship, they widened the scope of economic freedom. By relaxing restrictions on geographic mobility, educational and career choice, and job changes, they increased people's latitude to design their personal lives.

In the domain of politics, the reformers reduced mutual surveillance by citizens (compensating to some extent by increasing police surveillance) and diminished the role of ideological campaigns; diversified and commercialized the media; and introduced a system of laws, including a criminal law and a criminal procedure law, to regulate state-society and citizen-citizen relations in a more formal manner than had been the case under Mao. The reformers introduced semi-competitive elections of village committees and of the two lowest levels of the four-level system of people's congresses. They gradually gave greater power over legislation and some elements of policy to the formerly rubber-stamp National People's Congress.

These initiatives brought far-reaching change to the tenor of everyday life and even of political life. But none of them established a realm of freedom that was reliably protected in principle or in practice. In fact, the party shied away from doing this at the apex of political reform in 1987, when a high-ranking committee was asked to consider more fundamental changes in the political system. The story of these secret deliberations has been revealed by a staff member of this committee, which was called the Political Reform Discussion Small Group.[27] It was convened in 1987 by then party secretary Zhao Ziyang to discuss proposals that might be submitted to the upcoming Thirteenth Party Congress. The committee worked by taking testimony from ranking Party and even some non-Party figures in academia and government. The presentations were frank and unconstrained by political orthodoxy and give us a sense of the outer limits of the Party's conception of political reform.

Perhaps the most radical (in the Chinese context) person called to testify before the committee was Professor Gong Xiangrui of Peking University, a non-Party liberal educated—like Luo Longji—at the London School of Economics under Harold Laski. Gong had been released from twenty years' imprisonment as a "rightist" at the outset of the reform era, and he frequently used his Peking University pulpit to criticize the excesses of Party dictatorship. Meeting with the committee, Gong argued that the economic reforms had to be matched with political reforms: a market economy does not function properly without an environment of freedom and equality. To give substance to democratic institutions, the regime must grant political freedoms. These in turn he defined as the guarantee that the individual's person, speech, and actions will not suffer any invasion and are limited only within the scope of law for the purpose of protecting them. Tacitly criticizing the tradition we have identified as dominant from Liang Qichao through Mao Zedong, Gong suggested that the idea of sacrificing the rights of the individual for the group and those of the group for the state might have been appropriate when China was oppressed by imperialism and sought independence from oppression for the state and the race. But under commodity reform (the regime's preferred term for the market reform) the formula should be reversed, with the citizen placed in first position. Softening his attack at the last moment, Gong summarized his recommendation as "pluralistic politics under monolithic leadership," which he glossed as keeping party leadership in place but allowing the activities of many parties and groups.

It was remarkable that a committee of top Party leaders summoned Gong and listened to him respectfully, but his voice was isolated among those they consulted. No one else defended freedom as central to the healthy functioning of the political system, much less as occupying a high position among the ends-in-themselves that a good political system ought to deliver. Zhao Ziyang expressed the committee's sense of its limits at one point by remarking that "On the one hand we can't carry out bourgeois liberalization [a tag phrase for critical and oppositionist views], we can't have a two party system, we can't have anarchy. On the other hand, we must actively increase socialist democracy, since people demanding democracy is a trend." Perhaps, he thought, a good middle point was what was called "autonomy" in Eastern Europe, systems in which the masses participate in management without gaining influence over policy.

Although the reformers used the language of democracy, they had in mind something more like a streamlining of government organizations. The committee and its staff shared the view that political power was overly concentrated and that this concentration presented an obstacle to economic reform. The core of political reform should therefore consist of measures to rein in the power of the Party, not, however, in order to strengthen the autonomy of the individual citizen but to give more power to other branches of the administrative system. Because of political exigencies the committee's proposals were later watered down before presentation to the Party Congress, and many of these more cautious proposals were left unimplemented or reversed after the 1989 Tiananmen incident. But even had they been implemented in full they would have done little to change the citizen's relationship to the state.

By century's end, officially sponsored political reform thus remained constrained by the assumption of the primacy of collective over individual interests familiar from Liang Qichao. As Deng Xiaoping put it in 1979, in order to realize modernization in a country as crowded and poor as China, freedom must be constrained by "four basic principles"—the socialist road, proletarian dictatorship, communist party leadership, and Marxism-Leninism-Mao Zedong thought.[28] These principles were written into the 1982 Chinese constitution and throughout the 1980s and 1990s the claim that they were being challenged served as the basis for criminal convictions of dissidents who sought more extensive freedoms and who in consequence were charged with crimes against the state.

≺ V ≻

The Democracy Movement

Despite such risks of repression, democratic dissent, driven underground by the Maoist dictatorship, had reemerged in the more hospitable environment of Deng Xiaoping's reforms. According to Hu Ping—the liberal thinker with whom we began this chapter—so-called democracy activists after the death of Mao were liberals more than democrats. That is, they were more concerned with establishing limits to governmental power than with establishing mechanisms for popular participation in or control over government.[29] Yet most of them expressed much the same hope for the compatibility of individual freedom and the strong state as did Liang Qichao and Mao Zedong.

Hu Ping himself devoted most of his famous Democracy Wall essay, "On Freedom of Speech," to extolling the benefits of the exercise of this freedom for society.[30] Freedom of speech "helps us perceive and develop truth." It "helps people develop into true Marxists." It "strengthens national unity" and "helps us [the regime] consolidate our political power." It trains the people to be open and honest, diminishes apathy, and is the key to national progress.

The use of the word "us" highlights Hu's rhetorical decision to argue from within rather than outside the regime's framework.[31] This was a common approach at Democracy Wall (in Beijing, 1978–79). The writers on the wall were hoping to find an ally in the reformist Deng Xiaoping, who was just coming to power and whose policy positions were unknown. Hu Ping thus placed himself on what he supposed to be the side of the newly emerging reformist faction against the Maoist conservatives who still defended the kind of ideological discipline that had led to the excesses of the Cultural Revolution. Basing himself on the grant of freedom in the Chinese constitution, Hu argued against those who would restrict its exercise. He quoted Marxist classics and Mao Zedong at length, although out of context, to establish the legitimacy of free speech as a Chinese communist value. If the argument was for total free speech and the attack on the conservatives strong, the posture nonetheless was of one supporting, not challenging, the new leadership.

The echo in Hu's argument of John Stuart Mill's foundational essay *On Liberty* is unmistakable, yet there are some subtle differences which help locate Hu's argument as a distinctively Chinese form of utilitarian liberalism, with much in common with Liang Qichao and his successors. This is partly a matter of historical context: where Mill was arguing against Christian self-righteousness and bourgeois propriety, Hu takes on an even stronger antagonist—an ideologically-based political regime. And it is partly a matter of goals: while Mill argues for the supreme value of convictions internally arrived at for truth and human fulfillment, Hu argues for the supreme value of talents fully mobilized for national unity and strength. While Mill has to defend utilitarianism as a premise, Hu does not need to do so. There was no Chinese natural rights controversy to escape from. Since Marx was himself strongly influenced by British political economy, it is easy to be a utilitarian in a Marxist debate, and Chinese Marxism had established a set of national goals that could be used to legitimate Hu's conclusions.

Yet, as it happens, Hu had not needed to read Mill to arrive at his arguments; indeed, he did not read Mill until after writing the fourth draft of the essay. There was enough raw material in the modern Chinese intellectual tradition, combined with the traumatic personal experiences of Hu's generation in facing political repression, to enable Hu to construct his argument on his own. Hu's essay is thus an important document in the history of Chinese liberalism, not just for its clear alignment with one of the most influential Western rationales for liberty, but even more for the fact that this rationale could have a parallel origin within the contemporary Chinese tradition. "Living under dictatorship," Hu told me, "we had to retrace the ground others had already traversed in order to struggle for our freedom."[32]

If Hu's rediscovery of freedom occurred recognizably within the boundaries set down by such distinguished predecessors as Liang Qichao, the example of another Democracy Wall essayist, Wei Jingsheng, shows how the idea of freedom can also reemerge with a freshness that seems to defy any attempt to discover historical origins.

Wei by his own testimony was deprived of systematic exposure to previous political thinkers, Chinese or Western. What his writings lack in sophistication they make up in clarity and eloquence. In his second essay on "The Fifth Modernization—Democracy," Wei wrote,

> Autocratic rulers of all ages have invariably taught the people that since men are social beings, social interests should predominate; that since social interests are common to all people, centralized management or administration is necessary; that since rule by a minority, or even by a single person, is most centralized, autocracy is the most ideal form . . . [But] society is composed of different individuals, and in his natural condition, each individual exists independently of the others. People's social nature is formed of the common characteristics and common interests of many different individuals. . . People's individuality is a component of human nature which is prior to their sociality.[33]

Although he often refers in his writings to various social benefits of democracy, Wei Jingsheng was unusual even among Chinese democratic activists for his clean, clear vision of freedom as grounded in a human nature that is instinctively free and individualistic, rather than intrinsically social and yielding. This was a break with classic as well as with most twentieth-century Chinese thought. "From the moment he is born," Wei wrote,

> a human being has the right to live and the right to strive for a better life. These are what people call heaven-given [natural] human rights. For they are not bestowed by any external thing. Just like the right of any object to exist, they are bestowed by the fact of existence itself. This is like the case of a stone: since it occupies a bit of space by virtue of its existence, it has its right of existence relative to the things around it.[34]

Appealing though it is, there are difficulties with this grounding of a claim to the right to freedom. It ignores the fact that humans are social beings and that the freedoms of speech, association, publication, and the like are social claims, not unchallenged facts of mere passive existence. As such, the analogy fails to resolve the classic dilemma over how the human desire for freedom gains the status of a universal moral claim: through its social utility or through some metaphysical sanction, whether religious or logical?

But on a sympathetic reading, one can see that Wei's argument rests on the same psychological foundation that we noticed earlier in some classical authors and in Luo Longji: that the freedom to express one's individuality is essential to human growth and development. If this is a reading-into of Wei's words, it is validated by a reading-out of his life as one of China's longest-serving and its most famous political prisoner. (He served fourteen years for circulating essays critical of Deng Xiaoping during the 1978–79 Democracy Wall movement and was imprisoned again in 1994–97 for continuing to advocate democracy after release from his first term.) Throughout his long stay in prison Wei insisted on exercising his capabilities to read, think, conduct small scientific experiments, raise rabbits, and write—even if only family letters and unsolicited, critical memoranda to the nation's leaders. "Man is not a product of his social relations," Wei points out in one of these memos,

> nor indeed of any relations. He is not a robot, nor is he a product created by other people based on a pattern for man. Rather, he is a product of nature. Thus, his essential qualities are likewise a product of nature. These are "instinctive" and very basic and they constitute a human "commonality" which is inborn and possessed by all and on which all other human natures and social relations are based. Human rights and basic freedoms refer to the satisfying or realizing of this part of human nature. They are the sum of hopes and aspirations that emerge naturally and do not need to be taught.[35]

The examples of Luo and Wei suggest that Chinese culture is far from lacking in strong reasons to make freedom a transcendent value. The most accessible Chinese source for a strong defense of freedom lies in an active, questing, and often ethically demanding conception of what it means to develop into a full human personality. If this is a less philosophically elaborate argument than Western appeals to natural law, religious sanction, or social utility, it may nonetheless be stronger and also more universal in its very immediacy.

< VI >

Recent Chinese Liberalism

While Wei sat in prison, Chinese society was becoming more mobile, plural, prosperous, and individualistic—in a sense, more Westernized. Did the mainstream of Chinese liberal thought accordingly move closer to relatively Western-sounding ideas of freedom like Hu's and Wei's?

At the mass level, the opening of the economy, the increase in mobility, and the rise of consumerism have affected attitudes toward freedom. In a 1990 national sample survey, 54.8 percent of respondents agreed that "China needs more democracy now." Two-thirds of respondents disagreed with the proposition that "If people's ideas are not united, there will be chaos in society." On the other hand, levels of tolerance measured in the same survey were relatively low. Only 17.4 percent of respondents believed that persons espousing an ideologically unpopular viewpoint should be allowed to express their views at a public meeting. Although the absence of earlier surveys makes it impossible to calculate how large a change these percentages represented from attitudes in the past, statistical analysis supports the idea that reforms helped change attitudes. The highest levels of support both for political freedoms and for further freeing up of the national economy existed among those sections of the public that had benefited most from the reforms—the better educated, younger, and more urban residents, especially males. Yet the blunt instrument of survey research disguises the nuances of meaning in such attitudes. For example, among those who wanted more democracy most nonetheless agreed with the proposition, "The realization of democracy in our country depends upon the leadership of the Party."[36] Thus it would be hard to tell from survey research alone how much change had occurred at the mass level in the conception of, as opposed to the level of support for, democracy.

Within the Party, during the reform era liberal intellectuals resumed a search that dated back to the 1930s for the liberating potentials of Chinese Marxism.[37] Again, as with Luo Longji and Wei Jingsheng, the Chinese conception of a morally autonomous human nature demonstrated its appeal as a value alongside and sometimes in competition with the Liangist-Maoist tradition of freedom as a value serving mainly social ends. The senior Communist Party intellectuals of the Deng Xiaoping era were specialists in ideology, propaganda, and literature, who had joined the Party in the 1930s, 1940s, and 1950s out of a belief that communism would bring justice, equality, and a flowering of freedom in the service of the nation. (Although they could not have been unaware of Mao's "On Liberalism," they took more seriously his later pronouncement of a "New Democracy."[38]) Up to the mid-1960s they tried to develop a role as autonomous yet loyal and constructive partners of the Party authorities—a role akin to the Confucian idea of the selfless yet morally independent scholar-official. Many of them were punished during the anti-Rightist movement of 1957 for speaking too freely during the Hundred Flowers period; others became objects of "struggle" during the Cultural Revolution. But under Deng they were restored to influential positions in the Party's theoretical and propaganda apparatuses. Invited to provide the theoretical superstructure to accommodate the market reforms, they glimpsed anew, as Jing Wang puts it, "the theoretical possibility of the autonomous and infinitely open self."[39]

High-ranking Party liberals founded a magazine called *New Enlightenment* that promised, "the fate of theory lies in courage and truth, not in bowing to power or fawning on fashion." Theorist Ruan Ming argued in the journal's pages that the new forces of production require that each social citizen be bestowed with the freedom and power to obtain knowledge and information, and to realize creativity. New questions of subjectivity, identity, and the individual were raised. Party journalist Wang Ruoshui placed the traditional Chinese conception of the morally autonomous human being on a Marxist footing with his theory of "Marxist humanism." He argued that man is by nature free and that socialism goes astray when it deprives him of this freedom, thus creating "the alienation of man under socialism." Intellectuals followed Wang's lead in debating human nature and "socialist humanism."[40] For the first time since 1949 it was permissible to ask, as in the title of one short story, "Who am I?"[41]

In response to such trends, conservative Party ideologists launched a series of four campaigns against "bourgeois liberalization," understood as tendencies toward intellectual and creative freedom reflecting values characteristic of the West. Even though the intellectual class continued to be employed overwhelmingly by the state, most of its members resisted these campaigns and gradually developed something resembling the oppositionist stance of an independent intelligentsia. In the aftermath of the 1989 crackdown, 60-odd years after Mao Zedong had denounced "freedom-ism," a Party member and philosophy professor at Nanjing University, Guo Luoji, broke precedent by actually suing his university's Party committee for violating his rights. It had, he charged, punished him for his support of the student movement by depriving him of the right to teach, direct graduate students, and go abroad for academic exchange. Guo's suit was unsuccessful; in fact, the court refused to accept it. He left China in 1992. But his quixotic action symbolized both the new independence of the Party intellectuals and the potential contradiction between Party rule and the evolving legal system.[42]

For senior party liberals, these struggles forced a very personal rethinking of the meaning of freedom versus organizational discipline in the context of their long careers in the service of the Party. Dramatist Wu Zuguang recalls a moving hospital bedside conversation with his senior colleague Cao Yu in 1994. When Cao expressed dissatisfaction with his lifetime of writing at the behest of the apparatus, Wu blurted out, "You were too obedient."

> Cao's response surprised me! He almost shouted, "Well said! Exactly what I've been thinking! I was too obedient! I always obeyed the leadership, whatever the leadership said, I did, sometimes I even had to guess at what the leaders wanted . . . But how can creative writing follow the wishes of the leadership?" As his agitation decreased his voice grew quieter. Obviously, he had become clear. But there was no time left, his health was gone, his creative years were behind him.[43]

In 40 years of thought campaigns under the People's Republic, how many intellectuals straightened their backs and preserved their individuality? asks senior party liberal Li Honglin. There were a few, he concludes. They were either expelled from the Party, or suffered even more grievously. Li's prime example is Gu Zhun.[44]

Li's reference to Gu Zhun is significant. Gu Zhun was a Party member who was designated a rightist in 1957 and spent most of the next seventeen years until his death living among the peasants and in conditions of deprivation. He lost his family and his livelihood. He nonetheless preserved his independence of thought, and in the darkest days of late Maoism in the early 1970s, he wrote a series of crystalline short essays on revolution, democracy, Marxism, Greek and Roman philosophy, and Daoism and Confucianism, which were informed by a lucid liberal sensibility and a critical but unrancorous view of revolutionary dictatorship.[45] The posthumous publication of Gu's works in the 1990s created a brief vogue in which intellectuals celebrated Gu as an example of intellectual integrity.

But Gu makes an ambiguous model of intellectual freedom because of the very quietism or recessiveness of his liberalism, which was in turn made necessary by the conditions of extreme repressiveness under which he lived. By contrast, those who openly resisted ended up in prison and labor camp, an experience few survived, and they left no posthumous publications.[46] Gu's liberalism thus in effect embraced his political helplessness. The limits of his assertiveness—to be sure, sufficiently dangerous under the circumstances—consisted in using private writings, never intended for publication and marked by a pronounced moderateness of language, to think through the historical origins of the repression in terms of comparative history.

For the Party liberals, Gu thus represented the perfect contrast both with intellectuals who served the Party too well and with those who refused to serve it at all. For it would have been difficult for those who were both Party members and advocates of freedom to reconcile their lifetimes of service to the socialist cause with approval of the anti-communist resisters who ended up in the labor camps or even of rhetorically fellow-traveling but essentially anti-communist wall-poster writers like Hu Ping. Perhaps that is why the common Western liberal contrast between criminal complicity with a dictatorial regime and heroic resistance is replaced in contemporary China with the contrast between the good person who tries to achieve good ends by cooperating with the state and goes too far in blind obedience, versus the person who preserves his integrity in private without carrying out overt resistance.[47]

Here one finds the same tension as in the Confucian archetype of the integrity of the sage. To be a good public servant, it is essential to say what you think. But one should not go to the point of selfishly insisting on one's own views in a public confrontation with the authorities. But under the more individualist view of human nature reemerging in post-Mao China, the delicate combination of intellectual integrity and non-opposition seems more and more difficult to maintain. Li Honglin explains why.

> Thought can only be produced in the brains of people. Of course, it will reflect the outer world, but it will also reflect the inner person. Thought is not only cognition, it also includes emotion, will, aesthetic concepts and moral judgments, as well as other aspects of the subjective world. The essence of thought is freedom, so the content and manifest forms of thought are richly diverse. It follows that thought in society must be pluralistic. Once Marxism, which has been the main melody, can no longer drown out all others, pluralization of the intellectual world becomes possible. To acknowledge this pluralization, to acknowledge the freedom of thought, and to give legal protection to the expression of free thought—that is to say, to freedom of speech—is a necessary condition of a modernized society.[48]

To put Li's point in less Marxist terms, modernization makes inevitable a clash between the intellectuals and the ideologically monovocal state.

If Li does not choose to put his point in non-Marxist terms, it is probably because he still honors his lifelong commitment to Marxism. Yet the history he has lived through has forced him to abandon the once-orthodox Stalinist "reflectionist" epistemology, in which knowledge is only a reflection of the outside world; and, perhaps at a deeper level, to abandon as well a neo-Confucian epistemology of potentially perfectible knowledge. One thus glimpses in Li's remarks a sense of loss along with a sense of liberation. Li makes freedom of thought sound not so much like an end in itself as like a necessary accommodation to the newly acknowledged imperfection of human cognition. But it remains his view that the struggle against dictatorship is properly carried out by those who wish to contribute positively to the social cause, not by those who have self-serving motives, who wish to weaken authority just to have more leeway to exercise their selfish desires. What Li seeks is liberation of the individual, to be sure, but *for*, not against and not neutral about, the creation of a modernized—that is prosperous—society and a strong state. Thus Li still expresses a distinctively Chinese-liberal, as opposed to Western-liberal, conception of what freedom is and why it is to be valued.

≺ VII ≻

Conclusion

By the 1990s, the simple trichotomy of Party authorities/Party liberals/non-Party dissidents gave way to a more complex structure of discourse made possible by the commercialization and diversification of the media, growing mobility, declining Party control of education and careers, and the impact of globalization. Issues of human nature and freedom could be explored not only within but also outside the bounds of any form of Marxian thought, so long as there was no overt challenge to the Four Basic Principles. For example, freedom was a subtext in the 1990s' "hoodlum culture"—fiction, movies, music, and even T-shirts that celebrated an attitude of hedonism and detachment. Writers in this culture affected an attitude of being "fed up" and chose to treat the painful puzzles of the 1980s ironically. Thus, in a short story by the hoodlum author Wang Shuo, one of the characters spurns a petition for human rights, saying, "We've got more than enough human rights. Any more and we wouldn't know what to do with 'em." And an author in one of this school's stories proposes to write a book with the title, *Don't Treat Me Like a Human.*[49]

Yet for all its added complexity, the Chinese discourse on freedom remains centered on the problem of political freedom; it was not only the decision to focus this chapter on the political dimension that makes it seem so prominent.[50] Aesthetic, theological, and metaphysical conceptions of freedom have found little place in the Chinese discourse. The issue of women's liberation was seriously discussed early in the century but was effectively banned under Mao by his declaring it resolved under socialism. It has still not been revived as anything but a slogan. As elsewhere in Asia and Africa, the state has been an overwhelming problem in China, whether as an absence in the first half of the century or as a presence in the second half. It is understandable that Chinese have focused a large part of their thinking about the individual on the question of his (seldom her) relationship to this looming entity.

A century's thought has demonstrated the staying power of some old ideas. Chinese thinkers continue predominantly to conceive of freedom as something valued for its utility to the national project. Freedom in modern Chinese thought remains ethically linked to discipline and even self-sacrifice. What we have been calling a Chinese liberal ideal of freedom is almost closer to a republican ideal, so closely linked is it with notions of responsibility and citizenship instead of finding its basis in an affirmation of individual selfishness or hedonism.

That is to say that mainstream Chinese thought remains "Liangian" on the question of freedom. To be sure, the consensus on the primacy of order and the collective has been shaken by internal events like the Tiananmen crackdown of 1989 and by external events like the worldwide spread of democracy from the 1970s through the 1990s. Social change has also had an impact. Industrialization and growth of GNP have brought about social pluralization and new values and ideas. China is no longer an agrarian society; the transition was made at the low point of freedom under Mao, but the social impact was delayed until the Deng opening. And China has been affected by increasingly intensive influences from outside via international trade, human movement, and the Internet. With increasing insistence, the mainstream Chinese idea of freedom is challenged by more liberal conceptions, some closely resembling the liberalism of the West but most reflecting the strong influence of distinctively Chinese ideas about human nature and its ethical potential.

On the whole, the Chinese experience has shown both an openness to considering external ideas and a tendency to interpret these outside messages in the light of its own tradition. Thus, we must conclude that both of our initial hypotheses are correct. China has been influenced by the West in its ideas of freedom; it has at the same time continued to address this problematic idea from the ground of its own cultural preconceptions and preoccupations. Do cultures converge, or do they remain always fundamentally themselves even as they adopt similar language in a shrinking world? The story we have told can be read in either way, or both.

Yet the most direct lesson that emerges is that dictatorship itself creates the desire for freedom, through the very instrumentality of oppression. People who are oppressed think about freedom. And this speaks to a universality of freedom that underlies the diversity of ways of thinking about it. Freedom is an idea that is not merely discovered once and spreads from there, but that emerges and reemerges out of the concrete circumstances of people's lives in history.

REFERENCE MATTER

Notes

CHAPTER I

1. Among others, J. H. Hexter, ed., *Parliament and Liberty: From the Reign of Elizabeth to the English Civil War* (Stanford, 1992); J. R. Jones, ed., *Liberty Secured? Britain Before and After 1688* (Stanford, 1992); Isser Woloch, ed., *Revolution and the Meanings of Freedom in the Nineteenth Century* (Stanford, 1996); Philip T. Hoffman and Kathryn Norberg, eds., *Fiscal Crises, Liberty, and Representative Government, 1450–1789* (Stanford, 1994); Dale Van Kley, ed., *The French Idea of Freedom: The Old Regime and the Declaration of Rights of 1789* (Stanford, 1994).

2. The seminal work documenting its numbers remains Philip D. Curtin, *The Atlantic Slave Trade: A Census* (Madison, WI, 1969).

3. Suzanne Miers and Igor Kopytoff, eds., *The End of Slavery in Africa* (Madison, WI, 1988).

4. See the illuminating studies by James Searing, *West African Slavery and Atlantic Commerce: The Senegal River Valley, 1700–1860* (Cambridge, 1993); and Paul E. Lovejoy and Jan S. Hogendorn, *Slow Death for Slavery: The Course of Abolition in Northern Nigeria, 1897–1936* (Cambridge, 1993).

5. Searing, *West African Slavery*, 2.

6. Chisanga N. Siame, "'Two Concepts of Liberty' Through African Eyes," *Journal of Political Philosophy* (forthcoming).

7. Slavery, for Patterson, is the "permanent, violent, and personal domination of natally alienated and generally dishonored persons," cut off completely from kin and under the total control of the owner: thus without social existence. Orlando Patterson, *Slavery and Social Death: A Comparative Study* (Cambridge, MA, 1982), 13. He goes on to argue that, in the Greek world, the idea of personal liberty, or freedom, first arose as the antithesis of slavery; Patterson, *Freedom in the Making of Western Culture* (New York, 1991).

8. Lovejoy and Hogendorn, *Slow Death for Slavery*, 77.

9. Gabriel Warburg, *The Sudan under Wingate: Administration in the Anglo-Egyptian Sudan, 1899–1916* (London, 1978), 51.

10. See the engaging extended interview with a Harratin lawyer now based in the United States, documenting his unrelenting efforts to publicize and combat what he and his followers believe to be the persisting real-

ity of unfree status; William Finnegan, "A Slave in New York," *New Yorker* Jan. 24, 2000, 50–61. The issue of slavery also resurfaced in southern Sudan in the late 1990s, when an evangelical Christian group began purchasing enslaved southern Sudanese to free them. For detail on slave-raiding by Baggara Arab militia armed by the Sudanese government, see Sharon Elaine Hutchinson, "A Curse from God? Religious and Political Dimensions of the Post-1991 Rise of Ethnic Violence in South Sudan," *Journal of Modern African Studies* 39, 2 (2001): 307–32.

11. The most thorough study is by Senegalese scholar Abdoulaye Diop, *La société wolof: Tradition et changement: Les systèmes d'inégalité et de domination* (Paris, 1981).

12. For the argument that African precolonial political forms were essentially consensual, see Kwame Gwekye, *Tradition and Modernity: Philosophical Reflections on the African Experience* (Oxford, 1997); and Fred M. Hayward, ed., *Elections in Independent Africa* (Boulder, CO, 1987).

13. The thesis that state weakness is a central theme in African political history, from the precolonial era until present times, is the core argument in the important work by Jeffrey Herbst, *States and Power in Africa* (Princeton, NJ, 2000). He suggests, in an arresting although controversial analysis, that historical continuities in the constraints limiting state centralization projects help explain the relative weakness of contemporary sub-Saharan African states.

14. Victor Azarya, *Nomads and the State in Africa: The Political Roots of Marginality* (Avebury, UK, 1996).

15. To use the analytical narrative of Goran Hyden, *Beyond Ujamaa in Tanzania: Underdevelopment and an Uncaptured Peasantry* (Berkeley, 1980).

16. One finds here distant echoes of the contrasting notions of freedom and land found among Indians and settlers on the American frontier, with Indians perceiving land as an area to be roamed at will to hunt, fish, or cultivate, and settlers seeing absolute ownership of land (and thus extinguishment of Indian rights) as the core of freedom. Alan Taylor, "Land and Liberty on the Post-Revolutionary Frontier," in David Thomas Konig, ed., *Devising Liberty: Preserving and Creating Freedom in the New American Republic* (Stanford, 1995), 83–90.

17. Julius K. Nyerere, *Ujamaa: Essays on Socialism* (Oxford, 1968).

18. Illustrative of more recent skepticism of indigenous authenticity of socialism is Gwekye, *Tradition and Modernity*.

19. Kwame Anthony Appiah, *In My Father's House: Africa in the Philosophy of Culture* (Oxford, 1992), 22.

20. Crawford Young, *The African Colonial State in Comparative Perspective* (Madison, WI, 1994).

21. Shanti Marie Singham, "Betwixt Cattle and Men: Jews, Blacks, and Women, and the Declaration of the Rights of Man," in Van Kley, ed., *The French Idea of Freedom*, 114–53; Raymond Betts, *Tricoleur: The French Overseas Empire* (London, 1978).

22. For the classical statement of the colonial doctrine of indirect rule, see F. J. Lugard, *The Dual Mandate in British Tropical Africa* (Edinburgh, 1922). Lugard had served as Uganda Governor at the moment of incorporation into the British Empire in 1894 and had served subsequently in Nigeria, where his administrative theories were systematized.

23. Mahmood Mamdani, *Citizen and Subject: Contemporary Africa and the Legacy of Late Colonialism* (Princeton, NJ, 1996).

24. Young, *The African Colonial State*, 124–33.

25. Ibid., 144.

26. Martin Chanock, *Law, Custom, and Social Order: The Colonial Experience in Malawi and Zambia* (Cambridge, 1985), 47.

27. Mamdani, *Citizen and Subject*, 51.

28. For detail on these exceptional enclaves, see Wesley Johnson, *The Emergence of Black Politics in Senegal: The Struggle for Power in the Four Old Communes, 1900–1925* (Stanford, 1971); Iba Der Thiam, *Evolution politique et syndicale du Sénégal colonial de 1840 à 1936* (Thèse de Doctorat d'Etat, Univ. de Paris I, 8 vols., 1983); Christopher Fyfe, *A History of Sierra Leone* (Oxford, 1962).

29. See the subtle analysis of this process by David Robinson, "France as a Muslim Power in West Africa," *Africa Today* 46, 3/4 (1999): 105–27.

30. Paul Marty, *Etudes sur l'Islam au Sénégal* (Paris, 1917), 208.

31. The atrocities of the Congo Free State find a diligent chronicler in Adam Hochschild, *King Leopold's Ghost* (Boston, 1998).

32. Kwame Nkrumah, *I Speak of Freedom: A Statement of African Ideology* (New York, 1962), 175.

33. Michael Clark, *Algeria in Turmoil* (London, 1960), 17.

34. Julius K. Nyerere, *Freedom and Development: A Selection from Writings and Speeches 1968–1973* (Oxford, 1973), 58.

35. Nkrumah, *I Speak of Freedom*, 117.

36. Lionel Cliffe, ed., *One Party Democracy: The 1965 Tanzania General Election* (Nairobi, 1967), 467. Substantial extracts from the document are reprinted in this book.

37. Tony Killick, *Development Economics in Action* (London, 1978), 25.

38. Bismarck U. Mwansasu and Cranford Pratt, eds., *Towards Socialism in Tanzania* (Toronto, 1979), 19–45.

39. See the interesting parallels drawn between early modern absolutism in Europe and patrimonial autocracy in Africa by Thomas Callaghy, *The State-Society Struggle in Zaire in Comparative Perspective* (New York, 1984).

40. Donald Rothchild and Naomi Chazan, eds., *The Precarious Balance: State and Society in Africa* (Boulder, CO, 1988).

41. Celestin Monga, *The Anthropology of Anger: Civil Society and Democracy in Africa* (Boulder, CO, 1996), 2.

42. The debates over "civil society" in Africa are usefully assembled in John Harbeson, et al., eds., *Civil Society and the State in Africa* (Boulder, CO, 1994).

43. For a fascinating demonstration of the consequences, see Aili Mari Tripp, *Changing the Rules: The Politics of Liberalization and the Urban Informal Economy in Tanzania* (Berkeley, 1997).

44. Aili Mari Tripp, "Political Reform in Tanzania: The Struggle for Associational Autonomy," *Comparative Politics* 32, 2 (2000): 191–214.

45. Sylvia Tamale, *When the Hens Begin to Crow: Gender and Parliamentary Politics in Contemporary Uganda* (Boulder, CO, 2000).

46. Claude Ake, *Democracy and Development in Africa* (Washington, 1996), 132.

CHAPTER 2

1. Julius K. Nyerere, "The Process of Liberation," address given by President Julius K. Nyerere to the Convocation of Ibaden University, Nigeria, Nov. 17, 1976.

2. Mahmood Mamdani, *Citizen and Subject* (Princeton, NJ, 1995). Crawford Young, *The African Colonial State in Comparative Perspective* (New Haven, CT, 1994).

3. Nyerere, "Process."

4. Kwame Nkrumah, *Neo-Colonialism: The Last Stage of Imperialism* (New York, 1965).

5. Jules Gérard-Libois, *Katanga Secession* (Madison, WI, 1963), 277–83.

6. Jeffrey D. Sachs and Andrew W. Warner, "Sources of Slow Growth in African Economies," *Journal of African Economies* 6, 30 (1997): 355–76.

7. Nicholas van de Walle, "Neo-Patrimonialism and Democracy in Africa, with an Illustration from Cameroon," in J. Widner, ed., *Economic Change and Political Liberalization in Sub-Saharan Africa* (Baltimore, 1994), 129–57.

8. Robert H. Jackson, *Quasi-States Sovereignty, International Relations and the Third World* (Cambridge, 1990).

9. Elena M'buyinga, *Pan Africanism or Neo-Colonialism: The Bankruptcy of the OAU* (London, 1982); Zdenek Cervenka, *The Unfinished Quest for Unity: Africa and the OAU* (London, 1977).

10. C. L. Sulzberger, *New York Times*, Apr. 23, 1964.

11. Gilbert Khadiagala, *Allies in Adversity: The Frontline States in Southern African Security* (Athens, OH, 1994).

12. Richard Hall, *The High Price of Principles: Kaunda and the White South* (London, 1973).

13. Nyerere, "Process."

14. William J. Foltz and J. Widner, "The OAU and Southern African Liberation," in Y. El-Ayouty and I. W. Zartman, eds., *The OAU After Twenty Years* (New York, 1984), 249–72.

15. Christopher Clapham, *Africa and the International System* (Cambridge, 1996).

16. Michael Clough, *Free at Last? U.S. Policy Toward Africa and the End of the Cold War* (New York, 1992).

17. Victor T. LeVine, *The Arab-African Connection: Political and Economic Realities* (Boulder, CO, 1979).

18. H. S. Aynor, "Black Africa's Rediscovery of Israel: Motivations and Expectations," *Jerusalem Journal of International Relations* 12, 1 (1990): 102–11.

19. Margaret Levi, *Of Rule and Revenue* (Berkeley, 1988).

20. Thomas M. Callaghy, *The State-society Struggle: Zaire in Comparative Perspective* (New York, 1984).

21. Jean-Francois Bayart, *L'Etat en Afrique: la Politique du Ventre* (Paris, 1989).

22. Abdul Rashid Na'allah, *Ogoni's Agonies: Ken Saro Wiwa and the Crisis in Nigeria* (Trenton, NJ, 1998).

23. Sachs and Warner, "Sources of Slow Growth."

24. Ruth Iyob, *The Eritrean Struggle for Independence: Domination, Resistance, Nationalism, 1941–1993* (Cambridge, 1990).

25. William J. Foltz, "Reconstructing the State of Chad," in W. Zartman, ed., *Collapsed States: The Disintegration and Restoration of Legitimate Authority* (Boulder, CO, 1994), 15–32.

26. Max Gluckman, *Ritual of Rebellion in South Eastern Africa* (Manchester, 1954).

27. United Nations High Commissioner for Refugees, *UNHCR Global Report* (*www.unher.ch/fdrs/gr98/review*, 1999).

28. Goran Hyden, *Beyond Ujamaa in Tanzania* (Berkeley, 1980).

29. Robert Bates, *Markets and States in Tropical Africa* (Berkeley, 1981).

30. Janet MacGaffey, "Fending-for-Yourself: The Organization of the Second Economy in Zaire," in Nzongola-Ntalaja, ed., *The Crisis in Zaire* (Trenton, NJ, 1986); Catharine Newbury, "Survival Strategies in Rural Zaire: Realities of Coping with Crisis," in Nzongola-Ntalaja, ed., *Crisis in Zaire*, 99–122.

31. Crawford Young and Thomas Turner, *The Rise and Decline of the Zairian State* (Madison, WI, 1985).

32. Clapham, *Africa*.

33. Michael Bratton and Nicolas van de Walle, *Democratic Experiments in Africa* (Cambridge, 1997).

34. Freedom House, *Freedom in the World: Political Rights and Civil Liberties* (New York, 1986–87, 1999–2000).

35. A. M. Babu, "Africa's Interpretation of Soviet Policy Since *Perestroika*: Facing the Challenge," in Marion E. Doro, ed., *Africa Contemporary Record: 1988–1989* (New York, 1992): A159–75.

36. Alison Des Forges et al., *Leave None to Tell the Story: Genocide in Rwanda* (New York, 1999).

37. Marina Ottaway and Theresa Chung, "Debating Democracy Assistance: Toward a New Paradigm," *Journal of Democracy* 10, 1 (1999): 99–113.

38. Philippe Marchesin, "Mitterrand l'Africain," *Politique Africaine* 58 (1995): 5–24.

39. Fréderic Lejeal, "Le Président Chirac en Afrique," *Marchés Tropicaux* (1999): 1516.

40. World Bank, *A Continent in Transition: Sub-Saharan Africa in the Mid-1990s* (Washington, 1995).

41. Thomas Hodgkin, *Nationalism in Colonial Africa* (London, 1956).

42. Carol Lancaster, *Aid to Africa: So Much to Do, So Little Done* (Chicago, 1999).

43. Pearl Robinson, "The National Conference Phenomenon in Francophone Africa," *Comparative Studies in Society and History* 36 (1994): 575–610.

44. *Who Rules The Airwaves: Broadcasting in Africa* (London, 1995), Article 19 and Index on Censorship.

45. Dorothea E. Schulz, "In Pursuit of Publicity: Talk Radio and the Imagination of a Moral Public in Urban Mali," *Afrika Spectrum* 34, 2 (1999): 161–85.

46. Thomas L. Friedman, "Low-Tech Democracy," *New York Times*, May 1, 2001, 23.

47. James Manor, *The Political Economy of Democratic Decentralization* (Washington, 1999).

48. Cédric Mayrargue, "Le Point de Vue de Cédric Mayrargue," *Politique Africaine* 74 (1999): 289–92.

49. Aili Mari Tripp, *Women and Politics in Uganda* (Madison, WI, 2000).

50. Samuel P. Huntington, *The Third Wave: Democratization in the Late Twentieth Century* (Norman, OK, 1991), 266–67.

51. Frederick Schaffer, *Democracy in Translation: Understanding Politics in an Unfamiliar Culture* (Ithaca, NY, 1998).

52. Mikael Karlstrom, "Imagining Democracy: Political Culture and Democratisation in Buganda," *Africa* 66, 4 (1990): 448–505.

53. Chisanga Siane, "Two Concepts of Liberty Through African Eyes," *Journal of Political Philosophy* 81, 1 (2000):53–67.

54. Ibid., 53.

55. *Marchés Tropicaux*, July 23, 1999; 1507.

56. Organization of African Unity, Assembly of Heads of State and Government, AHG, Decl. 3 (XXIX), Rev. 1 (June 1993): 28–30.

57. *Business Day*, June 9, 1998.

58. *New York Times*, Sept. 21, 1999.

59. Jonathan Derrick, "African Union: One More Lap," *West Africa* 12–18 (Mar. 2001): 10.

60. Monde Muyangwa and Margaret A. Vogt, "An Assessment of the OAU Mechanism for Conflict Prevention, Management and Resolution, 1993–2000" (New York, 2000), 1.

61. Herbert M. Howe, *Ambiguous Order: Military Forces in African States* (Boulder, CO, 2000).

CHAPTER 3

1. Lisa Anderson, "Democracy in the Arab World: A Critique of the Political Culture Approach," in Rex Brynen et al., eds., *Political Liberalization and Democratization in the Arab World*, vol. 1, *Theoretical Perspectives* (Boulder, CO, 1995), 77.

2. Rex Brynen, "Theoretical Perspectives on Arab Liberalization and Democratization," in Brynen et al. eds., *Political Liberalization* 1:5. See, for example, Guillermo O'Donnell et al., eds., *Transitions from Authoritarian Rule: Prospects for Democracy* (Baltimore, 1986); Samuel P. Huntington, "Will More Countries Become Democratic?," *Political Science Quarterly* 99 (1984): 193–218.

3. See, for example, chap. 2 above.

4. Edward W. Said, *Orientalism* (New York, 1978). For "Islam's bloody borders," see Samuel P. Huntington, *The Clash of Civilizations and the Remaking of the World Order* (New York, 1996); for the equation of "Islamic civilization" with "history gone wrong," see David S. Landes, *The Wealth and Poverty of Nations: Why Some Are So Rich and Some Are So Poor* (New York, 1999).

5. See, for example, Bryan S. Turner, *Capitalism and Class in the Middle East: Theories of Social Change and Economic Development* (London, 1984); id., *Orientalism, Postmodernism, and Globalism* (London, 1994).

6. Muhammad [c]Imara, *al-Hiwar al-qawmi al-dini* (Beirut, 1989); [c]Abbas Mahmud al-[c]Aqqad, *Dimuqratiyya fi al-Islam* (Cairo, 1964); Khalid Muhammad Khalid, *Difa[c] [c]an al-dimuqratiyya* (Cairo, 1985).

7. Saad Eddin Ibrahim, "Liberalization and Democratization in the Arab World: An Overview," in Brynen et al., eds., *Political Liberalization* 1:36.

8. Kiren Aziz Chaudhry, *The Price of Wealth: Economies and Institutions in the Middle East* (Ithaca, NY, 1997), 80, 85–96.

9. Elizabeth Picard, *Lebanon, A Shattered Country: Myths and Realities of the Wars in Lebanon*, trans. Franklin Philip (New York, 1996), 90–91.

10. [c]Isam al-Khafaji, "State Incubation of Iraqi Capitalism," *Middle East Report* 142 (1986): 4–9; F. Gregory Gause III, "Regional Influences on Experiments in Political Liberalization in the Arab World," in Brynen et al., eds., *Political Liberalization* 1:292.

11. See Hazem Beblawi and Giacomo Luciani, eds., *The Rentier State* (London, 1987).

12. J. C. Hurewitz, *The Middle East and North Africa in World Politics: A Documentary Record* (New Haven, CT, 1975), 1:269–71, 315–18.

13. Selim Deringil, *The Well-Protected Domains: Ideology and the Legitimation of Power in the Ottoman Empire, 1876–1909* (London, 1998), 171.

14. Ibid.; Hasan Kayali, *Arabs and Young Turks: Ottomanism, Arabism, and Islamism in the Ottoman Empire, 1908–1918* (Berkeley, 1997).

15. Suraiya Faroqhi et al., *An Economic and Social History of the Ottoman Empire* (Cambridge, 1994), 2:876.

16. Ibid.; Fatma Muge Gocek, *Rise of the Bourgeoisie, Demise of Empire: Ottoman Westernization and Social Change* (New York, 1996), 111.

17. Yahya M. Sadowski, "Political Power and Economic Organization in Syria: The Course of State Intervention, 1946–1958," (Ph.D. diss., Univ. of Calif., Los Angeles, 1984), 40–42.

18. Hanna Batatu, *The Old Social Classes and the Revolutionary Movements of Iraq: A Study of Iraq's Old Landed and Commercial Classes and of its Communists, Baᶜthists, and Free Officers* (Princeton, NJ, 1978), 320–21.

19. Marion Farouk-Sluglett and Peter Sluglett, *Iraq Since 1958: From Revolution to Dictatorship* (London, 1987), 37.

20. Daniel Chirot, *Social Change in the Twentieth Century* (New York, 1977), 35.

21. James L. Gelvin, "Napoleon in Egypt as History and Polemic," in Irene Bierman, ed., *Napoleon in Egypt* (forthcoming).

22. Roger Owen, "The Ideology of Economic Nationalism in its Egyptian Context: 1919–1939," in Marwan R. Buheiry, ed., *Intellectual Life in the Arab East, 1890–1939* (Beirut, 1981), 2–3.

23. Robert Vitalis, *When Capitalists Collide: Business Conflict and the End of Empire in Egypt* (Berkeley, 1995), 39–40; Roger Owen and Sevket Pamuk, *A History of Middle East Economies in the Twentieth Century* (Cambridge, MA, 1999), 36.

24. Hurewitz, *Middle East* 2:179.

25. See, for example, Afaf Lutfi al-Sayyid Marsot, *Egypt's Liberal Experiment, 1922–1936* (Berkeley, 1977); Selma Botman, "The Liberal Age, 1923–1952," in M. W. Daly, ed., *The Cambridge History of Egypt*, vol. 2, *Modern Egypt from 1517 to the End of the Twentieth Century* (Cambridge, 1998), 285–308.

26. Marius Deeb, *Party Politics in Egypt: the Wafd and Its Rivals, 1919–1939* (London, 1979), 80, 349.

27. Sadowski, "Political Power," 204–5; Vitalis, *When Capitalists Collide*, 172–73; Robert L. Tignor, *State, Private Enterprise, and Economic Change in Egypt, 1918–1952* (Princeton, NJ, 1984), 12–13, 78–79; Samira Haj, *The Making of Iraq, 1900–1963: Capital, Power and Ideology* (Albany, NY, 1997), 65–66.

28. Robert Springborg, "The Arab Bourgeoisie: A Revisionist Interpretation," *Arab Studies Quarterly* 15 (1993): 13–39.

29. Owen, "Ideology," 9.

30. Elizabeth Thompson, "The Climax and Crisis of the Colonial Welfare State in Syria and Lebanon during the Second World War," in Steven Heydemann, ed., *War, Institutions, and Social Change in the Middle East* (Berkeley, forthcoming).

31. Robert Mabro and Samir Radwan, *The Industrialization of Egypt, 1939–1973: Policy and Performance* (Oxford, 1976), 82; Sadowski, "Political Power," 162.

32. Robert Vitalis and Steven Heydemann, "World War II and the Poli-

tics of Economy Building in Egypt and Syria," in Heydemann, ed., *War, Institutions, and Social Change.*

33. Rashed el-Barawy, *The Military Coup in Egypt: An Analytic Study* (Cairo, 1952), 89–90; Tignor, *State*, 184, 213; Alan Richards and John Waterbury, *A Political Economy of the Middle East* (Boulder, CO, 1998), 119.

34. Joel Gordon, "The False Hopes of 1950: The Wafd's Last Hurrah and the Demise of Egypt's Old Order," *International Journal of Middle East Studies* 21 (1989): 197; Joel Gordon, *Nasser's Blessed Movement: Egypt's Free Officers and the July Revolution* (New York, 1992), 21, 24.

35. "La Constitution Syrienne" (Damascus, 1950); Sadowski, "Political Power," 203–4.

36. See texts in Hisham Sharabi, *Nationalism and Revolution in the Arab World* (Princeton, NJ, 1966), 156–68.

37. Gordon, *Blessed Movement*, 59.

38. Eliezer Be'eri, *Army Officers in Arab Politics and Society* (New York, 1970), 59; Farouk-Sluglett and Sluglett, *Iraq*, 84.

39. Gamal ʿAbd al-Nasr (Abdul Nasser), *Falsafat al-thawra* (Cairo, 1966), 37–43.

40. el-Barawy, *Military Coup*, 75–80; Manfred Halpern, *The Politics of Social Change in the Middle East and North Africa* (Princeton, NJ, 1963), 278; Morroe Berger, *Bureaucracy and Society in Modern Egypt* (Princeton, NJ, 1957), 185.

41. Gabriel Baer, "Egyptian Attitudes towards Land Reform, 1922–1955," in Walter Z. Laqueur, ed., *The Middle East in Transition: Studies in Contemporary History* (New York, 1958), 98.

42. el-Barawy, *Military Coup*, 37.

43. Joel Beinin and Zachary Lockman, *Workers on the Nile: Nationalism, Communism, Islam, and the Egyptian Working Class, 1882–1954* (Princeton, NJ, 1987), 421–26.

44. Kirk James Beattie, "Egypt: The Struggle for Hegemony, 1952–1981," (Ph.D. diss., Univ. of Mich., 1985), 131.

45. William Roger Louis, *The British Empire in the Middle East, 1945–1951: Arab Nationalism, the United States, and Postwar Imperialism* (Oxford, 1984), 604.

46. Sa'id B. Himadeh, "Social Awakening and Economic Development in the Middle East," in Laqueur, ed., *Middle East*, 58; el-Barawy, *Military Coup*, 83.

47. See *The Economic Development of Iraq: Report of a Mission Organized by the International Bank for Reconstruction and Development at the Request of the Government of Iraq* (Baltimore, 1952); International Bank for Reconstruction and Development, *The Economic Development of Syria* (Baltimore, 1955).

48. Raymond William Baker, *Egypt's Uncertain Revolution under Nasser and Sadat* (Cambridge, MA, 1978), 49.

49. David Waldner, *State Building and Late Development* (Ithaca, NY, 1999), 78; Farouk-Sluglett and Sluglett, *Iraq*, 51–54.

50. Vitalis, *Capitalists*, 24, 208.

51. Richards and Waterbury, *Political Economy*, 182–83.

52. Jean Vigneau, "The Ideology of the Egyptian Revolution," in Laqueur, ed., *Middle East*, 131.

53. Beattie, "Egypt," 228–29.

54. Gamal ʿAbd al-Nasr (Abdul Nasser), *al-Dimuqratiyya: Min aqwal al-raʾis Gamal ʿAbd al-Nasr* (Cairo, n.d.). For an analogous redefinition of freedom by Kwame Nkrumah, see chap. 1 above.

55. Waldner, *State Building*, 79.

56. Kamel S. Abu Jaber, *The Arab Ba'th Socialist Party: History, Ideology, and Organization* (Syracuse, NY, 1966), 167–74.

57. Ibid., 157–65.

58. Phillipe C. Schmitter, "Still the Century of Corporatism?," *Review of Politics* 36 (1974): 93–94.

59. Beattie, "Egypt," 246–47.

60. Robert Bianchi, *Unruly Corporatism: Associational Life in Twentieth-Century Egypt* (New York, 1989), 65, 74–76; Sadowski, "Political Power," 236.

61. Bianchi, *Unruly Corporatism*, 76; Waldner, *State Building*, 86; Farouk-Sluglett and Sluglett, *Iraq*, 139.

62. See Joel S. Migdal, *Strong Societies and Weak States: State-Society Relations and State Capabilities in the Third World* (Princeton, NJ, 1988).

63. I am using the terms "Islamist" and "Islamism" to refer to individuals and associations commonly referred to as "Muslim (Islamic) fundamentalist" and "Muslim (Islamic) fundamentalism." The use of the terms "fundamentalist" and "fundamentalism" implies a closer correlation between these individuals and associations with Protestant fundamentalists and Protestant fundamentalism than actually exists.

64. Mervat F. Hatem, "Economic and Political Liberalization in Egypt and the Demise of State Feminism," *International Journal of Middle East Studies* 24 (1992): 231–51.

65. See, for example, chaps. 7 and 8 below.

66. Daniel Brumberg, "Authoritarian Legacies and Reform Strategies in the Arab World," in Brynen et al., eds., *Political Liberalization* 1:234.

67. Richard P. Mitchell, *The Society of the Muslim Brothers* (New York, 1993); Sadowski, "Political Power," 275; Waldner, *State Building*, 86.

68. Sami Zubaida, *Islam, the People, and the State: Political Ideas and Movements in the Middle East* (London, 1989), 92; Batatu, *Old Social Classes*, 699–705.

69. Fred H. Lawson, "Social Bases for the Hamah Revolt," *Middle East Report* 110 (1982): 24–28.

70. Owen and Pamuk, *Middle East Economies*, 154–55, 171–72.

71. See, for example, Steven Heydemann, "Taxation without Representation: Authoritarianism and Economic Liberalization in Syria," in Ellis Goldberg et al., eds., *Rules and Rights in the Middle East: Democracy, Law, and Society* (Seattle, WA, 1993), 69–101.

CHAPTER 4

1. I. Berlin, "Two concepts of liberty," *Four Essays on Liberty* (Oxford, 1969). Although Berlin was primarily concerned with a different distinction between "negative" and "positive" liberty in this essay, and much of his other political work, and this distinction is made in passing, it is of immense utility in analyzing the history of ideas in India. The historical account offered here does not follow Berlin's line of thought—in two senses. First, in the sense that in Berlin, this is a minor point; but I believe this must play a major role in Indian intellectual history. Secondly, Berlin wanted the two not to be confused. This chapter argues that while they are obviously analytically distinct, an historically sensitive reading must try to explain why, in certain circumstances, the two questions are seen as inter-linked.

2. One of the major concerns in modern liberal theory is the attempt to formulate arguments that accommodate the idea of liberal rights enjoyed integrally by groups. Indian political reflection of the early twentieth century grapples with similar problems, though its cultural and intellectual context is quite different. For an argument on this point, referring to the process of constitution-making in India, see Rajeev Bhargava, "Democratic Vision of a New Republic: India 1950" in Francine Frankel et al., eds., *Transforming India* (Delhi, 1999).

3. I would call the methods advocated by scholars like Quentin Skinner "contextualism," although in his own initial statement of this position he uses that term to refer to marxist reductionism. Quentin Skinner, "Meaning and Understanding in the History of Ideas," in James Tully, ed., *Meaning and Context: Quentin Skinner and His Critics* (Cambridge, 1988), chap. 2.

4. The best and the most detailed exposition of this method is to be found in the works of Quentin Skinner and J. G. A. Pocock. See Tully, ed., *Meaning and Context*; J. G. A. Pocock, *Politics, Language and Time* (New York, 1971). I am not interested here in the critical discussions that have surrounded contextualist intellectual history since the 1970s. It is sufficient to recognize its distinct methodological techniques. Some of the main critical arguments against this style can also be found in Tully, ed., *Meaning and Context*.

5. For a defense of this method, and a wonderful example of its practice, see Q. Skinner, *Foundations of Modern Political Thought* (Cambridge, 1978).

6. Skinner, *Foundations*; J. G. A. Pocock, *The Machiavellian Moment* (Princeton, 1975), and the latter's recent studies of early modern British thought can be seen in this fashion.

7. Reinhart Koselleck, *Futures Past* (Cambridge, MA, 1989). See especially his essay on "Begriffsgeschichte and social history."

8. If Bengalis did not practice caste in their daily life, it would collapse as a practical concept and would be replaced, I expect, by something like class.

9. These concepts are new in two different ways: some are new words, others older terms given a new signification related to the relevant social practice.

10. Quite a lot has been written on the discovery of an ontologically distinct field of an "economy" by Adam Smith, or of "society" by the French Enlightenment. Keith M. Baker, "Enlightenment and the Institution of Society," in W. Melching and W. Velema, eds., *Main Trends in Cultural History* (Amsterdam, 1994); and Johan Heilbron, *The Rise of Social Theory* (Cambridge, 1993).

11. Western theoretical ideas of utilitarianism or positivism become widely used and debated by the mid-nineteenth century. One of the first and most impressive attempts at developing a distinctively "Indian" social theory, highly critical of both the Western civilization and its legitimizing modes of thought, was by Bhudev Mukhopadhyay in his *Samajik Prabandha* (*Essays on Society*), ed. Jahnabi Kumar Chakraborty (Calcutta, 1981). For discussions of his arguments in English, see Tapan Raychaudhuri, *Europe Reconsidered* (Delhi, 1989), and Sudipta Kaviraj, "A reversal of Orientalism," in H. von Stietencron and V. Dalmia, eds., *Reconstructing Hinduism* (New Delhi, 1994).

12. Although there is a substantial literature tracing the development of modern thinking in India, especially nationalism, this literature does not take a strictly "historical semantic" approach tracing the transformation of singular ideas. Usually, these offer a general picture of the transformation of intellectual styles and sensibilities, or provide histories of individual theories like "liberalism" or socialism. Early attempts at history of political ideas by nationalists are also vitiated by the misconceived "nationalist" project of proving that every single theoretical development in European social theory, like utilitarianism, liberalism, or socialism, had its strict Indian equivalents—preferably showing that Indians developed these theories either independently or, even better, before the Europeans. For an extreme example of this kind, where considerable detailed scholarship is framed by this improbable nationalist story, see Biman Bihari Majumdar, *A History of Political Thought in India* (Calcutta, 1934). This kind of writing was very influential before independence, falling away slowly afterward.

13. It is true, for instance, that Machiavelli startlingly changes the use of the term virtue; but that term comes to him through the continuity of an intellectual tradition. Machiavelli's intellectual operation on the Ciceronian connotations of virtue is fundamentally different from the intellectual predicament of a Bengali intellectual, formed by Brahminical pedagogy, reading the compelling arguments on individual liberty in Mill.

14. To take an example: to understand what the idea of private property does to colonial Bengali society, we must look for earlier conceptions of ownership, entitlement, and use around the more neutral and generic concept of "wealth," which designate the kinds of specific social relations of

legitimate control that individuals or groups could have—for example, *sampatti*—and map out their connotations precisely.

15. An example would be the different ways in which the German tradition and English utilitarians define and develop the ideals of freedom, in massively influential texts like Kant's *Groundwork of the Metaphysics of Morals* and John Stuart Mill's *On Liberty*.

16. This can be clarified by an example chosen from the everyday language of modern politics. In some modern Indian languages, such as Hindi, often the adjective "governmental" or "state" as in "government /state vehicle" would be translated as *rajakiya vahan* in which the word "*rajakiya*" literally means "royal." So the associations of the term become confusing, the intended, European-derived meaning suggesting impersonal, institutional authority and the traditional meaning connoting personal power.

17. For a recent discussion on the problem of "translation," see Gyan Prakash, *Another Reason* (Princeton, NJ, 1999), chap. 3.

18. A final difficulty comes from the erroneousness of the assumption that we are writing the history of a single social and political unit and describing how it changed over a period of time. In fact, we are writing the history of its slowly, through these processes, coming to be a single unit, at least at the upper levels of this society. Politically, there is no India to write a history of; it is being written into existence by these devices we describe. Apart from the rhetoric, the basic methodological problem is to come to terms with and tackle the internal diversity of the colonial empire. Before the British came, different areas of what was to become India had experienced radically different political cultures. To take an obviously stark contrast, Calcutta and Bombay played significant roles in the shaping of the empire in its early stages: yet the immediately preceding history of Bengal and the Maratha kingdom were vastly different. Bengal had been under an effete *Nababi* and *dewani* rule under the formal tutelage of the Mughal empire; Maharashtra, by contrast, was going through a sudden decline of a highly successful political authority under the Peshwas. It is essential, in writing a history of ideas, to respect the diversity of intellectual cultures of different Indian regions.

19. Written, according to tradition, by Chanakya, the astute counselor to the Maurya emperor Chandragupta, around 300 BC, though some parts are supposed to have been added subsequently, as late as 300 AD.

20. Probably written in the second or third century AD.

21. The Indian tradition had literary texts which raised important dilemmas of social life, occasionally of the use of political power. The epics, the *Ramayana* and the *Mahabharata*, are both concerned centrally with the nature of royal power; and some sections of the *Mahabharata*, like the Shantiparva, offer direct discussions about the rules of good government.

22. The *Mahabharata* uses the following *sloka* to illustrate the hazards of leading a good life:

Veda vibhinnah smrtayoh vibhinnah/
nasau muniryasya matam na bhinnam/

dharmasya tattvam nihitam guhayam/
majano yena gatah sa pantha/

There are differences among the Vedas; the books of moral rules give conflicting advice; a sage is one whose opinions are by definition different from others'; the real rules of goodness are buried in a dark cave; the only path is the way great men have lived their lives. But Arindam Chakravarti has recently pointed out that Nilakantha in his commentary rejects the translation of *mahajana* as "great men," and prefers "the great numbers of men," grammatically equally correct, on the ground of greater internal consistency. Since the earlier clauses deplore the conflicting evidence of other possible sources of the good, if lives of great men are set up as examples, they could hardly avoid the same puzzling plurality and lack of decisiveness. The argument that morality consists in the patterns contained in lives that the great number of men have lived takes a Hegelian route, to solve the indeterminacy.

23. There is a vast literature on the sociology and theology of caste. The modern debates have primarily revolved around the forceful interpretation of Louis Dumont, *Homo Hierarchicus* (Delhi, 1981). For a brief introduction, see Ursula Sharma, *Caste* (Buckingham, 1998).

24. The texts, which lay down common codes of social behavior, are collectively called the *Smrti*.

25. The Hindu moral system however admitted one deviation from this minutely-detailed moral world, which was awesome in its radical consequences. It is always possible to make use of the underlying dichotomy between a *grhi* (householder) and the *sannyasi* (renouncer) to go away from home and establish the radical autonomy of the recluse. To the renouncer, the intricate and suffocating rules of caste-bound domesticity did not apply; but the model was evidently meant to be used as an exception rather than the rule. And in one sense this merely confirmed the unconditional obligation of the householder to follow caste rules.

26. The use of Weber's central thesis about this-worldly and other-worldly asceticism is not inappropriate here, as Bengali intellectuals, as we see below, came to apply a very similar, if not exactly identical, argument.

27. Deliverance from these entanglements could be found either in renunciation or in death. Indian cultures abound in poems and songs celebrating death as a cessation of desires, frustration, and the aggravation of human existence.

28. The poem itself is called "*Mukti*," deliverance/freedom; and its propositions provide a great example of the struggle to translate other-worldly concepts into mundane ones, declaring the superior complexity and dignity of the latter.

Mukti? Ore mukti kothay pabi, mukti kothay acche
apni prabhu srstibandhan pare bandha sabar kacche

(where can you find liberation? Does it exist at all?
The Lord himself is bound to all beings by wearing the
bonds of creation.)

What is interesting here is the direct and explicit suggestion that God accepts obligations with his created beings by the act of creation itself. Rabindranath Tagore, "Dhulamandir," in *Sanchayita* (Calcutta, 1972), 510.

29. Tagore, "Mukti," in *Sanchayita*, 437.

30. In the mature stage of Indian nationalism, Bengali writing uses the term *mukti* as equivalent to *svadhinata*, to refer to the liberation of the nation. It is interesting that the "freedom fighters" during the Bangladesh secession from Pakistan used the term *mukti-vahini* (army of freedom), and the liberation movement was called *mukti-yuddha* (war for freedom/liberation). This shows precisely how far a single term had traveled during this period.

31. Characteristically, it was not merely poor, recourseless subjects who had to throw themselves at the mercy of the law. Ram Mohan Roy was once humiliated by the collector of Bhagalpur district and wrote to the governor general for redress, couching his appeal precisely in those terms. *Essential Writings of Raja Ram Mohan Roy*, ed. Bruce Carlisle Robertson (Delhi, 1999) (hereafter *EWR*).

32. See for more details, "The pursuit of reason in colonial Bengal," in Tapan Raychaudhuri, *Perceptions, Emotions, Sensibilities* (Delhi, 1999).

33. One particularly interesting example was the debate not merely about sati, but also about the remarriage of widows, and the age of consent for women's marriage.

34. *EWR*.

35. *EWR*, 273. Ram Mohan Roy was directly influenced by a reading of John Locke, in particular, his arguments about religious toleration. See Robertson's introduction to *EWR*, xxxiv.

36. It is essential to be circumspect on this point, because the colonial administration did not follow a consistent policy of support to radical reform of native society. Quite often it feared that excessive reformist initiative might stir up discontent, and this was often a point of contention between the colonial administration and Christian missionaries. The enthusiasm of the new middle class toward Western ways should not be overestimated either. Alongside groups which were enthusiastic about the Western civilization, there were others who split their social conduct into two spheres. In one, they offered utter conformity to the external demands of colonial authorities, but maintained traditional practices inside an inner, domestic sphere. There were still others who were openly hostile to the Western ideas and practices.

37. Set up in 1817.

38. Established in 1857.

39. Again, Bhudev Mukhopadhyay distinguished between learning sci-

ence and learning stories about science, and complained that the current teaching in Calcutta University inclined excessively toward the latter; consequently, this kind of science education was unlikely to create real growth of indigenous experimental science. Mukhopadhyay, *Samajik Prabandha.*

40. In Ram Mohan Roy's intellectual formation reading Locke played an important part; but by the middle of the nineteenth century, the modern intelligentsia was fascinated by utilitarian and positivist ideas. The introduction to positivism was most probably mediated by John Stuart Mill. But in Bhudev Mukhopadhyay's careful critical arguments about Western social theory there are discussions of a wide range of writers, from the British traditions of political economy, Mill, and Spencer to other strands like Kant and Hegel. Derozio, a charismatic teacher in Hindu College's early days, used to give lectures on Hume and Kant and wrote a review of the first critique. In Bankimchandra Chattopadhyay's famous essay on equality, there are references to relatively minor figures like Feuerbach, and a remark about the First International. Mukhopadhyay, *Samajik Prabandha*; and Bankimchandra Chattopadhyay, *Samya*, in *Bankim Rachanavali* (Bankim's Collected Works) 2 (Calcutta, 1971): 381–406.

41. One of the most potent influences on the early modern Bengali intelligentsia, Henry Vivian Derozio, a Eurasian teacher, discussed Kant and Hume, and in the works of authors who have a more specialized interest in social theory, references to Kant and Hegel are common.

42. For the most detailed analysis of the social context and intellectual arguments in the Bengali re-evaluation of the West, see Tapan Raychaudhuri, *Europe Reconsidered* (Delhi, 1989).

43. One of the classics of social thought in this period, Bankimchandra Chattopadhyay's essay on equality, *Samya*, was deeply influenced by Rousseau.

44. Similarly, in Mukhopadhyay's *Samajik Prabandha* there are detailed critiques of both the mechanistic and organic conceptions of society, and discussion of Locke and Hegel. Ibid., 41–52.

45. One of the most intellectually creative suggestions in this respect came from Bhudev Mukhopadhyay who produced the first serious social-theoretical analysis of colonial modernity in Bengal. He argues that to discuss Western theories is not to do theory at all, but to tell stories about theory. To do "theory" is to clarify the conceptual understandings underlying Indian social practices, formulate a conceptual system out of them, and then proceed to judge through this new conceptual apparatus the relative claims of Western and Indian social practices.

46. *Bankim Rachanavali* (Bankim's Collected Works) 2 (Calcutta, 1971), 381–406, esp. 382–85.

47. Ibid., 85–87.

48. Mukhopadhyay, *Samajik Prabandha*, 65ff.

49. A leading Brahmo intellectual, Shivnath Shastri, produced a closely reasoned work that argued the new form of companionate marriage was

morally superior to traditional arranged marriages. Shivnath Shastri, *Grhadharma* (Calcutta, 1963).

50. Emma Tarlo, *Clothing Matters* (London, 1994), gives a fascinating account of sartorial changes.

51. Ibid.

52. In a brutally frank Sanskrit saying: *putrarthe kryate bharya*—literally, one takes wives in order to beget children.

53. Jogesh Chandra Bagal, *Banglar Navya Sanskriti* (The New Culture of Bengal) (Calcutta, 1958).

54. This is generally argued in many studies on the rise of sociology, since the separation of the identity of that discipline required the distinctiveness of its object of study. See Johan Heilbron, *The Rise of Social Theory* (Cambridge, 1994). For an excellent account of the semantic change, see Keith Michael Baker, "Enlightenment and the Institution of Society," in Sudipta Kaviraj and Sunil Khilnani, eds., *Civil Society: History and Possibilities* (Cambridge, 2001).

55. To take a random example, in the aesthetic texts of Abhinavagupta, the celebrated aesthetic theorist from the thirteenth century, "samajika" means simply man in society.

56. However, this is obviously because of the dependence of the language of sociability on the social practices historically available. Such ideas were inconceivable because social practices did not demand such ideas. When they started doing so, a particular term was selected (in this case *samaj*) and its semantic connotation slowly displaced until it covered this emerging sociological need.

57. The word *samaj* was used at that time to mean the English term "society," "institution," or meetings and associations. Bagal's book, on the new culture of Bengal, is in fact a collection of historical notes on nineteen associations of this kind. To explain the simultaneous emergence of these new types of groups, Bagal says: "As a result of new education and establishment of a new education system Bengalis slowly became acquainted with Western ideas. They applied themselves to form associations to pursue activities which were for the good of humanity and the welfare of the country. There was no dearth of examples in front of them which showed how fruitful collective efforts/undertakings could be in a short time" (my translation). The entire introduction extols the virtues of collective effort or association of individuals in collective objectives of various kinds. Bagal, *Banglar Navya Sanskriti*, 1.

58. "Appeal to the King in Council" (1824), *EWR*, chap. 25.

59. It is essential to point to the immense historic significance of these developments and to their restrictedness. Statistically, the number of people imbued with the new spirit and having access to the means to try out new ways of living was small; but historically, they set up a model whose historic significance was incalculable. Their ability to live their lives free of older restrictions undermined the traditional system, eventually, for all groups. In European discussions of modernity the "restrictive" character of

the liberal models has been strongly emphasized in recent discussions, for example, in Peter Wagner, *A Sociology of Modernity* (London, 1994). Evidently, it is even more important to emphasize this in the colonial context.

60. For an excellent discussion on Phule's thinking and practical initiatives, see Rosalind O'Hanlon, *Caste, Conflict and Ideology* (Cambridge, 1985).

61. Phule, *Ghulamgiri* (Eng. trans. Bombay, 1991).

62. I have discussed the problems about teleological representations in nationalist history in my "Imaginary Institution of India," in Gyanendra Pandey and Partha Chatterjee, eds., *Subaltern Studies* 7 (Delhi, 1992).

63. Sir Sayiid Ahmad Khan [Syed Ahmad Khan], the eminent leader of modernist Muslims, wrote an interesting analysis of the events about a year later, which sought to interpret the disaffection of the Muslim elite differently. Syed Ahmad Khan Bhadaur, *Causes of the Indian Revolt* (Benares, 1873).

64. Lelyveld, *Aligarh's First Generation*, quoted in Kenneth W. Jones, *Socio-Religious Reform Movements in British India* (Cambridge, 1989), 65.

65. Jones, *Socio-Religious Reform Movements*, 65.

66. C. A. Bayly, *Local Roots of Indian Politics, Allahabad, 1880–1920* (Oxford, 1975).

67. Though not always in English. As in Bengal, there was a rich debate about the medium of instruction and the appropriate language for learning of the native students.

68. Bhudev Mukhopadhyay, for instance, believed that Indians should learn two subjects from the Europeans, nothing else: natural science and political economy.

69. In the Bengali discussions too there were obvious influences of the arguments of British political economy. The first issue of *Tattvabodhini Patrika*, the highly influential Brahmo journal, thanked the almighty and the power of commerce for bringing the blessings of modernity to India. But it remained, largely, a theoretical argument which authors often invoked but rarely developed with great interest on their own in unexpected and original directions.

70. The most thorough and detailed account of this strand of thinking can be found in Bipan Chandra, *Rise of Economic Nationalism in India* (Delhi, 1973).

71. J. S. Mill, *On Liberty*, in J. S. Mill, *Utilitarianism, On Liberty and Representative Government*, ed A. D. Lindsay (London, 1962), 73.

72. "The progress of ruralization in modern India means its rustication, i.e., a loss of power, and intelligence, and self-dependence, and is a distinctly retrograde move." M. G. Ranade, "Indian Political Economy," *Essays on Indian Economics* (Bombay, 1898), 19.

73. For a direct use of Mill in an early argument for self-government, though at the local level, see M. G. Ranade, *Essays on India Economics* (New Delhi, 1982); 109.

74. Ranade, *Essays on Indian Economics*.

75. Ranade, "Inaugural address at the first Industrial Conference, Poona, 1980," in id., *Essays*, 79.
76. Ibid., 82.
77. Ibid., 83.
78. The title of Naoroji's famous book was *Poverty and the Un-British Rule in India*.
79. Ranade sounded a slightly discordant note in his address to the Industrial Conference in 1890 when he said "What we have chiefly to avoid is the pursuit of impracticable objects. We should husband our little resources to the best of our power, and not exhaust them by vain complaints against the drain of Indian tribute, or by giving battle with free trade." However, this does not imply that the charge of the drain is false, just that the attempt to convince the British about its unfairness is a vain attempt.
80. G. K. Gokhale saw this quite clearly. In a lecture to the National Liberal Club in London, on Nov. 15, 1905, he said: "Political reformers in India are, in one sense, the natural allies of the Liberal Party in England; for we in India are struggling to assert in our own country those very principles which are now the accepted creed of the Liberal Party in England. Peace, retrenchment and reform are our watchwords, as they are yours. We are, like you, seeking to throw open to the many the advantages which at present are the monopoly of the privileged few; and we are fighting against the predominance of interests of a class over the mass of the people." This was surely a greatly exaggerated description of the liberal program in India; but he was right in stressing the commonness of principles. G. K. Gokhale, "England's Duty to India," in R. P. Patwardhan, ed., *The Select Gokhale* (New Delhi, 1968), 194.
81. Tapan Raychaudhuri, *Perceptions, Emotions, Sensibilities* (Delhi, 1999).
82. For an excellent detailed analysis of Hindu nationalist ideology, see Christophe Jaffrelot, *Hindu Nationalism and Indian Politics* (New York, 1996).
83. M. K. Gandhi, *Hind Swaraj*, ed. Anthony Parel (Cambridge, 1996) (hereafter *GHS*).
84. In Hindi, the largest of the Indian vernaculars, *swaraj* (or *svaraj*) meant freedom, though general usage would subsequently settle on the term *svatantrata*; in Bengali, similarly on *svadhinata*. Etymologically, in all these homonyms the prefix *sva* (self) is linked to some form of rule (*raj/rajya*), government (*tantra*), legality, subjection (*adhinata*), control. *Svaraj* literally means rule over oneself, *svatantrata*, giving rules to oneself /living under rules created by one's own self, *svadhinata*, subjection to one's own self. All these terms have meanings close to the European meanings of autonomy.
85. *GHS*, 39.
86. *GHS*, chap. 6.
87. *GHS*, 67.
88. *GHS*, 71.

89. For an excellent concise account, see Bhikhu Parekh, *Gandhi* (Oxford, 1997). More detailed analyses can be found in Bhikhu Parekh, *Gandhi's Political Philosophy* (London, 1983); Bhikhu Parekh, *Colonialism, Tradition and Reform* (Delhi, 1986); and Raghavan Iyer, *The Moral and Political Thought of Mahatma Gandhi* (New York, 1973).

90. *GHS* contains direct references to Mill as well: 28n, 29n.

91. Gandhi would not agree with Mill that "man's way of doing something is good because it is his own way." Also his thinking is different from Kant's strong universalism: he accepts the Hindu view that people of different types have different *svabhava*, not a common practical reason.

92. Though at times he would defend authority or tradition by rationalistic arguments, as ways of doing things that have been found rational by a long line of generations, and which therefore had an immense rational weight.

93. *GHS*, 77.

94. The Communist Party of India was established in 1921 in Tashkent and restarted in India in 1925. Until the early 1930s, however, it remained a marginal group within Indian nationalist opinion. The Congress Socialist Party was formed in 1934.

95. In his presidental address to the annual session of the Congress at Lahore, Nehru said: "[T]he real thing is the conquest of power by whatever name it may be called. I do not think that any form of Dominion Status applicable to India will give us real power. A test of this power would be the entire withdrawal of the alien army of occupation and economic control. Let us, therefore, concentrate on these and the rest will follow easily. We stand, therefore, for the fullest freedom of India." Jawaharlal Nehru, Presidential address to the Lahore Congress, Dec. 1929.

96. Ibid.

97. Nehru, *Whither India?* (London, 1962), 21.

98. Ibid., 21.

99. Ibid., 21.

100. Ibid., 22.

101. Ibid., 30.

102. Ibid., 31.

103. Granville Austin, *The Indian Constitution: Cornerstone of a Nation* (Oxford, 1964), provides a clear and concise account of some of these theoretical and legal debates.

104. The surprising degree of agreement among all sections—from conservatives to communists—must have been helped by radical acceptance of a theory of stages. Marxists often argued that until conditions ripened, a socialist revolution was impossible; all that was feasible was a democratic revolution. Communists, in fairness, criticized the "bourgeois" character of the constitution and supported the inclusion of social and economic rights in the constitutional document. But they were too weak in the Constituent assembly to influence its formulations.

105. Important cases like Romesh Thapar v. The State of Madras helped the courts to define the terms of constitutional rights more precisely.

106. How closely Indian political disputes followed the obligatory conceptual terminologies of the ideological cold war can be seen from the language used for instance in Nehru's major programmatic statement after independence, *The Basic Approach*, 1958. It showed through its calm indifference to caste and religious questions its firm conviction that such traditional problems were over, in the past. The vital political debate was about the claims of communist impatience about economic redistribution.

107. Since the 1980s, the intellectual world of Indian politics has changed so fundamentally that it is unrecognizable in terms of the earlier ideological categories of capitalism, socialism, social democracy, communism, and welfare state. In fact, one of the fundamental changes is in terms of the forms of expression of political ideas themselves. As politicians represent more underprivileged political groups, they have much less social capital in education, control of English, or even seriously discursive prose. All these appurtenances of elegant upper-class politics have been binned in favor of a politics that is less voluble in its inarticulate urgency. Politicians make quick shifts in alliances, which they do not or cannot defend in elevated ideological terms. But underlying this is perhaps a significant rejection of the politics of the chattering classes, in favor of the undiscursiveness of those who do not chatter and mistrust it. The second phase of Indian politics in which indiscriminate populist gestures undermined the value of ideological positions contributed to this state of affairs. An argument offered by most politicians would be that those earlier promises were essentially deceptions on a grand scale. By contrast, their new kind of politics without pretensions of high ideals, was, in an ironical way, a politics of truth.

108. In some respects, the same is true of the communal hostility of the Bharatiya Janata Party toward Indian Muslims: it is constantly split between a rhetoric of hatred against Muslims and a desire for liberal respectability in claiming that it practices real secularism while other parties like the Congress are pseudo-secularists. It is intellectually remarkable that even the BJP cannot express explicit hostility toward secular principles, and has to look for excuses.

109. "Although the revolution that is taking place in the social condition, the laws, the opinions, and the feelings of men is still very far from being terminated, yet its results already admit of no comparison with anything that the world has ever before witnessed. I go back from age to age up to the remotest antiquity, but I find no parallel to what is occurring before my eyes; as the past has ceased to throw light on the future, the mind of man wanders in obscurity." Alexis de Tocqueville, *Democracy in America* (London, 1994), 331.

110. Since the story of freedom has traditionally been associated with some lyricism, let me end with the poetry of liberty in the Indian context.

The fullest expression of the ideal of liberty that animated the Indian national movement was the famous poem by Tagore which Nehru, with his entire generation, admired: the poem is nameless, but its subtle unpronounced title is liberty:

> citta jetha bhayshunya uccha jetha shir/gnan jetha mukta, jetha grher prachir/apan prangan-tale dibasa sharbari/ vasudhare rakhe nai khanda hshudra kari/ jetha tuchcha acharer maruvalurashi/ vicharer srotahpath phele nai grashi/paurushere kareni shatadha nitya jetha/ tumi sarva karma chinta anander neta/nijahaste nirday aghat kari pitah/ bharatere sei svarge kara jagarita/
>
> (where the soul is fearless, the head is held high, where knowledge is free, where the walls of the household courtyard have not broken up the earth night and day into unsurpassable fragments, divided and poor, where the sands of mere custom have not swallowed up the pure stream of reason, or have not broken manliness into tiny shards, where always you lead/inspire all action, thought and happiness, O father, through suffering caused by your own hands raise India to that state of bliss/ make India awake in that heaven.)

CHAPTER 5

1. Burma was renamed Myanmar in 1989 but the older colonial term Burma will be used in this chapter, which largely concentrates its discussion on the country's history before that time.

2. S. J. Tambiah, *World Conqueror and World Renouncer: A Study of Buddhism in Thailand Against its Historical Background* (Cambridge, 1976), 102–13.

3. Michael Adas, "From Avoidance to Confrontation: Peasant Protest in Precolonial and Colonial Southeast," *Comparative Studies in Society and History* 23, 2 (Apr. 1981): 217–47.

4. E. R. Leach, *Political Systems of Highland Burma* (London, 1954).

5. Like *ahmudan* and *athi, phrai* and *lek* were categories of "free" men with different obligations to the monarch and his agents.

6. This discussion relies heavily on the insights of J. S. Furnivall, particularly his classic *Colonial Policy and Practice: A Comparative Study of Burma and Netherlands India* (Cambridge, 1948). See also the same author's masterly "The Fashioning of Leviathan: The Beginnings of British Rule in Burma," *The Journal of the Burma Research Society* 29, 1 (Apr. 1939): 3–137.

7. See Thant Myint-U, *The Making of Modern Burma* (Cambridge, 2001).

8. For an account of the history of elections in Burma, see R. H. Taylor, "Elections in Burma/Myanmar: For whom and why?", in R. H. Taylor, ed., *The Politics of Elections in Southeast Asia* (Cambridge, 1996), 164–83.

9. Still the best single account of this process for these purposes is Fred

W. Riggs, *Thailand: The Modernization of a Bureaucratic Polity* (Honolulu, 1966).

10. *Ibid.*

11. Thak Chaloemtiarana, *Thailand: The Politics of Despotic Paternalism* (Bangkok, 1979).

12. See Benedict R. O'G. Anderson, "Murder and Progress in Modern Siam," *New Left Review* May/June 1990, 34–48; James Ockey, "Crime, Society and Politics in Thailand," in Carl A. Trocki, ed., *Gangsters, Democracy and the State in Southeast Asia* (Ithaca, NY, 1998), 39–54; and Ruth McVey, ed., *Money and Power in Provincial Thailand* (Copenhagen, 2000).

13. See Suchit Bunbongkarn, "Elections and Democracy in Thailand," and Anek Laothamatas, "A Tale of Two Democracies: Conflicting perceptions of elections and democracy in Thailand," in Taylor, ed., *The Politics of Elections*, 184–200 and 201–30.

14. See R. H. Taylor, "Politics in Late Colonial Burma: The Case of U Saw," *Modern Asian Studies* 10, 2 (Apr. 1976): 161–94.

15. Mary P. Callahan, "Sinking the Schooner: Murder and the State in Independent Burma, 1948–1958," in Trocki, ed., *Gangsters, Democracy and the State*, 17–37.

16. R. H. Taylor, "Change in Burma: Political Demands and Military Power," *Asian Affairs* 22, pt. 2 (June 1991): 131–41.

CHAPTER 6

I am grateful to Melinda Tria Kerkvliet and Pham Thu Thuy for assisting me with research for this chapter. For sources, suggestions on numerous specific points, and constructive criticisms, I thank Helen Chauncey, Kit Collier, John Dunn, David Elliott, Mai Elliott, Natalie Hicks, Hue-Tam Ho Tai, Rey Ileto, Sudipta Kaviraj, David Koh, Victor LeVine, David Marr, Andy Nathan, David Rosenberg, Drew Smith, Bob Taylor, Alex Woodside, Fred Yap, and all participants in the October 1998 and 1999 workshops at Washington University, seminars at the Australian National University in October 1999 and the University of California at Los Angeles in March 2000, and panel discussion at the Association for Asian Studies' annual meeting in March 2000. I also thank the Center for the History of Freedom, Washington University, which encouraged me to delve into this topic.

1. For background, see Anthony Reid, *Southeast Asia in the Age of Commerce, 1450–1680* 1 (New Haven, CT, 1988): 137–72 passim.

2. Alexander B. Woodside, *Community and Revolution in Modern Vietnam* (Boston, 1976), 14; also see 15–17.

3. Orlando Patterson, *Freedom in the Making of Western Culture* (New York, 1991).

4. Here and elsewhere, when referring to vernacular material for the Philippines, I use Tagalog because I do not know the country's other languages. Tagalog is the base for Pilipino, the country's national language.

5. William Henry Scott, *Barangay: Sixteenth Century Philippine Culture and Society* (Quezon City, 1994), 222–25. Scott's book describes similar social groups, frequently with the same terminology, for the Bisayas, Bicol, and other parts of the archipelago.

6. "Vocabulario Hispano-Tagalog," in Juan de Noceda and Pedro de Sanlucar, *Vocabulario de la Lengua Tagala* (Vocabulary of the Tagalog Language), 3d ed. (Manila, 1860), 544. Contrast this situation to the survival in Indonesia of "*merdeka*," which originally had the same meaning as *maharlika* (*maharlica*), and became the Indonesian word for freedom. (Anthony Reid, "Merdeka: The Concept of Freedom in Indonesia," in David Kelly and Anthony Reid, *Asian Freedoms: The Idea of Freedom in East and Southeast Asia* [Cambridge, 1998], 141–60.) In the Philippines today, the Tagalog word *maharlika* is sometimes used, but refers to an aristocrat or nobleman. In some other Philippine languages today, the words for "free" or "freedom" appear not to have roots in old terminology for unbonded or not enslaved people; in other languages, however, the words may have a connection to such earlier usage.

7. *Sa sariling baya't upang matimawa sa madlang pahirap.* The poem is reprinted and translated into English in Bienvenido L. Lumbera, *Tagalog Poetry 1570–1898* (Quezon City, 1986), 217–34; see 233 for the stanza.

8. Virgilio S. Almario, *Panitikan ng Rebolusyon(g 1896)* (1896 Revolutionary literature) (Quezon City, 1997), 60.

9. Reynaldo Clemeña Ileto, *Pasyon and Revolution: Popular Movements in the Philippines, 1840–1910* (Quezon City, 1979), 107–8. Also see *Diksyunaryo ng Wikang Filipino* (Filipino language dictionary) (Manila, 1989), 398.

10. Noceda and Sanlucar, *Vocabulario*, 177. The dictionary does have the words "*laya*," meaning extend one's arm (*estender el brazo*), and "*laya*," referring to rubbish (*vasura*) or being dry or withered (*vide* "*tuyò*," "*lanta*"), neither of which seems connected to *laya* in the sense of liberty or freedom, although students of etymologies should pursue the matter. (I thank Melinda Tria Kerkvliet for translating the Spanish definitions.)

11. Nancy Kimuell-Gabriel, *Ang Timawa sa Kasaysayang Pilipino: "Malaya Noon, Dayukdok Ngayon"* (The *Timawa* in Filipino History: "before free, now starving") (Lunsod Quezon, 1999), 53–54.

12. Ileto, *Pasyon*, 108–9.

13. Greg Lockhart, "Vietnam: Democracy and Democratisation," *Asian Studies Review* 17 (July 1993): 136–37.

14. Alexander Woodside, "Freedom and Elite Political Theory in Vietnam Before the French," in Kelly and Reid, *Asian Freedoms*, 207.

15. Ibid., 218.

16. Ileto, *Pasyon*, chap. 2; Nicholas P. Cushner, *Spain in the Philippines* (Quezon City, 1971), 210–29 inter alia.

17. Cesar A. Majul, *The Political and Constitutional Ideas of the Philippine Revolution* (Quezon City, 1967), 187–90; John N. Schumacher, *The Propaganda Movement, 1880–1895* (Manila, 1973), 17–52 passim; David

G. Marr, *Vietnamese Anticolonialism, 1885–1925* (Berkeley, 1971), 5, 110–11, 133, 271; Hue-Tam Ho Tai, *Radicalism and the Origins of the Vietnamese Revolution* (Cambridge, MA, 1992), 23, 62, 72–73, 152–53; Vinh Sinh, "Phan Boi Chau and Fukuzawa Yukichi: Perceptions of National Independence," in Vinh Sinh, ed., *Phan Boi Chau and the Dong Du Movement* (New Haven, CT, 1988), 110, 119, 126–27, 136–37. Chapters 7 and 8 below have more to say about Liang Qichao and Fukuzawa Yukichi.

18. This discussion draws on Almario, *Panitikan*, 58, 82–92; Ileto, *Pasyon*, 37–140 passim; John Schumacher, "The 'Propagandists' Reconstruction of the Philippine Past," in Anthony Reid and David Marr, eds., *Perceptions of the Past in Southeast Asia* (Singapore, 1979), 269, 274; Hue-Tam Ho Tai, *Radicalism*, 20, 90, 114–15, 142–43; Marr, *Vietnamese Anticolonialism*, 44–119 passim.

19. Neil Jamieson, *Understanding Vietnam* (Berkeley, 1993), 49.

20. Schumacher, *Propaganda*, xi, 49. Leon Ma. Guerrero argues that Jose Rizal taught his compatriots in the 1880s that instead of being Bisayan, Tagalog, Ilokano, etc., "they could be something else, Filipinos who were members of a Filipino Nation. He was the first who sought to 'unite the whole archipelago' and envisioned a 'compact and homogeneous' society of all the old tribal communities from Batanes to the Sulu Sea." *The First Filipino: A Biography of Jose Rizal* (Manila, 1963), 496.

21. Quoted in O.D. Corpuz, *The Roots of the Filipino Nation* 2 (Quezon City, 1989): 568.

22. See, for instance, F. A. Hayek, "Freedom and Coercion," in David Miller, ed., *Liberty* (Oxford, 1991), 80–81; Patterson, *Freedom*, 3–4.

23. See chaps. 7 and 8.

24. Corpuz, *Roots*, chaps. 15, 16.

25. Bernard B. Fall, ed., *Ho Chi Minh on Revolution: Selected Writings, 1920–1966* (New York, 1967), 29–30, 68–69, 90–92, 141–42.

26. Pierre Brocheux, *The Mekong Delta: Ecology, Economy, and Revolution, 1860–1960* (Madison, WI, 1995), 180; Marr, *Vietnamese Anticolonialism*, 187–93; Phan Chu Trinh, *A Complete Account of the Peasants' Uprising in the Central Region*, trans. Beter Baugher and Vu Ngu Chieu (Madison, WI, 1983), 45–51.

27. Jayne Susan Werner, *Peasant Politics and Religious Sectarianism: Peasant and Priest in the Cao Dai in Viet Nam* (New Haven, CT, 1981), chaps. 3 and 4.

28. Constitution of the Philippine Republic, Jan. 1899, article 5. For debates leading up to this provision, see Majul, *Political*, chap. 7; and Teodoro A. Agoncillo, *Malolos: The Crisis of the Republic* (Quezon City, 1960), 298–306.

29. Hue-Tam Ho Tai, *Radicalism*, 58.

30. For debates about Vietnamese family and gender relations in the 1910s–30s, see Hue-Tam Ho Tai, *Radicalism*, 196–223; David Marr, *Vietnamese Tradition on Trial 1920–1945* (Berkeley, 1981), 131–32, 190–251, 333–34; Jamieson, *Understanding Vietnam*, 106–7, 171–75.

31. Marr, *Vietnamese Anticolonialism*, 246–47, 269–71; Tran Van Giau, *Su Phat Trien cua Tu Tuong o Viet Nam tu The Ky XIX den Cach Mang Thang Tam* (The development of ideas in Vietnam from the nineteenth century to the August revolution), vol. 2 (Hanoi, 1975), 446–48, 454–55; Hue-Tam Ho Tai, *Radicalism*, 77–80.

32. Quoted in Majul, *Political*, 30; also see 27–31, 109–12. For Rizal, education was also a means for eventually getting independence from Spain without resorting to violence, which he opposed. See Schumacher, *Propaganda*, 213, 226, 243, 251.

33. Schumacher, *Propaganda*, 122–53 passim, 180, 197; Majul, *Political*, 47–48.

34. Phan Boi Chau, "Tan Viet Nam" (New Vietnam), in Chuong Thau, ed., *Phan Boi Chau Toan Tap* (Collected Works of Phan Boi Chau), vol. 2 (Hue, 1990), 257.

35. Woodside, *Community*, 5.

36. Hue-Tam Ho Tai, *Radicalism*, 153.

37. Cesar Adib Majul, *Apolinario Mabini Revolutionary* (Manila, 1964), 62–65; Constitution of the Philippines, 1899, article 20.

38. Constitution of the Democratic Republic of Vietnam, Nov. 1946, chap. II:B. Quotations from the Viet Minh publication are in Marr, *Vietnamese Tradition*, 98–99.

39. Majul, *Political*, 63–64.

40. Hue-Tam Ho Tai, *Radicalism*, 82, 83, also 85–86, 173. Neil Jamieson argues that a major feature of Vietnam's history during the twentieth century was the ongoing effort to balance diversity and uniformity, freedom and order, and individual rights and common welfare. Jamieson, *Understanding Vietnam*, 374–75.

41. George G. Brenkert, *Political Freedom* (London, 1991), chap. 7.

42. Ileto, *Pasyon and Revolution*, 144; also see 145–54.

43. Ileto, *Pasyon and Revolution*, 230–31.

44. Christine Pelzer White, "Agrarian Reform and National Liberation in the Vietnamese Revolution: 1920–1957" (Ph.D. diss., Cornell Univ., 1981), 66. These actions were taken, argues White, even before Communist Party members in the province started sending directives. Also, see William J. Duiker, "The Red Soviets of Nghe-Tinh: An Early Communist Rebellion in Vietnam," *Journal of Southeast Asian Studies* 4 (Sept. 1973): 186–98; Martin Bernal, "The Nghe-Tinh Soviet Movement 1930–1931," *Past and Present* 92 (Aug. 1981): 148–68.

45. Hoang Nhat Tan, *Xo Viet Nghe-Tinh* (The Nghe-Tinh soviets) (Hanoi, 1962), 105, as quoted in Greg Lockhart, *Nation in Arms: The Origins of the People's Army of Vietnam* (Sydney, 1989), 60.

46. Marr, *Vietnamese Anticolonialism*, 205.

47. Majul, *Mabini*, 203. Although a necessary condition, independence was not for Mabini a sufficient condition for other freedoms and national development. See ibid., 206.

48. Regarding Rizal, see Corpuz, *Roots*, 119, 131; and Majul, *Political*,

26. Regarding Phan Chu Trinh, see Marr, *Vietnamese Anticolonialism*, 162–63, 198–99. Numerous apparent similarities between Rizal and Phan Chu Trinh merit careful study.

49. Quoted in Guerrero, *First Filipino*, 497. Also see Majul, *Political*, 26.

50. The full name was *Kataastaasan Kagalanggalang Katipunan ng mga Anak ng Bayan* (The Highest and Most Honorable Society of Sons of the Nation).

51. Bonifacio S. Salamanca, *The Filipino Reaction to American Rule, 1901–1913* (Quezon City, 1984), 14–16; Ileto, *Pasyon*, 144, 225–26.

52. Indicative of this contrast are the declarations of independence in the two countries (the Philippine one issued June 12, 1898, the Vietnam one issued Sept. 2, 1945). In the course of outlining the justifications for revolution against and independence from colonial rule, the Philippine document barely mentions economic adversities. They are emphasized, however, in the Vietnam declaration, which also specifically condemns French rule for reducing "our people, especially our peasantry, to a state of extreme poverty." "Declaration of Independence of the Democratic Republic of Viet Nam," in Fall, *Ho Chi Minh*, 141–43; "Act of Proclamation of Philippine Independence," in Alfredo B. Saulo, *Emilio Aguinaldo* (Quezon City, 1983), 509–12.

53. The Viet Minh's full name was *Viet Nam Doc Lap Dong Minh* (League for the Independence of Vietnam).

54. Not that all Vietnamese supporting the Viet Minh against France subscribed to the socio-economic remaking of the country. Many who were wealthy people did not, which made the Viet Minh leadership initially proceed somewhat cautiously with land reform for fear of alienating nationalists in the upper classes. For an extended analysis, see White, "Agrarian Reform," 89–132.

55. Kim Ngoc Bao Ninh, "Revolution, Politics and Culture in Socialist Vietnam, 1945–1965" (PhD diss., Yale Univ., 1996), 18–20; Hue-Tam Hoi Tai, *Radicalism*, 4, 260–63.

56. Ileto, *Pasyon*, 240.

57. Some Muslims even said they would rather remain under U.S. rule than end up part of an independent Philippines. Peter Gordon Gowing, *Muslim-Filipinos: Heritage and Horizon* (Quezon City, 1979), 168–70.

58. The paragraph with these words vows that the Vietnamese people will never surrender. Ho Chi Minh, "Loi Keu Goi Dong Bao va Chien Si ca Nuoc" (A call to compatriots and fighters across the land), in Ho Chi Minh, *Vi Doc Lap Tu Do vi Chu Nghia Xa Hoi* (For independence, freedom, and socialism) (Hanoi, 1970), 282. Ho had used the same expression to inspire compatriots at least twenty years earlier. See Truong Nhu Tang, with David Chanoff and Doan Van Toai, *A Vietcong Memoir* (San Diego, CA, 1985), 15.

59. For an account of the NLF by one of its leaders, who was not a Communist Party member and had many differences with the party, see Truong Nhu Tang, *Vietcong Memoir*. Also see Douglas Pike, *Viet Cong:*

The Organization and Techniques of the National Liberation Front of South Vietnam (Cambridge, MA, 1966).

60. See, for instance, "Declaration of the Government of the State of Vietnam on Reunification," Aug. 9, 1955, in Gareth Porter, ed., *Vietnam: A History in Documents* (New York, 1979), 181–82. School textbooks, which the Saigon government authorized, talked about all of Vietnam, not just the southern zone. Thaveeporn Vasavakul, "Schools and Politics in South and North Viet Nam: A Comparative Study of State Apparatus, State Policy, and State Power (1945–1965)" (Ph.D. diss., Cornell Univ., 1994), chap. 3.

61. This was also a key part of U.S. government officials' argument for waging war in Vietnam. How many Vietnamese believed it is unclear. One who seems to have come to identify with South Vietnam as a nation is Bui Diem, who was the Saigon government's ambassador to Washington, D.C., for several years. Bui Diem, with David Chanoff, *In the Jaws of History* (Boston, 1987), 103, 159, 337–38. An explicit argument for South Vietnam "as a nation" appears in Nguyen Duy Hinh and Tran Dinh Tho, *The South Vietnamese Society* (Washington, DC, 1980, 1984).

62. For elaboration on one or both of these, see Gabriel Kolko, *Anatomy of a War: Vietnam, the United States, and the Modern Historical Experience* (New York, 1983), 212–13, 226–29; James Walker Trullinger, Jr., *Village at War: An Account of Revolution in Vietnam* (New York, 1980), 153–55, 168, 171, 182, 185; William S. Turley, *The Second Indochina War* (Boulder, CO, 1986), 192–93; Woodside, *Community*, 302–3.

63. Carlyle Thayer said it well: the "concept of a 'South Vietnamese nationality' was only tenable by those who chose to ignore the facts." *War by Other Means: National Liberation and Revolution in Viet Nam 1954–60* (Sydney, 1989), xxviii.

64. For the Philippines, see President McKinley's 1900 instructions to the new colony's first commissioners (repr. in Salamanca, *Filipino Reaction*, 237–45) and the 1935 Constitution of the Philippines, particularly the "Bill of Rights." For Vietnam under the DRV, see sections regarding citizens' rights and duties in its 1946 and 1960 constitutions; for Vietnam under the Saigon-based government, see the discussion of its 1958 constitution in Bernard B. Fall, *The Two Viet-Nams: A Political and Military Analysis*, 2d ed. (London, 1967), 261.

65. Hernando J. Abaya, *The CLU Story: Fifty Years of Struggle for Civil Liberties* (Quezon City, 1987), 21.

66. Ileto, *Pasyon and Revolution*, 210–12, 219–22, 225, 230–31, 233, 270, 276, 287.

67. "An Interview with Pedro Calosa," in David R. Sturtevant, *Popular Uprisings in the Philippines, 1840–1940* (Ithaca, NY, 1976), 274.

68. Mamerto J. Ponce's article in the newspaper *Sakdal*, Feb. 13, 1937, 3. Economic and social oppression were pronounced themes in rural unrest during the 1930s. See Benedict J. Kerkvliet, *The Huk Rebellion* (Berkeley, 1976), 26–60.

69. Sturtevant, *Popular Uprisings*, 291; also see 278–83. For elaboration of Sakdalista aspirations, see *Pamahayag at Patakaran ng Lapiang Sakdalista* (Manifesto and platform of the Sakdalista Party) (n.p., Oct. 29, 1933).

70. Regarding the PKP case, see Philippine Supreme Court decision, "The People of the Philippine Islands vs Crisanto Evangelista, Jacinto G. Manahan and Dominador J. Ambrosio," No. 36275, Oct. 26, 1932, in *Official Gazette* (Manila), Feb. 6, 1934, 302–7; and Crisanto Evangelista, "Communism and Capitalism: Before the P.I. Supreme Court" (Manila, 1932). For an overview of this and other struggles involving civil liberties in the 1930s, see Ramon C. Aquino, *A Chance to Die: A Biography of Jose Abad Santos* (Quezon City, 1967), 76–121 passim, 149–50. Also see Abaya, *CLU Story*, 4–37.

71. For analyses of rural movements in the 1920s–1930s and government responses, see Milagros C. Guerrero, "The Colorum Uprisings: 1924–31," *Asian Studies* 5 (April 1967): 65–78; Kerkvliet, *Huk Rebellion*, chap. 2; Sturtevant, *Popular Uprisings*, chaps. 9, 11–13.

72. Quang Truong, *Agricultural Collectivization and Rural Development in Vietnam: A North-South Study* (Amsterdam, 1987), 35.

73. For elaboration, see Thaveeporn Vasavakul, "Vietnam: The Changing Models of Legitimation," in Muthiah Alagappa, ed., *Political Legitimacy in Southeast Asia: The Quest for Moral Authority* (Stanford, 1995), 265–66; Benedict J. Tria Kerkvliet, *Land Struggles and Land Regimes in the Philippines and Vietnam During the Twentieth Century* (Amsterdam, 1997), 19–20.

74. Robert Sansom, *Economics of Insurgency in the Mekong Delta of Vietnam* (Cambridge, MA, 1970), 656–69, 228–45; Charles Stuart Callison, *Land-to-the-Tiller in the Mekong Delta* (Berkeley, 1983), 46–51, 74–78; Nguyen Tran, *Cong va Toi: Nhung Hoi Ky Lich Su Chinh Tri Mien Nam Viet Nam 1945–1975* (Merits and Faults: memoirs of politics in south Vietnam, 1945–1975) (Los Alamitos, CA, 1992), 368, 555–56; Woodside, *Community*, 292–93, 302; Turley, *Second Indochina War*, 192–93; Charles A. Joiner, *The Politics of Massacre: Political Processes in South Vietnam* (Philadelphia, 1974); Fall, *Two Viet-Nams*.

75. Nguyen Chanh Thi, *Viet Nam: Mot Troi Tam Su* (Vietnam: world of sorrows) (Los Alamitos, CA, 1987), 122–23. The author, as an officer in the Saigon army, participated in an unsuccessful coup attempt in 1960.

76. Thich Nhat Hanh, *Vietnam: Lotus in a Sea of Fire* (New York, 1967), 26–31, 55–83 passim; Pjero Gheddo, *The Cross and the Bo-Tree: Catholics and Buddhists in Vietnam*, trans. Charles Underhill Quinn (New York, 1970), 177–85, 265–74.

77. For recent discussions of this episode, see Nguyen Hung Quoc, *Van Hoc Viet Nam Duoi Che Do Cong San, 1945–1990* (Vietnamese literature under the communist regime) (Westminster, CA, 1991), chap. 2; Kim Ngoc Bao Ninh, "Revolution, Politics and Culture," chap. 4; Georges Boudarel, "The Nhan Van Giai Pham Affair: Intellectual Dissidence in the 1950s," *Vietnam Forum* 13 (1990): 154–74; Georges Boudarel, *Cent Fleurs Ecloses*

dans la Nuit du Vietnam: Communisme et Dissidence, 1954–1956 (Paris, 1991); Russell Hiang-Khng Heng, "Of the State, For the State, Yet Against the State: The Struggle Paradigm in Vietnam's Media Politics" (Ph.D. diss., Australian National Univ., 1999), chap. 3.

78. Truong Tuu, "Tu Do Tu Tuong cua Van Nghe Si" (Freedom of thought of artists), *Giai Pham*, Winter, 1 (1956): 68–70. Also see articles by Q. Ngoc and T. Hong and by Nguyen Duc Tieu in *Dat Moi* 1 (1956): 3–19, 59–64. *Dat Moi* (New Land) was another short-lived publication in 1956 criticizing overly restrictive and domineering behavior of authorities in various institutions, including universities.

79. One satirical story talks about mechanically produced poetry that soon drives villagers to boredom. Cham Van Biem, "The Robot Poet," *Nhan Van*, Nov. 20, 1956. The author's name, probably a pseudonym, is a play on the Vietnamese word for ridicule (*cham biem*). The story is in Hoa Mai, ed., *The "Nhan Van" Affair* (n.d., n.p.), 146–55. This book has some of the articles, translated from Vietnamese, that appeared in the 1956 Hanoi publication *Nhan Van*.

80. Truong Tuu, "Benh Sung Bai Ca Nhan trong Gioi Lanh Dao Van Nghe" (The personality cult among leaders of arts and culture), *Giai Pham*, Autumn, 2 (1956): 7, 12–14. Also see Dao Duy Anh, "Muon Phat Trien Hoc Thuat" (To develop scholarship), *Giai Pham*, Autumn, 3 (1956): 44–45.

81. See *Nhan Van* writings by Dao Van Ngu, Nguyen Huu Dang, Tran Duy, and Tran Duc Thao in Hoa Mai, *Nhan Van Affair*, 84–87, 109–16, 128–29.

82. Tran Duc Thao, "Noi Dung Xa Hoi va Hinh Thuc Tu Do" (Social content and forms of freedom), *Giai Pham*, Winter, 1 (1956): 20–21, also see 15, 18.

83. I am drawing on attacks against the writers and artists compiled in *Bon "Nhan Van—Giai Pham": Truoc Toa An Du Luan* (The Nhan Van—Giai Pham gang: facing the tribunal of public opinion) (Hanoi, 1959), especially articles by To Huu, 156–77; Quang Dam, 180–211; Hong Chuong, 211–26; Ban Chap Hanh Trung Uong Dang Lao Dong Viet Nam (Executive Committee of the Vietnam Worker's Party aka Vietnam Communist Party), 344–53; and Truong Chinh, 362–64.

84. ... *tu do sang tac hoa doc, hoa thoi*, which literally means "freedom to create poisonous and rotten flowers," a slam against those who said that Vietnam should let a hundred flowers bloom, as China was reportedly then doing.

85. Phan Khoi, "Phe Binh Lanh Dao Van Nghe" (Criticizing leadership in the arts and literature), *Giai Pham*, Autumn, 1 (1956): 6.

86. Tran Duy, "The Sincere Struggle for Democratic Freedoms," *Nhan Van*, Nov. 5, 1956, in Hoa Mai, *Nhan Van Affair*, 115.

87. In Hoa Mai, *Nhan Van Affair*, 165–67.

88. Ho Chi Minh, *Vi Doc Lap Tu Do*, 203–5.

89. Succumbing to intense pressure from the U.S. government and business groups, the newly independent Philippine government in 1946 gave

Americans the same rights as Filipinos—"parity"—to do business in the country and exploit the country's resources.

90. Truong Nhu Tang, *Vietcong Memoir*, 285–89, 309–10 passim.

91. See, for instance, articles in *Nhan Dan*, the daily newspaper of the Communist Party (e.g., a series on human rights, June 2, 3, 28, 1993), and "Bai Noi cua Dong Chi Tong Bi Thu Do Muoi tai Hoi Nghi Can Bo do Ban Bi Thu Trieu Tap tai Ha Noi, ngay 3–3–1994" (Speech by Comrade Secretary General Do Muoi at a conference for cadres convened by the secretariat, Hanoi, Mar. 3, 1994). Also see Benedict J. Tria Kerkvliet, "Politics of Society in the Mid 1990s," in id., ed., *Dilemmas of Development: Vietnam Update 1994* (Canberra, 1995), 35–38.

92. See, for instance, Thich Quang Do, *Nhan Dinh ve Nhung Sai Lam Tai Hai cua Dang Cong San Viet Nam doi voi Dan Toc va Phat Giao* (Grave mistakes of the Vietnam Communist Party against the nation and Buddhism) (Paris: 1995); Le Da Duong, "Phat Giao Viet Nam va cuoc Dau Tranh vi Dao Phap, Dan Toc va Dan Chu" (Vietnamese Buddhism and the struggle for Buddha's teachings, the nation, and democracy), *Thong Luan* 63 (Sept. 1993): 13 15.

93. One prominent advocate is Doan Viet Hoat, a prisoner of conscience whom Amnesty International brought to the world's attention. In September 1998, Vietnam government authorities released him and several other prisoners and insisted that he leave Vietnam. He went to the United States. For his writings, see *Doan Viet Hoat va Nhom Dien Dan Tu Do* (Doan Viet Hoat and the freedom forum) (Garden Grove, CA, 1993).

94. "Nha Van Hoang Tien Phan Doi Ha Noi Dan Ap Tu Do Ngon Luan" (Literary figure Hoang Tien opposes Hanoi for suppressing free speech), *Tivi Tuan San*, Sept. 16, 1998, 56. *Tivi Tuan San* (TV Weekly), published in Melbourne, is a weekly magazine that frequently carries articles about and by people in Vietnam who criticize the government.

95. Nguyen Ho, *Quan Diem va Cuoc Song* (Outlook and life) (Paris, 1994), 29. Once a member of the Communist Party and a veteran of the war to overthrow the government in Saigon and reunite Vietnam, Nguyen Ho was arrested in 1990.

96. Tran Do, "Tinh Hinh Dat Nuoc va Vai Tro cua Dang Cong San" (The state of the nation and role of the Communist Party—an undated [circa December 1997] letter to Communist Party leaders), *Tivi Tuan San*, Feb. 18, 1998, 60. Tran Do is a retired general in Hanoi who was expelled from the Communist Party in January 1999. His long 1997 letter, followed in subsequent years by several more missives, appeared in Vietnamese language publications outside the country but apparently has yet to be published in Vietnam itself. *Tivi Tuan San* serialized the letter in its Feb. 11, 18, and 25, 1998, issues. An English translation was put on the internet in early January 1998 (http://www.fva.org/document/dissident/trando.htm).

97. Nguyen Thanh Giang, "Trao Doi Voi Nha Cach Mang Lao Thanh Tran Do ve Tinh Hinh Dat Nuoc va Vai Tro cua Dang Cong San" (Interacting with veteran revolutionary Tran Do on the state of the nation and role

of the Communist Party), *Tivi Tuan San*, Apr. 8, 1998, 60. Nguyen Thanh Giang is a geophysicist working in a state research institute. Written in Vietnam in February 1998, Nguyen Thanh Giang's essay was serialized in *Tivi Tuan San*, Mar. 25 and Apr. 1 and 8, 1998. Also see Hoang Tien's argument in "Nha Van Hoang Tien," *Tivi Tuan San*, Sept. 16, 1998, 56, and Sept. 23, 1998, 42.

98. *Doc lap ma khong co tu do, hanh phuc thi doc lap cung khong co y nghia*. Tran Do, "Tinh Hinh Dat Nuoc," *Tivi Tuan San*, Feb. 25, 1998, 66. The national motto is *Doc Lap, Tu Do, Hanh Phuc* (Independence, Freedom, Happiness).

99. Phan Dinh Dieu, "Ve Yeu Cau Tiep Tuc Doi Moi trong Giai Doan Hien Nay" (On the need to continue the current renovations), *Tivi Tuan San*, Feb. 18, 1998, 84. Phan Dinh Dieu, a mathematician in Hanoi who has often spoken out on behalf of civil liberties, originally presented this paper to a Hanoi conference of the Central Committee, Fatherland Front of Vietnam, Dec. 12–13, 1997. Also see Hoang Tien's argument in "Nha Van Hoang Tien."

100. Duong Thu Huong, "Tuong Trinh voi Chi Bo Dang Xuong Phim Truyen I" (Report for party officials of Film Workshop I), in *Nhung Van De Viet Nam* (Vietnam problems) (Garden Grove, CA, 1992), 437–46. Required by local party officials in 1990 to explain statements she had been making, Duong Thu Huong, a novelist in Hanoi, wrote this bitter critique of socialism and the Communist Party, both of which she had supported but later concluded had failed to live up to their promises.

101. Tran Do, "Tinh Hinh Dat Nuoc," *Tivi Tuan San*, Feb. 11, 1998, 28, 60.

102. *Tien Phong* (Vanguard, a newspaper in Vietnam), Oct. 2, 4, 7, 9, 1997; Tuong Lai, "Bao Cao so bo ve cuoc Khao Sat Xa hoi tai Thai Binh cuoi Thang Sau, dau Thanh Bay nam 1997" (Preliminary report of a sociological investigation of Thai Binh, late June-early July 1997) (http://members.aol.com/tdxanh/th-binh.htm, accessed Oct. 14, 1998); *Nhan Dan*, Sept. 8, 9, 10, 11, 1997; Tran Do, "Tinh Hinh Dat Nuoc," *Tivi Tuan San*, Feb. 11, 1998, 30, 58. The study by Tuong Lai summarizes a series of reports done at the request of the Vietnamese government.

103. Elsewhere I have argued that such democratic institutions and liberties, however flawed in practice, have been important to political legitimacy of governments in the Philippines since independence. Kerkvliet, *Land Struggles*, 21–23.

104. See Kerkvliet, *Huk Rebellion*, chap. 4; Richard J. Kessler, *Rebellion and Repression in the Philippines* (New Haven, CT, 1989), 136–61 passim; Gregg R. Jones, *Red Revolution: Inside the Philippine Guerrilla Movement* (Boulder, CO, 1989), 106–9; Christopher James Collier, "The Politics of Insurrection in Davao, Philippines" (Ph.D. diss., Univ. of Hawaii, 1997).

105. A poignant example is Ditto Sarmiento, editor of the student newspaper *Philippine Collegian*. For not abiding by the new rules, he was questioned in 1976 by authorities. Then, because he refused, in his words,

"to temper the editorial policy of my paper—which would be a blatant infringement on the freedom of expression (authorities) so hypocritically proclaim exists under martial law," he was imprisoned. See his letter in *Pintig: Poems and Letters from Philippine Prisons* (Hong Kong, 1979), 19.

106. One popular slogan chanted by demonstrators from wide-ranging class and social backgrounds called Marcos both a dictator and "*tuta,*" meaning a lap dog of foreign interests. See Jose Diokno, "Sovereignty and Democracy," Mar. 19, 1983, in Priscila S. Manalang, ed., *A Nation for our Children: Human Rights, Nationalism, Sovereignty: Selected Writings of Jose W. Diokno* (Quezon City, 1987), 167–68; Abaya, *CLU Story*, 125–47.

107. "*Ang Panahon ni Cristy*" (Cristy's time), by Edgar B. Maranan, performed in January 1979 at the University of the Philippines, Diliman, directed by Behn Cervantes. I saw the performance and have a printed program with notes by the playwright, director, and other commentators.

108. Lualhati Bautista, *Dekada '70* (The '70s) (Mandaluyong, 1992), 3d printing. Originally printed and distributed around 1982 or 1983.

109. "*Balita,*" written by C. Banares, Jr., performed and recorded by Asin in its album "*Himig ng Pagibig*" (Melodies of love) (Cinema Audio, Philippines, 1979).

110. Written by Jose Corazon de Jesus and Constancio de Guzman in 1928, probably aimed then at American colonial rule, the song's plaint about "*dalita*" (destitution) and "*dusa*" (suffering) in the country resonated with the economic depression and political repression many Filipinos experienced during martial law. As in many other anti-martial law writings, a bird symbolizes freedom. Put a free bird in a cage and "it will cry,"the lyrics say. "What more a country of splendor. Would it not also desire to escape?", the song asks rhetorically. "My ambition," goes the last line, "is to see that you (my country) are completely *free*" (*aking adhika makita kang sakdal laya*). Reflecting about the song's impact, one anti-Marcos political prisoner wrote the bird "had become so associated with freedom from detention and dictatorship that its original nationalist intent is somewhat overlooked." (Edicio de la Torre, *Touching Ground, Taking Root* [Quezon City, 1986], 149.) The date of the song's composition and first appearance is cited in Felipe Padilla de Leon, "Poetry, Music and Social Consciousness," *The Urian Lectures* (Manila, 1969), 281.

111. My observations in the Philippines, late 1984-early 1985; articles in *Mr. and Ms.* (a weekly newspaper), 1983–86; Mark R. Thompson, *The Anti-Marcos Struggle* (New Haven, CT, 1995), chaps. 7 and 8.

112. These ideas were published first in Ferdinand E. Marcos, *Today's Revolution: Democracy* (place not provided, 1971), followed by id., *The Democratic Revolution in the Philippines* (Englewood Cliffs, NJ, 1974).

113. O. D. Corpuz, "Liberty and Government in the New Society" (Manila, ca. 1974), 6–9, 19–20, 30. A slightly different version appears in the *Philippine Political Science Journal* 3 (June 1976): 5–35. A respected professor at the University of the Philippines, Corpuz became a cabinet member in the Marcos regime.

114. See chap. 3.

115. The Civil Liberties Union of the Philippines, "The State of the Nation after Three Years of Martial Law," Sept. 21, 1975, repr. in David A. Rosenberg, ed., *Marcos and Martial Law in the Philippines* (Ithaca, NY, 1979), 286–98. Also see Jose Diokno, "Human Rights Make Man Human," Dec. 31, 1981, in Manalang, *Nation*, 4–5; and Bonifacio Ilagan's play "Pagsambang Bayan" (Mass of the people), in *Collegian Folio*, Summer 1978, 23–41.

116. For a succinct summary by one vocal critic, see Jose Diokno, "Martial Law in the Philippines," Sept. 21, 1978, in Manalang, ed., *Nation*, 32; also see 43. The song "*Pangako*" (Promise), written by popular folk singer Freddie Aguilar, asks "where is that economic development / spoken about at length with such lovely sounding words?" Meanwhile, the song says, "there you are," meaning Marcos, "hiding in your palace" (*sa iyong palasyo at nagtatago*), where the sound of money being counted means "you're unable even to hear" the pleas of hungry people. (The song, probably written in the early 1980s, is in Freddie Aguilar's album "*Katarungan*" (Justice), Ivory Records, Philippines, 1988.) The song "*Ikaw-Kayo-Tayo*" (You, you guys, and we), taped in 1983 by the group called Asin, says, referring to Marcos, "you're fond of fooling people who believed in you" (*Mahilig kang manloko ng taong may tiwala sa iyo*). But, the last stanza says, "our eyes are opening to see the truth." (Asin's album "*Himig ng Lahi*" [Native Melodies], Ivory Records, Philippines, 1983.)

CHAPTER 7

Following East Asian practice, Japanese surnames precede given names, excepting those of Japanese whose English-language works have been cited.

1. See chap. 8.

2. Robert A. Scalapino, *Democracy and the Party Movement in Prewar Japan: The Failure of the First Attempt* (Berkeley, 1953); for a somewhat different perspective, see Tatsuo Arima, *The Failure of Freedom: A Portrait of Modern Japanese Intellectuals* (Cambridge, MA, 1969).

3. Scalapino, *Democracy*, 3, 5–7, 37.

4. Daikichi Irokawa, *The Culture of the Meiji Period*, trans. and ed. Marius Jansen (Princeton, NJ, 1985), 119.

5. Italics mine. Miyachi Masato, "Ōmotokyō fukei jiken: Shinkō shōkyō to tennōsei ideorogii," in Wagatsuma Sakae, ed., *Nihon seiji saiban shiroku: Taishō* (Tokyo, 1969), 297; for an overview of "emperor-system ideology," see Carol Gluck, *Japan's Modern Myths: Ideology in the Late Meiji Period* (Princeton, NJ, 1985), 4–6.

6. Stephen Vlastos, *Peasant Protests and Uprisings in Tokugawa Japan* (Berkeley, 1986), 42–43; David L. Howell, "Ainu Ethnicity and the Boundaries of the Early Modern Japanese State," *Past & Present* 142 (Feb. 1994): 72–73.

7. Masanao Nakamura, "An Outline of Western Culture," no. 12 (June

1874), in William R. Braisted, trans., *Meiroku Zasshi: Journal of the Japanese Enlightenment* (Cambridge, MA, 1976), 162.

8. See chaps. 6 and 8 in this volume; and Vera Mackie, "Freedom and the Family: Gendering Meiji Political Thought," in David Kelly and Anthony Reid, eds., *Asian Freedoms* (Cambridge, 1998), 121.

9. Rinshō Mitsukuri, "Liberty," no. 9 (June 1874), and Nakamura, "Outline of Western Culture," in Braisted, trans., *Meiroku Zasshi*, 117–18, 162, also xxvii, xx.

10. Quoted in Irokawa, *Culture of the Meiji Period*, 61; also, Braisted, trans., *Meiroku Zasshi*, 21, 29 n. 1.

11. Amane Nishi, "On Religion (Part Two)," no. 5 (n.d.), Arinori Mori, "Religion," no. 6 (n.d.), and Nishi, "On Religion (Part Five)," no. 8 (May 1874), in Braisted, trans., *Meiroku Zasshi*, 59–62, 78–85, 109–11.

12. Mackie, "Freedom and the Family," 125–27; Arinori Mori, "On Wives and Concubines (Part Five)," no. 27 (Feb. 1875), in Braisted, trans., *Meiroku Zasshi*, 331–33.

13. George Akita, *Foundations of Constitutional Government in Modern Japan, 1868–1900* (Cambridge, MA, 1967), 16–20, 113.

14. Scalapino, *Democracy*, 69–71; also David L. Howell, "Visions of the Future in Meiji Japan," in Merle Goldman and Andrew Gordon, eds., *Contemporary East Asia: China, Japan, and Korea* (Cambridge, MA, 2000), 101.

15. Mackie, "Freedom and the Family," 124–25.

16. See Irokawa, *Culture of the Meiji Period*.

17. Scalapino, *Democracy*, 101.

18. Sheldon Garon, *Molding Japanese Minds: The State in Everyday Life* (Princeton, NJ, 1997), 36–37.

19. Italics mine. The texts of the Meiji and postwar constitutions appear in Hugh Borton, *Japan's Modern Century*, 2d ed. (New York, 1970), 569–88.

20. Gregory J. Kasza, *The State and Mass Media in Japan, 1918–1945* (Berkeley, 1988), 14.

21. Quoted in Ivan Parker Hall, *Mori Arinori* (Cambridge, MA, 1973), 322–23.

22. Kasza, *State and Mass Media*, 15.

23. *Kin-gendaishi jiten*, 1978 ed., s.v. "Shōkai oyobi seishahō"; Sotozaki Mitsuhiro, *Nihon fujinronshi* 1 (Tokyo, 1986): 202–5.

24. See Ian Neary, *Political Protest and Social Control in Pre-war Japan: The Origins of Buraku Liberation* (Atlantic Highlands, NJ, 1989).

25. Garon, *Molding Japanese Minds*, 103, also 98–102.

26. Masumi Junnosuke, *Nihon seitōshi ron* 4 (Tokyo, 1968): 230, 267, 293.

27. Sheldon Garon, *The State and Labor in Modern Japan* (Berkeley, 1987), 30–31, 35.

28. Kasza, *State and Mass Media*, 15–17.

29. Quoted in Roger W. Bowen, *Rebellion and Democracy in Meiji Japan: A Study of Commoners in the Popular Rights Movement* (Berkeley, 1980), 210.

30. Gluck, *Japan's Modern Myths*, 97–99; Andrew Gordon, *Labor and Imperial Democracy in Prewar Japan* (Berkeley, 1991).

31. Peter Duus, *The Abacus and the Sword: The Japanese Penetration of Korea, 1895–1910* (Berkeley, 1995), 10–11, 49–53.

32. Quoted in Marlene Mayo, ed., *The Emergence of Imperial Japan* (Lexington, MA, 1970), ix.

33. Quoted in Albert M. Craig, "Fukuzawa Yukichi: The Philosophical Foundations of Meiji Nationalism," in Robert E. Ward, ed., *Political Development in Modern Japan* (Princeton, NJ, 1968), 129–30.

34. See Kenneth B. Pyle, *The New Generation in Meiji Japan* (Stanford, 1969), chap. 8; Andrew Nathan describes similar tendencies in China (chap. 8 below).

35. See Garon, *Molding Japanese Minds*, 18–21; Gluck, *Japan's Modern Myths*, 25, 112–13; Andrew E. Barshay, *State and Intellectual in Imperial Japan: The Public Man in Crisis* (Berkeley, 1988), 8–9, 16.

36. Garon, *Molding Japanese Minds*, 41.

37. Bowen, *Rebellion and Democracy*, 203–4.

38. See Garon, *State and Labor*, chaps. 2–3; Andrew Gordon, *Labor and Imperial Democracy*, chap. 5.

39. Garon, *State and Labor*, 64.

40. Quoted in Garon, *State and Labor*, 88–89.

41. Quoted in ibid., 134.

42. Quoted in Garon, *Molding Japanese Minds*, 125.

43. Quoted in ibid., 138, 140

44. Kasza, *State and Mass Media*, 20–27.

45. Sheldon Garon, "Rethinking Modernization and Modernity in Japanese History: A Focus on State-Society Relations," *Journal of Asian Studies* 53, 2 (May 1984): 352–54.

46. Quoted in Garon, *Molding Japanese Minds*, 80; see also 69–70, 79–80.

47. Yosuke Matsuoka, "Dissolve the Political Parties," *Contemporary Japan* 2 (Mar. 1934): 662.

48. Japan, Ministry of Education, "The Way of Subjects," 1941, in David John Lu, ed., *Sources of Japanese History* 2 (New York, 1974): 155–56.

49. Byron K. Marshall, *Academic Freedom and the Japanese Imperial University, 1868–1939* (Berkeley, 1992), 147–57; also Richard H. Mitchell, *Censorship in Imperial Japan* (Princeton, NJ, 1983), chap. 6; Kasza, *State and Mass Media*, chaps. 6–7.

50. Quoted in Garon, *State and Labor*, 202.

51. William Miles Fletcher, *The Search for a New Order: Intellectuals and Fascism in Prewar Japan* (Chapel Hill, NC, 1982), 112–13, 56, 61, 86; also Andrew Barshay, *State and Intellectual*, 28.

52. Garon, *State and Labor*, 190–98, 219–20.

53. Quoted in Barshay, *State and Intellectual*, 28–29.

54. Garon, *Molding Japanese Minds*, 142–43.

55. Abe Isoo, quoted in Garon, *Molding Japanese Minds*, 108, see also 106–14.

56. John W. Dower, *Embracing Defeat: Japan in the Wake of World War II* (New York, 1999), 67–68, 81–82, 347; for Occupation reforms, see also Lawrence Ward Beer, *Freedom of Expression in Japan: A Study of Comparative Law, Politics, and Society* (Tokyo, 1984), 72–77.

57. Beer, *Freedom of Expression*, 76–77.

58. Dower, *Embracing Defeat*, 351–64, 392.

59. Ibid., 255, also 369.

60. Beer, *Freedom of Expression*, 74, 79, 281.

61. Ivan P. Hall, *Cartels of the Mind: Japan's Intellectual Closed Shop* (New York, 1998), chap. 2.

62. *Nihon kin-gendaishi jiten*, 1978 ed., s.v. "Hakai katsudō hōbō"; Beer, *Freedom of Expression*, 80–81.

63. Anthony Woodiwiss, *Law, Labour and Society in Japan: From Repression to Reluctant Recognition* (London, 1992), 137; also Garon, *State and Labor*, 235–40; William B. Gould, *Japan's Reshaping of American Labor Law* (Cambridge, MA, 1984), 34.

64. Garon, *Molding Japanese Minds*, 207–11.

65. Beate Sirota Gordon, *The Only Woman in the Room: A Memoir* (Tokyo, 1997), 107, 110; Dower, *Embracing Defeat*, 357, 392; for the influence of the Weimar constitution on the Japanese constitution's labor-related articles, see Takemae Eiji, *Sengo rōdō kaikaku* (Tokyo, 1982), 81–83, 84–85, n. 13.

66. Beer, *Freedom of Expression*, 220.

67. Italics mine.

68. See Sheldon Garon and Mike Mochizuki, "Negotiating Social Contracts," in Andrew Gordon, ed., *Postwar Japan as History* (Berkeley, 1993), 145–66.

69. Frank K. Upham, "Unplaced Persons and Movements for Place," in Gordon, ed., *Postwar Japan as History*, 327–30.

70. Walter L. Ames, *Police and Community in Japan* (Berkeley, 1981), 44–45; Yoshio Sugimoto, *An Introduction to Japanese Society* (Cambridge, 1997), 246–51.

71. Garon, *Molding Japanese Minds*, 201–5.

72. Ibid., 211–15.

CHAPTER 8

1. Hu Ping, "Ziyouzhuyi sichao zai Zhongguo de mingyun" (The fate of the liberal stream of thought in China), in his *Zhongguo minyun fansi* (Reflections on the Chinese democracy movement) (Hong Kong, 1992), 159.

2. Andrew J. Nathan, *Chinese Democracy* (New York, 1985); R. Randle Edwards et al., *Human Rights in Contemporary China* (New York, 1986).

3. Wm. Theodore de Bary, *Asian Values and Human Rights: A Confucian Communitarian Perspective* (Cambridge, MA, 1998).

4. W. J. F. Jenner, "China and Freedom," in David Kelly and Anthony Reid, eds., *Asian Freedoms: The Idea of Freedom in East and Southeast Asia* (Cambridge, 1998), 65–92.

5. The position is well stated by Chenyang Li, *The Tao Encounters the West: Explorations in Comparative Philosophy* (Albany, NY, 1999), 163–89.

6. *Zhongwen dazidian* ("The encyclopedic dictionary of the Chinese language"), rev. and expanded ed. (Taipei, 1975), 7:1176. Also, commentary by Jenner in Kelly and Reid, *Asian Freedoms*, 85.

7. Li Yu-ning, *The Introduction of Socialism into China* (New York, 1971), 84.

8. Liang Qichao, *Xinmin shuo* (On the new citizen), published serially 1902–1904, chap. 9. I am using the edition published by the Zhonghua shuju, Taibei, 1959; my quotes are from 40–46.

9. The major works in English on Liang's thought are Hao Chang, *Liang Ch'i-ch'ao and Intellectual Transition in China, 1890–1907* (Cambridge, MA, 1971); Philip C. Huang, *Liang Ch'i-ch'ao and Modern Chinese Liberalism* (Seattle, 1972); and Joseph R. Levenson, *Liang Ch'i-ch'ao and the Mind of Modern China* (Berkeley, 1970).

10. Edmund S. K. Fung, *In Search of Chinese Democracy: Civil Opposition in Nationalist China, 1929–1949* (New York, 2000), 36.

11. Ch'ien Tuan-sheng, *The Government and Politics of China, 1912–1949* (Stanford, 1970), chap. 9.

12. Until the 1980s, that is, in Taiwan under Kuomintang rule. Unfortunately, space prohibits treatment of this part of the story. But see Linda Chao and Ramon H. Myers, *The First Chinese Democracy: Political Life in the Republic of China on Taiwan* (Baltimore, 1998).

13. Fung, *In Search*, 185–86, citing Wang Jingwei and Chiang Kai-shek.

14. Luo Longji, "Lun renquan" (On human rights), in Hu Shi, ed., *Renquan lunji* (Essays on human rights) (Shanghai, 1930), 39, 43, quoted in Fredric J. Spar, "Human Rights and Political Engagement: Luo Longji in the 1930s," in Roger B. Jeans, ed., *Roads Not Taken: The Struggle of Opposition Parties in Twentieth-Century China* (Boulder, CO, 1992), 64. Besides Spar, the best treatment of Luo's thought is Marina Svensson, *The Chinese Conception of Human Rights: The Debate on Human Rights in China, 1898–1949* (Lund, Sweden, 1996), 214–27.

15. Spar, "Human Rights and Political Engagement," 64–67.

16. Svensson traces Luo's functionalist theory of rights to the influence of Harold Laski. Edmund Fung argues that Luo views freedom both as an end in itself and as a means to social health (Fung, *In Search*, 58–65). Writing about another liberal, Liang Shuming, Hung-Yok Ip suggests a useful distinction among a "nation-oriented utilitarian" commitment to freedom as a way to strengthen the state, an "individual-oriented utilitarian" commitment to freedom as a condition for the happiness and fulfillment of the

individual, and a non-utilitarian commitment to freedom as an end in itself. Luo Longji might be seen as combining all three. Hung-Yok Ip, "Liang Shuming and the Idea of Democracy in Modern China," *Modern China* 17,4 (Oct. 1991): 469–508. For more discussion of the same issue in relation to additional thinkers, also see Hung-Yok Ip, "The Origins of Chinese Communism—A New Interpretation," *Modern China* 20,1 (Jan. 1994): 34–63.

17. Jeans, ed., *Roads Not Taken*, articles by Edward S. Krebs, Marilyn A. Levine, and in general, passim, for the whole spectrum of views.

18. Summarized in Svensson, *Chinese Conception*, 253–90.

19. Fung, *In Search*, 16.

20. This analysis draws on Thomas A. Metzger, *Escape from Predicament* (New York, 1977); and Baogang He, *The Democratization of China* (London, 1996), esp. chap. 5.

21. Li Zhisui, *The Private Life of Chairman Mao* (New York, 1994).

22. "Talk at an Enlarged Central Work Conference," Jan. 30, 1962, in Stuart Schram, ed., *Chairman Mao Talks to the People: Talks and Letters: 1956–1971* (New York, 1974), 162, 167, 187.

23. "Our very purpose is to let people think for themselves," *The Secret Speeches of Chairman Mao: From the Hundred Flowers to the Great Leap Forward*, ed. Roderick MacFarquhar et al. (Cambridge, MA, 1989), 292.

24. "On the Correct Handling of Contradictions Among the People," Feb. 27, 1957, in *Selected Works of Mao Tsetung* 5 (Peking, 1977): 412.

25. "Combat Liberalism," *Selected Works of Mao Tse-tung* 2 (Peking, 1965): 31–33. I have replaced the word liberalism with freedom-ism throughout.

26. "Reading Notes on the Soviet Union's 'Political Economics,'" in *Miscellany of Mao Tse-tung Thought (1949–1968)*, pt. 2, Joint Publications Research Service JPRS 61269–2 (Feb. 20, 1974), 290.

27. Wu Guoguang, *Zhao Ziyang yu zhengzhi gaige* (Zhao Ziyang and political reform) (Hong Kong, 1997). Wu worked for the Political System Reform Office (Zhengzhi tizhi gaige bangongshi) from October 1986 to February 1989. The office staffed the work of the five-man Political Reform Discussion Small Group (Zhengzhi tizhi gaige yantao xiaozu), consisting of Zhao, Hu Qili, Tian Jiyun, Bo Yibo, and Peng Chong. After Wu left China, he published the account of the in camera discussions based on four volumes of his work notes.

28. "Jianchi sixiang jiben yuanze" (Uphold the four basic principles), Mar. 30, 1979, *Deng Xiaoping wenxuan* (Selected works of Deng Xiaoping) 2 (Beijing, 1983): 164–65.

29. Hu, "Ziyouzhuyi sichao," 161.

30. Citations are from the version of this essay published in Hu Ping, *Gei wo yige zhidian* (Give me a fulcrum) (Taibei, 1988). In a telephone conversation on August 31, 1998, Hu told me that this is the authoritative version. The essay went through several revisions. In 1980, when Hu ran for the post of people's deputy in the election district comprising Peking

University, he tripled the length of the essay and fully developed its positive arguments for freedom, which were less thoroughly discussed in the Democracy Wall version.

31. In fact, Hu Ping had been harboring even more radical ideas ever since his experience as a "sent-down youth" (urban middle school graduate sent to live among the peasants) in the early 1970s. Author's interview with Hu Ping, New York City, Aug. 12, 1987.

32. Interview, Aug. 12, 1987.

33. "Xu 'diwuge xiandaihua—minzhu yu qita'" (Sequel to the fifth modernization—democracy and other things), in *Tansuo* (Explorations) No. 1, Jan. 8, 1979; repr. in Claude Widor, ed., *Documents on the Chinese Democratic Movement 1978–1980: Unofficial Magazines and Wall Posters* 1 (Paris, 1981): 61.

34. "Renquan, pingdeng, yu minzhu" (Human rights, equality, and democracy), in *Tansuo* No. 3. (Mar. 11, 1979), in Widor, *Documents*, 115.

35. *The Courage to Stand Alone: Letters from Prison and Other Writings*, ed. and trans. Kristina M. Torgeson (New York, 1997), 175.

36. Andrew J. Nathan and Tianjian Shi, "Cultural Requisites for Democracy in China," and "Left and Right in Deng's China," in Andrew J. Nathan, *China's Transition* (New York, 1997), 152–73 and 174–97.

37. On the earlier and later phases of this struggle, see respectively Merle Goldman, *China's Intellectuals: Advise and Dissent* (Cambridge, MA, 1981); and Merle Goldman, *Sowing the Seeds of Democracy in China: Political Reform in the Deng Xiaoping Era* (Cambridge, 1994).

38. "On New Democracy" (1940), in Mao Tse-tung, *Selected Works* 2 (Peking, 1965): 339–84.

39. Jing Wang, *High Culture Fever: Politics, Aesthetics, and Ideology and Deng's China* (Berkeley, 1996), 32.

40. Wang Ruoshui, *Zai zhexue zhanxianshang* (On the philosophical front) (Beijing, 1980); Zhongguo shehui kexueyuan zhexue yanjiusuo "Guonei zhexue dongtai" bianjibu (Editorial department of "Domestic philosophical trends" of the Institute of Philosophy of the Chinese Academy of Social Sciences), eds., *Renxing, rendaozhuyi wenti taolunji* (Collection of articles on problems of human nature and humanism) (Beijing, 1983).

41. Jing Wang, *High Culture Fever*, chap. 1, and Li Honglin, *Zhongguo sixiang yundongshi, 1949–1989* (History of Chinese ideological campaigns, 1949–1989) (Hong Kong, 1999), 387–91. As a senior Party theorist Li was both an observer and a participant in the events he describes.

42. Guo Luoji, *Gongchandang weifa'an jishi* (The story of how the Chinese Communist Party violated the law) (Hong Kong, 1997).

43. Li Honglin, *Zhongguo sixiang yundongshi*, 422.

44. Ibid., 423.

45. Gu Zhun, *Gu Zhun wenji* (Collected works of Gu Zhun) (Guiyang, 1994), esp. 223–426.

46. Yang Xiguang and Susan McFadden, *Captive Spirits: Prisoners of the Cultural Revolution* (Hong Kong, 1997).

47. Of course one cannot absolutize this comparison. For example, in his reportage entitled "The Second Kind of Loyalty," Liu Binyan contrasted the first kind of person with a second kind of person whose dissent is not private but public, and he praised the latter. See Goldman, *Sowing the Seeds,* 147–50.

48. Li Honglin, *Zhongguo sixiang yundongshi,* 428.

49. Geremie R. Barmé, *In the Red: On Contemporary Chinese Culture* (New York, 1999), chaps. 4–6, quotations from 89–90. On the diversity of discussions of freedom in the 1990s, see also David Kelly, "The Chinese Search for Freedom as a Universal Value," in Kelly and Reid, *Asian Freedoms,* 93–119.

50. Kelly and Reid argue that political freedom has been at the center of all modern Asian discussions of freedom. Kelly and Reid, *Asian Freedoms,* 3

≺ ≻

Index

In this index an "f" after a number indicates a separate reference on the next page, and an "ff" indicates separate references on the next two pages. A continuous discussion over two or more pages is indicated by a span of page numbers, e.g., "57–59." *Passim* is used for a cluster of references in close but not consecutive sequence.